CONTESTED ISSUES IN
STUDENT AFFAIRS

Academic Affairs Theory-Practice Student Affairs Civil Discourse
Parents Knowledge
Alcohol Politics Gender Educators
Social Justice Diverse Perspectives
Identity Contested Issues Social Networking Mental Health
Collegians
Professional Boundaries Language Free Speech Accountability Spirituality Religion
Values Respectful Dialogue Ideology
Learning Race
Supervision
Difference Partnerships

CONTESTED ISSUES IN STUDENT AFFAIRS

Diverse Perspectives and Respectful Dialogue

Edited by
PETER M. MAGOLDA
and
MARCIA B. BAXTER MAGOLDA

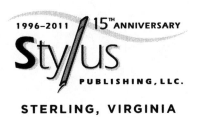

1996–2011 15TH ANNIVERSARY
Stylus
PUBLISHING, LLC.

STERLING, VIRGINIA

COPYRIGHT © 2011 BY
STYLUS PUBLISHING, LLC.

Published by Stylus Publishing, LLC
22883 Quicksilver Drive
Sterling, Virginia 20166-2102

Library of Congress Cataloging-in-Publication-Data
Contested issues in student affairs : diverse perspectives
and respectful dialogue / edited by Peter M. Magolda and
Marcia B. Baxter Magolda.—1st ed.
    p.   cm.
    Includes bibliographical references and index.
ISBN 978-1-57922-583-4 (cloth : alk. paper)
ISBN 978-1-57922-584-1 (pbk. : alk. paper)
ISBN 978-1-57922-585-8 (library networkable e-edition)
ISBN 978-1-57922-586-5 (consumer e-edition)
    1. Student affairs services—United States.   I. Magolda,
Peter Mark.   II. Baxter Magolda, Marcia B., 1956–
LB2342.92.C67   2011
378.1'97—dc22
                                        20110121

13-digit ISBN: 978-1-57922-583-4 (cloth)
13-digit ISBN: 978-1-57922-584-1 (paper)
13-digit ISBN: 978-1-57922-585-8 (library networkable
e-edition)
13-digit ISBN: 978-1-57922-586-5 (consumer e-edition)

Printed in the United States of America

All first editions printed on acid free paper
that meets the American National Standards Institute
Z39-48 Standard.

Bulk Purchases

Quantity discounts are available for use in workshops
and for staff development.
Call 1-800-232-0223

First Edition, 2011

10 9 8 7 6 5 4 3 2

To two of our late colleagues and friends.

Terry Piper, who spent his professional career tirelessly working with students and colleagues to mediate contested issues in the academy.

Doug Toma, a scholar notable for his irrepressible curiosity about all things contestable in higher education.

CONTENTS

PART THREE
Achieving Inclusive and Equitable Learning Environments

PART FOUR
Organizing Student Affairs Practice for Learning and Social Justice

ACKNOWLEDGMENTS

O ver the past 35 years we have encountered a seemingly endless number of contested issues in higher education as undergraduates, graduate students, student affairs educators, and as faculty members. While many of these issues—teaching, learning, inequalities, academic integrity, human development, supervision, race, gender, community standards, and student success, to name a few—have perplexed us, we have been fortunate to have encountered students, practitioners, policy makers, researchers, supervisors, mentors, and friends who have offered us keen insights about how to think differently and more complexly about these matters. We are forever grateful for these chance encounters that continue to educate us each day.

In this edited volume, we invited over 50 colleagues—many of whom have profoundly influenced higher education and us—to share their insights about a series of critical issues facing the academy in general and student affairs in particular. Contributors include graduate students, a university chancellor, several chief student affairs officers, numerous new and midcareer professionals, faculty, a psychologist, and a community organizer. These scholars have worked in public and private higher education in large and small institutions, including traditional 4-year degree-granting colleges as well as community colleges. Although their areas of expertise are too numerous to mention, suffice it to say they are sufficiently sensible and modest to recognize there are no simple solutions to these complex problems, and that their solutions can be thought provoking, helpful, and imperfect. We sincerely appreciate the contributors' honesty and willingness to act as public intellectuals and submit their ideas for national consumption and scrutiny, for the betterment of higher education.

Over the years, students enrolled in the Miami University Student Affairs in Higher Education (SAHE) program (formerly the College

Student Personnel program) have gently and persistently reminded us that resolving contested issues, such as fraternity pledging or a university changing its mascot's name from Redskins to Redhawks, is not merely an administrative task but also a political act. Current and former students' enthusiasm and encouragement for us to write a book that illuminates the politics of student affairs is a major impetus for this volume. We appreciate their feedback and recognition of the importance of such a book.

In particular, eight current Miami University SAHE students who have been instrumental in the conceptualization and production of this book are Craig Berger, Sue Ann Huang, Ashya Majied, Jeffrey Manning, Sarah Meagher, Nyamugurwa Ami Rubango, Kerry Thomas, and Amanda Wilson. These individuals helped identify the 24 contested issues showcased in the book, critiqued the 48 essays, compiled annotated bibliographies, and will act as online bloggers/catalysts for continuing the conversations about these topics.

Celia Ellison and Sarah Meagher carefully read and copyedited the book. Their conceptual and practical suggestions and attentiveness to detail helped to fine-tune contributors' arguments and improve the overall readability. Craig Berger conceptualized and implemented the innovative online blogging component and will serve as its editor.

John von Knorring, president and publisher at Stylus, embraced the idea of the book and has been highly supportive of creating meaningful dialogues through the online components. He was a constant, creative, and candid counsel offering superb suggestions for the book and website content and organization. We especially appreciate John's commitment to publishing an affordable work that prioritizes the needs of readers. All these individuals' labors have helped us immensely and have enhanced the quality of this book and of our lives. For this we are thankful.

PREFACE

How do graduate preparation program faculty prepare future student affairs educators to address the complexities of higher education? What kinds of continuing education opportunities do divisions of student affairs offer to optimize staffs' effectiveness with students and colleagues? *Contested Issues in Student Affairs,* a collection of essays by student affairs faculty, administrators, and graduate students, answers these two questions. The book includes 24 contemporary, critical, and contentious questions (e.g., Why is it so difficult for collegians and student affairs educators to talk about race?). Essayists introduce diverse ideological and political conceptualizations of and responses to these 24 questions by situating them historically in the professional literature, summarizing the diverse ideological and theoretical responses to the questions, making explicit their perspectives and responses, and discussing political implications. Each chapter contributor invites readers to contemplate and disseminate their reactions to the commentaries by contributing posts on our book-sponsored blog at contestedissues.word press.com. The target audiences for this text are graduate students enrolled in student affairs preparation programs and leaders of divisions of student affairs that sponsor professional development workshops for staff.

Seminal Introductory Texts

Historically, graduate preparation programs require students to enroll in an introductory seminar that introduces and socializes graduate students to the profession. Although the number of Introduction to Student Affairs texts has grown over the past 50 years, the essential knowledge these books transmit to students has remained relatively constant. A brief review of a few seminal introductory texts written during the past 50 years illuminates topics of importance that have withstood the test of time and reveals voids this text aims to fill.

Kate Mueller's *Student Personnel Work in Higher Education* introduced foundations of student personnel work (e.g., the nature and objectives of higher education, overviews of different kinds of American colleges and universities, historical overviews of student personnel work, student typologies, and organizational structures), personnel services basic to campus life (e.g., housing and programs for students' mental and physical health), personnel services aimed at student growth and success (e.g., student government, literary societies, and religious programs), personnel services for special groups (e.g., married students, international students), and the personnel worker (e.g., tending to the mental health of the personnel worker and research about personnel work).[1]

E. G. Williamson's *Student Personnel Services in Colleges and Universities: Some Foundations, Techniques, and Processes of Program Administration* resembles Mueller's framework, highlighting routine administrative practices, special administrative practices (e.g., judiciary and counseling services), and new services and politics (e.g., academic freedom, extracurriculum).[2] This genre of introductory texts, aimed at orienting and socializing graduate students, typically illuminated the profession's past and present as well as speculated about the future, identified unique student personnel functional areas and services, and focused on the evolving needs of students and student affairs staffs.

Lawrence Litwack, June Holmes, and Jane O'Hern published *Critical Issues in Student Personnel Work: A Problem Casebook,* which reflects a second genre of introductory book.[3] This text augments Mueller's and Williamson's texts by introducing 45 real-life case studies that reveal the challenges, potential conflicts, and ethical dilemmas student affairs staff encounter when they interact with their surrounding communities, universities, and students.[4] Although these authors intentionally offer no solutions, they encourage readers to translate scholarly and personal theories into practice.

Robert Shaffer and William Martinson's *Student Personnel Services in Higher Education* and William Packwood's *College Student Personnel Services* exemplify a third genre of introductory texts that showcase the numerous discrete functional areas in student affairs, such as housing, financial aid, and student activities.[5] These texts provide comprehensive overviews of each unit, revealing daily practices and challenges. E. G. Williamson and Donald Biggs in *Student Personnel Work: A Program of Developmental Relationships* present a variation of previous works, focusing on functional skills such as staffing, budgeting, advising, psychological counseling, disciplinary arbitration, financial aid advice, research, and residence hall management that transcend student affairs offices or units.[6]

James Appleton, Channing Briggs, and James Rhatigan's *Pieces of Eight: The Rites, Roles, and Styles of the Dean, By Eight Who Have Been There* augments the technical and scholarly overviews of student affairs with personal reflections from eight senior student affairs officers.[7] These narratives offer keen insights into how universities and divisions of student affairs work, as well as the senior student affairs officers' daily problems and preoccupations.

During the past 30 years, *Student Services: A Handbook for the Profession*, now in its fifth edition, has refined, updated, synthesized, and expanded topical discussions contained in introductory texts.[8] This handbook, written by faculty and student affairs administrators, identifies the functions and purposes of the profession and its members, clarifies the importance of theory and practice, introduces various theoretical perspectives and management techniques, and includes best practices. This compendium also includes discussions about professional roots and commitments (e.g., historical foundations, evolution of the student services profession, guiding standards, legal issues), theoretical traditions (e.g., student development and organizations), roles and models for practice (e.g., administration, advising, ecology management), administration (e.g., planning and budgeting, managing data), and emerging roles and opportunities (e.g., student diversity, outcome assessments).

Editors Gregory Blimling and Elizabeth Whitt in *Good Practice in Student Affairs: Principles to Foster Student Learning* de-emphasize functional areas and skills while emphasizing student learning.[9] Contributors to the book make explicit the profession's shifting focus on learning and the implications for this shift.

Three Noteworthy Historical Trends

Three noteworthy trends transcend these diverse approaches to introductory texts, which influence the unique content and organization of *Contested Issues in Student Affairs*. First, these introductory texts reveal three distinct approaches to student affairs work during the past 50 years, focusing on student services, student development, and student learning.[10] According to the student services tradition, the student affairs professional's role is to support the academic mission of the university by providing high-quality services to students in nonacademic functional areas. Over time, the academy recognized that noncognitive student development issues occurring outside the classroom (e.g., student's identity development) complicated students' learning inside the classroom and their overall satisfaction with college. This realization resulted in a shift in student affairs professionals' primary role from service providers to noncognitive human development specialists. Robert Brown discussed this second tradition in *Student Development in Tomorrow's Higher Education: A Return to the Academy*, and authors of numerous volumes expounded on the developmental foundations of the profession.[11] "The Student Learning Imperative," *Powerful Partnerships*, and *Learning Reconsidered*, by national higher education and student affairs associations, all advocated for a holistic approach to learning.[12] This third student affairs tradition situated learning at the epicenter of the cocurriculum, with development and service as its foundation. This tradition recommends faculty and student affairs educators integrate student learning and development, de-emphasizing in-class/out-of-class and cognitive/noncognitive dichotomies.[13]

Second, these introductory books—regardless of how one conceptualizes his or her work as a service provider, student development specialist, or student learning advocate—provide primarily technical advice to graduate students. For example, they offer historical milestones for the profession, models for effective practice, and best practices. Often muted in these technical and rational discussions are moral, ideological, and political discussions. For example, conceptualizing student affairs work as providing nonacademic support to students is a moral decision based on a particular ideology that has political ramifications. Past generations of introductory texts seldom explicitly or substantively discuss moral, ideological, and political aspects of the student affairs enterprise.

A third theme that transcends these introductory texts is implicit acknowledgment of boundaries that frame and influence student affairs work. In each of the introductory text genres, the authors of these books implicitly yet frequently discuss boundaries: boundaries differentiating different kinds of colleges, boundaries distinguishing between student affairs and academic affairs, boundaries within student affairs separating functional units, boundaries separating basic groups (e.g., governing organizations) from special groups (e.g., athletes, international students), boundaries between ethical and unethical behaviors and practices, boundaries separating theory and practice, boundaries delineating faculty and student affairs staff responsibilities, theoretical boundaries, and boundaries dividing the curriculum and cocurriculum.

Contested Issues in Student Affairs returns to a tradition pioneered by Esther Lloyd-Jones and Margaret Smith in their *Student Personnel Work as Deeper Teaching*.[14] Lloyd-Jones and Smith brought together 25 authorities in the field and asked them to offer insights about how to attain students' fullest development. The essays acknowledge and blend technical, moral, ideological, and political issues as contributors reflect on the changing nature of student personnel work, examine who should go to college, explore the challenges associated with orienting new collegians, encourage learning outside the classroom, encourage students to live a healthy life, support students from other countries, support spirituality, evaluate practice, and most importantly, improve the quality of human relations on campus.

Contested Issues in Student Affairs, in the spirit of *Student Personnel Work as Deeper Teaching*, focuses on student affairs educators as learning specialists; extends technical aspects of our work to reveal moral, ideological, and political issues; and blurs boundaries by examining issues that transcend content areas. *Contested Issues in Student Affairs* augments traditional introductory handbooks that focus on functional student affairs areas (e.g., residence life, career services) but underemphasize contested issues (e.g., the value of diversity education) that transcend these functional student affairs units.

Desired outcomes for readers of this book are that they explore the many different theoretical and ideological approaches that student affairs scholar practitioners employ when addressing complex questions and situations, and that professionals are encouraged to generate and disseminate their responses to these perspectives about professional challenges through participating in a sustained online dialogue.

Book Format

We organize the 24 questions into four parts. Part One, Philosophical Foundations of Student Affairs in Higher Education, explores the implications and complications of student affairs educators' placing learning at the epicenter of their professional work. These four chapters focus on the tensions between theory and practice, the curriculum and cocurriculum, and academic affairs and student affairs. Part Two, Challenges of Promoting Learning and Development, explores the challenges associated with learning-centered practice, including consumerism versus learning, the value of taking risks and failure, and the role of policy, overinvolved parents, and assessment. Part Three, Achieving Inclusive and Equitable Learning Environments, addresses crafting learning environments that include students whose needs are often labeled *special*. These students or student subcultures are often marginalized and encouraged to adapt to normalizing expectations. These chapters explore race, ethnicity, sexual orientation, spirituality, and physical, learning, and psychological needs. Part Four, Organizing Student Affairs Practice for Learning and Social Justice, addresses the organizational and professional implications of placing learning and social justice at the epicenter of student affairs practice. These chapters explore the professional's, institution's, and student's organizational transformations, as well as the educator's transformation needed to enact learning for a global world.

Each chapter begins with a single question in the title and includes four subsections: a 4,000-word essay written by an author (who was selected based on that person's expertise) that responds to the question, a 2,000-word essay response written by another scholar, an annotated bibliography, and a URL link to the book's website.

Each essay situates the issue historically in the professional literature, presents background information and context, defines key terms, summarizes the diverse ideological and theoretical approaches to responding to the question, makes explicit the author's perspectives about the question, and discusses political implications.

Response essays critique the essays, note areas of agreement, introduce and discuss relevant issues not addressed in the essay, make explicit the author's perspectives about the question, and discuss political implications. Authors of the essays and responses identified seminal works that provide readers with additional information. Graduate students and essay authors composed the bibliographic annotations.

Extending the Face-to-Face and Virtual Conversations

Our intention is to initiate a sustained conversation about the content of this book that allows educators to converse with each other respectfully regardless of ideology. We invite faculty of graduate preparation programs to use the chapters in introductory, special topics, supervised practice, or capstone courses. The primary and response essays model for graduate students how to explore complex issues and engage in respectful dialogue. The online blog offers opportunities for graduate students to exchange perspectives with those in other programs or with professionals around the world. We encourage student affairs staff to read and discuss individual essays, which transcend most functional areas, in staff development meetings and discussions and post their perspectives in this book's blog.

Each chapter concludes with a link to a website that allows readers to teach and learn from each other as they continue the dialogue about contested issues. We encourage readers to post blogs commenting on and critiquing the essays and responses. Readers will also have the opportunity to upload relevant resources to share with colleagues. Too often dialogue is limited to people in close proximity. The blog site is a unique opportunity to engage in dialogue with professionals in multiple preparation programs, multiple student affairs divisions at diverse institutions, and contexts around the world. It encourages dialogue across disciplines, functional roles, and moral, political, and ideological perspectives. The blog invites professionals who share an interest in particular contested issues to join a sustained conversation about how to navigate the complexities of those issues in various contexts. This online forum also provides emerging and veteran educators with opportunities to share perspectives from the vantage point of their professional career paths.

The book's overarching goal is for readers to consider the following questions: What is your level of understanding of these moral, ideological, and political issues that student affairs educators regularly encounter? What is your personal responsibility in addressing these issues? What are the rationales behind your decisions? What are the theoretical options you might choose and why? How do your responses compare with those of colleagues?

We hope you will consider this book as an invitation to explore the contested issues in student affairs work, and we hope you will join the online blogs to interact with colleagues beyond your campus regarding these complex issues. Engaging in dialogue on contested issues is a crucial part of inclusive learning-centered practice in student affairs.

Peter M. Magolda and Marcia B. Baxter Magolda
Miami University

Notes

1. Mueller, K. H. (1961). *Student personnel work in higher education*. Boston, MA: Houghton Mifflin.

2. Williamson, E. G. (1961). *Student personnel services in colleges and universities: Some foundations, techniques, and processes of program administration*. New York, NY: McGraw-Hill.

3. Litwack, L., Holmes, J. E., & O'Hern, J. S. (1965). *Critical issues in student personnel work*. Chicago, IL: Rand McNally.

4. Mueller, *Student personnel work in higher education*; Williamson, *Student personnel services*.

5. Shaffer, R. H., & Martinson, W. D. (1966). *Student personnel services in higher education*. New York, NY: Center for Applied Research in Education; Packwood, W. T. (1977). *College student personnel services*. Springfield, IL: Charles C. Thomas.

6. Williamson, E. G., & Biggs, D. A. (1975). *Student personnel work: A program of developmental relationships*. New York, NY: Wiley.

7. Appleton, J. R., Briggs, C. M., & Rhatigan, J. J. (1978). *Pieces of eight: The rites, roles, and styles of the dean, by eight who have been there*. Portland, OR: NASPA Institute of Research and Development.

8. Delworth, U., & Hanson, G. R. (Eds.). (1980). *Student services: A handbook for the profession* (1st ed.). San Francisco, CA: Jossey-Bass; Delworth, U., & Hanson, G. R. (Eds.). (1989). *Student services: A handbook for the profession* (2nd ed.). San Francisco, CA: Jossey-Bass; Komives, S. R., & Woodard, D. B., Jr., (Eds.). (1996). *Student services: A handbook for the profession* (3rd ed.). San Francisco, CA: Jossey-Bass; Komives, S. R., & Woodard, D. B., Jr., (Eds.). (2003). *Student services: A handbook for the profession* (4th ed.). San Francisco, CA: Jossey-Bass; Schuh, J. H., Jones, S. R., & Harper, S. R. (Eds.). (2011). *Student services: A handbook for the profession* (5th ed.). San Francisco, CA: Jossey-Bass.

9. Blimling, G. S., & Whitt, E. J. (Eds.). (1999). *Good practice in student affairs: Principles to foster student learning*. San Francisco, CA: Jossey-Bass.

10. Ender, S. C., Newton, F. B., & Caple, R. B. (1996). Contributions to learning: Present realities. In S. C. Ender, F. B. Newton, & R. B. Caple (Eds.), *Contributing to learning: The role of student affairs* (pp. 5–17). San Francisco, CA: Jossey-Bass.

11. Brown, R. D. (1972). *Student development in tomorrow's higher education: A return to the academy*. Washington, DC: American Personnel and Guidance Association; Creamer, D. G. (1990). *College student development: Theory and practice for the 1990s*. Alexandria, VA: American College Personnel Association; Evans, N. J., Forney, D. S., & Guido-DiBrito, F. (1998). *Student development in college: Theory, research, and practice*. San Francisco, CA: Jossey-Bass; Knefelkamp, L., Widick, C., & Parker, C. A. (Eds.). (1978). *Applying new developmental findings: New directions for student services*. San Francisco, CA: Jossey-Bass; Parker, C. A. (1978). *Encouraging development in college students*. Minneapolis: University of Minnesota Press.

12. American College Personnel Association. (1996). The student learning imperative: Implications for student affairs. *Journal of College Student Development, 37*(2), 118–122; American Association for Higher Education, American College Personnel Association, & National Association of Student Personnel Administrators. (1998). *Powerful partnerships:*

A shared responsibility for learning. Washington, DC: Author; Keeling, R. P. (Ed.). (2004). *Learning reconsidered: A campus-wide focus on the student experience.* Washington, DC: National Association of Student Personnel Administrators and the American College Personnel Association.

13. Ender et al., Contributions to learning; King, P. M., & Baxter Magolda, M. B. (1996). A developmental perspective on learning. *Journal of College Student Development, 37*(2), 163–173.

14. Lloyd-Jones, E. M., & Smith, M. R. (1954). *Student personnel work as deeper teaching.* New York, NY: Harper.

PART ONE

Philosophical Foundations
of Student Affairs
in Higher Education

1

What Counts as "Essential" Knowledge for Student Affairs Educators?

Intellectual Curiosity and Lifelong Learning

Marcia B. Baxter Magolda and
Peter M. Magolda, Miami University

What do student affairs educators need to know to effectively work with students? This question permeates our daily lives as faculty members. Prospective students ask this question during our informational interviews as they work to understand what they will learn and gain from graduate school. Our colleagues in other disciplines ask this question in the hope of better understanding the roles student affairs educators might play on campus. We too ask ourselves this question as we continually revise our graduate program's core curriculum. Regardless of the context, we work continually to combat the myth that success in student affairs simply requires a genuine interest in working with people. After all, careers ranging from barista to medical doctor all require a genuine interest in working with people. With a desire to build meaningful relationships being necessary but insufficient for success in student affairs, what other knowledge and skills must student affairs educators possess?

Reports published by two key student affairs organizations—the American College Personnel Association (ACPA) and the National Association of Student Personnel Administrators (NASPA)—have influenced our thinking about essential knowledge. These reports collectively focus on the concepts of holistic, transformative learning. Holistic refers to promoting growth not only in terms of how students understand knowledge

---

We work continually to combat the myth that success in student affairs simply requires a genuine interest in working with people.

---

but also in terms of how they understand themselves and their relationships. Transformative learning refers to "Formulating more dependable beliefs about our experience, assessing their contexts, seeking informed agreement on their meaning and justification, and making decisions on the resulting insights."[1] "The Student Learning Imperative" (SLI), a document published in 1996 to spark dialogue about how student affairs educators could enhance learning and development, recommended that student affairs educators be experts about students, environments, teaching, and learning:

> Student affairs staff should know how students spend their time and whether students are using the institution's resources to educational advantage. . . . Moreover, they [should] integrate data about student performance from faculty and others with their own observations of students' experiences and disseminate this information to stakeholders.[2]

Another national report, *Powerful Partnerships: A Shared Responsibility for Student Learning,* further emphasized collaboration between student and academic affairs to enhance learning.[3] Finally, *Learning Reconsidered: A Campus-Wide Focus on the Student Experience* reiterated that learning and development are inseparable because one process cannot occur without the other.[4] The contributors to *Learning Reconsidered* argued that today's college learning outcomes, which include (among others) the ability to integrate knowledge from multiple sources and adapt to changing environments as well as the ability to enact civic values, require transformative education. Transformative education places learning "in a much larger context that requires consideration of what students know, who they are, what their values and behavior patterns are, and how they see themselves contributing to and participating in the world in which they live."[5] Collectively, these reports call upon student affairs educators to carefully select knowledge relevant to context and bring this knowledge to the foreground of their consciousness for their day-to-day practices. Adopting learning as our central mission and the integration of student and academic affairs as essential ingredients of higher education, we underscore the SLI's call for student affairs educators to be experts on students, their environments, and the teaching and learning process, and we add to that list becoming an expert on oneself as a teacher and learner.

But given the complex and messy problems that characterize 21st-century higher education, no sole knowledge base will solve the challenges of higher education. Rather, multiple and diverse knowledge bases enrich understanding about students, learning environments, and learning. The breadth, depth, and ever-changing nature of these knowledge sources preclude the ability of an individual to acquire and master them. Student affairs educators must learn how to locate, evaluate, and integrate knowledge as well as create it. We need to cultivate a passion and thirst for acquiring knowledge, not simply during graduate school but throughout life. We have to understand the history of students, higher education, teaching and learning. We need to become familiar with the moral, ideological, and political perspectives embedded in our work settings and become aware of our own moral, ideological, and political stances. We need to understand the capacities for learning that people (including ourselves) and organizations bring to teaching and learning processes and how to enhance those capacities. We need to understand how people, organizations, and cultures function and evolve by bringing relevant knowledge to bear on particular situations.

From this perspective, what is *essential* is an intellectual curiosity. This is the single most important quality for success in graduate preparation programs and subsequently in student affairs. Recognizing one's intellectual curiosities and having the passion to explore them is a foundation for one's graduate studies and professional career. What is essential is the recognition that multiple sources of knowledge underlie and inform the actions of student affairs educators; the ability to access, integrate, and apply multiple sources of knowledge; and the capacity to continually reflect on the intersections of knowledge and action. All these require intellectual curiosity as well as knowing ourselves as teachers and learners.

Essential Knowledge

Student affairs is an interdisciplinary field drawing on many academic traditions, such as developmental or counseling psychology, sociology, history, law, and organizational development, to understand students, college environments, and the learning and teaching process. Understanding, integrating, and applying these multiple sources of knowledge in practice is essential for success in student affairs.

Recognizing Multiple Sources of Knowledge

Prospective students conducting informational interviews often express concern with whether our theory-oriented academic program will provide them with the practical experience to succeed in student affairs. We usually interject into these conversations the idea that it is impossible for student affairs educators to act without the influence of theory (i.e., knowledge), but also acknowledge it is possible and often highly probable one can act without consciously understanding theories that influence actions. For example, when patrons enter a campus eatery and contemplate an entrée (i.e., action) they base decisions on a theory—for example, consuming baked rather than fried food and passing on dessert are foundations for a heart-healthy theory. It is impossible to select an entrée that is not influenced by theory; the goal then is for diners to bring their theories to the forefront of their consciousness. In student affairs, acting without a conscious understanding of the theories that influence action complicates and diminishes the effectiveness of our work.

This conversation often leads to questions about "essential" theories one must know. Many prospective students recognize the role student development theory has played in student affairs but are less familiar with sociological, cultural studies, management, or learning theories (to name a few). Prospective students often envision themselves as either counselors or administrators and want to know which theories will best prepare them for the future. We offer an expanded version of student affairs roles that include aspects of counseling and administration and then explain that educators can use a multitude of theories to understand issues. For example, many student affairs professionals involve themselves in assisting international students with their transition to university life in the United States. Developmental psychology offers insights about identity and relational transitions many collegians experience. However, an understanding of international students' cultures must refine these insights. Sociological theories offer insight on how family relationships influence transitions, again considered in the particular cultural context.

The particular campus community they are joining also mediates these students' transition. Understanding learning theories faculty endorse is important in helping international students succeed academically. Organizational and management theories help student affairs educators better understand institutional and government policies affecting international students. Our life experiences as well as our student affairs roles influence which knowledge sources are most relevant to practice. For example, an academic adviser or residence hall director interacting directly with international students may choose different sources than an administrator working at the policy level.

In student affairs, acting without a conscious understanding of the theories that influence action complicates and diminishes the effectiveness of our work.

Thus, there is no one essential knowledge source; instead, it is essential for educators to use multiple theoretical lenses to analyze and assess the utility of the diverse bodies of knowledge. Student affairs educators must be aware of bodies of knowledge that influence their actions, and graduate school is an ideal setting to bring to the forefront of students' consciousness their existing knowledge, the diverse (and contested) bodies of knowledge that guide the student affairs profession, and help them identify their knowledge passions. We encourage students to cultivate their intellectual curiosity to probe what sources of knowledge best resonate with their passions and interests as well as with the particular roles they aspire to.

Accessing, Integrating, and Applying Multiple Sources of Knowledge

How educators decide on a course of action—in the face of multiple knowledge sources—baffles some prospective (and current) students. They are even more taken aback at our suggestion to critique these knowledge sources. We explain that no one theory can explain every situation, and that theories are context specific and ever changing. Each perspective has benefits and limitations that must be assessed relative to the context.

Skilled educators integrate multiple sources of knowledge to form a more complex understanding of students, learning, and teaching. For example, students use knowledge sources they study in class, such as student development, to analyze situations in their assistantships. However, sometimes the dynamics of the situations do not precisely fit the knowledge source. Easing transitions of international students is a good example. Sociological and anthropological theories that center on socialization enrich understanding about the culture these international students find themselves in, but interacting with international students is crucial to assess the extent to which these theories are relevant to their home culture. Similarly, what we know about the developmental transitions involved in going to college is based on U.S. students. Educators need to explore the extent to which these insights are relevant to international students and search for additional relevant knowledge sources that can then be integrated into a more complex understanding to guide practice. Pursuing knowledge sources about intercultural interactions, the effects of socioeconomic status, and international students' aspirations enhances understanding their transitions. Educators must use their interactions with international students to refine their theoretical perspectives.

We explain during informational interviews that a goal of graduate school is to become familiar with the many disciplinary knowledge bases and delve into a few of them. We highlight that their specific learning aspirations should be a deciding factor in their graduate school choice, since different programs focus on different knowledge bases. Our advice aligns with the 2009 Council for the Advancement of Standards (CAS) that specifies broad areas of expertise student affairs master's graduates should achieve, noting the importance of flexibility regarding disciplinary approach and expertise of faculty. For example, CAS notes that "graduates must be able to demonstrate knowledge of how student learning and learning opportunities are influenced by student characteristics and by collegiate environments so that graduates can design and evaluate learning experiences for students."[6] Designing and evaluating learning experiences requires using one's intellectual curiosity to access, integrate, and apply multiple sources of knowledge.

Many student affairs graduate preparation programs mirror this perspective. Although most graduate preparation programs include an organizational or administrative emphasis, the degree to which faculty members emphasize student development, cultural studies, or counseling varies based on the program's history, perception about student affairs work, and faculty expertise. Thus although it may seem to graduate students who are attempting to digest large bodies of knowledge that there is essential knowledge for becoming a student affairs professional, graduate preparation programs mirror the CAS approach of addressing key areas of knowledge without mandating essential knowledge.

Preparation programs and professional development opportunities are political acts, shaped by moral, ideological, and political considerations. Practice takes place in particular institutional contexts with particular missions. Context-based divergence thus requires professionals to examine their moral and ideological perspectives, bring their knowledge bases to consciousness, and consider political dynamics prior to action. Students and professionals alike should use their intellectual curiosity to access, use, and fit together knowledge in new and creative ways to solve real-world issues.

Continual Reflection on the Intersections of Knowledge and Action

Knowledge and action are synergistic. Knowledge informs action, and the results of action in turn refine knowledge. Robert Coles wrote, "Theory is an enlargement of observation."[7] People interpret what they see in their everyday experiences to form perspectives—or theories—about how the world works. Thus theory is the systematic organization of observations. In the context of student affairs, observations from practice (action) yield theories (knowledge) about students, environments, learning, and teaching. These theories inform future practice, and the outcomes of that practice lead to additional observations to continue the cycle. Reflection on how existing knowledge interacts with and is further informed by action helps educators refine their expertise.

We frame our informational interviews as a learning partnership, a process for teaching and learning that embodies this continual reflection on the intersections of knowledge and action. Learning partnerships emphasize respecting learners' thinking, engaging learners in a mutual exploration of the complexities of knowing, and collaborating to solve problems.[8] Respecting learners' thinking draws out their experiences and observations to inform their graduate school decisions. Mutual exploration increases learners' awareness of theories that influence their decisions and exposes them to new theories that might inform their decisions. Collaboration provides students with additional perspectives, yet emphasizes their personal authority in choosing the best graduate program given their values and passions. However, as Ira Shor eloquently noted, "Mutual dialogue is not a know-nothing learning process."[9] Shor advocated for educators to bring their knowledge and expertise to the learning relationship and integrate it with the knowledge and expertise of learners.

We bring our expertise to the teaching/learning process, yet we engage students in continual reflection on the intersections of knowledge and action so they can build their expertise. Helping them frame their graduate school decisions through this kind of reflection is a precursor to prospective students' owning their own work and being "accomplished masters of [their] particular work roles, jobs, or careers."[10]

The Role of Self-Authorship

Gaining the complex capacities necessary for becoming accomplished masters of student affairs work depends on more than sophisticated knowledge and skills. Success requires a high level of intellectual, personal, and social maturity, or *self-authorship*.[11] Self-authorship supports the pursuit of multiple perspectives, critical analysis of knowledge sources, careful reflection on beliefs and values, and dialogue across difference because it creates a sense of internal security in a chaotic world.

Another explicit agenda of our informational interview, and of our stance on what counts as essential knowledge, is to convey the importance of self-authorship in graduate school and beyond. Taking context into account, analyzing multiple and often divergent ideologies and knowledge bases, acting interdependently in partnerships, defining one's professional perspective, using relevant knowledge to guide action, and acting with integrity all require complex cognitive, intrapersonal, and interpersonal meaning-making capacities. Meaning-making capacities are the assumptions we use to make sense of knowledge (i.e., cognitive), our identities (i.e., intrapersonal), and our relationships (i.e., interpersonal). Complex cognitive capacities enable acknowledging multiple perspectives, critically analyzing knowledge, and judging relevant evidence in context to make informed decisions about what to believe. Complex intrapersonal capacities enable critical analysis of one's values and social identities to construct a coherent, internal sense of self. Complex interpersonal capacities enable authentic interdependent relations with diverse others in which perspectives and needs are mutually negotiated. These complex capacities enable us to craft an internal compass to guide professional and personal action. Self-authorship is a precursor to being able to read context, craft an informed perspective, and act on that perspective in full awareness of its moral and political implications without undue fear of others' perceptions. Prior to developing self-authorship capacities, educators rely uncritically on authorities for knowledge and struggle to integrate multiple perspectives. Moving from dependence to interdependence as educators is crucial to form the learning partnerships that promote college students' holistic learning. Intellectual curiosity about oneself is again an essential ingredient in this process.

Possibilities and Perils

Our perspective on what counts as essential knowledge offers exciting possibilities that are simultaneously fraught with perils for graduate preparation and professional development.

Learning-Centered Graduate Preparation

During informational interviews we encourage prospective students to craft learning goals they want to achieve during their graduate studies. Respecting their prior experience and personal authority is the first step in their becoming masters of their own work. We explain, however, that we will expose them to new theoretical perspectives and give them the opportunity to explore those and ultimately form their own theoretical perspectives. We also promise to expose them to research processes to help them learn how to learn so they can continue to refine their knowledge and action throughout their professional lives. We explain that they will be able to use these explorations to make sense of the practical experience they will gain during graduate school and to refine their beliefs and vision about their practice. We forewarn prospective students that this kind of graduate preparation will involve exploring, critically analyzing, and deciding upon their beliefs, identity, and relationships.

Inviting students to bring their personal authority to map their own learning outcomes and form their own perspectives reflects our core values and beliefs about professional preparation.[12] Enacting the mutual dialogue that is the centerpiece of learning partnerships is complicated because learners are not accustomed to participating in developing course agendas or evaluating their work. It is difficult to craft a curriculum that encompasses study of multiple in-depth knowledge bases yet focuses on how students critically analyze and choose their own knowledge-based perspectives to guide action. A curriculum and teaching/learning environment to cultivate lifelong learning is more difficult to construct (and to experience) than one focused on essential bodies of knowledge.

Learning-Centered Professional Practice

In today's economy and climate of accountability, student affairs must be central to the learning mission of higher education. Student affairs educators must demonstrate expertise in promoting and assessing student learning. Our perspective positions student affairs educators as interdisciplinary experts who interact with diverse constituents, critically analyze multiple perspectives, and act with integrity. Emphasis on knowledge-based action entails lifelong learning and thoughtful practice that promote critical analysis and integrative and lifelong learning as the essential outcomes of higher education.[13] These benefits require significant changes in the way student affairs professionals have traditionally viewed themselves, their roles, and articulated their areas of expertise.

Because the profession came into being primarily to provide counseling and services to help students develop beyond intellectual training, it has historically been characterized as addressing the nonacademic components of college life. Despite its long-standing conceptualization of holistic learning, the profession is largely organized around discrete, nonacademic functional areas. Although national organizations endorsed learning as student affairs' central mission in the past 20 years, some professionals remain hesitant to conceptualize their work under the learning umbrella.

Many student affairs professionals believe that faculty members regard them as second-class citizens who merely provide nonacademic services to students. Some faculty members maintain these perceptions. However, other faculty members are either unaware of the issue or open to any expertise that will help them meet their desired goals. When student affairs educators can articulate their expertise and how it applies to contexts of interest to faculty, faculty members are enthusiastic collaborators to advance student learning. If we frame our functions in the context of how they contribute to the larger goal of learning, academic affairs colleagues are more likely to understand the importance of student affairs.

Articulating learning goals for all student affairs functions is a necessary first step.[14] Thus it behooves leaders of student affairs divisions to encourage staff to use their intellectual curiosity to integrate and apply multiple knowledge sources to guide practice. The perspective we advocate complicates this process by focusing on the nebulous nature of valuing intellectual curiosity, knowledge-based action, lifelong learning, and self-authorship—all concepts more difficult to articulate and enact than learning concrete bodies of knowledge.

Our proposal is messy. Staff members who subscribe to differing knowledge bases and ideologies will encounter frustration working together, despite our belief that contemplating diverse perspectives leads to better practice. The mutual partnerships we advocate are difficult to enact, particularly under the pressure of resolving immediate issues. Student affairs educators will encounter resistance from faculty who believe learning is exclusively their purview.

Student affairs practitioners who wish to avoid knowledge-based practice will use the lack of essential knowledge as a rationale to continue to practice without intentionally considering the theory that guides them. Some will balk at the suggestion that self-authorship is a necessary foundation for effective practice. Yet we have no hesitation to desire that our physicians, our elementary school teachers, or our attorneys use wisely crafted internal perspectives to assess external pressure and act according to their beliefs and values. Self-authored student affairs educators who are intellectually curious, lifelong learners, thoughtful and reflective scholar practitioners, and who are able to communicate across difference, are excellent role models for students for whom we desire these same outcomes.

Conclusion

A number of obvious conclusions emerge from perusing the 24 questions in this book: complexities in higher education are inevitable; addressing these issues by simply supporting students or being responsive is necessary but insufficient; *knowing* how to learn is essential; knowing everything is impossible; and no single person or disciplinary perspective can solve these challenges. Actively pursuing our intellectual curiosities to gain knowledge to satisfy these curiosities for the common good is a prudent course of action. If we want to meaningfully enhance the college learning experience, as well as the student affairs graduate experience, we will have to wield the kind of essential knowledge advanced in this essay.

Notes

1. Mezirow, J. (Ed.). (2000). *Learning as transformation: Critical perspectives on a theory in progress.* San Francisco, CA: Jossey-Bass, p. 4.

2. American College Personnel Association. (1996). The student learning imperative: Implications for student affairs. *Journal of College Student Development, 37*(2), 118–122, p. 121.

3. American Association of Higher Education, American College Personnel Association & National Association of Student Personnel Administrators. (1998). *Powerful partnerships: A shared responsibility for learning.* Washington, DC: Author.

4. Keeling, R. P. (Ed.). (2004). *Learning reconsidered: A campus-wide focus on the student experience.* Washington, DC: National Association of Student Personnel Administrators & American College Personnel Association.

5. Ibid., p. 9.

6. Council for the Advancement of Standards. (2009). *CAS standards and guidelines.* Washington, DC: Author, p. 307.

7. Coles, R. (1989). *The call of stories: Teaching and the moral imagination.* Boston, MA: Houghton Mifflin, p. 20.

8. Baxter Magolda, M. B. (2009). *Authoring your life: Developing an internal voice to navigate life's challenges.* Sterling, VA: Stylus.

9. Shor, I. (1992). *Empowering education: Critical teaching for social change.* Chicago, IL: University of Chicago Press, p. 247.

10. Kegan, R. (1994). *In over our heads: The mental demands of modern life.* Cambridge, MA: Harvard University Press, p. 153.

11. Robert Kegan coined this phrase to describe this phase of adult development. See Kegan, *In over our heads.* For an expansion of this concept related to college students, see Baxter Magolda, M. B. (2001). *Making their own way: Narratives for transforming higher education to promote self-development.* Sterling, VA: Stylus.

12. See http://www.units.muohio.edu/csp/sahe/page1708.html

13. For example, see Association of American Colleges and Universities. (2007). *College learning for the new global century.* Washington, DC: Author.

14. For example, see Piper, T. D., & Buckley, J. A. (2004). Community standards model: Developing learning partnerships in campus housing. In M. B. Baxter Magolda & P. M. King (Eds.), *Learning partnerships: Theory and models of practice to educate for self-authorship* (pp. 185–212). Sterling, VA: Stylus.

What Do Student Affairs Educators Need to Know?

A Conversation Involving Two Senior University Leaders

Jill Ellen Carnaghi, Washington University in St. Louis, and Victor John Boschini Jr., Texas Christian University

Associate Vice-Chancellor Jill Carnaghi (JC): Vic, if we were *wise*, our response to how Marcia [Baxter Magolda] and Peter [Magolda] addressed the opening question, "What counts as 'essential' knowledge for student affairs educators?" would simply be a resounding "Amen!" And, then we could go back to the meetings, memos, and messy desks that we know all too well as underpaid, overworked administrators.

Chancellor Victor Boschini (VB): I like the idea of taking a break from my day-to-day demands of never-ending e-mails and crises to discuss and critique their essay. What struck me most about their comments is—"Our proposal is messy." While I am not sure I can succinctly answer their question about what counts as "essential" knowledge in student affairs, I am certain senior and new student affairs professionals need to know something to respond to these never-ending messy situations.

JC: For me, the messiness is a primary reason why I immensely enjoy and am passionate about my work. I wouldn't trade it for the world; and if truth be told, we are neither underpaid nor overworked. Yes! How many of us on a daily basis interact, work, and learn from future leaders? Being on a college campus in the 21st century is exciting. Where else in the span of less than 12 hours can you dress in full academic regalia and welcome new students and their parents to campus during a convocation, meet student leaders to discuss student engagement and learning outcomes, serve on a panel with students to discuss the merits of Greek life, respond to criticisms from a disgruntled alumnus who thinks the university is allowing itself to be manipulated for political reasons, and consult with legal counsel regarding an event that involves sending seniors to a nearby city for a weekend?

VB: Messy activities and events fill every workday. Our professional lives would be even messier if we fail to identify and articulate (to ourselves

15

and others) why and how we do what we do. What do we need to (and want to) know to perform our seemingly disparate tasks as part of a larger educational gestalt?

JC: To answer these questions, Marcia and Peter suggest that student affairs folks need to use multiple sources of knowledge that will chart clear, long-term directions for our institutions and ourselves. I concur. What they failed to explicitly state in their essay is that there is no clear-cut answer or right path for creating thriving institutions and ensuring student success. There is no right way to welcome new students to an academic community. There is no right way to discuss the merits of Greek life. You have to know something, but that something emerges from book learning, practical experience, and professional judgment.

VB: I agree, and there are some basics that graduate students need to know. They need to know that some strategies are better than others. The nexus of knowledge, practical experiences, and reflection are keys to enacting best practices and optimally serving students.

JC: Still, it is not possible during graduate school to gain all the knowledge and tools necessary to understand, for example, the nuances of legal liability for a class field trip. I did not learn it all during my time in graduate school. I still don't know it all, nor will I ever. So what do graduate students need to know?

VB: For me, graduate students need to use their academic and student affairs experiences during their graduate studies to mature and cultivate a passion for learning for the rest of their lives. This affirms Peter and Marcia's argument. They also need to learn to listen. Listening is a great way to learn. While there is no definitive body of knowledge that aspiring student affairs educators need to acquire during graduate school, there are some things that are really important for them to ponder. First and foremost, you need to become expert in human development—not simply student development, which is too narrow. You need to know how people operate and the psychology of human interactions, and you can get this by listening and watching.

JC: For me, there is essential content knowledge that people need to know. This seems contrary to the views Marcia and Peter expressed. Intellectual curiosity is a good start, but it's not enough. Context matters. It is essential for graduate students to understand the importance of context. My work context at Washington University is very different from my work at University of Vermont. If new professionals don't understand institutional context, their expertise in human development won't be as effective.

Graduate students need to use their academic and student affairs experiences during their graduate studies to mature and cultivate a passion for learning for the rest of their lives.

VB: I agree. Too often, graduate students and new professionals lack an understanding of organizational context and the importance of culture. The concept of lifelong learning, intellectual curiosity, and interdisciplinary theories learned and applied are great foundations to build one's career—and the new professional needs to learn to apply these ideas to specific contexts. It would beneficial for graduate students and new professionals to learn more about organizations and campus culture.

JC: Graduate school was a selfish time for me, and I think this is true for many graduate students. While in graduate school, I read whatever I wanted to read. I dabbled with theory and pondered case studies. I learned a lot about myself—essential knowledge—which was great. Unfortunately, my graduate preparation programs did not assist me in communicating such theories about college students to staff and faculty who did not have formal student affairs training. I probably sounded egocentric and too by-the-books.

New professionals may find themselves in uncharted water with colleagues who have not read the same literature or had the same assignments; with hierarchy and supervisors—many of them seemingly telling you what to do, and at the same time encouraging you to think critically and be creative; with competing as well as outside interests—yours and those of others. The rose-colored glasses have come off, and it's no longer learning for learning's sake. It's during these challenging times that student affairs educators can and should call upon their more formal classroom learning *and* think critically, reflect, and assess variables to take into consideration to make small adjustments to their ways of operating in their new environment.

VB: Excellent point. While in graduate school, we surround ourselves with like-minded people who speak the same language. When I accepted my first student affairs job, I encountered people—faculty and student affairs colleagues—who knew nothing about student development theory. Simply stated, graduate preparation programs and supervisors of new professionals need to work with new professionals to educate colleagues (in layperson terms) as well as learn from colleagues.

JC: I would add effective communication skills (written and verbal) and strong interpersonal skills to your list of topics worthy of exploration during graduate school. Graduate students and new professionals need to be able see beyond themselves; they have to cultivate an interest in others around them. They need to become comfortable with themselves and understand group dynamics. Finally, they have to have a working knowledge about differences—centering on the importance of diversity, multiculturalism, and ethic and racial sensitivity. We all, including seasoned professionals, need to learn to celebrate differences—based on differing learning styles, gender, ethnicity, sexual orientation, to name a few.

VB: Jill, you just named about nine additional things new professionals need to know. Can graduate preparation programs substantively address all these critical issues? Is there enough time? Are students ready to learn? I've concluded over the years that some staff members, even with graduate work in student affairs, are not ready to tackle complex issues such as identity development. Some student affairs professionals will never get it. Over the years, I have encountered people who will never work well with others no matter how many degrees they earn or workshops they attend. There is not much graduate preparation faculty and supervisors can do except to encourage them to pursue a different career.

JC: Yes, I've encountered a few of these folks as well. For most graduate students and new professionals, having a mentor or coach can go a long way toward helping them acquire and refine these professional qualities.

VB: Tell me more about self-authorship. It was a centerpiece of the essay, but I am still not sure I fully understand this concept. It's an idea I don't hear much about in my world of work.

JC: Many new professionals start with an external view of the world; they let others define their identity. They don't have their own voice; they don't trust themselves. For example, many new resident directors want to be liked by their peers and residents. This was true of me in my earlier years in residential life. Now I don't worry about being liked. Instead, I strive to be respected and to focus on the needs of students— not my own needs. Self-authorship means that we trust ourselves to make decisions about what we believe and are secure enough in our own identity to engage in interdependent relationships with others. Navigating these competing demands is stressful for new professionals and their supervisors.

VB: Good point. I see a lot of age 30 staff who are wounded. They can't get past themselves to understand the other and address bigger things. The *personal is professional* for many of these staff members. We need to address the personal along with the professional in graduate school as well as in the work world.

JC: For me, learning and personal maturing do not end when someone earns a graduate degree. We need to provide ongoing professional development opportunities for all staff. Many contemporary needs of students didn't even exist when we were in school. Hence I agree with Marcia and Peter that intellectual curiosity is important; however, what bothers me about their argument is the implicit belief that being curious is enough.

VB: We all need to stay curious and current about relevant issues to do our jobs well. I was a speaker for a student affairs program a few years ago. While on campus I learned about the program's curriculum. It looked almost identical to my graduate curriculum in the 1970s. This concerns me. Graduate preparation programs and professionals responsible for staff development need to be on the cutting edge of new knowledge and find ways to inspire students to continue to learn.

JC: Technology is a good example. Facebook and Twitter—not e-mail or brochures—are ways students communicate, interact with each other, and learn. Student affairs educators can't influence students' development unless we can effectively connect with them. We need to be continually learning.

VB: What is essential today—for example, Facebook—did not exist a decade ago. Each day I am reminded of what I do not know; a learning-centered paradigm is critical. How many administrators of student affairs preparation programs think of themselves as learning centered?

JC: I don't know, but even those who subscribe to a learning-centered curriculum struggle to enact this agenda. How do we impart knowledge to students but not from on high? How do we challenge students and encourage them to challenge us—inside and out of the classroom? Answering these questions has to start in graduate school and continue in student affairs work. I may embrace a learning-centered organization, yet young staff may still defer to my views, no matter how many times I remind them that learning is content specific and I am not always the expert. Old habits are hard to break. For example, we need forums for staff to share their expertise—what they do and why they do it. We need to create learning organizations.

VB: I agree with your vision of a learning organization, but what you propose is boring. The profession needs something more. We need something more dynamic than forums, internships, and practica.

JC: What did you think about Peter and Marcia's emphasis on theory?

VB: Nice idea, but I don't think it is realistic. I use theory every day, but not the way scholars make it sound. For me, theory is second nature. The key is to be aware of our personal theories and help colleagues bring to the foreground their theories in use. We need to remind staff that theory is fluid, not discrete, sometimes informal and often unconscious.

JC: Good point. I think we need to help colleagues realize the invisible values (theories) that guide our actions. These theories and models come from classroom discussions, books, professional opportunities, training sessions, and everyday practice.

VB: When graduate students become full-time professionals, they come loaded with contemporary research, theories, and implementation models. However, we're growing increasingly concerned about how they see and understand themselves as educators in large, complex organizations filled with hierarchy, bureaucracy, and political quagmires.

JC: We need to cultivate professional maturity and help staff to process life lessons. Some graduate students and new professionals are not ready to understand or even see politics. Politics are often beyond their sight line. Navigating politics is something that has to happen in the field. Thus we need coaches and partners to talk about these issues and allow new professionals space to voice their views and process their experiences. We need to identify allies as well as land mines. We need a new model for professional development.

VB: Maybe we should dramatically alter graduate school internship opportunities and completely revamp professional development in divisions of student affairs. For example, graduate preparation programs can shift from a model of practical supervision to problem-solving meetings. Here students would bring in problems and then talk with peers and faculty about options.

JC: I like this idea. We could have staff bring in real everyday problems for us to solve collaboratively. These could lead to many ah-ha moments. This would be more meaningful to their work, would model lifelong learning using multiple perspectives, and hopefully not be so boring!

VB: An essential but often overlooked role for student affairs/higher education preparation programs is for faculty and student affairs educators to model ways for students and professionals to learn *how to learn*.

JC: Agreed. We need to get graduate students and new professionals to see themselves as architects, boundary spanners, team players, theoretical practitioners, conceptual thinkers, institution builders, doers, jugglers of an overwhelming and disparate array of tasks. Perhaps the term *reflective practitioner* captures it.

VB: Our conversation certainly reinforces the "it's messy" theme! We have named many components of an essential body of knowledge, including human development, organizational development, and culture, yet it is clear from our experiences that this knowledge is not static. Applying knowledge in context and in ever-changing circumstances requires lifelong learning, expert listening and communication skills, and personal maturity. This has been a great conversation, Jill, but I have an appointment with a potential donor.

JC: I understand! I'm off to a student government meeting. Talk with you soon!

Further Reading and Related Blog

Kerry Thomas, Oregon State University

Baxter Magolda, M. B., & King, P. M. (Eds.). (2004). *Learning partnerships: Theory & models of practice to educate for self-authorship.* Sterling, VA: Stylus.

The editors of this book advocate developmental maturity in the form of self-authorship as crucial for adults to meet the demands of their professional and personal lives. They offer a model of learning partnerships to promote self-authorship, illustrated by several chapter authors in diverse contexts that include curricular, cocurricular, and organizational settings. A step-by-step process for assessing and designing practice is included.

Keeling, R. P. (Ed.). (2004). *Learning reconsidered: A campus-wide focus on the student experience.* Washington, DC: National Association of Student Personnel Administrators and American College Personnel Association.

This volume calls for comprehensive, transformative, holistic learning experiences in higher education. The contributors reexamine previously held practices and outline various theoretical possibilities in the future of student affairs. Additionally, *Learning Reconsidered* outlines learning outcomes for undergraduate students, preparation for student affairs professionals, and competencies for student affairs organizations.

Lloyd-Jones, E. (1954). Changing concepts of student personnel work. In E. Lloyd-Jones & M. R. Smith (Eds.), *Student personnel work as deeper teaching* (pp. 1–14). New York, NY: Harper.

The author of this chapter provides a historical review of higher education highlighting the evolution of student affairs work, potential threats to the profession, and the importance of using theoretical constructs in education. Her analysis of the role of an educator in 1954 was visionary. Many of her ideas including holistic education, the importance of learning in and out of the classroom, the integration of knowledge and experience, and the role of higher education in preparing individuals to participate in modern society are key contemporary concepts.

Blog URL: contestedissues.wordpress.com
Corresponding Chapter Post: tinyurl.com/contestedissues01

2

How Does the Perception That Learning Takes Place Exclusively in Classrooms Persist?

Expanding the Learning Environment

*Mimi Benjamin, Cornell University, and
Florence A. Hamrick, Rutgers University*

Full-time, part-time, residential, and commuting students may have markedly different postsecondary experiences, complicating discussions of typical student experiences. Beliefs associating student learning with particular times and classroom spaces are persistent and long standing, and in this essay we refer to the more traditional residential college and university settings where boundaries, space differences, and campus hierarchies can be quite stark. However, the majority of these observations also apply to a range of campuses and student experiences where many traditional boundaries regarding learning have become even more indistinct.

Student affairs professionals frequently encourage new college students to practice effective personal management skills, while their campus role and temporal and space boundaries help students organize their weeks and their energies. For example, a full-time student is typically in class about 15–20 hours per week. Many engage in outside academic activities, such as research or study groups, adding to their time spent on academics. As a result, it can be easy to characterize college/university life as academic time and then everything else. With the potential exceptions of the availability of academic assistance programs, the financial aid package, and the relative proximity of residence halls to central campus buildings, student affairs staff and programs may not factor heavily into prospective students' and families' decisions about college selection. Because work in the classroom is what presumably leads students to pursue higher education, and because the goal of higher education is frequently earning a degree within a certain time frame, it is not surprising that learning at colleges and universities can be perceived as: (a) academic and (b) occurring only, or primarily, in classroom settings—perceptions that echo the question in the chapter title.

Perception of Where Learning Occurs

The first question we raise is: Who believes that learning takes place exclusively in the classroom? Admittedly, this perception is not likely to be shared by the majority of contemporary student affairs professionals. The 1996 "Student Learning Imperative" called upon student affairs units to form broad campus partnerships and assume shared responsibility for students' learning and personal development.[1] In 1999 Elizabeth Whitt and her colleagues offered frameworks and strategies for explicitly centering student affairs work and programs on learning.[2] More than 15 years after student affairs leaders proposed this shift in perspective, student affairs professionals are still met with skepticism or indifference when discussing their contributions to student learning. Concurrently, student affairs professionals can probably also identify faculty members who get it and enthusiastically become partners and sponsor, for example, student leadership, service learning, and internship opportunities. To further complicate the situation, some student affairs professionals themselves may question their legitimate roles in advancing student learning, especially when affiliated with institutions where supporting roles at best are envisioned for student affairs programs and staff.

The belief that learning occurs *exclusively* in academic classrooms (and related sites such as laboratories, studios, or field settings that are under the direction or supervision of faculty members) is a perspective that is largely consistent with Western academic traditions, roles, boundaries, and hierarchies. And this perspective is in turn grounded in the broader scope of Western social, cultural, and economic structures and practices, particularly assumptions about hierarchies and boundaries related to work, domesticity, and traditional gender role ascriptions. We explore in this essay how organizational structures and practices at colleges and universities privilege faculty members' content expertise as central to, if not exclusively responsible for, advancing students' learning, leaving student affairs educators' claims to partnerships in advancing student learning to appear as misguided hubris or naïveté. Such a dynamic can be particularly stark at more traditional colleges and universities and at colleges and universities aspiring to high-status recognition.

The Intersections of Work, Domesticity, and Gender Roles

How do Western assumptions about work, domesticity, and gender roles intersect to influence perspectives about classrooms and student learning? We anchor this brief overview in two watershed eras in the United States: the Industrial Revolution and post–World War II. Prior to the middle 18th through early 19th centuries, people frequently worked at home or with small family-based enterprises. With the rise of industrialization and capitalism, work became bounded by time (e.g., factory shifts) and space (e.g., workplaces). Child labor restrictions and worker safety provisions further specified times and places for work as well as who could work. After World War II, employers replaced or dismissed large numbers of women employed in the civilian labor force and replaced them with returning veterans. During the baby boom years (1946–1964), women disproportionately occupied the private sphere of domestic management and family caregiving while men disproportionately occupied the public sphere of paid work and family financial support. Middle- to upper-class work included set weekday hours, with weekends and evenings identified as leisure and family time.

Persistent gender role ascriptions and stereotypes are consistent with such a separate spheres approach, as are pervasive assumptions about "men's work" (e.g., expertise, leadership) and "women's work" (e.g., caregiving, domestic management) regardless of whether men or women perform the work. The spheres are also hierarchically related, as Joan Acker noted in her classic 1990 article: The largely invisible, repetitive,

and unacknowledged women's work enables the success of public, challenging, and remunerated men's work.[3] These same gendered assumptions about work extend to higher education. For example, Shelley Park in
1996 described how the largely unacknowledged and less well-remunerated
flow of academic women's work (e.g., advising, teaching, nurturing) frees
up other faculty members to succeed at academic men's work (e.g.,
researching, analyzing, theorizing).[4] Faculty traditionally engage in three
types of work—research, teaching, and service—but research (or teaching, at some undergraduate institutions) tends to factor most heavily in
career advancement and reward determinations, while traditional reward
structures often regard advising undergraduate students or groups as a
distraction from research or scholarship.

The gendered nature of work is a whole separate topic for study, but
the preceding broad overview may reveal how these same perceptions and
ascriptions can give rise to analogous assumptions about student affairs
professionals performing, for the most part, the women's work of caring
for students while faculty members perform the men's work of academics
and education. Indeed, these same roles and boundaries are also evident
in the very early years of student affairs work. According to Elizabeth
Nuss, although faculty members in early U.S. colleges and universities
performed the contemporary equivalents of student affairs functions, by
the early 20th century, universities hired directors or counselors to
assume the primary responsibility for advising and disciplining students.[5]
If directing or overseeing programs that advise, feed, shelter, or counsel
students is regarded as women's work requiring no particular skills or
expertise but instead reflecting natural or instinctual caregiving, Park
asserted the negative perception may attach itself irrespective of education levels or degrees earned by student affairs professionals.[6] Additionally, while engaging in research and disciplinary scholarship is widely
assumed to be a routine part—and many times the major part—of the
faculty job description, rarely is research a routine expectation for student
affairs staff, although becoming a practitioner scholar or scholar practitioner may be encouraged as a way to increase effectiveness.[7]

Expanding the Definition of Learning

If student learning, or a major part of student learning, is regarded as
achieving appropriate levels of content mastery, academic learning

becomes the principal work of college students. Contact with experts in the content area(s) becomes critical, and as Shils noted in *American Scholar*, faculty members have earned their expert status through extended years of study *as well as* demonstrated capabilities to create and advance knowledge through research.[8] The times and places for students' academic work throughout the term—usually during weekday, daytime hours—are prescribed in students' course schedules, yet encroachment of academic work into students' unassigned evening and weekend hours (i.e., study, independent project work) is assumed. Additionally, indicators of learning such as grades and class attendance can be readily tabulated, and monitoring systems can easily determine whether the student is making adequate progress toward a degree. Consequences for inadequate progress can be severe, so attention to work (academic study) becomes the student's highest priority.

Such a restrictive definition of student learning (i.e., content mastery) and positing grades and degree completion as the principal determinants and outcomes of learning aligns with the notion of student learning as an exclusively academic undertaking that rightly occurs in classrooms or related settings under faculty supervision. In such a scenario, although student affairs offices operate during daytime weekday hours, many programs, events, and advising contacts also occur during evening and weekend hours and away from buildings designated as academic.

If student learning is thought to occur only in classrooms or only under faculty direction, many student affairs offices or divisions can be regarded as providing food and shelter, offering leisure opportunities, and nurturing or disciplining students. Consequently, administrators of student affairs programs and staff may support learning by, for example, maintaining domestic order, providing social outlets, and ensuring students' overall well-being. However, student affairs programs may also be accused of diverting students' attention from academic learning priorities and to less-important cocurricular involvements. In either case, student affairs professionals and programs are axiomatically unrelated to student learning if learning is narrowly associated with classroom or academic experiences.

While collaboration may be desirable, different perceptions about learning may make collaborative efforts to educate challenging. In their chapter in a 1999 National Association of Student Personnel Administrators monograph, Arnold and Kuh noted the various mental models that are held by faculty, staff, students, and external stakeholders.[9] Using concentric circles to depict the various models, the authors highlight that some derivative of learning is central in all stakeholders' mental models, but other central elements are very different for each group. Faculty research is critical in the faculty mental model but exists on the outside circle on the mental model of the student affairs staff member, while the formal cocurriculum in the form of clubs and organizations is one of the center elements for student affairs but is in the outer circle for faculty. What is central suggests not only what the individual perceives as most important but also what is critical to the work he or she does. Such compartmentalized views of the educational process do not serve students well when opportunities abound for a more holistic student learning experience that includes intellectual as well as personal development.

Student affairs professionals generally maintain that robust cocurricular opportunities represent a legitimate aspect of a preferred, more expansive definition of student learning. Personal development is a critical factor in student affairs work as professionals teach students about interpersonal communication, leadership skills, citizenship, critical thinking, and the like. The cocurriculum serves as an applied curriculum that often presents students with the opportunity to put into action what they have learned in the classroom, whether that learning is content based (e.g., accounting major serving as student government treasurer) or interpersonally based (e.g., students availing themselves of cultural knowledge that may be taught or alluded to in class by interacting with a diverse group of peers). Student affairs professionals might consider the developmental level of students as well, which may require highlighting the learning element of cocurricular experiences. For example, some students may be dualistic in their thinking early in their college careers, leading them to define classroom experiences as learning and activities outside the classroom as not learning. In addition, providing students with feedback about their performance in their cocurricular activities may help them recognize this participation as measurable, similar to their in-class performance.

At some institutions, efforts to span the boundaries of curriculum and cocurriculum and structure the work of the faculty and the staff as complementary are evident. Learning communities are one example of collaborative, boundary-spanning opportunities on some campuses. Faculty programs in residence halls also may provide a similar, albeit differently focused, opportunity. When faculty members live in the residence halls with students through faculty-in-residence programs, faculty participate in the out-of-class experience not only for the students they teach but also for those they live with. Collaborative work between the faculty member and the residence hall staff can reinforce the variety of learning experiences students can access in college. Other opportunities for collaboration to reiterate the message that learning takes place throughout the entire student experience and not just in the classroom might include having faculty serve as advisers to student organizations and asking them to draw members' attention to the learning they experience, or having faculty note those opportunities in their classrooms to connect what students have learned more directly to the perceived learning space.

Student Affairs Professionals as Educators

Student affairs staff members must view themselves as educators to refute the belief that learning takes place only in the classroom. Viewing our work through a learning lens suggests some potentially different approaches to our everyday work. Directly asking students we work with what they have learned through their experiences highlights for students the educational potential of their out-of-class activities. Regarding programmatic interventions, Saunders and Cooper noted research suggesting that "students tend to pay more attention to the outcomes of their experiences when administrators spend time discussing with students their growth and learning. Simply having institutional staff members talk to students regularly about their growth and learning progress fosters a greater degree of reflection, thus encouraging students to . . . learn how to learn and develop."[10]

According to Astin's 1996 article in the *Journal of College Student Development*, most faculty talk about student learning, while student affairs staff talk about student development.[11] Perhaps student affairs staff should talk about *student learning and development* to reinforce the multiplicity of growth areas for students in higher education. Approaching the coordination of these opportunities with attention to the learning and development elements is critical. Creamer, Winston, and Miller acknowledged in *The Professional Student Affairs Administrator: Educator, Leader, and Manager* that while student affairs functions may offer personally meaningful and educational experiences, "that will not likely be the case unless they are intentionally planned and executed with educational goals at their foundation."[12] Careful consideration to what students can learn through these offerings should guide student affairs professionals to establish explicit outcomes for their work.

These learning and development experiences do not simply happen *to* students, they happen with their active involvement. There is a disconnect between the belief that students learn most from their peers and through the traditional classroom structure, yet most individuals view learning as occurring when a teacher leads a group through an experience that equates to a classroom activity. A professional staff member may provide guidance or have ultimate oversight of a program or service, but in many cases, such as student governance organizations, students themselves can and are expected to take the lead. This is consistent with what Barr and Tagg identified as a "learning-centered approach" of creating conditions for discovery and knowledge construction; through the cocurriculum, student affairs administrators create those very conditions.[13] Students participate in the programs and services offered through student affairs offices, but students play roles in the creation and implementation of programs and services as well. As Saunders and Cooper explained, students involved in designing programs with student affairs staff members use and enhance their skills in critical thinking and problem solving, skills more often associated with classroom learning but clearly experienced through their out-of-class activities as well.[14]

With the advent of distance and on-line learning, the concept of the classroom has been expanded. Expanding that concept to include residence halls, administrative buildings, student unions, and even the surrounding community may lead to a greater belief that learning occurs well beyond the walls of those spaces identified as classrooms. Service-learning experiences expand the space considered the classroom by placing students in the community to provide services based on what they learned in class. Learning communities structured around academic interests or disciplines can remind students that learning occurs in and out of the classroom, and they can provide collaborative opportunities for faculty and staff. While there are various ways to structure learning communities, many do require student and faculty participation outside the classroom through such activities as field trips, service projects, or community-building activities. These application-based learning experiences demonstrate how much learning can and does occur outside the confines of the classroom.

Support—for internships, practica, or clinical experiences as opportunities for students to apply their newfound knowledge to a variety of work settings—is pervasive in higher education. Internships help students prepare for real life (a related boundary assumption that sets apart life in college as unreal). Although adult and part-time students may have had significant work and community leadership experience prior to enrolling in college, internships provide reasonably high-benefit and low-risk ways for students to try on a desired social identity. More importantly, students can identify matches or mismatches with their sets of skills, values, and preferences. Students get an initial sense not simply about whether they can be successful but also whether they can thrive in particular organizational cultures, meet work expectations, connect with colleagues, and build satisfying careers.

Learning communities structured around academic interests or disciplines can remind students that learning occurs in and out of the classroom, and they can provide collaborative opportunities for faculty and staff.

However, students' lives while in college—in addition to formal internship or practicum experiences—are no less real and substantive. Practica or internships are far from the only opportunities students have to apply their growing knowledge and understanding. The following are examples of learning outcomes in the relatively high-benefit and low-risk environment of college:

- Students in shared living spaces have opportunities to develop respectful and effective approaches to interacting and negotiating with peers.
- Members of student organizations have opportunities to motivate themselves and others toward achieving shared goals.
- In disciplinary hearings students have opportunities to examine situations, impulses, and actions; meet the consequences of their actions; and plan toward future decision-making opportunities.
- Through interactions with people representing different backgrounds and social identities, students have opportunities to appreciate complexities in individuals and societies.
- Students involved in political campaigns and principled dissent have opportunities to challenge leaders or structures, envision alternatives, and enact changes.

In these situations, civility, leadership, critical thinking, accountability, forbearance, and civic responsibility reflect some of the learning possibilities—about students themselves, their local communities, and the world. Student affairs professionals foster these outcomes through programs and interpersonal interactions, such as coaching, advising, listening, questioning, and encouraging students to reflect on their efforts, to yield learning. Although none of the learning outcomes in the list entails content in an academic, disciplinary sense (although some are certainly suggestive of, for example, political science or psychology), these reflect some of the crucial learning experiences offered—typically under the auspices of student affairs programs and professionals.

Maintaining a Focus on Student Learning

Despite the authors' shared renunciation of perspectives that restrict student learning to classroom settings or to academic content, new and aspiring student affairs professionals may regard the current circumstances as perplexing and potentially deflating. Student affairs professionals and programs clearly contribute to student learning, but widespread acknowledgment of these contributions—much less validation—may not be forthcoming from faculty, parents, community members, or even students themselves. While it is tempting to view affirmation or recognition from others as a sign of a job well done, our challenge as professionals is to do our best work advancing student learning regardless of the level of affirmation or acknowledgment from others. We have little control over others' beliefs, assumptions, or mental models regarding learning. Additionally, undue preoccupation with perceptions of low status ascriptions can overshadow the more urgent priorities of focusing on students and learning. Our advice: Let it go and focus instead on adopting learning-centered perspectives and doing our best possible work.

However, despite this advice, student affairs professionals and units should vigorously challenge persistent beliefs about the lack of contributions or irrelevance to student learning from student affairs staff. Student affairs professionals should be ready to articulate—broadly as well as specifically—how their work provides critical learning opportunities for students. Assessment efforts have become widespread on college and university campuses. Accordingly, academic departments and student affairs units are being asked to identify targeted goals or outcomes for assessment, and much of the emphasis lies with demonstrations and evidence of student learning. On individual campuses, assessment teams

---

While it is tempting to view affirmation or recognition from others as a sign of a job well done, our challenge as professionals is to do our best work advancing student learning regardless of the level of affirmation or acknowledgment from others.

---

include faculty members along with student affairs professionals. These working groups may provide opportunities to redefine learning that incorporates the entire student experience and encompasses multidimensional and complementary opportunities for students to learn while enrolled at the college or university. These assessment discussions may create conceptions of learning that challenge the reflexive belief that learning occurs exclusively in classrooms, and such discussions may also reveal just how tenaciously the more traditional beliefs are held.

And so we end where we started: Exactly whose belief is it that learning only occurs in the classroom? It is not the belief of student affairs professionals. And in discussions with students, it is likely not their belief either, although they may need to be asked to reflect on their experiences to specifically identify the learning that has occurred in their out-of-class activities. In many ways, that clearly demonstrates the achievement of seamless learning that we hope for: Learning occurs while students are actively engaged in their lives as college/university community members, through the very real lives they are experiencing as students, in and outside the classroom.

Notes

1. American College Personnel Association. (1996). The student learning imperative: Implications for student affairs. *Journal of College Student Development, 37*(2), 118–122.

2. Whitt, E. J. (Ed.). (1999). *Student learning as student affairs work: Responding to our imperative.* Washington, DC: National Association of Student Personnel Administrators.

3. Acker, J. (1990). Hierarchies, jobs, bodies: A theory of gendered organizations. *Gender & Society, 4*(2), 139–158.

4. Park, S. M. (1996). Research, teaching, and service: Why shouldn't women's work count? *Journal of Higher Education, 67*(1), 46–84.

5. Nuss, E. M. (2003). The development of student affairs. In S. R. Komives, D. B. Woodard Jr., & Associates (Eds.), *Student services: A handbook for the profession* (4th ed., pp. 65–88). San Francisco, CA: Jossey-Bass.

6. Park, Research, teaching, and service.

7. Komives, S. R. (1998). Linking student affairs preparation with practice. In N. Evans & C. Phelps (Eds.), *The state of the art of professional education and practice in student affairs: Another look* (pp. 177–200). Washington, DC: American College Personnel Association.

8. Shils, E. (1978). The academic ethos. *American Scholar, 47*(2), 165–190.

9. Arnold, K., & Kuh, G. D. (1999). What matters in undergraduate education? Mental models, student learning, and student affairs. In E. J. Whitt (Ed.), *Student learning as student affairs work: Responding to our imperative* (pp. 11–34). Washington, DC: National Association of Student Personnel Administrators.

10. Saunders, S. A., & Cooper, D. L. (2001). Programmatic interventions: Translating theory to practice. In R. B. Winston Jr., D. G. Creamer, T. K. Miller, & Associates (Eds.), *The professional student affairs administrator: Educator, leader, and manager* (pp. 309–340). New York, NY: Brunner-Routledge, p. 314.

11. Astin, A. W. (1996). Involvement in learning revisited: Lessons we have learned. *Journal of College Student Development, 37*(2), 123–134.

12. Creamer, D. G., Winston Jr., R. B., & Miller, T. K. (2001). The professional student affairs administrator: Roles and functions. In R. B. Winston Jr., D. G. Creamer, T. K. Miller, & Associates (Eds.), *The professional student affairs administrator: Educator, leader, and manager* (pp. 3–38). New York, NY: Brunner-Routledge, p. 15.

13. Barr, R. B., & Tagg, J. (1995). From teaching to learning: A new paradigm for undergraduate education. *Change, 27*(6), 12–25.

14. Saunders & Cooper, Programmatic interventions.

Student Affairs and Integrated Learning

Laura Blake Jones, University of Michigan

The perception that learning takes place exclusively in classroom settings has persisted over time for a variety of complex and interrelated reasons highlighted by Mimi Benjamin and Florence Hamrick. This limited view of where and how learning takes place has not been systemically challenged by the work of student affairs educators, in spite of the existence of well-documented educational practices and a body of research and writing that suggests it should be. It is commonly understood that we have moved from a teaching-centered pedagogy to a learning-centered environment with the 2004 *Learning Reconsidered* document calling for "a holistic process of learning that places the student at the center of the learning experience."[1] Reports from the student affairs national association advocate a new identity for student affairs educators centered on holistic and integrative student learning.

Student affairs educators have always been committed to supporting students to face the developmental tasks of early adulthood. Their focus, however, has been on identity and relational tasks that are prevalent in out-of-class activities. Despite the fact that the cocurriculum offers a vast array of opportunities to advance cognitive development, student affairs educators have deferred to faculty in supporting students to understand multiple perspectives and learn to judge evidence to decide what to believe. Thus the significance of students moving toward self-authorship via integrative and reflective learning practices that allow them to develop the capacities needed to become keenly aware, highly engaged, and fully functioning, interculturally effective global citizens is obscured, at best, en route to graduation requirements, degree attainment, graduate school, or a career.

Student affairs educators have made great strides in this work over time but have stopped short of comprehensively advancing student learning to its fullest potential. Because student affairs educators understand the relativism of learning modalities and the value of a multifaceted, integrative student learning experience, expanding the perception of where learning occurs, for others and us, should be our aspiration.

Resolving the Student Affairs Identity Crisis

Student affairs educators continue to confront the discouraging reality that faculty and academic affairs administrators may remain unaware, misunderstand, or benevolently ignore the role of their student affairs colleagues. Benjamin and Hamrick offered a variety of explanations for this. These circumstances appear to persist in part because as student affairs educators we are not always sure of our purpose, or we fail to convincingly represent our roles as educators to others. It is easy to understand how student affairs educators could become distracted by the sheer volume of administrative and management tasks inherent in their daily work or be overwhelmed by the constant struggle to develop and maintain progressive programmatic advances within the constraints of emerging needs and limited resources. Underneath these dynamics, our identity as professionals may mediate our ability to create integrative learning environments for students.

Like students who may graduate and leave our institutions having failed to synthesize their learning experiences and fully ground themselves in a developing self-authored identity, we also graduate and employ student affairs professionals who may not be sure how to actualize their core purpose as partners in the educational enterprise. In *Authoring Your Life* Baxter Magolda cites the importance of developing self-authorship, heeding the "internal voice" to navigating life's challenges.[2] She notes that the ability to internally generate values, beliefs, and perceptions of self and others is central to managing multiple perspectives and interdependence with those whose perspectives differ from one's own. As Baxter Magolda argues, mature student affairs professionals may need developmental supervision and the "good company" of mentors, supervisors, and colleagues along the way to support their continuing professional development and evolving practice as educators.[3] Absent this, one could easily struggle to challenge traditional perspectives of student affairs work. Mid- and later-career professionals may also be consumed by the increasing complexity of their responsibilities and the magnitude of balancing work and family life, or become discouraged or deflated by years of experiencing marginalization of their roles in the learning environment. If we as student affairs educators have not progressed in our individual identity development work to a level of introspective personal reflection that allows us to become comfortable in our own skin and confident in our educational craft, we may not be able to embrace the new learning-centered identity for the profession or challenge the limited perspectives of our colleagues. We therefore may not be well equipped to illuminate developmental pathways for our students.

Integrative Learning as a Frame for Our Work

To rethink the perception of where learning occurs, student affairs educators must continue to expand their effectiveness by drawing more comprehensively on integrative learning theory. Schneider has described integrative learning as "a shorthand term for teaching a set of capacities—capacities we might also call the arts of connection, reflective judgment, and considered action—that enable graduates to put their knowledge to effective use."[4] Schneider argues that "reflective learning should also lead students to connect and integrate the different parts of their overall education, to connect learning with the world beyond the academy, and, above all, to translate their education to new contexts, new problems, new responsibilities."[5] Applying integrative learning theory as a tool to facilitate student growth can enable student affairs educators to bring sharply into focus the more blurred and undefined tasks confronting student learners and the role student affairs educators play in facilitating these critical learning experiences. Schneider advocates for "integrative and culminating studies," which she said can be achieved through a variety of means including interdisciplinary study, portfolios and e-portfolios, capstone experiences, and culminating projects and assessments.[6]

To rethink the perception of where learning occurs, student affairs educators must continue to expand their effectiveness by drawing more comprehensively on integrative learning theory.

The authors of *Greater Expectations: A New Vision for Learning as a Nation Goes to College* call on us to provide students with "the kind of education that develops their intellectual and ethical capacities, deepens their understanding of the world around them (the social world as well as the physical world), cultivates their sense of civic and social responsibilities to others and prepares them to thrive in a world characterized by innovation, complexity and change."[7] In their report the authors argue that students must become intentional integrative learners. Unfortunately this type of learning experience does not occur in most formal classroom learning environments, and while it does occur with greater regularity in the cocurricular environment, student affairs educators often fall short of creating awareness of the learning that is occurring and of intentionally facilitating the learning moments. Too few of our learning organizations are providing a consistent framework, guidance, or expectations that students should synthesize and integrate their learning experiences. And, if we do articulate the importance of integrative learning, we often continue to fail to have structures in place to assist students with this process or to make it widely available to the entire student population.

Benjamin and Hamrick offer a partial blueprint for how student affairs educators may become more fully participatory in the educational experiences of their students. They suggest that student affairs staff members make the educational content of interactions explicit to their students, and they encourage student affairs educators to take time to provide feedback to students so they recognize in a measureable way that they are interacting with another teacher. They also highlight and promote the boundary-spanning educational partnerships between faculty and student affairs educators that exists in intentionally created learning communities, residential colleges, and living-learning enterprises. They challenge student affairs professionals to shift the focus from just student learning to student learning and development.

We know that our students want to be challenged by big questions. What makes life worth living? What kind of difference will you make in the world? How can you learn from and demonstrate that you value the perspective of those who are different from you? And how does what you have learned in one setting translate to another? Student affairs educators are uniquely poised—usually outside the walls of the formal classroom—and able to interact with students about these questions and shape the expectation that students should be thinking and learning on this expansive and integrative level.

We can foster this type of thinking and reflection with students in large and small ways on a daily basis. This could occur in a hallway conversation with a student leader, in a developmentally directed supervision meeting with a staff member, in a more formal program within a living-learning community, or in a reflective moment when a narrowly considered action has resulted in unfortunate consequences. Student affairs educators are usually at their best with students in these moments yet can still fall short of fully illuminating and facilitating the reflective piece of the integrative learning opportunity. To do the latter, we must prioritize it as being equally important to the tangible content of the encounter. If we do not encourage our students to recognize and approach their learning experiences with intentionality and to subsequently engage in reflection about their learning, who will?

The curriculum for student affairs educators is vast and expansive, as are the connections between and among the learning experiences of our students. We have traditionally thought of our work with students in terms of developing a variety of skills, including personal management, interpersonal communication, conflict management, leadership, and health and wellness behaviors. We have also commonly participated in educational experiences promoting service learning, internships, and various opportunities that foster critical thinking skills. Our continuing evolution as educators, however, has taken us to working with our students in the expanded arenas of applied learning, such as teaching intercultural maturity and effectiveness, civic mindedness, and global citizenship skills. A framework for successfully advancing our work to this level is integrative learning, and as documented in *Learning Reconsidered,* student affairs educators are uniquely positioned and must play "broad roles in implementing transformative, integrated liberal education."[8]

The Value of an Intentional Road Map

Achieving these higher-order educational opportunities with our students will not happen without intentionality. Certainly on a one-on-one basis, individual student affairs educators have always had transformative educational experiences with students. These interactions could be with our student employees, student leaders, or individual students with an internal motivation or need that causes them to seek advice. If our goal is to have these transformative experiences with all our students, however, we need to create intentional opportunities for entering students to realize the breadth of the developmental tasks in front of them. We could accomplish this by offering a road map to assist in crafting a plan, cultivating learning opportunities along the way, and then allowing for capstone synthesis moments or experiences as students make the transition from our campuses to graduate school or their careers. While many institutions have initiated innovative programs for select groups of students, we need to see that these reflective learning experiences are more broadly received by students and commonly understood within the academy. Indeed, this is how we could succeed in changing the perception about where and how learning occurs and achieve our goals as educators.

Failure to expand the learning opportunities of our students will leave us right where we have been—working diligently with our students to achieve lofty goals—but with our roles misunderstood or relegated to the periphery. Student affairs educators can actively challenge the misperception about where and how learning occurs and actively work to create the structures and intentionality necessary for all students to have the opportunity to plan for and synthesize their educational experiences and be able to cohesively construct and reflect upon their learning. Embodying this in our daily work with students would reposition and emphasize the role of student affairs educators at the dynamic intersection of learning moments with our students. To succeed at this we must be personally grounded and intentional about our purpose and remain sharply focused on our intended outcomes, capitalizing on our ability to forge strong connections and interdisciplinary partnerships and brightly illuminating all the places where learning can and does occur.

Notes

1. Keeling, R. P. (Ed.). (2004). *Learning reconsidered: A campus-wide focus on the student experience*. Washington DC: National Association of Student Personnel Administrators and American College Personnel Association.

2. Baxter Magolda, M. B. (2009). *Authoring your life: Developing an internal voice to navigate life's challenges*. Sterling, VA: Stylus, pp. xi–xx.

3. Ibid., p. 311.

4. Schneider, C. G. (2003). Liberal education and integrative learning. *Issues in Integrated Studies, 21*, 1–8.

5. Ibid.

6. Ibid.

7. Association of American Colleges and Universities. (2002). *Greater expectations: A new vision for learning as a nation goes to college*. Washington, DC: Association of American Colleges and Universities.

8. Keeling, *Learning reconsidered*.

Further Reading and Related Blog

N. Aminatu Rubango, Loyola University Chicago

American College Personnel Association. (1996). The student learning imperative: Implications for student affairs. *Journal of College Student Development, 37*(2), 118–122.

This article describes how student affairs educators can intentionally create conditions to promote learning and personal development in the curriculum and cocurriculum. It includes five features of learning-oriented student affairs divisions, addresses questions and challenges inherent in transforming to a learning focus, and advocates student learning as the core of student affairs work.

Magolda, P. M., & Quaye, S. J. (2011). Teaching in the co-curriculum. In J. H. Schuh, S. R. Jones, & S. R. Harper (Eds.), *Student services: A handbook for the profession* (5th ed., pp. 385–398). San Francisco, CA: Jossey-Bass.

Authors discuss the role of student affairs professionals as educators who facilitate student learning in the cocurriculum. The chapter begins with a discussion on institutional influences on student learning. The authors discuss the importance of student affairs professionals understanding their role as educators and conclude with practical suggestions to foster learning in the cocurriculum.

Taylor, K. B., & Haynes, C. (2008). A framework for intentionally fostering student learning. *About Campus: Enriching the Student Learning Experience, 13*(5), 2–11.

The authors describe their reform of the curriculum and cocurriculum of a university honors program to emphasize student learning. They present a three-tiered framework that sequences learning outcomes and provides a means to measure progress.

Blog URL: contestedissues.wordpress.com
Corresponding Chapter Post: tinyurl.com/contestedissues02

3

How Are Dichotomies Such as Scholar/ Practitioner and Theory/Practice Helpful and Harmful to the Profession?

Developing Professional Judgment

Gregory S. Blimling, Rutgers University

I count myself among the group of professionals who tries to be reflective about the practice of student affairs; I work to apply human development and student learning theories to my daily practice, and I use theory to inform my judgment about a range of issues as a senior student affairs officer (SSAO). Despite my predisposition to implement theory through practice, everyday management issues of budgets, personnel, construction, student crises, meetings, and community relations consume most of my time. For every one conversation I have about an educationally substantive topic, I am engaged in at least 100 other conversations about management issues related to leading a student affairs division. I also found this to be true when I was a department head in student affairs and in less senior roles earlier in my career.

Even though theory informs my decision making, I rarely stop and think about using theory as a way to solve a particular problem. It has simply become part of how I think about student affairs work. Yet, in our field, we discuss theory as something that is separate from practice. We publish articles about how to use theory in practice as if it were a tool borrowed from a rack when needed and returned when finished.

In this essay I argue that theory and practice are not separate but are merged into what I refer to as professional judgment. I start this discussion by briefly explaining how the history of student affairs played a role in why our profession debates the value of using theory in practice. I also challenge the notion that student affairs educators are divided into two camps—practitioners and scholars. Such broad classifications oversimplify a more nuanced pattern of using theory through practice. To support this viewpoint, I discuss various styles student affairs professionals use to combine theory and practice into professional judgment. I conclude with a discussion and examples about how professional judgment manifests itself through the work of being a professional in student affairs.

Throughout this essay, I use the term *theory* to refer to the general body of theories customarily referred to in student affairs that help describe, understand, and engage students in college. I use the term *experience* to define what a person learns through the practice of student affairs and the accumulation of that knowledge over a career. I define *practice* as the application of theory and experience to student affairs work. When I mention student affairs professionals, I am referring to college administrators and educators who completed graduate work in college student affairs or a closely related field and who work at a college or university in a position usually associated with student affairs work.

The Theory Practice Debate

Questions about the need for using theory in student affairs have strong historical roots. Robert Schwartz's brief history of the importance of deans of women published in 1997 reports that one of the issues that separated deans of men from deans of women was the belief by the deans of men that they were born to the job.[1] Thomas Clark (as cited by Schwartz) in his speech to the National Association of Deans of Women in 1936 articulated this belief when he said, "There is no satisfactory training [to be a dean], at least from the academic standpoint, for the simple reason that the best deans are born that way and not trained that way."[2] Deans of men saw experience and the force of personality as the best qualifications for the position. Apprenticeships with a dean of men or relevant work experience were the only qualifications deans of men viewed as appropriate training for student affairs work.

In contrast, deans of women believed that graduate education grounded in theory and research was critical to becoming a student affairs professional. Built on a commitment to theory, research, and publication, the deans of women used scholarship as a way to legitimize their positions on male-dominated campuses.[3] They acted on this commitment to scholarship by writing the first book about student affairs work in 1915;[4] establishing the first graduate program in student affairs at Teachers College, Columbia University in 1916; and establishing the first student affairs professional association in 1917.

In Chapter 2, Benjamin and Hamrick explain some of the gender-related issues that placed less value on the caretaking roles deans of women were given and greater value on the leadership and management roles deans of men were believed to exercise. For these and related historical reasons, deans of men consolidated administrative authority over student affairs programs and became the SSAOs on most campuses. Their philosophy of practice and personality over education and theory prevailed, bringing Melvene Hardee to lament in 1964 that many student affairs offices had been staffed with retired military people, discarded football coaches, elderly housemothers, and random others who had what she described as "scout-like" qualities.[5]

The value of the reliance by deans of men on practice over theory received support from Paul Bloland in 1979, when he wrote that the role of the SSAO required no special knowledge or theoretical foundation in student affairs because the position was nothing more than the administration of a division of the university that only required good leadership and organizational skills.[6]

Some student affairs educators continued to question the value of theory to student affairs practitioners. For example, Bloland, Stamatakos, and Rogers wrote a monograph in 1994 that discounted the value of using student development theories in student affairs practice.[7] Their argument was not about whether theory is good or bad; instead, they argued that student development theory had limited utility in its application to the daily practice of student affairs work. They also claimed that the complexity of the application of these theories was beyond the understanding of most practitioners without a strong academic background in the social sciences. They believed that practitioners only gave lip service to these theories and instead functioned in administratively pragmatic ways. Hundreds of SSAOs adopted this view, many of whom were active in national professional associations.

One concern about the usefulness of theory was that student affairs practice is highly contextualized. Judgments about students are frequently influenced by students' circumstances, institutional policies, regional difference, institutional history, and financial resources, rather than by a critical review of students' developmental issues. In addition, many in student affairs work have no formal academic training in the field. A shared foundation of theories, research, and philosophy is difficult to achieve in an organization composed of people from different academic backgrounds. Career services professionals might come from business or counseling roots, individuals responsible for student leadership might be recreation professionals, and the staff responsible for student conduct might have formal legal training with no academic preparation for student affairs work.

University organizational structures further complicate the issue of theory in student affairs practice. Traditional student affairs functions may or may not report organizationally within a student affairs division. Financial aid, career services, recreation, cultural centers, international student services, and disability services are a few examples of student affairs functions that are sometimes in student affairs divisions and sometimes not. Although administrative organizations do not determine who is and is not a student affairs professional, organizational structures influence who is hired to perform those functions, the philosophy of the program, and its direction.

Good reasons exist to question the use of theory in student affairs if theory is viewed as a tool to solve student issues rather than something student affairs professionals make part of their way of thinking about their work with students. Most of the concerns about theory rest on the premise that theory is separate from practice rather than an integral part of it. These concerns dissipate when one changes the premise to suggest that theory and experience are merged to inform student affairs practice.

Professional judgment is the result of merging experience and theory to guide practice. It evolves from using experience in applying theory to refine one's way of thinking about practice.

Merging Theory and Experience

If we were to draw a continuum that showed at one end scholars who were exclusively theory oriented and at the other end practitioners who were exclusively experience oriented, the most interesting elements of the continuum would not be those extremes, which probably exist only in the abstract. The interesting parts would be between these extremes where professionals balance theory and experience. For the purpose of demonstrating the interconnections of theory and experience in student affairs practice, I created a four-cell matrix that juxtaposes the use of theory or experience with orientation as a scholar or practitioner (see Table 3.1). For each of the four styles, I assigned percentages to illustrate the relative balance between use of theory and experience represented. These percentages are intended to show relative weights that theory or experience might play in decision making for each of the four styles.

Table 3.1   **Four Styles of Integrating Theory and Practice**

	Practitioner	*Scholar*
Theory	Reflective-Practitioner	Scholar-Researcher
Experience	Experienced-Practitioner	Scholar-Practitioner

Reflective-practitioners use theory to inform practice. They read books and journals, attend professional meetings, share their knowledge through conference programs, and use research to analyze issues in their work. They think about student affairs practice in the context of research and theory and use this knowledge coupled with their work experience to inform and modify their practice. Balance of theory to experience: 40% theory, 60% experience.

Experienced-practitioners rely heavily on personal experience and the experience of others to guide decision making in student affairs. Although not averse to reading research about college students, they are more often guided by the informal theories they have constructed based on their past work experiences. Their primary interest in attending national meetings in the field may be networking and getting a broad overview of current issues of interest in the field. Balance of theory to experience: 20% theory, 80% experience.

Scholar-researchers derive their knowledge about student affairs from published studies, theories, and their own research. They may have limited experience in student affairs and only an abstract idea of what the daily practice of student affairs involves. Their engagement in the student affairs field is often devoted to better understanding the student experience rather than directly providing services to students. Balance of theory to experience: 80% theory, 20% experience.

Scholar-practitioners are educators with a history of practical experience in student affairs as well as practitioners who actively engage themselves in the creation of knowledge. These two types of educators may be indistinguishable. The difference is in how they devote their educational efforts. Where one might teach full-time as a professor in higher education, conduct research, and advise student affairs staff on program development, the other might be employed in student affairs as a practitioner, teach part-time, and contribute to scholarship through research, authorship, and program presentations. Balance of theory to experience: 60% theory, 40% experience.

These four styles are benchmarks on the continuum between the extremes of exclusively using theory or only using experience to guide practice. They suggest that the use of theory is not all or nothing, and that the nomenclature of scholar and practitioner only serves to define the tilt in the balance between using theory or experience in making professional judgments. Student affairs professionals merge theory and experience to construct knowledge that informs their professional judgment. The continuum represents only one dimension of understanding how theory and experience can come together in practice. Student affairs work is highly varied, and professionals may balance the use of theory and experience in different ways depending on topics, circumstances, and knowledge.

What Is the Value in Knowing Theory?

Knowledge of theory in student affairs helps student affairs professionals develop the habits of the mind that define how to think about the educational needs of students. It is a tool professionals use to analyze problems and build programs, and it helps to define membership in the field. Theory also provides an efficient means of transmitting knowledge from one generation to the next and from one professional to another. Because it is not possible for every person to have a close mentor relationship with the most knowledgeable people in the field, published research and theory is an invaluable way to share what is known about students and how best to promote their learning.

It is difficult to argue against mastering theory and having it available to use when needed. Perhaps the question should be asked in a different way. What is the practical value of knowing theory for student affairs professionals?

Theory has a practical and cognitive dimension. Knowing a theory is different from knowing how to apply it in the same way that having information about something is different from knowing how to use it. For example, I know how the game of hockey is played, but I cannot actually play hockey. The reverse is also true. It is possible to know how to do something but not understand how it works. Many people know how to use a computer, but they may not be able to explain how it works. Similarly, a person may be able to implement a program that successfully facilitates students' learning and development but not understand the theory behind why the program works.

In 2005 Kuh, Kinzie, Schuh, Whitt, and others published the results of a study they conducted with 20 colleges and universities using the National Survey of Student Engagement.[8] They identified a number of practices that enhanced student opportunities for academic and personal success. They concluded from their research that there were multiple paths to student success and no single blueprint existed for all campuses. Engaging students in ways that required them to put more time and effort into their studies and other activities, allocating financial resources, and organizing learning opportunities and services that facilitated student involvement were the critical elements in defining successful colleges. Doing what was educationally right was more important than knowing the theory and research behind why it worked. Successful programs can operate regardless of how well practitioners are able to articulate the research and theory explaining why they work, but when they know why the theory works, it empowers them to enhance, improve, evaluate, and create programs and experiences that further enrich the lives of their students.

Knowing a theory is different from knowing how to apply it in the same way that having information about something is different from knowing how to use it.

Many university policies and programs are based on research and theory about how to advance the academic and personal success of students. For example, living in a residence hall the first year in college is known to have a positive effect on retention, campus involvement, autonomy, and student satisfaction for traditionally aged undergraduates.[9] For these reasons, many universities require undergraduates to reside in a residence hall their first year in college. Various theories explain the reasons for these educational benefits. Students are likely to acquire the same educational benefits by living in a residence hall even when a residence life administrator cannot articulate the theory and research behind the policy that requires students to live on campus. However, without understanding the theory, that administrator may not be able to clarify the importance of the policy, defend the policy, or employ the types of educational experience in the residence halls that engage students in attaining the full educational value of the experience.

Our field has many gifted administrators with no formal training in student affairs who care deeply about students and work hard to help students succeed. They do what is educationally right for students and often accomplish much. The student affairs field also has gifted student affairs professionals who have formal training in student affairs and understand how theory influences the academic and personal success of students and how to use that knowledge to help students learn, grow, and develop. When professionals fuse this knowledge of theory with experience gained through a career in student affairs, they develop professional judgment about how to apply what they know, and it influences the way they think about their work with students.

Although people can perform tasks and implement programs without fully understanding the theory behind what they are doing, having information is almost always better than not having it. In many ways, it is this very knowledge that separates the professional from the amateur.

How Theory Shapes Practice

Knowing theory does not substitute for judgment anymore than knowing the alphabet substitutes for knowing how to write. Mastering theory alone does not make a person a student affairs professional. Being a professional also includes what one learns from interacting with other student affairs professionals, being a part of an organization engaged in the practice of student affairs, and a career of experience working with students. It includes having the mind-set and disposition of a student affairs professional, reflected in an ethic of caring, the habit of working out what is possible in a given time, self-knowledge, a spirit of advocacy on behalf of students, empathy, and the energy for and knowledge of how best to respond to students. It is shown by professional judgment, including knowing when to react, what to react to, when to watch, when to get involved, when to take action, when to look the other way, how to advocate for institutional resources, and how to best put those resources to use for the interests of students.

The combination of these experiences built on a foundation of knowledge about student learning, human development, and organizations, shapes the judgment of a student affairs professional.

Integrating theory with experience about how to advance the success of students is at the core of student affairs work. In the same way that physical training helps an athlete improve performance, knowledge of theory trains the mind of the student affairs professional to the disposition and demeanor of the profession. Being a student affairs professional is not about holding a job in student affairs. It is about having the necessary knowledge to think and act like a member of the profession.

In *Blink: The Power of Thinking Without Thinking*, Malcolm Gladwell explores how professionals develop an intuitive knowledge of correct responses to judgments that need to be made in their area of expertise.[10] Professionals from various fields were not always able to say at first why they reacted the way they did; they just knew what they knew. Their judgments were based on the ability to thin-slice experiences from first impressions, and these judgments were usually correct. The reason was that the depth of knowledge and experience in their field of expertise had fused to become part of their adaptive unconscious. One can see this phenomenon in professional athletes who not only know well how a sport is played but through experience have developed an almost instinctive knowledge of where to position themselves and how to move to help the success of their team.

I would describe this phenomenon among student affairs professionals as professional judgment. It is the mind-set or predisposition of knowing how to respond. Professional judgment evolves with experience and new information. Experiences such as responding to student suicides, hazing, arsonists, parents, cheating scandals, protests, pressure from politicians for favors, roommate conflicts, racial unrest, advising student groups, and helping students with special needs shape professional judgment, and over time, those experiences become fused with knowledge of theory and research. Being able to recite from memory various theories is less important to professional judgment than knowing what those theories teach us about how students embrace the college experience. Student affairs professionals may not always be able to say why they reacted in a particular way or be able to recite the theory and research behind a decision. But they have internalized those theories and merged them with their experience, mentoring, and associations into who they are and the way they think about the practice of student affairs.

The mind-set or disposition of a student affairs professional manifests itself in other ways. Consider this example. Student government is one vehicle for active learning by students. It allows students to acquire functionally transferable skills such as how to work in a policy structure, manage budgets, negotiate, speak in large groups, and conduct a meeting. I know student government is more about what students learn through their participation than what legislation student government enacts. In almost every case, what students learn through the experience is more meaningful and longer lasting than what the organization produces. However, to someone with minimal experience in student affairs, the measure of a student government's success is likely to be what it produces. This difference in focus changes how one works with the organization, how advising is done, and how one measures the success of the experience.

When theory is combined with experience gained through the practice of student affairs, it produces professional judgment that ultimately distinguishes the thinking of the professional from that of the amateur.

Understanding that the work of student affairs is the education of students is part of what it takes to be a student affairs professional. To be a professional one also needs to know how to structure educational experiences for students to help facilitate their learning and their psychosocial, emotional, and cognitive growth and development. To successfully fulfill the responsibilities of a professional in student affairs, one needs to understand how students learn, how they mature, how environments influence their development, and how organizations help and hinder those processes. Theory can enrich understanding on why some approaches work and others do not, why some students challenge every decision and others work to please, and why some students lose interest in organizations while others remain committed. Theory opens doors to finding the answer to those questions and more. When theory is combined with experience gained through the practice of student affairs, it produces professional judgment that ultimately distinguishes the thinking of the professional from that of the amateur.

Conclusion

When I started working in student affairs more than 35 years ago, many of the theories now considered foundational were just entering the dialogue about the role, scope, and mission of the profession. For me, these theories opened doors to learning why students behaved the way they do and how I could use that knowledge to help educate them. Theories became more useful after I taught them to others, wrote about them, and used them to understand students better.

Today I do not think about theory as something that is separate from what I do. Although I could explain human development theories that support decisions I make, I do not consult these theories before I make decisions and I usually do not explain the rationale for those decisions by reciting theories. Instead, I use my professional judgment, of which theory is a part, to make decisions and explain why they will promote student learning.

I base my professional judgment on an amalgamation of research I have read, theories I have learned, student affairs positions I have held, books I have written, discussions with colleagues, students I have helped, and decisions—good and bad—I have made. In the same way that it is difficult for students to identify which college experience helped them become the person they are when they graduate, it is difficult for me to separate my professional judgment from my knowledge of theory in student affairs. What I do know is that I make better decisions because I have that knowledge, and that as a result, students have benefited.

Notes

1. Schwartz, R. A. (1997a). Reconceptualizing the leadership roles of women in higher education: A brief history on the importance of deans of women. *Journal of Higher Education, 68*(5), 502–522.

2. Ibid., p. 512.

3. Schwartz, R. A. (1997b). How deans of women became men. *The Review of Higher Education, 20*(4), 419–436.

4. Mathews, L. K. (1915). *The dean of women.* Cambridge, MA: Riverside Press. Lois Kimberly Mathews was dean of women and associate professor of history at the University of Wisconsin.

5. Hardee, M. (1964, November). *The residence hall: A locus for learning.* Paper presented at the Research Conference on Social Science Methods and Student Residence, University of Michigan, Ann Arbor, MI.

6. Bloland, P. A. (1979). Student personnel training for the chief student affairs officer: Essential or unnecessary? *NASPA Journal, 17*(2), 57–62.

7. Bloland, P. A., Stamatakos, L. C., & Rogers, R. R. (1994). *Reform in student affairs: A critique of student development* (ERIC Counseling and Student Services Clearinghouse). Greensboro: School of Education, University of North Carolina.

8. Kuh, G. D., Kinzie, J., Schuh, J. H., Whitt, E. J., & Associates. (2005). *Student success in college: Creating conditions that matter.* San Francisco, CA: Jossey-Bass.

9. Pascarella, P. T., & Terenzini, P. T. (2005). *How college affects students: A third decade of research* (Vol. 2). San Francisco, CA: Jossey-Bass.

10. Gladwell, M. (2005). *Blink: The power of thinking without thinking.* New York, NY: Little, Brown.

Moving Beyond Dichotomies

Integrating Theory, Scholarship, Experience, and Practice

Ellen M. Broido, Bowling Green State University

As Blimling writes in his essay, debates about the role of theory in practice have an almost century-long history in student affairs. Similar conversations about the differences between and the integration of scholarship and practice are pervasive in a wide variety of academic disciplines, including music, political science, nursing, psychology, and especially in education. Even the American Association of Colleges and Universities has a project titled Bringing Theory to Practice.[1] In our own field, the American College Personnel Association's (ACPA) *Developments* newsletter has begun a series about ways of being a scholar-practitioner.[2]

I agree there is a useful distinction between research/scholarship and practice; they are activities with different goals. Theory is by definition general; practice is always context bound. However, theory and experience inform good scholarship and good student affairs practice. What is problematic is the perception that theory and practice are mutually exclusive or adversarial and the perception that each lacks value for the other. Scholarship and practice, at least in applied fields like student affairs, are two sides of the same coin.

I agree with most of Blimling's arguments. We agree that theory and experience are constitutive elements of effective student affairs practice; that people vary in the extent they use each, but that it is rare when people use only one or the other; that reflection is critical to integrating theory and practice; that knowing how to apply theory is as important as knowing theory; and that knowing theory "empowers [practitioners] to enhance, improve, evaluate, and create programs and experiences that further enrich the lives of their students" (p. 48). His distinction between the terms *experienced practitioner, reflective practitioner, scholar practitioner, and scholar researcher* is useful and I use his definitions in this essay.

I depart from Blimling's position in two regards. First, in addressing his reasons student affairs educators seldom use theory, he points out many student affairs professionals received their academic training in fields other than student affairs and so are unfamiliar with theories that might support their work. This argument has two limitations. First, it presumes that the theories these practitioners learned in other academic disciplines are minimally useful when working with collegians. Backgrounds in other social sciences are the most obvious source of relevant theories, but business and the humanities also provide insights into the human and organizational dynamics of campuses. Second, Blimling presumes that student affairs educators' interest in theory ends when their employment begins. Options for learning theory while working are plentiful, providing the opportunity to expand knowledge of theories and gain experience with how to use them to design and evaluate programs, to understand the needs and development of students, to explain the dynamics of our organizations, and to improve the quality of our students' experiences.

As Upcraft notes, faculty and student affairs practitioners work best when they understand and address theory and practice, but doing so "will require a change in attitude and behavior on the part of both theoreticians and practitioners if theory and practice are to be melded for the benefit of institutions of higher education, student affairs services and programs, and most of all students."[3] Both parties must change, as must our institutional contexts.

What Faculty Must Do

Student affairs faculty can enhance the development of reflective scholars and scholar practitioners in two ways. The first is to enable our graduate students to use theory to guide their practice. The second is to make our scholarship useful for practitioners. Most student affairs preparation program faculty make a concerted effort to understand and address practitioners' concerns. I must listen to current practitioners to understand their concerns, pressures, and imperatives. I volunteer for campus committees and initiatives that help me become aware of concerns and accomplishments of undergraduate students. Most colleagues contributing the newest theories in student affairs work are former practitioners themselves. Many of those who are not have worked hard to understand the day-to-day realities of student affairs practitioners.

What Practitioners Must Do

To be an effective practitioner do you need to memorize Chickering and Reisser's seven vectors?[4] No. Do you need to know the major ways students change while in college, what facilitates those changes, and how those ways differ for different types of students and those who have different experiences while students? Absolutely. While it will be far easier to communicate with professional colleagues if you know icons and lexicons, understanding and being able to implement the concepts are far more important to work effectively with students. ACPA: College Student Educators International and NASPA: Student Affairs Administrators in Higher Education's Joint Task Force on Professional Competencies have identified the ability to use theory to design programs and practices as intermediate-level competencies[5] and "utilize theory to inform divisional and institutional policy and practice" as an advanced-level competency.[6]

Many practitioners who believe they operate without theory are in fact using informal ad hoc theories, what Blimling refers to as experience. Widick, Knefelkamp, and Parker consider informal theory as "the body of common knowledge that allows us to make implicit connections among the events and persons in our environments and to act upon them everyday."[7] As McEwen writes,

> Each one of us has our own informal theories about people, environments, students, human development, and how to work with students, although those theories or perspectives may not always be a conscious or clear part of our awareness. Thus people turn to theory—both formal and informal—to make the many complex facts of experience manageable, understandable, meaningful, and consistent rather than random.[8]

What is problematic is when those informal theories are not challenged and tested; Widick, Knefelkamp, and Parker note that we tend to ignore evidence that contradicts our informal theories and pay attention to data that support them, making it critical we be aware of those assumptions and consciously evaluate them.[9] That self-reflective testing can come from empirically derived theories, from conversations with colleagues, and from close attention to our experiences. As important as knowing *what* to do, is knowing *why*. And those *whys* are theory, sometimes formal, sometimes informal.

Many models have been proposed to help practitioners apply formal theory to practice (e.g., Upcraft).[10] I encourage my students to answer five questions to help them understand how to use theory to guide practice: What issue or problem am I looking to solve? What theories speak to that problem? Who are my students, and what characteristics do they exhibit in light of those theories? What do these theories tell us about how to promote development for students with these characteristics? and Which of those approaches are feasible in light of other important considerations (legal/ethical, policy, resources, political, and goals and priorities of the institution)?[11] Being intentional about asking these questions can develop the kind of reflexivity Blimling describes. Using these questions to assess the adequacy of one's informal theories will enhance their effectiveness.

As important as knowing what to do, is knowing why. And those whys are theory, sometimes formal, sometimes informal.

With practice, awareness of the answers to the preceding questions leads to what Blimling calls *professional judgment.* Dean writes that for her,

> Both the scholar and the practitioner now co-exist. . . . this change was not defined by a degree, a title, or a role, but rather it is a way of thinking and doing. . . . A primary characteristic of scholar-practitioners is that they value knowledge as a means to improve practice, and understand that the research-based literature has relevance for both program and policy.[12]

Dean and Kidder both argue that to effectively integrate scholarship into practice one must make the time to read research literature, and they suggest that engaging in assessment of one's own practices furthers development as a reflective practitioner.

What Institutions Must Do

Among notable student affairs scholar-practitioners, those who have gone beyond using theory in their design and implementation of programs to the production of scholarship, I observe a preponderance of White men. If we want to encourage the development of scholar-practitioners we should consider what institutional structures and expectations have impeded women and people of color from producing scholarship.

What systems might we build into our institutions that would value and foster the scholarly contribution of all student affairs practitioners? How can those opportunities be extended to everyone who has an interest? What other aspects of people's work might be reformulated to allow them the time to develop their scholarship?

Leaders must be explicit about modeling the use of theory, must require theoretical and data-based justification for the allocation of resources (which will have the benefit of creating more compelling justification for our work), and reward the development of scholarship by people within their divisions. They can enhance this through providing opportunities for their staff to learn and apply theory—encouraging attendance at professional conferences and workshops and campus-based reading groups and staff development sessions.

What systems might we build into our institutions that would value and foster the scholarly contribution of all student affairs practitioners?

Translating My Own Theory Into My Own Practice

Someone once asked me how I used a model I had developed when teaching general education courses for first-year undergraduates. That is, they asked how did I apply my own theory to my practice? Ouch. I had not consciously tried to do so but quickly set out to rectify this situation.

I learned how difficult it was to constantly intentionally use theory when teaching, to keep in the forefront of my consciousness a model I knew better than anyone else did. So yes, integrating theory and practice takes effort. I returned to the questions I posed earlier in this essay: What outcomes was I hoping students would achieve? Which theories (not just my own) helped explain that kind of learning? What did theory tell me about how to foster that kind of development? What did those efforts look like when integrated with all the other things I wanted my students to learn, with all the other things I was concentrating on? While for a variety of reasons—inattention, distraction, time—I did not always consider these questions, it was what I strove for, and when I was able to be this intentional, I was most effective with students.

The question posed for consideration in this essay was, How are dichotomies such as scholar-practitioner and theory-practice helpful and harmful to the profession? No, I do not find such dichotomies useful to our profession. Many such dichotomies pervade our language and thinking: qualitative/quantitative, pragmatist/idealist, teacher/student, U.S./foreign, 2-year/4-year, hard/soft, leader/disengaged, traditional/nontraditional. Rarely do such distinctions effectively represent the range of our experiences or of those we serve. It is more useful to consider the ways both aspects are and can be present in our work.

Notes

1. American Association of Colleges and Universities. (n.d.). *Bringing theory to practice.* Retrieved from http://www.aacu.org/bringing_theory/index.cfm

2. Kidder, R. (2010, Spring). Part I: The scholar practitioner. *Developments, 8*(1). Retrieved from http://www.myacpa.org/pub/developments/archives/2010/Spring/article.php?content = kidder

3. Upcraft, M. L. (1994). The dilemmas of translating theory to practice. *Journal of College Student Development, 35,* 438–443, p. 438.

4. Chickering, A. W., & Reisser, L. (1993). *Education and identity* (2nd ed.). San Francisco, CA: Jossey-Bass.

5. ACPA: College Student Educators International, & NASPA: Student Affairs Administrators in Higher Education. (2010). *ACPA/NASPA professional competencies for student affairs practitioners.* Washington, DC: Author. Retrieved from http://www2.myacpa.org/img/Professional_Competencies.pdf

6. Ibid., p. 28.

7. Widick, C., Knefelkamp, L., & Parker, C. A. (1980). Student development. In U. Delworth, G. Hanson, & Associates, *Student services* (pp. 73–116). San Francisco, CA: Jossey-Bass, p. 111.

8. McEwen, M. K. (2003). The nature and uses of theory. In S. R. Komives, D. B. Woodard Jr., & Associates (Eds.), *Student services: A handbook for the profession* (4th ed., pp. 153–178). San Francisco, CA: Jossey-Bass, p. 154.

9. Widick, Knefelkamp, & Parker, Student development, p. 111.

10. Upcraft, The dilemmas of translating theory to practice.

11. Coomes, M. D. (1994). Using student development to guide institutional policy. *Journal of College Student Development, 35,* 428–443.

12. Dean, K. L. (2010, Summer). Part II: The scholar practitioner. *Developments, 8*(2). Retrieved from http://www.myacpa.org/pub/developments/article2.php?content = scholar, p. 2.

Further Reading and Related Blog

Amanda Wilson, University of Iowa

Association of American Colleges and Universities. (2011). *Bridging Theory to Practice Newsletter.* Retrieved from http://www.aacu.org/bringing_theory/newsletter/index.cfm

This newsletter series reports activities of the Bringing Theory to Practice Project that encourages people in higher education to advance learning and discovery, to advance students' potential and well-being, and to advance education as a public good that sustains a civic society.

Jones, S. R., & Abes, E. S. (2010). The nature and uses of theory. In J. H. Schuh, S. R. Jones & S. R. Harper (Eds.), *Student services: A handbook for the profession* (5th ed., pp. 149–167). San Francisco, CA: Jossey-Bass.

The authors' overview of theories provide the foundation for student affairs practice. They describe the creation process, constant evolution, and the importance of using theory to guide practice. They also summarize the theoretical families that guide the student affairs profession, such as development, students, social identities, organizations, campus environments, student success, and typology. This chapter also introduces paradigms for theory construction and application, such as positivism, constructivism, critical theory, and post-structuralism.

Strange, C. C., & King, P. M. (1990). The professional practice of student development. In D. G. Creamer (Ed.), *College student development: Theory and practice for the 1990s* (pp. 9–24). Alexandria, VA: American College Personnel Association.

This seminal article articulates theory as the formulation of a reasonable explanation for experience and observation, the role of research in assessing the accuracy of that explanation, the nature of practice guided by theory and values, and the role of evaluation in assessing the effectiveness of practice. This cycle of experience, theory, research, practice, and evaluation is offered as a framework for professional practice.

Blog URL: contestedissues.wordpress.com
Corresponding Chapter Post: tinyurl.com/contestedissues03

4

If Student Affairs–Academic Affairs Collaboration Is Such a Good Idea, Why Are There So Few Examples of These Partnerships in American Higher Education?

Transforming Our Approach to Education: Cultivating Partnerships and Dialogue

Victor J. Arcelus, Gettysburg College

Why do some faculty and staff believe it is a good idea to develop academic and student affairs partnerships? At many universities people have reevaluated their goals for the future and aspire to create a learning-centered environment within an organizationally and programmatically seamless campus community. Their goal is for students to appreciate the interconnectedness among components of their lives, strengthen their intellectual development, and cultivate a disposition toward lifelong learning. To achieve this shift, faculty and student affairs staff need to rethink their roles and consider ways to develop a campus ethos that encourages students to become more actively involved in their education while integrating their disciplinary and experiential learning.

This rich educational experience is possible when faculty, staff, and students engage in substantive interactions that help students develop a sense of self through increased understanding of others. Some faculty and staff have navigated their way toward increased partnership, but for many it has been difficult to plot a course through complex campus climates and deeply entrenched cultures that often limit our ability to work collaboratively across campus to develop an integrated approach to higher education.

Richard Hersh explained that "the best education takes place at the nexus of profound intellectual and social/emotional development. Yet most institutions dichotomize the various facets of learning, as if our intellectual, emotional, and ethical lives were compartmentalized."[1] To develop an integrated and transformational educational experience, faculty and staff must work together to create synergistic relationships across institutional divisions, particularly those responsible for educating students—academic affairs and student affairs. According to Hersh, the modus operandi for colleges should be to undo the "false dichotomies and foster a more global and holistic version of education."[2]

George Kuh advocated for the development of a seamless learning environment, one in which a college campus strives to be a "tapestry of previously unconnected experiences carefully stitched together by policies and practices," thus allowing students to merge their in- and out-of-class learning.[3] Alexander Astin, Ernest Pascarella, Patrick Terenzini, and Vincent Tinto support the seamless learning approach, for their research demonstrates that students' whole collegiate experience provides a platform for learning. The student's intellectual and social integration plays a key role in satisfaction, persistence, and learning.[4]

Pascarella and Terenzini in *How College Affects Students* noted that educational research disseminated since 1990 shows "the broad scope of the dimensions of students' lives that change with exposure to college."[5] They identified many areas where students developed through participation in higher education: academic and cognitive, psychosocial, attitudes and values, career and economic, and quality of life. Most importantly for the purpose of this essay, they stated that "the evidence strongly suggests that these outcomes are interdependent, that learning is holistic rather than segmented, and that *multiple forces* operate in *multiple settings* to shape student learning and change in ways that cross the 'cognitive-affective divide.'"[6] As a result, institutions should dissolve the deeply entrenched division of labor between faculty (attending to students' intellectual development) and student affairs (focusing on students' social and emotional development), acknowledging, as Patrick and Anne Love stated, "intellectual development does not happen exclusively in the class and that social and emotional development does not happen exclusively out of class."[7]

The Kellogg Commission on the Future of State and Land Grant Universities published a report that encouraged institutions of higher education to integrate the out-of-classroom "hidden curriculum" into the learning experience.[8] Marcia B. Baxter Magolda supported this recommendation:

> [Students] cannot be expected to connect the cognitive, intrapersonal, and interpersonal dimensions of their adult lives if their education has led them to believe these dimensions are unrelated. It is clear—and it has been for some time—that our current approach to bifurcating the cognitive and affective dimensions of learning does not work.[9]

These studies suggest that university administrators need to examine how they can develop an educational approach that acknowledges students' many ways of learning, engages them as active participants in knowledge construction, and capitalizes on the concurrent learning occurring in and out of class. Terenzini and colleagues succinctly declared that "ways must be found to overcome the artificial, organizational bifurcation of our educational delivery systems."[10]

Why Is Cross-Divisional Collaboration So Challenging to Accomplish?

As the United States population grew and access to higher education expanded, universities rapidly became more complex, forcing institutions increasingly to divide tasks. Robert Zemsky, Gregory Wegner, and William Massy introduced the concepts of *administrative lattice* and *academic ratchet* to describe the emerging tension and unproductive competition for resources between academic and administrative units from 1940 to the end of the 20th century.[11] During this period, institutions expanded their administrative staffs and became more specialized. These administrative structures established an increasingly important role in the daily operations of institutions as their administrators defined their own goals and justified their growth with evidence of their initial successes on campus. Rather than "growth by substitution," institution officials continued to add administrative functions in their pursuit of continued improvement, which led to faculty becoming "an important minority."[12]

Simultaneously, the academic ratchet led faculty members progressively to disengage from their home institutions as they redefined their roles in terms of "the more specialized concerns of research, publication, professional service, and personal pursuits."[13] Zemsky and colleagues make clear that faculty came to believe that professional status often depended more on their contributions to a discipline than their roles as master instructors at their institution. Thus faculty members began to disengage from their campus communities, which then justified the development of administrative units designed to perform tasks formerly assigned to faculty. As faculty became more specialized and discipline centered, they were seldom rewarded for time spent with students outside the classroom. Over time, student affairs has assumed more of the out-of-classroom roles with students and differentiated itself from academic affairs to the extent that it is not unusual for the two divisions to compete with each other.

Nevertheless, student affairs as a profession has been attempting to collaborate with academic affairs for more than two decades. However, the cross-divisional collaborative opportunities that have emerged since the 1990s have been largely perceived to be one-sided, for the attempt by student affairs to reach out to involve faculty in their initiatives has seldom been reciprocated. While administrators of academic affairs divisions have also been focusing in the past two decades on collaboration, they have not strengthened their relationship with student affairs. Instead, faculty members have been focusing on developing valuable cross-disciplinary programs and departments.

Cultural differences between the divisions, as well as the real and perceived differences in the deeply held values and beliefs about students and their education, hamper the pursuit of cross-divisional partnership. As specialization among academic departments deepened and student affairs became more professionalized, academic and student affairs staffs experienced dramatically different training and assumed distinct roles. As a result, student affairs practitioners and academicians do not always understand one another's discourse, nor do they accurately comprehend each other's roles and responsibilities. The resulting cultural differences often lead to "misunderstandings, mistrust, disrespect, conflict, disdain, and antagonism."[14] These sentiments become magnified when people at an institution focus on difference rather than on the commonalities that exist in their values and goals for educating students. In fact, the way people define *educator* can be one of the most significant barriers impeding faculty and student affairs partnerships, and it may be deeply embedded in the cultural norms of both divisions.[15]

In cases where the campus culture is neither conducive to collaborative ventures nor to substantive cross-divisional dialogue, the two divisions can operate in isolation, seeking to advance their own goals at the perceived expense of the other. Often, faculty members conclude that student affairs needs to be "reined in" or the academic program will suffer. Student affairs staff members pursue their work independently of academic affairs because the climate does not support collaboration. They also simultaneously resent academic affairs staff for isolating themselves and not engaging in an inclusive dialogue about the educational mission of the institution. At the root of this struggle is the debate over the mission of the college or university; some believe that the answer is a polarizing one—the institution pursues either an academic mission or an educational mission.

One can trace the origins of this institutional struggle to the debate over whether an undergraduate experience should be about the life of the mind or about educating the whole person. The argument is not new, and one can refer to the writings of Robert Hutchins[16] and John Dewey[17] to see that their different philosophies and theories of education reflect the conflicting perspectives shared by faculty and staff today. In the 1930s, the debate focused on the nature and purpose of liberal education and how institutional leaders should design undergraduate education. Dewey advocated a constructivist approach to education in which students, through experience, made meaning for themselves through personal connections with others. He spoke of a collaborative educational setting rich with interactions and with students engaged in cooperative arrangements. Hutchins, however, promoted an educational approach based in reading and discussing the great books of the Western world facilitated by a moratorium on experiences in society. Hutchins's intellectual inquiry model conflicted with Dewey's experiential model.

Hutchins's concern that faculty and administrators did not believe in the "cultivation of the intellect for its own sake" led him to propose his theory for the design of higher education.[18] He maintained that institutions of higher learning should stand firm in their "single-minded pursuit of the intellectual virtues" and their "single-minded devotion to the advancement of knowledge."[19] Hutchins's answer to higher education's anti-intellectualism was to propose an academically focused general educational program that would provide all students with a common intellectual training.

In contrast, Dewey's philosophy was that colleges and universities have a broad educational mission, one that seeks to enhance students' intellectual development through the acquisition of knowledge and skills, and accomplishing this goal by linking knowledge with experience while learning through social interactions. Dewey's belief that an effective education extends beyond subject matter learning to include personal experience required careful attention to the many conditions and circumstances within the educational environment that exist beyond the classroom. The environment surrounding students, Dewey affirmed, provides abundant academic and psychosocial learning opportunities to help students make meaning of academic content and vice versa. Dewey cautioned that subject matter and skills learned in isolation from experience are disconnected from reality in a way that makes the material less accessible under real-world conditions.

The application of these philosophies to the modern university reflect very different pedagogies and faculty and student roles in the learning process. In addition, the particular philosophy followed will affect how student affairs staff approach their work. At an institution that adheres to an educational philosophy consistent with Hutchins's approach, the student affairs division would likely be a very small service-oriented operation supporting the academic affairs division. At an institution with a progressive approach consistent with Dewey's philosophy, student affairs would likely operate in tandem with academic affairs to accomplish two things: promoting educational experiences that engage students as active participants in their education and cultivating opportunities for continuity and integration within and between the in- and out-of-class aspects of students' lives.

Challenges Facing Institutions

My years as a practitioner and my research centering on the relationship between academic and student affairs influence my current thinking about cross-divisional collaboration. In 2003 I conducted an ethnographic study that investigated the cultures of academic and student affairs divisions in one residential liberal arts institution to consider the barriers and opportunities when trying to develop a mutually supportive educational program.[20] My research questions focused on how faculty and student affairs staff members perceive their own and each other's roles as educators and how these perceptions influence the potential for cross-divisional collaboration. At Crossroads University (a pseudonym), I immersed myself in the campus culture for one academic year, seeking to understand the institutional culture, the divisional cultures, and their interactions.

I found a fragmented and competitive campus. The academic and student affairs divisions operated independently of each other, and administrators and staff of each division appeared to be most concerned with issues that pertained primarily to themselves and their work. The intellectual climate preoccupied faculty, who felt that the student affairs division was diminishing academic primacy. Student affairs professionals expressed concern that faculty neither valued their roles on campus, nor recognized their roles as educators. Weak institutional leadership fueled the preoccupations of academic and student affairs, which contributed to fragmentation and competition.

The academic and student affairs divisions competed over what I call the *core elements* (i.e., institutional mission and philosophy, resources as money, and resources as student time). Ideally, the institutional mission and philosophy should drive budgetary decisions, which in turn influence the types of programs developed and thus the ways that students spend their time; the circular relationship among these factors is stable and reinforcing in healthy institutions. At Crossroads, however, the sense of competition destabilized the system, limiting institutional progress in planning for the future and undermining the university's educational impact on students. With the academic and student affairs divisions at odds over the core elements and the executive leadership providing insufficient institutional direction, the university struggled to mobilize its resources in a coordinated manner to enhance student engagement on campus.

The Crossroads case depicts a campus climate where one must choose between Hutchins's or Dewey's philosophy of education. Different perspectives on education and the learning process influenced the debate on campus that pitted academic primacy against educating the whole person.

My research concluded that these problems should be addressed in campuswide conversations that focus on learning, rather than on the merits of academic primacy (perceived to privilege academic affairs) or educating the whole student (perceived to privilege student affairs). These phrases pulled people apart at Crossroads rather than bringing them together.

The research evidence justifies consideration of educational strategies that link students' lives in the classroom with their lives outside the classroom. Exploring how Dewey's philosophy of education might assist institutions in advancing student learning does not mean that a commitment to intellectual development is curtailed. Adopting a vision of education where faculty, staff, and students come together as a community of learners enriches the intellectual climate. Institutions that can achieve a campuswide focus on learning are ones that do not minimize the academic mission of the institution, but surround it with a broader and reinforcing educational mission.

Paths Toward Partnerships

Because institutions struggle with fostering cross-divisional partnerships, they perpetuate a campuswide ethos of separation that maintains a divide between academic and student affairs, and thus students' in- and out-of-class experiences. Kuh explained that *ethos* derives from the Greek for "habit," and he defines ethos as "a belief system widely shared."[21] If the habit is separation, then actions are necessary to break the habit. The cultures and roles of academic and student affairs are different enough that there is a natural tendency for the two to remain separate. It is critical to design multifaceted ways to encourage personnel in the two divisions to come together in the shared purpose of improving student learning.

Adopting a vision of education where faculty, staff, and students come together as a community of learners enriches the intellectual climate.

When I began to study Crossroads, I defined *partnership* in terms of *initiatives*. I focused on understanding how people's perceptions of their own and each other's roles facilitated or hindered the potential for collaborative projects that enhance student learning. I based my preconception that the goal is to develop a cross-divisional collaborative project on the fact that much of the published scholarship on cross-divisional partnership focuses on specific programs often in isolation of the broader campus ethos. Thus faculty and staff evaluate the effectiveness of partnership-based initiatives as stand-alone components that do not take into consideration the broader institutional context.

As my year in the field progressed, my definition of partnership changed. I eventually concluded that partnership is not about developing a program together; partnership is exhibiting mutual understanding and together developing an ethos where people value integrative learning. Of course, the campus ethos does not develop on its own. As Adrianna Kezar explained, "Educators must tend their institution's ethos on an ongoing basis and constantly work to align policies and practices with it."[22] Developing mutual understanding and tending to the ethos together makes it possible for people to recognize their shared purpose and allows for collaborative programs to then emerge from a foundation built of trust and respect, acceptance and appreciation.

We must therefore resist the temptation to quickly initiate cross-divisional collaborative projects because a stand-alone project will have limited influence on the campus ethos. If the goal is to create broad-based partnership, an integrative educational experience, and a learning-centered campus, then we must challenge each other to delve deeply into understanding the purpose and goals of our own divisional work and then engage each other across divisions in dialogue.[23] Conversation moves us beyond bias and competition to a place where we can understand how academic and student affairs work can complement each other to provide students with a rich educational experience.

At Crossroads, a senior student affairs professional acknowledged that faculty members, administration, and students all do things differently, "but all three need to be involved if Crossroads will really reach its fullest potential." To foster integration, a faculty member spoke about the necessity to "remove the attitudes and egos and personal agendas" and instead attend to what is in the best interest of the student. An academic affairs administrator echoed this point, expressing that "we need to, as an institution, be focusing on what the best thing for our students is, and stop this conversation about what's best for student affairs, [and] what's best for academic affairs."[24]

Why Engage in Dialogue?

Why are there so few examples of these partnerships in American higher education? Put simply, it is because we do not know *why* we need to speak with each other, and we do not know *how* to speak with each other. We need to organize our institutions in a way that engages mixed groups of people and forces us to venture outside traditional silos. In this alternative setting, individuals can lay the foundation for change by rethinking their beliefs, assumptions, and ideas. Our collaborations, our pursuit of a cohesive community, and our desire for a learning-centered campus must be built on a solid foundation of mutual understanding. This is largely not the case at most institutions of higher education, and as a result, a campus's ethos does not cultivate cross-divisional partnerships.

The ethos can be changed through dialogue because people have the opportunity to view the organization through different lenses, evaluate their interpretation of their world, and identify new paths to achieve their shared goals. Ethos can be influenced through a two-stage process that engages faculty and staff as learners through intragroup dialogue and intergroup dialogue. These dialogues facilitate change and create the foundation for the development of a learning-centered campus.

Intragroup dialogue serves as the foundation; academic and student affairs leaders facilitate an internal, reflective evaluation of their divisions regarding their roles on campus, their philosophies and approaches to education, as well as outsiders' key criticisms of their division. Intragroup dialogue allows people in a particular group to ponder their own segment of the institution and discuss the diverse perspectives that emerge within their particular group.[25] It is a pivotal yet often overlooked step toward building ongoing partnerships. Peter Magolda emphasized the importance of developing greater self-awareness through a self-evaluative process:

> I argue that there is a far greater need for these two subcultures [academic and student affairs] to understand themselves before embarking on a quest to learn about the other. One of the most disappointing aspects of partnerships between these two subcultures is members' lack of awareness of the norms and values that guide their own everyday practices.[26]

Internal audits will reveal the ways academic and student affairs sub-cultures influence administrators' and faculty members' actions and their interpretations of their own and each other's work. In the case of student affairs, it is essential for student affairs administrators to reflect on faculty members' claim that student affairs distract students from the university's academic mission. For faculty, it is important to consider student affairs' criticism that faculty members are not sufficiently engaged in integrating students' academic experience with their lives beyond the classroom. Starting down the path to partnership through the development of greater self-awareness is likely to bring increased clarity of purpose that intends to make the subsequent phase—intergroup dialogue—more productive.

Intergroup dialogue aims to develop trust and mutual understanding among groups defined by their different social identities.[27] Before academic and student affairs personnel can create meaningful collaborative initiatives, they need to engage in cross-divisional dialogue to discuss each other's roles, values, priorities, perspectives on student learning, and ultimately the areas where they can identify philosophical overlap. It is critical that we engage in discussions that help us better understand students: who they are, societal trends, as well as what the literature and campus specific data tell us about students and how higher education affects them. In addition, many of the same student issues appear across contexts (e.g., bystander behavior, concerns with integrity and civility, lack of engagement, and dissatisfaction with the intellectual climate) and frustrate student affairs practitioners and faculty. Discussing topics of mutual interest and developing mutual understanding allows for collaborative programs to emerge from a recognition that the two divisions share common purpose and aspirations.

Conclusion

People in each division operate within overwhelmingly different cultures, and this generates misunderstandings, mistrust, and conflict. Despite the differences between academic and student affairs, they share a critical common goal—advancing student intellectual and personal development. Given that they share an interest in student success and given what we know about ways to enhance student learning, it is no longer acceptable to simply say the two groups of people are different and then tolerate separation as the status quo.

An institution's potential will reveal itself once people develop relationships with each other that move them beyond their biased positions to find common ground regarding student learning. The strength of the partnership must be based on divisional self-awareness (through intragroup dialogue) and understanding of the perspectives shared by members of the other division (through intergroup dialogue). A foundation of mutual understanding allows collaborative initiatives to emerge more naturally and lead to successful, long-lasting, and meaningful opportunities for student learning in a coherent and connected learning-centered campus. To develop partnerships between academic and student affairs, institution officials need to cultivate a synergistic relationship between academic and student affairs that goes beyond a potentially successful collaborative project. Faculty and staff should relentlessly pursue campus dialogue that fosters deep institution-wide commitment to a shared approach for student learning.

Despite the differences between academic and student affairs, they share a critical common goal—advancing student intellectual and personal development.

Admittedly, many people may not know how to structure and facilitate the type of dialogue I propose. Faculty and staff would benefit from a higher education research agenda that further explores fundamental philosophies of education and cultural differences on campus while testing, evaluating, and developing the best practices for dialogue. The intent is to cultivate a campus culture where faculty and staff exhibit confidence and trust in each other, support each other's work, create a coherent campus life for students, and implement engaging pedagogies that help students see the connections across disciplinary fields and between their in- and out-of-classroom lives.

Notes

1. Hersh, R. H. (1999). Generating ideals and transforming lives: A contemporary case for the residential liberal arts college. *Daedalus, 128*(1), 173–194, p. 182.

2. Ibid., p. 182.

3. Kuh, G. D. (1996). Guiding principles of creating seamless learning environments for undergraduates. *Journal of College Student Development, 37*(2), 135–148.

4. Astin, A. W. (1993). *What matters in college: Four critical years revisited.* San Francisco, CA: Jossey-Bass; Pascarella, E. T., & Terenzini, P. T. (2005). *How college affects students: A third decade of research.* San Francisco, CA: Jossey-Bass; Tinto, V. (1987). *Leaving college: Rethinking the causes and cures of student attrition.* Chicago, IL: University of Chicago Press.

5. Pascarella & Terenzini, *How college affects students,* p. 628.

6. Ibid., p. 629.

7. Love, P. G., & Love, A. G. (1995). *Enhancing student learning: Intellectual, social, and emotional integration* (ASHE-ERIC Higher Education Report No. 4). Washington, DC: George Washington University, Graduate School of Education and Human Development, p. 6.

8. Kellogg Commission on the Future of State and Land Grant Universities. (2000). *Returning to our roots: The student experience.* Washington, DC: National Association of State and Land Grant Colleges, p. 22.

9. Baxter Magolda, M. B. (1996). Cognitive learning and personal development: A false dichotomy. *About Campus, 1*(3), 16–21, p. 21.

10. Terenzini, P. T., Springer, L., Pascarella, E. T., & Nora, A. (1995). Influences affecting the development of students' critical thinking skills. *Research in Higher Education, 36*(1), 23–39, p. 36.

11. Zemsky, R., Wegner, G. R., & Massy, W. F. (2005). *Remaking the American university: Market-smart and mission-centered.* New Brunswick, NJ: Rutgers University Press.

12. Ibid., p. 23, 24.

13. Ibid., p. 25.

14. Engstrom, C. M., & Tinto, V. (2000). Developing partnerships with academic affairs to enhance student learning. In M. J. Barr & M. K. Dresler (Eds.). *The handbook of student affairs administration* (2nd ed., pp. 425–452). San Francisco, CA: Jossey-Bass, p. 428.

15. Arcelus, V. J. (2008). *In search of a break in the clouds: An ethnographic study of academic and student affairs cultures.* (Unpublished doctoral dissertation). Pennsylvania State University, State College.

16. Hutchins, R. M. (1936). *The higher learning in America.* New Haven, CT: Yale University Press.

17. Dewey, J. (1938). *Experience and education.* New York, NY: Macmillan.

18. Hutchins, *Higher learning in America,* p. 31.

19. Hutchins, *Higher learning in America,* p. 32.

20. Arcelus, *In search of a break in the clouds.*

21. Kuh, G. D. (1993). Ethos: Its influence on student learning. *Liberal Education, 79*(4), 22–31, p. 22.

22. Kezar, A. (2007). Creating and sustaining a campus ethos encouraging student engagement. *About Campus, 11*(6), 13–18, p. 14.

23. See, for example, Koester, J., Hellenbrand, H., & Piper, T. D. (2005). Exploring the actions behind the words "learning-centered institution." *About Campus, 10*(4), 10–16;

Koester, J., Hellenbrand, H., & Piper, T. D. (2008). The challenge of collaboration: Organizational structure and professional identity. *About Campus, 13*(5), 12–19.

24. Arcelus, *In search of a break in the clouds*, p. 380.

25. Schoem, D. L. (Ed.). (1991). *Inside separate worlds: Life stories of young Blacks, Jews, and Latinos.* Ann Arbor: University of Michigan Press.

26. Magolda, P. (2005). Proceed with caution: Uncommon wisdom about academic and student affairs partnerships. *About Campus, 9*(6), 16–21, p. 20.

27. Schoem, D. L., Hurtado, S., Sevig, T., Chesler, M., & Sumida, S. H. (2001). Intergroup dialogue: Democracy at work in theory and practice. In D. L. Schoem & S. Hurtado (Eds.), *Intergroup dialogue: Deliberative democracy in school, college, community, and workplace* (pp. 1–21). Ann Arbor: University of Michigan Press; Pettigrew, T. F., & Tropp, L. R. (2006). A meta-analytic test of intergroup contact theory. *Journal of Personality and Social Psychology, 90*(5), 751–783.

Supporting Intragroup and Intergroup Dialogues

A Model for Collaborative Campuses

Jaime Lester, George Mason University

I largely agree with the work of Victor Arcelus—academic and student affairs in higher education remain divided because of competition for resources, specialization, professional status of faculty, and cultural differences.[1] The root of the division lies in the expansion of higher education that created large and complex organizations with internal competition for resources, specialization among administrative staff, and faculty who redefined their roles by emphasizing professional status as opposed to identities rooted in their home institutions. These changes resulted in significant cultural differences between student and academic affairs. Arcelus argues that the path toward more collaboration involving student and academic affairs includes intragroup and intergroup dialogues. These dialogues provide many opportunities for individuals to engage in relationship building, create a common language and philosophy, foster understanding, and, most important, create opportunities for cognitive complexity—a perspective of a problem or issue with nuanced solutions that represents multiple perspectives.[2]

I argue that for dialogue to develop and be sustained over time, administrators of higher education institutions need to consider structural and cultural changes to remove barriers, create opportunities, and provide incentives to bring together the fragments in organizational life. Fragmented cultures are an outgrowth of complex and multiple cultural identities. Cultural identities (e.g., race, gender, class) shape individuals—who belong to many subcultures. An individual may identify himself or herself as a person of color, have strong ties to religious organizations, be a family member, and work for a university. Each of these identities and allegiances creates a split or fragment of identity that may overlap with other fragments and compete for attention, time, resources, and importance. Organizational contexts that lack a clear center, have unclear boundaries, and little distinction between insiders and outsiders characterize fragmentation.[3] This definition moves beyond Arcelus's observation of fragmented and competitive divisions of academic and student affairs to characterizing the entire campus and the perspective of individuals who may participate in dialogues. Intragroup and intergroup dialogues will be more successful if introduced in a context that acknowledges the complexity of multiple identities in organizational life and the need to integrate structures, and offers opportunities through networking that will bring together separate and fragmented spheres.

A Model to Enhance Partnerships

In our book *Organizing Higher Education for Collaboration*, Adrianna Kezar and I present a three-stage model that enhances internal partnerships and can address fragmentation and create an environment for dialogues to occur. The stages are building commitment, commitment, and sustaining commitment. In the first stage of building commitment, campus administrators need to convince the campus community of the importance and benefits of collaboration and relate collaboration to institutional values. On the collaborative campuses we examined, leaders and change agents identified messages from external groups that supported collaborative work and created public forums for discussion of new accreditation and foundation guidelines, business and industry proposals, and federal agency initiatives. Leaders also distributed research on the advantages of collaboration and held forums and workshops on various forms of collaboration they were trying to encourage, helping people to understand the benefits. During the forums, leaders were able to connect the collaboration to the values of the campus.

The second stage of commitment requires campus leaders to establish a sense of priority for collaboration by reexamining mission and values and articulating the philosophy of collaboration on the campus. In this second stage, the main work of senior executives was to revise the campus mission statement and make sure people were discussing the new mission and vision, creating a sense of priority on campus. On collaborative campuses, senior executives became vocal about the new direction for the campus and the new way work was being carried out. Leaders communicated a sense of collaboration using mission and values specifically through hiring and modeling. For example, several leaders used campus networks as a source of leadership, along with individual dedicated leaders with dynamic energy, enthusiasm, and momentum to push for collaboration and continue a message of interest initially expressed by leaders.

Finally, the third state of sustaining commitment includes macro- and microlevel changes to the institutional structure that will support and sustain collaboration. Sustained collaboration is highly dependent on redesigning campus systems, from computing systems to rewards and incentives to the creation of new structures such as institutes. On each collaborative campus particular structures emerged as most important for helping create an environment that supports collaboration, such as one or more central units for collaboration, a set of centers and institutes, cross-campus teams, presidential initiatives, and new accounting, computer, and budgetary systems. Each structure helped to integrate work and facilitate cross-functional activities and remove common barriers to collaboration. For example, new accounting processes ensured that divisions and departments could easily exchange money on joint research projects or full-time equivalents for team teaching.

Creating Opportunities for Collaboration

Although we did not develop this model to specifically address the divide between academic and student affairs, it implicitly reveals ways that colleges and universities can create opportunities to foster exchanges similar to intergroup and intragroup dialogues across fragmented cultures. First, colleges and universities must create reward structures to provide the incentive for individuals to collaborate. Faculty and student affairs professionals exist in separate spheres of professional influence and are constantly negotiating their identities and the norms and expectations of those spheres. Heavy teaching and advising loads and increased expectations for grant seeking and publishing burden faculty, particularly those who are on the tenure track. Collaborative campuses used rewards in stages two and three of the model to encourage participation to create a collaborative vision, participate in discussions about collaboration, and to sustain collaborative efforts over time. More specifically, the focus was on promotion and tenure requirements. If the tenure and promotion system supported collaboration, then the members of campus felt the context of collaboration would be fully sustained. Other important incentives included grants and administrative support. Student affairs professionals interested in engaging in collaborative work (e.g., interdisciplinary research, learning communities) need some relief from their day-to-day activities. Hiring, restructuring, small start-up grants, and release time from other duties all created incentives for collaboration and helped collaborative work to continue. Rewards also help create and maintain intra- or intergroup dialogues, as the development of trust and relationship building, as Arcelus describes, takes time and energy. Without rewards, there is little time or incentive for individuals to maintain their participation in a time-consuming, yet important, process of trust building.

Second, administrators of colleges and universities need to create networks across campuses that represent individuals from student and academic affairs. Networks maintain and generate more collaboration on campus. Participation in one collaboration may lead to other activities and ongoing connections and a greater degree of formality in the network. For example, at George Mason University, a group called MasonLeads seeks to inspire the development, emergence, and recognition of leadership throughout the Mason community. Not only is this committee cochaired by representatives from academic and student affairs, it is made up of people from across the campus, from alumni affairs to international programs to human resources. Other examples include a speaker series that addresses teaching and learning inside and outside the classroom, faculty fellowships in student affairs offices, student affairs professionals teaching in higher education programs, and the creation of new buildings that house academic and student affairs under one roof. Each example brings people together in the same space to meet and possibly connect regarding a similar interest. These networks help establish relationships, lead to a common language or shared understanding across units, and connect people who may be interested in dialogues.

Third, college and university officials must consider integrating structures across student and academic affairs. As previously noted, collaborative campuses developed particular integrating structures that appeared to be the most important in helping create an environment that supports collaboration—central unit(s) for collaboration, a set of centers and institutes, cross-campus teams, presidential initiatives, and new accounting, computer, and budgetary systems—helping to integrate work and facilitate cross-functional activities. These new structures were supportive of each other and solidified the new way of working collaboratively. Another less common practice is to staff student affairs with faculty who devote all their time to an administrative student affairs role. In our book, Adrianna and I introduce Collaborative University (pseudonym), which had a tenured faculty member as vice president for the student affairs division.

Another example is the creation of service-learning offices that unite faculty and student affairs professionals to create curricula with community engagement at the epicenter. The course may extend to a first-year experience with co-instructors from academic and student affairs. These partnerships create collaborations and capitalize on the strengths and skills of those involved. The integration of structures supports the dialogues Arcelus proposed. Without these structures, dialogues could be wrought with bureaucratic difficulties and frustration, making deep learning and relationship building more difficult.

We must be intentional about creating opportunities, rewards, networks, and structures to bridge the cultural divide.

Each of these recommendations is not without barriers. For collaborations between student affairs and academic affairs to develop in a sustained and significant way, campus leaders must understand the need for these collaborations and be willing to articulate the benefits and liabilities to the larger campus community. Campus leaders include positional leaders (e.g., presidents, provosts, and deans) and nonpositional leaders or change agents who advocate for collaboration. These campus leaders need to see the value of collaboration and how collaboration can assist the campus in achieving strategic priorities. Collaboration must have advocates who relate and embed collaboration within the institutional mission and values. While this second point has fewer barriers for those leaders in positional leadership roles, change agents may also tout the benefits of collaboration and create those links for positional leaders. Finally, campus leaders need to use either formal or informal power to create new structures for collaboration to be sustained over time. These structures come in the form of rewards for participation in collaboration, establishment of internal networks of people with similar interests and goals, and the integration of structures (e.g., creation of research centers or cross-campus teams). With efforts of just a few, a context can be created for successful intergroup and intragroup dialogue to occur and thrive.

Conclusion

Arcelus's essay and my response started with a simple question: Why are there so few partnerships between student and academic affairs? There is no single answer; rather, we must acknowledge that organizational life in higher education pulls us apart rather than together. We must be intentional about creating opportunities, rewards, networks, and structures to bridge the cultural divide. The benefits of collaboration are many. Principally, collaboration brings together different perspectives and helps to reframe problems and find new, creative solutions.[4] I doubt that any member of the higher education community would disagree that we need creative solutions to our increasingly complex problems.

Notes

1. Zemsky, R., Wegner, G. R., & Massy, W. F. (2005). *Remaking the American university: Market-smart and mission-centered.* New Brunswick, NJ: Rutgers University Press; Engstrom, C. M., & Tinto, V. (2000). Developing partnerships with academic affairs to enhance student learning. In M. J. Barr & M. K. Dresler (Eds.). *The handbook of student affairs administration* (2nd ed., pp. 425–452). San Francisco, CA: Jossey-Bass, p. 428; Arcelus, V. J. (2008). *In search of a break in the clouds: An ethnographic study of academic and student affairs cultures.* State College, PA: Pennsylvania State University.

2. Bensimon, E. M., & Neumann, A. (1993). *Redesigning collegiate leadership: Teams and teamwork in higher education.* Baltimore, MD: Johns Hopkins University Press; Googins, B. K., & Rochlin, S. A. (2000). Creating the partnership society: Understanding the rhetoric and reality of cross-sectoral partnerships. *Business and Society Review, 105*(1): 127–144.

3. Martin, J. (1992). *Cultures in organizations: Three perspectives.* New York, NY: Oxford University Press.

4. Mohrman, S., Cohen, S., & Mohrman, A. (1995). *Designing team-based organizations: New forms for knowledge work.* San Francisco, CA: Jossey Bass; Paulus, P. B., & Nijstad, B. A. (2003). *Group creativity: Innovation through collaboration.* New York, NY: Oxford University Press.

Further Reading and Related Blog

Sarah Meagher, Miami University

Arcelus, V. J. (2008). *In search of a break in the clouds: An ethnographic study of academic and student affairs cultures* (Unpublished doctoral dissertation). Pennsylvania State University, State College.

Arcelus provides insight to the institutional perceptions, biases, and connections between academic affairs and student services. After a year of observing Crossroads University (pseudonym), Arcelus constructs a possible framework for bridging the divide. This framework requires all professionals to engage in learning-centered education, where students encounter support toward learning in all higher education contexts.

Kezar, A. J., & Lester, J. (2009). *Organizing higher education for collaboration: A guide for campus leaders.* San Francisco, CA: Jossey-Bass.

The authors present findings from their empirical research, centering on campuses that create environments to support collaborative work. They discuss partnership possibilities, obstacles, and windfalls, and argue that genuine collaboration requires urgent action, new organizational structures, and the reallocation of campus resources.

Manning, K., Kinzie, J., & Schuh, J. (2006). *One size does not fit all: Traditional and innovative models of student affairs practice.* New York, NY: Routledge.

This book provides a historical context for the placement of student affairs in higher education and describes approaches for collaboration among higher education offices. The concluding chapter outlines the necessary collaboration of these offices to provide various perspectives that consider the needs of the diverse student populations entering higher education today and in the future. The authors claim that a more effective approach toward student affairs involves multiple perspectives contributing to problem solving for student needs, finding an overlap in learning goals among offices, and considering education more broadly—including students' engagements in and out of the classroom.

Blog URL: contestedissues.wordpress.com
Corresponding Chapter Post: tinyurl.com/contestedissues04

PART TWO

Challenges of Promoting Learning and Development

5

In This Age of Consumerism, What Are the Implications of Giving Students What They Want?

Have It Your Way U

Tracy Davis, Western Illinois University

This essay examines the tensions between the student affairs profession's contemporary focus on student learning and its historical focus on service. It explores the advantages and disadvantages of treating collegians as learners versus customers, and the implications for teaching and learning.

University officials are increasingly viewing students as consumers, and campus services are changing to cater to their needs. Given the rising tuition costs, it is neither inappropriate nor surprising that students demand a quality return on their investment. The problem lies not in students being savvy consumers of education, nor is there a problem with the return on the investment students receive from attending a higher education institute. Those acquiring a postsecondary degree enjoy a wealth of outcomes that demonstrate that education is one of the best investments a person can make, financially and otherwise. The problem is that in an environment of declining public support of higher education, corporate funding is encroaching into school matters and blurring important distinctions between business and educational practices.

Among the most important distinctions being obscured is the one between customers and students. Giving customers what they want in the marketplace fails miserably as an educational practice with students in higher education.

From naming rights of athletic arenas to exclusive soda contracts to huge entrepreneurial research grants, corporate influence is challenging the fundamental purposes of education and shaping the expectations of students, parents, and even higher education insiders. In student affairs, pressure on bookstores, residence halls, and food services to become profit centers is also increasing while public financial support of higher education continues its sharp decline.[1] It should come as no surprise that universities in the United States are increasingly shifting into businesslike enterprises.

In an environment of declining public support of higher education, corporate funding is encroaching into school matters and blurring important distinctions between business and educational practices.

The shift is not without consequences. Among the most damaging results is the belief that students should be treated like consumers. It is, however, as inappropriate to treat students like customers as it is to treat customers like students. Companies are in the business of promoting customer satisfaction, but educational institutions are called to promote learning. That is, while there are some valid parallels between students and customers, there are critical differences rooted in the mission of each that adversely influence collegians' learning if not mindfully considered. In today's higher education environment, especially in light of contemporary economic pressures, failing to articulate the essential differences is catastrophic. In this essay, I explore fundamental differences between industry and education, describe tensions caused by the diverse roles that student affairs professionals play, and outline critical errors we make if we embrace a customer service, students-as-consumers model, instead of a learning model when interacting with college students.

Mission Differences Making a Customer Service Model Inappropriate for Higher Education

Corporate influences and the related values of financial profit, loyal consumerism, and timely efficiency are prevalent in today's higher education environment.[2] These values are antithetical to the learning process and damaging to the fundamental purposes of educational institutions. The dangers associated with using a student-as-consumer, customer service model in higher education are evident in the most basic outcome and purpose differences sought by corporate versus educational enterprises. Higher education's primary purpose is to produce learning, while industry is essentially called on to produce profit. Commercial and social objectives are not necessarily mutually exclusive, but confusing the two can clearly damage the central focus of educational institutions—namely learning.

Outcomes associated with learning require processes that are quite distinct from processes associated with profit. For example, it is good business practice to treat customers as if they were always right. After all, a happy and satisfied customer is more likely to remain a customer, thus increasing profit. This is not generally the case in education where learning is a coveted outcome. While there are important power differences in education between student and teacher or student affairs professional that need to be ethically negotiated, the educator holds some level of content and process expertise the learner usually does not. If this were not the case, no one would pay tuition. In fact, we know that learning occurs through a process requiring dissonance; learning does not occur without some process that replaces previous understanding with new information. At the very least new information causes disequilibrium with what was previously known. In some cases, especially where values, ethics, and deeply ingrained traditions are associated, feelings of anger and resentment (natural to disequilibrium) often occur. Educational institutions are uniquely called on by society to not simply replace one dogma with another but to challenge students to more deeply integrate for themselves a more cogent, differentiated understanding. As Stephen Brookfield stated:

> Significant learning and critical thinking inevitably induce an ambivalent mix of feelings and emotions, in which anger and confusion are as prominent as pleasure and clarity. The most hallowed rule of business—that

the customer is always right—is often pedagogically wrong. Equating good teaching with a widespread feeling among students that you have done what they wanted ignores the dynamics of teaching and prevents significant learning.[3]

A second way that education and the marketplace differ is that the customer/consumer language establishes an inappropriate metaphor that leads to misunderstanding about the fundamental differences in purpose. Alexander Astin illustrated how an industrial or business model is inappropriate for measuring educational outcomes. He argued that "one consequence of this business orientation is that it portrays students and their degrees as 'produced' by the institution, in much the same way an automobile is produced at a factory."[4] The business model obscures the responsibility and involvement required by students in the learning process. Good students are responsible for reflecting critically, exploring ambiguities, giving and receiving feedback. A customer does not have responsibilities beyond the economic.

A third way that confusing the fundamental purposes of business and education is damaging relates to the increasing calls for accountability. Those not familiar with the unique processes associated with learning may expect, for example, that students progress in a unidirectionally upward or increasingly complex manner. What we know about learning and educational processes, however, is that sometimes students get worse before they get better. William Perry, in his well-known study of college students' intellectual development, used the terms *temporizing* and *retreat* to describe students who felt overwhelmed by a developmental challenge and who were either treading water in the face of the difficulty (temporizing) or actively moving in an opposite direction to avoid it (retreat).[5] What business or customer service models might categorize as negative, learning models may describe as naturally occurring phenomena.

In addition, the Astin metaphor of cars produced in a factory reinforces the fundamental differences in corporate arenas compared to educational measures of accountability.[6] In the former, we can use the number of car units produced in a day or year as one measure. But what does a unit of learning look like? What we do know is that learning generally escapes measurement in such tangible and simplistic ways. Even the most psychometrically adequate tests measure achievement, not learning. For example, which student has learned more, the one with a Graduate Record Exam (GRE) verbal score of 350 or the one with 450? We may be able to state with some confidence that the latter has a better verbal score, but we can't state which one learned the most in the content area. What if, for example, both students took the GRE a year prior to achieving the 350 and 450, and the first scored 200 the first time and the other 400? Anyone who is responsible for student learning knows the dramatic diversity of skill levels, characteristics, experiences, and histories represented by students that clearly elude the simplistic industrial outcome measures typically demanded in the corporate world. We know that student learning does not progress in the same manner. Affective, cognitive, identity, and other dispositional characteristics influence the unfolding of learning with different individuals. Moreover, efficiency measures—when applied to sentient, complex beings in the process of growth, learning, and development—are absurd. Learning outcomes cannot even be measured in the time students are engaged in their college education.[7] It is common for seeds planted in college to grow to fruition much later in life. What business has customers who have changed their minds over time about a service they received that was initially threatening, challenging, or otherwise negative? Businesses measure customer satisfaction; educational institutions, however, measure learning performance.

Is Student Affairs Supposed to Develop Students, Promote Learning, or Serve Customers?

The problems associated with using a business model in the context of higher education become even more complicated when applied to the student affairs profession. While most faculty are clear that learning is at the epicenter of their classes, most student affairs professionals have competing models upon which they base their practice. There have been at least three distinct approaches to student affairs work during the past 50 years: focusing on student services, student development, and student learning.[8] In addition, Blimling identified four communities—student administration, student services, student development, and student learning—that guide the practice of student affairs.[9] The student administration community of practice focuses on the distribution of resources, procedures, policies, and organizational leadership. Those coming from a student services community of practice perspective focus on a business model and cost efficiency with emphasis on student satisfaction. Professionals taking a student development approach focus on psychosocial growth of students and see out-of-class programmatic interventions as equally valuable as in-class learning. Finally, those with a student learning community of practice focus view student affairs professionals as partners in the learning process and the college environment as a seamless culture where learning can happen anywhere. Professionals are generally clear about which communities of practice dominate the expectations of their supervisors, which in turn influence the performance of their duties.

There have been times in the history of student affairs when a services mentality that operates separately from the central educational mission of the institution was dominant. The 1949 *Student Personnel Point of View* represents a clear administrative and services approach describing the supportive functions of student personnel work as supplementing the central tasks of "intensive class-room learning"[10] In addition, the 1987 National Association of Student Personnel Administrators in *A Perspective on Student Affairs* concluded that "the work of student affairs should not compete with and cannot substitute for that academic experience" and that "student affairs enhances and supports the academic mission."[11] The distinctions, however, between cognitive and psychosocial growth or between in- and out-of-class learning are artificial. Not only do noncognitive developmental issues outside the classroom have an impact on student learning inside the classroom, there is strong evidence that cognition and other forms of development (e.g., identity, moral) occur seamlessly. That is, those of us in academia may care who gets credit or what stimulates learning and development, but the recipient generally does not. Distinguishing cognitive learning from psychosocial development simply mischaracterizes the phenomena. As a result the authors of "The Student Learning Imperative," *Learning Reconsidered* and many student affairs scholars have called for the integration of student learning and development that reduces the artificial dualism of in-class and out-of-class growth.[12] With these artificial differences dissolved it should become clear that the work we do in higher education, whether as faculty or student affairs professionals, is centrally about educating students in a manner that honors the processes associated with learning rather than service.

The differences in communities of practice and the differing central purposes captured in each community are, however, not simply philosophical. Some of the work in student affairs does in fact need to operate more like a business. Areas of financial aid, building management, food services, and the like require business skills and are typically found in the same division as those who are charged with promoting student cocurricular learning and development. Residence life offices and food services are increasingly competing with private interests providing similar services and products. While it is legitimate that this causes some confusion, tension, and misunderstanding, it is not an excuse for failing to remember that even the most businesslike operation on campus must still function within an educational environment where learning is the central mission. If we cannot demonstrate the educational value of living in the residence halls then maybe we need to focus more on articulating and assessing appropriate outcomes than on increasing customer service. Fortunately, there is a movement on many campuses to more clearly identify learning outcomes and illuminate educational benefits for those engaging in out-of-class experiences. The American College Personnel Association, for example, holds an annual Residential Curriculum Institute aimed at grounding residential programs in an institution's educational mission, helping develop assessable learning outcomes, and examining the impact this shift has on campuses. Similarly, community standards models are gaining in popularity. At the University of Nevada, Las Vegas, new residents are challenged to clarify their expectations and to anticipate "working together toward common goals and through challenging differences" and to "learn how to negotiate, solve problems, and be a contributing member of a team—skills valued by graduate schools and future employers."[13] Learning-oriented expectations to work through challenges stand in stark contrast to consumer expectations for satisfaction. Moreover, the differences necessitate that employees in the marketplace know how to provide customer service, while educational institutions require professionals who can promote learning. McDonalds, Walmart, and Bank of America are employment possibilities for those frustrated by or incapable of honoring an educational mission and the related learning processes. What distinguishes student affairs from corporations are the learning specialists who go beyond the technical aspects of student affairs work to promote cognitive, affective, and psychosocial growth and development—not simply providing customer service.

Examples of Customer Service Mentality and Negative Impacts on Student Affairs

A few years ago, when higher education institutions were still publishing printed copies of course registration catalogs, I remember seeing large type, bulleted promises on the cover for single rooms in residence hall, wired (now wireless) capability, and dining facilities that provide carry out. There is nothing inherently wrong in providing these amenities, but it raised questions about whether we were concerned about students as customers or students as learners. What do we know about democratic engagement and learning outcomes that occur in the context of living with roommates and interacting with others in physical space? Are we considering the impact of learning to the same extent that we contort to meet consumer-driven desires? This is only one minor example of the potential problems raised by using a marketplace mentality in the context of higher education.

Faculty members have faced the conflict caused by the students-as-customers model in higher education and corporate encroachment for decades. Grade inflation has fueled student expectations for high grades with minimal effort and there is clear evidence that expectations are not receding.[14] The corporate-influenced customer service model, moreover, is at the heart of an unseemly connection between student evaluations of faculty and grades. Evidence shows that teachers can "buy" better evaluations through more lenient grading.[15] In addition, research into student expectations of their professors indicates that "students desire comfort-inducing activities that do not necessarily make them learn more."[16]

Just as faculty can be tempted by shortcuts to better student evaluations, student affairs professionals are seduced by the efficiency of treating students as customers. I have either experienced or witnessed firsthand how customer-service-influenced practice subverts a learning focus in student affairs in several ways. First, I have seen residence life policies and practices that allow roommate switching without consideration of underlying conflicts or even the requirement of meeting with staff to attempt reconciliation. It's not uncommon, for example, for roommates to experience tension with identity issues (e.g., sexual orientation, religious practices, or ethnicity). Rather than appropriately viewing these natural tensions as teachable learning moments, customer-service-influenced practices seek to efficiently satisfy consumers (parents and students), potentially subverting the learning mission of the educational institution.

A second example of how the customer service model is inappropriately applied in student affairs relates to strategies we use to evaluate our learning impact. When we design student programming, from homecoming events to sexual assault prevention programs, we tend to measure our success based on the number of people who attend. In fact, some funding algorithms focus exclusively on the number of students served. Learning

---

Not only does a corporate model risk confusing quality with quantity, but also there is an incentive to provide satisfying entertainment at the expense of the central learning outcomes.

---

eludes such simplistic measurement. More learning can occur in an intervention involving 3 people, hypothetically, than a program with 600 attendees. According to Alexander Astin, "Although it is possible to assess the impact of a plant in terms of the number and quality of its products, the actual impact of college is not necessarily reflected in the number of its graduates or even the quality of their achievements."[17] Not only does a corporate model risk confusing quality with quantity, but also there is an incentive to provide satisfying entertainment at the expense of the central learning outcomes.

In addition to efficient (rather than developmental) roommate conflict resolution and disproportionately quantitative outcome measures, the customer service model of student affairs practice fails to account for important phenomena associated with learning. For example, most of us who have been charged with the responsibility of advising a student group know that it would be more efficient and easier to outline responsibilities and lead the organization. Compared to producing learning, it is much simpler and much easier to satisfy others in the organization if we take the lead ourselves. But satisfaction is not what we are called to produce; rather, we are uniquely charged in education to create learning. Learning sometimes (and in my experience often) requires making mistakes and allowing students to learn deeply from those experiences. Paulo Freire reinforced the important distinctions between marketplace behavior and educational processes in his criticism of a banking metaphor of learning.[18] He claims that teachers using the banking metaphor will try to deposit knowledge into students hoping for good returns on their investment. Banking, however,

> attempts to maintain the submersion of consciousness; [while] problem-posing strives for the emergence of consciousness and critical intervention

in reality. Problem-posing education affirms men and women as beings in the process of becoming—as unfinished, uncompleted beings in and with a likewise unfinished reality.[19]

According to Freire, raising awareness of being incomplete, not our content expertise, is at the heart of the learning enterprise. Moreover, learning is often enhanced by mistakes and by posing problems. This process is rarely linear, almost never efficient, and stands in sharp contrast to general marketplace strategies related to customer service.

Conclusion

I know of no one who would claim that we should test or grade customers before allowing them to check out at the grocery store, but calls for treating students as customers abound. As budgetary constraints continue to choke off resources for education (ironically bailing out those who created the most recent financial crisis) college and university administrators are being forced to respond to increasing demands for accountability. Unfortunately we appear to be losing focus on the essential differences between corporate and educational purposes and processes. As such, "academic institutions have come to resemble the entities they now serve; colleges have been transformed into big businesses. Major research schools, particularly private ones, are also landlords, tax havens, and research-and-development surrogates, with administrators and fundraisers lauding it over faculty."[20]

The risks of continuing to misunderstand fundamental differences between education and business, and continuing to use a customer service model in higher education, are simply too great. While the business of higher education and student affairs has changed, the fundamental purposes related to learning have not. Applying an inappropriate metaphor and parallel terminology will have distinctly negative consequences. It will lead to a focus on satisfaction, not growth and development; to efficiency, not effectiveness; to quantity, not quality; and to a fundamental subversion of the most important thing that sets education apart from other civic enterprises: learning.

Robert Rhoads, in describing John Dewey's vision of higher education, said that "Dewey saw educated citizens as something more than a society of individuals with technical skills, vocational inclinations, and economic ambitions. And he saw democracy as more than a political economy of free markets, competition, and entrepreneurship."[21] If we continue to allow education to be commodified by corporate interests and a market mentality, we will lose the more fundamental broader focus on democracy. Our economic interests are important, but the proverbial tail should not be wagging the dog. It is our responsibility to be educators and not simply service providers, and it is the students' responsibility to be learners engaged in their own development and not simply customers. Therefore, we need to challenge and support students as they experience the anger, ambivalence, and unavoidable frustration involved in deep learning.

Notes

1. Archibald, R. B., & Feldman, D. H. (2006). State higher education spending and the tax revolt. *Journal of Higher Education, 77*(4), 618–644; Miller, T. (2003). Governmentality or commodification? U.S. higher education. *Cultural Studies, 17*(6), 897–904.

2. Bok, D. (2003). *Universities in the marketplace: The commercialization of higher education.* Princeton, NJ: Princeton University Press; Molnar, A. (1996). *Giving kids the business: The commercialization of America's schools.* Boulder, CO: Westview/Harper-Collins; Molnar, A. (2005). *School commercialism: From democratic ideal to market economy.* New York, NY: Routledge Falmer; Miller, Governmentality or commodification?

3. Brookfield, S. (1995). *Becoming a critically reflexive teacher.* San Francisco, CA: Jossey-Bass, p. 21.

4. Astin, A. (1993). *What matters in college?: Four critical years revisited.* San Francisco, CA: Jossey-Bass, p. 17.

5. Perry, W. G. (1970). *Forms of intellectual and ethical development in the college years: A scheme.* New York, NY: Holt, Rinehart, and Winston.

6. Astin, *What matters in college?*

7. Bowen H. (1977). *Investment in learning: The individual and social value of American higher education.* San Francisco, CA: Jossey-Bass; Pascarella, E. T., & Terenzini, P. T. (2005). *How college affects students: A third decade of research* (Vol. 2). San Francisco, CA: Jossey-Bass; Vaill, P. (2000). *Beware the idea of the student as a customer: A dissenting view.* Retrieved from http://www.people.vcu.edu/~rsleeth/NotCustomers.html

8. Ender, S. C., Newton, F. B., & Caple, R. B. (1996). Contributions to learning: Present realities. In S. C. Ender, F. B. Newton, & R. B. Caple (Eds.), *Contributing to learning: The role of student affairs* (pp. 5–17). San Francisco, CA: Jossey-Bass.

9. Blimling, G. (2001). Uniting scholarship and communities of practice in student affairs. *Journal of College Student Development, 42*(4), 381–396.

10. American Council on Education. (1949). *The student personnel point of view.* Washington, DC: Author, p. 4.

11. National Association of Student Personnel Administrators. (1987). *A perspective on student affairs.* Washington, DC: Author, p. 9.

12. American College Personnel Association. (1996). The student learning imperative: Implications for Student Affairs. *Journal of College Student Development, 37*(2), 118–122; Keeling, R. P. (Ed.). (2004). *Learning reconsidered: A campus-wide focus on the student experience.* Washington, DC: National Association of Student Personnel Administrators & American College Personnel Association; Ender, S. C., Newton, F. B., & Caple, R. B. (1996). Contributions to learning: Present realities. In S. C. Ender, F. B. Newton & R. B. Caple (Eds.), *Contributing to learning: The role of student affairs* (pp. 5–17). San Francisco, CA: Jossey-Bass; King, P., & Baxter Magolda, M. B. (1996). A developmental perspective on learning. *Journal of College Student Development, 37*(2), 163–173.

13. University of Nevada Las Vegas. (2009). *Your guide to community living 2009–10.* Las Vegas, NV: Author.

14. Rojstaczer, S., & Healy, C. (2010). Grading in American colleges and universities. *Teachers College Record.* Retrieved from http://www.tcrecord.org/Content.asp?ContentId=15928

15. Krautmann, A. C., & Sander, W. (1999). Grades and student evaluations of teachers. *Economics of Education Review, 18,* 59–63; Mehdizadeh, M. (1990). Log linear models and student course evaluations. *Journal of Economic Education, 21,* 7–21.

16. Chonko, L. B., Tanner, J. F., & Davis, R. (2002). What are they thinking? Student expectations and self-assessments may be the bane of teaching evaluations. *Journal of Education for Business, 77*(5), 271–281, p. 272.

17. Astin, *What matters in college?*

18. Freire, P. (1993). *Pedagogy of the oppressed.* New York, NY: Continuum Press. (Original work published 1970)

19. Ibid., p. 84.

20. Miller, T. (2003). Governmentality or commodification? p. 902.

21. Rhoads, R. A. (2003). How civic engagement is reframing liberal education. *Peer Review, 5*(3), 25–28, 26–27.

To Err on the Side of Learning

Lisa Boes, Harvard University

By clarifying the values and purposes that distinguish marketplace and educational language and metaphors, Tracy Davis illuminates the danger of adopting a consumer-driven approach to student learning and higher education outcomes. Davis articulates three fundamental differences between industry and education. First, consumer models overlook that the learning process involves challenging students in ways that create dissonance and disequilibrium, experiences that would be avoided from satisfaction approaches. Second, business perspectives obscure students' responsibility and involvement in the learning process by focusing on instruction and service delivery. And finally, profit measures can rarely be translated to educational outcome measures because student learning is inherently a complex human phenomenon that is multifaceted and iterative. Without disregarding calls for quality from students and efficiency and accountability from funding institutions, Davis reaffirms higher education's commitment to growth, development, effectiveness, and quality—all central to the learning mission of higher education. This response explores three additional tensions between learning and service: the limits of student satisfaction, a conceptualization of informational and transformational learning, and how one achieves the scholarly goals of higher education by recognizing and affirming a complex set of roles and relationships within that community.

The Limits of Student Satisfaction

Concern about student satisfaction with campus services and the academic experience should not be overlooked but should be weighed against other goals and concerns. Satisfied students are more likely to have a sense of belonging to the campus community and become alumni who remain connected to the institution.[1] Furthermore, these alumni have the potential to offer important forms of influence and financial support to their institution. However, administrators and faculty are also responsible for judging whether what is satisfying to students is also safe and supports educational goals. Although higher education has refuted an in loco parentis relationship with students, a move that treats students as adults in their own right, the ultimate responsibility for creating a safe and healthy environment for students still falls to the administration and faculty. For example, although students may request and be satisfied with libraries that offer 24-hour access, administrators can decide that 24-hour access does not symbolically communicate a healthy campus environment. Along with other programs that support well-being, university leaders can communicate to students a decision to close libraries from midnight to 6:00 a.m. as a structural form of support. Connecting practices to learning goals helps student affairs professionals and faculty create purposeful experiences and programs and achieve their goals.

Framing practices from a learning perspective also provides student affairs professionals, faculty, and administrators with a framework they can use to understand and work with dissatisfied students. In the case of displeasure with a campus service, such as limited library hours, student affairs educators can advise students about avenues to provide constructive feedback or ways to address the issue. As Davis has articulated, dissatisfaction may also arise from dissonance or disequilibrium to a student's existing frame of reference or way of knowing. In these cases, a problem-solving response has the potential of preventing rather than promoting learning. An alternative for administrators and faculty is to become curious about the dilemma, and to try to understand how a student constructs the issue as a way to promote a change in perspective.

Informational Versus Transformational Learning

The consumer-learner dichotomy lends itself to creating a dangerous dichotomy between higher education's goals of influencing *what* students know and *how* they know it. Building on Mezirow's work in *Learning as Transformation*,[2] Kegan distinguishes *in*formational from *trans*formation learning. A change in what a student knows is informational:

> Learning aimed at increasing our fund of knowledge, at increasing our repertoire of skills, at extending already established cognitive capacities into new terrain serves the absolutely crucial purpose of deepening the resources available to an existing frame of reference. Such learning is literally in-*form*-ative because it seeks to bring valuable new contents into the existing form of our way of knowing.[3]

In contrast, transformation learning involves qualitative differences in how students know. It is part of a process in which "taken for-granted frames of reference (meaning perspectives, habits of mind, mind-sets) [become] more inclusive, discriminating, open, emotionally capable of change, and reflective so that they may generate beliefs and opinions that will prove more true or justified to guide action."[4] This change in knowing is more than a matter of adding capacity or substituting one perspective with another. "Trans-*form*-ative learning puts the form itself at risk of change (and not just change, but increased capacity)."[5] Robert Kegan clarifies by saying that "genuinely transformational learning is always to some extent an epistemological change rather than merely a change in behavioral repertoire or an increase in the quantity of fund of knowledge."[6]

An example of the distinction between these two types of knowing can be seen in the experience of students enrolled in a physics course designed for first-year Harvard students with outstanding preparation.[7] The instructor of this course crafts complicated problem sets, designed to address the concepts he is teaching and new ways of approaching them. To force the students to think more coherently about problem solving, the problems have to be sufficiently novel and difficult to resist solution by standard cookbook techniques because these students are extremely facile and able to try out many standard approaches very quickly. This has worked for them through high school and they have never really had to think hard about what they were doing. A desired outcome from the instructor's vantage point is to create problems that Kegan and Lahey describe as "ones we don't so much solve as let solve us. They cause us, in some way, to change our minds."[8] The physics instructor hopes that in addition to teaching new tools, his assignments will promote transformative learning experiences, and that students' approaches to problem solving will become much more intentional.

While responsiveness to calls for accountability are important, consumer- and market-driven approaches to higher education risk being addressed by assessment measures that answer the question, Do students know more?—or informational learning—as a result of attending college. What is harder to assess, and arguably a more important goal of higher education, is, Do students also know differently?—that is, transformational learning. While it would be easy enough for the physics instructor to provide evidence that his students know dozens of ways to solve problems, documenting the development of an approach to problem solving that is conceptually more sophisticated is challenging. Developing these measures and remaining committed to the goal of creating transformative

---

Although higher education has refuted an in loco parentis relationship with students, a move that treats students as adults in their own right, the ultimate responsibility for creating a safe and healthy environment for students still falls to the administration and faculty.

---

learning experiences for college students is consistent with a learning-centered focus in practice, and it's a good reason to be cautious and nervous about institutional obsessions with a consumer-driven relationship with students.

Complex Learning Relationships

Marketplace approaches in higher education rest on clear consumer and producer roles. As Davis argued, these models are ill suited for higher education because they obscure the responsibility students have and the process by which they produce learning. Thinking about student learning as a product is also not appropriate in higher education because another product, knowledge creation, is also a central, and sometimes competing, goal. Within a community of scholarship—a complex intergenerational set of relationships between faculty, administrators, and students—knowledge creation flourishes. Through engagement in the classroom, being employed in campus offices, leadership on campus committees, and participation in research teams in laboratories, students make significant contributions to the learning experiences of the administrators and faculty members as well as the products of their work. Our commitment to learning-centered practice involves more than achieving measurable student learning outcomes, it is based on the commitment to developing a community of intergenerational relationships among those engaged in scholarly endeavors.

Calls for accountability—from students, parents, funders, alumni, and the public—to defend our use of resources in higher education have merit. Rather than being drawn into product-driven, customer service models, purposeful educational practice should shift the discourse to learning, development, and knowledge creation. Evidence to support this approach also necessitates the creation of assessment measures and programs that evaluate the kinds of learning we wish to promote at the level of the individual student, a program or course, and for graduates overall. Using the language of learning, rather than business-sector services and products, will help those in academe remain true to their mission.

Notes

1. Kuh, G. D. (1998). Strengthening the ties that bind: Cultural events, rituals, and traditions. In J. N. Gardner & G. Van der Veer (Eds.), *The senior year experience: Facilitating integration, reflection, closure, and transition* (pp. 152–170). San Francisco, CA: Jossey-Bass.

2. Mezirow, J. & Associates. (Eds.) *Learning as transformation: Critical perspectives on a theory in progress.* San Francisco, CA: Jossey-Bass.

3. Kegan, R. (2000). What "form" transforms? A constructive-developmental approach to transformative learning. In J. Mezirow & Associates (Eds.), *Learning as transformation: Critical perspectives on a theory in progress* (pp. 35–69). San Francisco, CA: Jossey-Bass.

4. Mezirow, *Learning as transformation*, pp. 7–8.

5. Kegan, What "form" transforms? p. 48.

6. Ibid.

7. Howard Georgi, Mallinckrodt professor of physics and master of Leverett House, teaches Physics 16 at Harvard University.

8. Kegan, R., & Lahey, L. (2001). *How the way we talk can change the way we work: Seven languages for transformation.* San Francisco, CA: Jossey-Bass, p. 64.

Further Reading and Related Blog

Craig Berger, Miami University

Bok, D. (2003). *Universities in the marketplace: The commercialization of higher education.* Princeton, NJ: Princeton University Press.

Bok, a former president of Harvard University, examines the problems associated with the commercialization of higher education, while acknowledging that occasionally the benefits that accompany commercialization can outweigh the risks. Bok laments the gradual erosion of the university's values as the largest issue, warning his audience of what can be lost with continued commercialization.

Kegan, R. (2000). What "form" transforms? A constructive-developmental approach to transformative learning. In J. Mezirow (Ed.), *Learning as transformation: Critical perspectives on a theory in progress* (pp. 35–69). San Francisco, CA: Jossey-Bass.

This chapter distinguishes between information and transformational learning, describing the latter as involving transformation of the way we know or make meaning of experience. Kegan explains the intersection of development and learning across the lifespan and offers insight into the implications for adult learning.

Miller, T. (2003). Governmentality or commodification? U.S. higher education. *Cultural Studies, 17*(6), 897–904.

Miller explores the tension in American higher education between two differing philosophies: viewing universities as an opportunity to encourage governmentality and recognizing that universities engage in commodification. Miller examines how administrators of universities approach research as being initiated for the public good and teaching as training the citizenry in self-regulation, while also viewing research as being increasingly driven by corporate needs and teaching as a consumer good.

Blog URL: contestedissues.wordpress.com
Corresponding Chapter Post: tinyurl.com/contestedissues05

6

What Are the Risks and Benefits Associated With Allowing Students to Fail If Learning Results?

Creative Learning for Challenging Times: The Promise and Peril of Risk

Michele M. Welkener, University of Dayton

We are in an unprecedented time when it comes to the world's complexity—never has the need been greater for students to be prepared to think for themselves and act creatively to solve perplexing problems. As an artist, faculty member and administrator in higher education, faculty developer, and researcher of creativity in college students, I am passionate about creating environments where students can exercise such skills. In the art culture, risk, experimentation, exploration, and even failure are expected routes that lead to finding one's own style, voice, and signature statement. My awareness of these expectations first began to intensify as I advanced from student to instructor of art. Early in my career when I taught introductory courses in drawing and painting I watched bright students act unsure of their efforts on the first days of class. Students would frequently confess a lack of creativity before I would even have a chance to talk with them about their work. When a pattern of these perceptions started to emerge, I began to question how and why students sometimes do not consider themselves creative and what they must think creativity is to hold this view. Finding a dearth of empirical research on creativity in the college environment, I set out to better understand how students' views of creativity influenced their sense of self and actions. In my dissertation, *Concepts of Creativity and Creative Identity in College: Reflections of the Heart and Head*, I investigated the various definitions of creativity students held, their sense of themselves as creative or not (what I came to call their *creative identity*), and how they came to think of these things as they did.[1]

The results of my qualitative study with students from a variety of majors convinced me that their creativity was often stifled by the time they reached college. Indeed, it was not even something that students gave much intentional thought to—they were puzzled by the request to reflect on creativity and its role in their lives. Despite these dynamics, I identified nine major themes from their responses related to creativity's meaning. They said creativity involves spontaneity, open-mindedness, imagination, seeing or doing something a new way, knowledge, self-investment, risk taking, emotion, and self-expression. While within these narratives students sometimes revealed a lack of confidence or familiarity with risk and creativity, they illuminated potential linkages between learning, creativity, risk taking, and fear. One participant, Taylor, provided an example of such an internal struggle and vulnerability in the learning process:

> When you make yourself vulnerable to new ideas, you really just make your entire ideology vulnerable. And when I have a discussion with someone about . . . some aspect of religion, my entire upbringing becomes vulnerable, and you know, one of the biggest parts of my foundation becomes vulnerable, and that's a huge risk. . . . [One] that a lot of people aren't willing to take. . . . Being different and standing up for new ideas, or just what you believe in, requires a certain amount of creativity, I think, to just be yourself. I think it's easy . . . to be just like everyone else. And it's hard to stand up for certain things.[2]

Taylor's conception of learning recognizes the risk to self and one's sense of knowledge when exposed to new ideas. To be sure, the college years are (or should be) a time when one's understanding grows in depth and breadth. New information calls prior knowledge into question, different perspectives add dimension and texture to one's point of view, and one's collection of resources grows exponentially. During such explorations, it is inevitable and assumed, at least to some degree, that collegians pursue the boundaries of new awareness, test knowledge claims, and venture into unfamiliar territory. Taylor's comments prompt us to be mindful of the empowerment and fragility that students can simultaneously feel during this period of growth. So then, what are the roles of student affairs educators when it comes to engaging students in creative explorations inside and outside the classroom? How can we assist students with discerning between purposeful risks and risks with consequences that may be too great? What conditions do we create for risk taking, and how do we help shape students' experience in ways that result in productive learning? To address these questions, I offer perspectives on learning centering on risk and creativity. Admittedly, this essay cannot comprehensively answer the aforementioned questions; instead it provides provocative thoughts and challenges to elicit in-depth conversation involving student affairs educators.

Changing to Learn/Learning to Change

Learning has always been the fundamental purpose of an American higher education, but historically, educators seldom considered risk taking and creativity as vital elements of learning. How the academy has defined and advanced learning has been in a state of flux since the origins of higher education based on empirical and practical discoveries in academic disciplines, including education, psychology, social psychology, and neuroscience. These changes can be seen most clearly in the literature that traces the evolution of thinking about teaching. Embedded in each new development in teaching is a revised conception of the features and expectations of successful learning.

---

*Creativity, once limited to the arts and constrained
in teacher-centered conceptions of education,
is now often recognized in institutions' mission
statements as requisite for success in our
increasingly global society.*

Wilbert McKeachie traced early attempts to understand the role of class size in learning, the debate about the effectiveness of lecture versus discussion, and research on teaching and technology.[3] Noticeable in his survey of literature is the trajectory of the conversation about learning that moves from more teacher-centered approaches (e.g., those that rely heavily on lecture, for instance) toward more student-centered approaches (e.g., independent study, or peer and cooperative learning).

In 1995 Robert Barr and John Tagg offered a landmark contribution to the discourse in their article "From Teaching to Learning: A New Paradigm for Undergraduate Education."[4] They suggested going a step beyond the shift mentioned in earlier works (i.e., from focusing on instruction to focusing on students) to a focus on *learning*, which has the promise to engage educators and students. A learning paradigm assumes that students will take increasing responsibility for their own learning. Thus, in this environment, the role of student moves from passive recipient to active creator of knowledge. A faculty member's role shifts from deliverer of content to facilitator of learning. Learning is recognized as fluid across experiences rather than classroom bound. Staff members act as educators who contribute to the achievement of student learning outcomes. These developments point to our current period in history, which is primed for building on the momentum to construct learning in new ways. Creativity, once limited to the arts and constrained in teacher-centered conceptions of education, is now often recognized in institutions' mission statements as requisite for success in our increasingly global society.

Risky Business

Student affairs administrators have wrestled with the issue examined in this essay—risk taking—from the emergence of the profession. Since the creation of residential colleges, faculty and staff have dealt with the myriad dilemmas precipitated by students' flirtations with risky behavior. However, just as we have transformed our ways of thinking about promoting learning over time (and need to continually do so because students and cultures change), we have undergone similar adjustments when responding to high-risk student behavior. For the various types of risks students take, it seems universities have devised measures to minimize these risks via the establishment of offices, services, or policies. Students' risks related to breaking the law or an institution's code of conduct are met with judicial sanctions from disciplinary boards. Residential life, wellness, or specific alcohol and other drug offices, committees, and programs address alcohol risks. Often, women's centers, campus safety, and health services initiate conversations about dangerous sexual behaviors.

For many years, administrators of American institutions operated under the assumption that colleges should act in place of parents and have the authority to do so. However, over time, faculty preferred to focus on intellectual pursuits and not respond to issues outside the classroom. Student affairs practitioners became the guardians and purveyors of risk management, responsible for student discipline, overall development, community living, conflict mediation, and safety, among other central aspects of campus life. Those in the student personnel movement, much like the shift in teaching/learning theory, began to recognize the role of students in their own learning, and, as a result, transferred increasing responsibility to students for self-regulation.

While popular culture portrayals of high-risk behavior (e.g., excessive drinking, sexual indiscretion, cheating) stereotype collegiate life, and, unfortunately, measures are necessary to manage such risks, not all risk is high, nor is all risk a bad thing. In fact, risk taking can help students learn to make good decisions. Consider this scenario: A resident assistant (RA) approaches her hall coordinator to request funding for a movie and pizza party scheduled on the night of the (traditionally well-attended) homecoming football game. While the coordinator could easily doubt the student staff member's programming skills and deny her request, it would be a teachable moment for the coordinator to engage the RA in a dialogue about the benefits and consequences of such a risk. What are the learning goals of the event? Why schedule it on that date? How might the football game compete for her intended audience? Why pizza? While it may seem like an ordinary example, risk taking can be promoted through similar, brief interactions with students that require them to construct an argument yet allow them the opportunity to test their ideas (and even fail); learning will result from the experience and a debriefing process about what worked and did not (and why).

It is difficult to think about how we should guide students through the tumultuous waters of risk without placing such situations in a developmental context. Risk requires the whole person and can have a positive or negative impact on every dimension of student development. These dimensions, as identified by Robert Kegan and Marcia Baxter Magolda include cognitive (involving the intellect), interpersonal (related to relationships with others), and intrapersonal (concerning one's sense of self and identity).[5]

Risk taking also requires the ability to tolerate ambiguity, since the outcome of the risk is unknown. Comfort with ambiguity is a developmental demand, requiring a certain level of complexity. For example, if we use the ways of knowing Baxter Magolda found in her study of college students, absolute knowers would likely take little (if any) risk in the classroom because they wish to be certain that their attempts are right according to authorities.[6] Only in independent and contextual knowing, when students can start to see themselves as a source of knowledge, can they truly take risks and step out from under the authority's primary influence. Even so, contextual knowing, when one can begin to take ownership of or self-author one's own experience and choices, is more ideally suited for successful risk taking, as evidence is used as a tool for weighing judgments. Independent knowing, where everyone's opinions are considered equal, may be the most tenuous place for college student risk taking, as there is no such mechanism in place for calculating risk.

For all of this talk about college student risk, it is possible that students are more reticent than ever to step into the unknown. The latest generations of college students have come of age in an era marked by fear. Terrorism, economic collapse, corrupt corporate leadership, and natural disasters have eroded the sense of safety, security, and stability Americans once felt. College students frequently turn to psychological counseling to cope, as shown in a review of literature by Martha Anne Kitzrow.[7] In *When Hope and Fear Collide*, Arthur Levine and Jeanette Cureton present the primary concerns plaguing college students, ranging from personal safety to finances and relationships. According to these authors, students often fear deep involvement, because "it presents a far greater potential for getting hurt, for adding to one's burden, or for personal failure."[8] I cannot help but wonder if the rise of technology has exacerbated (or perhaps has even helped to create) some of this sense of disengagement from others and retreat from risk.

This detached stance appears reflective of the larger culture's attitude about risk as purported by sociologist Frank Furedi in *Culture of Fear*. In this text, he described the trend toward "the fear of taking risks and the transformation of safety into one of the main virtues of society."[9] He further claimed:

> The celebration of safety alongside the continuous warning about risks constitutes a profoundly anti-human intellectual and ideological regime. It continually invites society and its individual members to constrain their aspirations and to limit their actions. . . . The advocacy of safety and the rejection of risk-taking have important implications for the future. If experimentation is discredited, society effectively acknowledges its inability to tackle—never mind to solve—the problems which confront it. The restrictions being placed on experimentation, in the name of protecting us and our children from risk, actually represent the dissipation of the human potential.[10]

More and more, it seems risk is cast in a negative light—in a contemporary culture rife with hazards, to some, risk taking seems to evoke images of recklessness and rebellion. The problem with this perspective is that to learn, one cannot stay perfectly safe; some risk is required. A participant in my study, Sydney, provides an example as she disclosed how risk taking and creativity were coupled with her adjustment to college.

> I think I've learned so many more new things, and . . . not only about like the classes I took in art history and my chemistry and biology classes, English and stuff like that—not only just in classes, but . . . living in a dorm and learning to live with other people. Just being aware of society and the people around me in relationship to myself. . . . Probably the most important aspect about creativity that I learned is the whole idea about taking risks.[11]

Had Sydney not taken the chance to explore, she would not have fully experienced college and made connections across these different domains. Failure is possible whenever risks are taken. However, failure is certain if risks are never ventured.

Managing Successful Failure

As educators, we are obligated to help students avoid risks that will result in serious crises. Mary Rolison and Avraham Scherman explored "College-student risk-taking from three perspectives."[12] Using a quantitative approach, they found that students who have a personality type that involves sensation seeking and those who perceive that peers are engaging in risky behavior are more likely to do so themselves. The students Jodi

Dworkin interviewed for her qualitative study described risk in terms of results, leading her to ask, "If a behavior cannot be identified as dangerous until after a negative outcome has been experienced, how can prevention efforts aimed at identifying and avoiding dangerous risk taking be successful?"[13] This is the paradox that practitioners face. She offers suggestions to "redirect [their] behaviors, provide [them] with alternatives to dangerous behavior, encourage [them] to take precautions when participating in potentially dangerous behaviors, and prevent [them] from experiencing real crisis."[14]

Failure is certain if risks are never ventured.

While it is imperative that we help students avoid dangerous risks, it is just as crucial that we encourage risks that promote positive learning and development. In my creativity study, those who viewed their creative potential as low held that a privileged few are gifted with creativity. These students' perceptions of being deficient in creativity mediated their ability to act on it. In contrast, students who had a highly creative self-view understood creativity as a central element of their identity they felt obligated to pursue. Lacking the skills in their first years of college to take ownership of their experience, social expectations, and other external influences as well as a fear of rejection were burdens many students brought to bear on their choices, which often resulted in conforming to others' standards.

According to another participant, Tammy, educators were guilty at times of imposing standards that limited her risk taking and creativity.

> I think sometimes we get disappointed, because, I guess . . . it goes back to being restricted. [Teachers are] like "okay be creative, but this, this, and this, and you can't do this. . . . And then I start to think, "well what's the point of being creative?" Then . . . I just get discouraged and don't give it my all and I really come to, "okay I don't care," you know, and then I'm just putting together something that will just please my teacher. . . . I end up doing what the teacher wants, and that doesn't make me too happy.[15]

Fear of being penalized for taking risks was a thread evident throughout many of my conversations with students. Taking chances with grades, especially in a competitive, global marketplace, can appear too dangerous. However, allowing students to stay safe from risk, vulnerability, and failure is doing a disservice to their learning and development, since these experiences can help shape essential competencies.

Interestingly, the word *failure* rarely appears in the higher education literature, except when referring to student attrition. Could this be because educators believe that failure is an inappropriate way of describing the process of taking unsuccessful risks that results in successful learning? Although it may be unspoken rather than explicitly communicated, many of us assume that some experience with failure is part of the learning journey. Perhaps a reason for this lack of exchange about student failure, however, has to do with educators' own bewilderment about the nature and role of risk and failure in our efforts to promote learning.

Given that learning is the fundamental charge of higher education, faculty and staff are increasingly shifting responsibility to students for their own learning, students inevitably face the promise and perils of risk, and we are just starting to understand the relationship between learning, risk, and creativity, how can we go about creating an environment that invites the kind of experimentation that can be so crucial for students' learning and growth?

Educators should strategically provide opportunities for exploration, in and out of the classroom, for students to find their boundaries and strengths and test possibilities. Since scaffolding will be necessary (to allay students' fears), starting with low-risk activities and projects will foster confidence. By low-risk I mean nongraded or formative occasions to practice building skills before moving to higher-risk learning. Intentionally targeting all dimensions of students' development will make their experience even more beneficial.

Educators should model creativity and risk-taking for students so they can understand that these components are part of the scholar's modus operandi and not limited by discipline or content. New knowledge doesn't emerge from merely supporting the status quo, so what does risk taking in the name of discovery look like? How do you decide if the consequences of failure are worth the learning involved? Sharing specific instances where we have dealt with challenges and failures will help students make their own judgments. For example, in my classes I regularly try new approaches to teaching in an effort to help my students learn. We discuss these approaches and their success (or failure) to invite everyone into thinking about how we can improve our educational practices.

Educators should provide students with *ill-structured problems*, issues with no easy or singular solutions, a developmental approach popularized by Patricia King and Karen Kitchener in their reflective judgment model.[16] This kind of dilemma is the mainstay of student affairs work, which can promote creativity and risk taking and cultivate students' internalization of learning.

A developmental perspective offers us an awareness that risk management is not a one-size-fits-all endeavor. Levels and types of risk are not all the same and neither should be our methods for fostering students' growth—choices for interventions should be based on an assessment of their development. Going back to the formative days of the student development literature, Nevitt Sanford's emphasis on striking a balance between challenge and support helps us understand that these notions are delimited by context.[17] One student's version of support may seem a challenge to another, so it is crucial to understand who you're trying to assist. Too much challenge and the student's confidence for risk taking can be dashed; too much support and his or her risks may become careless, if the student even has motivation to venture a risk. The appropriate amount of challenge and support needed for healthy risk taking is best gauged according to the student's developmental maturity and needs.

The reality of a contested issue, like the benefits and perils of risk, is that it presents a developmental challenge in the form of an ill-structured problem for educators as much as students. The effectiveness of risk as a learning aid is limited by an educator's ease with risk taking and perhaps even his or her creative identity. We learn about taking risks ourselves when making choices about how to teach students about risk. It requires us to be able to determine how to support students in the context of what we know about them and their development and perform a cost-benefit analysis. We just must be sure to temper students' risks (and failures) with our support, determining the spirit of our guidance by the potential for harm to students the risk could cause.

To encourage student risk, faculty and staff need to put learning first, even at the expense of revealing a program, event, or course's imperfections—not an easy thing to do in this age of accountability and competition for limited funds. The stakes of failure are high for faculty and staff, as they are for students. However, if facilitators make risk taking a learning outcome in their event or program designs, such efforts can reveal student progress and improve assessment results. Ultimately, educators cannot afford to avoid risk just as students cannot afford to avoid risk.

Therefore, administrators and staff supervisors must not only allow risk taking but also find ways to reward it.

While these ideas are not exhaustive, they represent a starting point for discussing the issue of risk and how we might take learning-centered and developmental action toward improving students' experiences in college. One glance at the news headlines can attest to the fact that we need to be vigilant about preparing future generations to deal with increasing complexity. If there ever was a time to embrace the ambiguity of creativity and risk, and their potential for learning, it is now. And what better laboratory for experimentation than higher education—where learning is our mission.

Notes

1. Welkener, M. M. (2000). *Concepts of creativity and creative identity in college: Reflections of the heart and head.* (Unpublished doctoral dissertation). Miami University, Oxford, OH.

2. Ibid., p. 147.

3. McKeachie, W. J. (1990). Research on college teaching: The historical background. *Journal of Educational Psychology, 82*(2), 189–200.

4. Barr, R. & Tagg, J. (1995). From teaching to learning: A new paradigm for undergraduate education. *Change, 27*(6), 13–25.

5. Kegan, R. (1994). *In over our heads: The mental demands of modern life.* Cambridge, MA: Harvard University Press; Baxter Magolda, M. B. (2004). Self-authorship as the common goal of 21st-century education. In M. B. Baxter Magolda & P. M. King (Eds.), *Learning partnerships: Theory and models of practice to educate for self-authorship* (pp. 1–35). Sterling, VA: Stylus.

6. Baxter Magolda, M. B. (1992). *Knowing and reasoning in college: Gender-related patterns in students' intellectual development.* San Francisco, CA: Jossey-Bass.

7. Kitzrow, M. A. (2009). The mental health needs of today's college students: Challenges and recommendations. *NASPA Journal, 46*(4), 646–660.

8. Levine, A. L., & Cureton, J. S. (1998). *When hope and fear collide: A portrait of today's college student.* San Francisco, CA: Jossey-Bass, p. 97.

9. Furedi, F. (2002). *Culture of fear: Risk-taking and the morality of low expectation* (Rev. ed.). New York, NY: Continuum, p. 47.

10. Ibid., p. 13.

11. Welkener, *Concepts of creativity and creative identity in college*, p. 149.

12. Rolison, M. R., & Scherman, A. (2003). College student risk-taking from three perspectives. *Adolescence, 38*(152), 689–704.

13. Dworkin, J. (2005). Risk taking as developmentally appropriate experimentation for college students. *Journal of Adolescent Research, 20*(2), 219–241, p. 235.

14. Ibid., p. 236.

15. Welkener, M. M. (2004). Helping students develop vision and voice: The role creativity plays. *About Campus, 8*(6), 12–17, p. 14.

16. King, P. M., & Kitchener, K. S. (1994). *Developing reflective judgment: Understanding and promoting intellectual growth and critical thinking in adolescents and adults.* San Francisco, CA: Jossey-Bass.

17. Sanford, N. (1966). *Self and society: Social change and individual development.* New York, NY: Atherton.

Fostering Creativity and Risk Taking
Essential Work in Student Affairs

Kelsey Ebben Gross, Central New Mexico Community College

Most higher education professionals can likely identify a moment in college when they took a risk and learning resulted. My study abroad experience in Spain in 2003 and a service trip to Mississippi in 2004 required me to venture outside my comfort zone and experience failure. Yet, they also shaped my emerging identity and sparked my interest in pursuing a career in student affairs.

I affirm Welkener's stance on the benefits of risk taking and failure for student learning. As she asserted, the essence of higher education is to challenge students, with learning as the end goal. Welkener outlines the numerous ways students benefit from risk taking, including enhanced personal growth and preparedness for a complex global society. Indeed, it is hard to argue against the merits of risk taking for student learning. Nevertheless, for many students, risk taking is often easier said than done. In this essay, I discuss two factors that inhibit student risk taking: fear of failure and financial pressure. Then, I highlight the importance of creativity for a quality liberal education and present ways student affairs professionals can help students develop creativity.

Fear of Failure

I agree with Welkener that fear of failure often deters students from taking risks that would enhance their growth. She notes that fear of failure leads to students' fear of engagement and avoidance of risky activities. In my work as an academic adviser, this fear of failure frequently materialized as procrastination; students felt their skills were inadequate compared to peers, so they did not fully engage with their course work. Likewise, Gordon Flett, Kirk Blankstein, Paul Hewitt, and Sponenka Koledin found that students who procrastinated feared peers' disapproval of their performance.[1] These data coincide with student development theories, such as Baxter Magolda's research concluding that many college students follow "external formulas" because of their desire for others' approval.[2] Thus, it can be difficult for students to break free of fear and disengagement until they develop confidence in their own skills and knowledge.

How can student affairs professionals help students move past their fear of failure? Welkener argues that creating scaffolding, or steadily increasing amounts of risk, will help students acclimate to pushing themselves outside their comfort zone. I concur. Scaffolding can also help them identify and develop confidence in their own voice. I encourage scaffolding by asking students to focus on *flow* activities. Mihaly Csikzent-mihalyi and Jeanne Nakamura identified flow as a mental state that many successful athletes, musicians, and artists embrace.[3] People who enter flow are fully engaged in a task, lose self-consciousness, and continue to deepen their enjoyment of an activity as they tackle a series of graded challenges.

When students feel stuck in procrastination and fear, I encourage them to recall times when they felt fully involved in a challenging task (i.e., in flow). For example, one student identified weight training as an activity that fully consumed him. Recalling his weight-training regimen reminded him that he *does* have the capacity to focus on and achieve goals; we worked together to transfer this experience to an academic training regimen. We can push students to deeper levels of engagement by first focusing on the skills and activities they are already comfortable with and then building the scaffold. By asking students to evoke times they were unafraid to take risks, we can help them marshal their skills for new challenges they encounter.

Because fear of failure can stem from fear of peer disapproval, it would also be wise to incorporate peer learning into the risk-taking scaffold. Michael Ignelzi, in "Meaning Making in the Learning and Teaching Process," recommends that students "travel together" as they learn.[4] Student affairs professionals can design programs that pair students who have not yet developed an internal voice with students who are more developmentally complex and are likely more open to risk taking and failure. This interaction could encourage more fearful students to take risks in their own collegiate experience, worrying less about how others perceive them.

Financial Pressure

In her essay, Welkener commented that societal pressures may make students more hesitant about risk taking than in the past. While this recognition is a good starting point, we must give more weight to the influences of environmental circumstances on students' risk taking. Whether students take risks in their learning has to do not only with personal characteristics (e.g., developmental complexity, tendency to procrastinate), but also the characteristics of the environment they live in. Thus, I now discuss students' financial reality—one environmental example that can deter their risk taking in college, especially in academics.

Students live in an economic environment that makes it preferable to avoid academic risks, particularly those that could lengthen their college career. Often my undergraduate advisees would say things like, "I would love to try art and philosophy classes, but that would mean graduating a semester later, and I can't do that financially." Or, "Even though I'm terrible at Chinese, I really want to take more classes. But I can't risk damaging my grade point average for scholarships or medical school." So-Hyun Joo, Dorothy Bagwell Durband, and John Grable in "The Academic Impact of Financial Stress on College Students" conclude that students who experience financial stress are significantly more likely to drop out of college than other students.[5] Knowing this fact, I am hesitant to encourage students to take academic risks that could increase their financial stress, even when I am confident it would be beneficial for their learning.

Students' financial concerns are not unfounded. According to the Project on Student Debt website, 67% of students graduating from 4-year colleges and universities in 2008 had student loan debt, which was up 27% from 2004.[6] (The average debt amount in 2008 was $23,200, up from 24% in 2004.) As a result of skyrocketing costs, many families now seek to limit students' time in college. Kirsten Kennedy in an *About Campus* article noted that parents now view their child's college experience as a financial investment, so they take a greater role in dictating how the experience should unfold.[7] Indeed, many parents I encounter pressure their children to complete their degrees as quickly as possible. Further, U.S. Senator Lamar Alexander in *Newsweek* highlighted that many schools have begun to offer shorter, 3-year baccalaureate programs to cater to highly motivated, financially concerned families.[8] The current economic reality has contributed to students', parents', and even higher education institutions officials' changing approach to higher education, thereby reducing opportunities for academic exploration—and risk taking and failure.

In addition, students carefully guard their GPAs because they worry that poor grades may translate to fewer career opportunities (and earning potential). The National Association of Colleges and Employers website makes the following assertion, "With the state of the job market leading employers to have higher expectations for the candidates they hire, there is increased emphasis on grade point average (GPA). . . . Currently three out of four say they screen for GPA." Further, of employers who screen for GPA, 63% use 3.0 as the cutoff.[9] For students planning to pursue professional degrees, GPA requirements are often even higher, with most schools on the American Association of Medical Colleges website accepting the greatest percentage of students in the 3.6 range and higher.[10]

However, despite these financial pressures, I will continue to encourage students to consider taking some risk, although it may take different forms than in the past. Welkener argues the best we can do is help students evaluate the various opportunities for risk and failure and encourage them to make an informed choice; this is sage advice. By helping students consider a variety of possibilities, we encourage the type of deliberative thinking necessary to build the capacity for risk taking in the future.

Student Affairs and the Creativity Imperative

I appreciate the way Welkener connected creativity with risk taking and argue that creativity training should be a cornerstone of student affairs work and a quality liberal education. In "The Creativity Crisis," Po Bronson and Ashley Merryman define creativity as "divergent thinking (generating many unique ideas) and then convergent thinking (combining those ideas into the best result)."[11] When defined as a divergent-convergent thinking process, creativity can be reframed as a nondisciplinary skill that can be developed in many contexts—not just the arts. In terms of risk taking, I suspect that students who are strong convergent-divergent thinkers are better able to envision new possibilities and may feel less inhibited by financial and other barriers that threaten their learning potential.

As Welkener indicated, many students currently lack the creativity skills they will need to solve complex societal issues. Higher education is beginning to respond to this need by providing creativity training for students and making creativity an essential learning outcome for graduates. For example, the Association of American Colleges and Universities' document *Greater Expectations* outlines the type of education that students need for the 21st century: "Complex capacities like creativity and reflection are honed as students encounter knowledge in new contexts and open-ended or unscripted problems. A student's sense of how knowledge relates to life grows by grappling with untidy social questions."[12]

By honestly acknowledging the complex nature of our society, and encouraging students to experiment with risk, failure, and creativity wherever possible, we can play a central role in preparing the creative future leaders our world desperately needs.

Student affairs professionals can play a major role in this mission to make creativity an essential part of a student's education. In fact, student affairs practice is primed for being a key provider of creativity training on campus. As a case in point, Bronson and Merryman also cited work by Northwestern University's Adam Galinsky in which people who had had cross-cultural experiences developed enhanced creativity.[13] Student affairs professionals can therefore reframe existing programs like diversity training, study abroad, service-learning, and student organizations as creativity building experiences that facilitate divergent and convergent thinking as students wrestle with new ideas and enter diverse environments. These programs provide cost-effective venues for students to experiment with risk and learn creativity—without delaying their graduation or damaging their GPA.

When talking with students and parents, we need to illuminate the value of student affairs programming for creativity development, and for fostering healthy, beneficial risk taking. The creativity-building nature of student affairs necessitates that the profession be viewed as an essential element of a quality liberal education and not merely a purveyor of fun or frivolous collegiate adventures. By honestly acknowledging the complex nature of our society, and encouraging students to experiment with risk, failure, and creativity wherever possible, we can play a central role in preparing the creative future leaders our world desperately needs.

Notes

1. Flett, G., Blankstein, K., Hewitt, P., & Koledin, S. (1992). Components of perfectionism and procrastination in college students. *Social Behavior and Personality*, *20*(2), 85–94.

2. Baxter Magolda, M. B. (2001). *Making their own way: Narratives for transforming higher education to promote self-development.* Sterling, VA: Stylus.

3. Nakamura, J., & Csikzentmihalyi, M. (2002). The concept of flow. In C. R. Snyder & S. J. Lopez (Eds.), *Handbook of Positive Psychology* (pp. 89–105). New York, NY: Oxford University Press.

4. Ignelzi, M. (2000). Meaning-making in the learning and teaching process. In M. B. Baxter Magolda (Ed.), *Teaching to promote intellectual and personal maturity: Incorporating students' worldviews and identities into the learning process* (pp. 5–14). San Francisco, CA: Jossey-Bass.

5. Joo, S. H., Durband, D. B., & Grable, J. (2008–2009). The academic impact of financial stress on college students. *Journal of College Student Retention*, *10*(3), 287–305.

6. Project on Student Debt. (2010, January). *Quick facts about student debt.* Retrieved from http://projectonstudentdebt.org/files/File/Debt_Facts_and_Sources.pdf

7. Kennedy, K. (2009). The politics and policies of parental involvement. *About Campus: Enriching the Student Learning Experience*, *14*(4), 16–25.

8. Alexander, L. (2009, October 17). The three-year solution: How the reinvention of higher education benefits parents, students, and schools [Electronic version]. *Newsweek.* Retrieved from http://www.newsweek.com/2009/10/16/the-three-year-solution.html

9. National Association of Colleges and Employers. (2010, January 6). *Job outlook: What do employers look for in candidates?* Retrieved from http://www.naceweb.org/Publications/Spotlight_Online/2010/0106/Job_Outlook__What_do_employers_look_for_in_candidates_.aspx

10. American Association of Medical Colleges. (2010). *MCAT and GPA grid for applicants and acceptees to U.S. Medical Schools, 2008–2010.* Retrieved from http://www.aamc.org/data/facts/applicantmatriculant/table24-mcatg pagridall2007-09.pdf

11. Bronson, P., & Merryman, A. (2010, July 10). The creativity crisis. [Electronic version]. *Newsweek.* Retrieved from http://www.newsweek.com/2010/07/10/the-creativity-crisis.html

12. Association of American Colleges and Universities. (2002). *Greater expectations: A new vision for learning as a nation goes to college.* Washington, DC: Author, p. 32.

13. Bronson & Merryman, The creativity crisis.

Further Reading and Related Blog

Sue Ann Huang, University of Washington

Newman, F. (1985). *Higher education and the American resurgence: A Carnegie Foundation special report.* Lawrenceville, NJ: Princeton University Press.

This Carnegie Foundation special report examines how American colleges and universities can contribute to the advancement of American society. In recognizing the influence that college graduates can have on society, the Carnegie Foundation proposes promoting creativity among students and educating students to be concerned with quality of life. The chapter author emphasizes the need to foster creativity in college students and encourage them to be willing to take risks. The Carnegie Foundation offers several suggestions for educators and institutions to encourage creativity, risk taking, and civic involvement in college students.

King, P. M., & Baxter Magolda, M. B. (2011). Student learning. In J. H. Schuh, S. R. Jones, & S. R. Harper (Eds.), *Student services: A handbook for the profession* (pp. 207–225). San Francisco, CA: Jossey-Bass.

The authors link learning and development, advocating self-authorship as the foundation for holistic, transformative learning. The authors offer an overview of the journey toward self-authorship, then explain how learning partnerships can be created to help students initiate and manage the risks involved in learning.

Sawyer, K. S., John-Steiner, V., Moran, S., Sternberg, R. J., Feldman, D. H., Nakamura, J., & Csikszentmihalyi, M. (2003). *Creativity and development.* New York, NY: Oxford University Press.

In this book, the authors make the connection between creativity theories and developmental theories. This book traces the history of creativity and development theories and brings them into the realm of education and reframes these theories to focus on the processes instead of end points and on finding the connections between processes. The book also examines individual and social processes as they relate to these different theories.

Blog URL: contestedissues.wordpress.com
Corresponding Chapter Post: tinyurl.com/contestedissues06

7

Does Social Networking Enhance or Impede Student Learning?

Social Networking and Student Learning: Friends Without Benefits

Mark R. Connolly, University of Wisconsin–Madison

Although its origin story has achieved nearly mythic status, allow me to recap. In October 2003 a wily Harvard College student named Mark Zuckerberg hacked into his university's network and stole his classmates' ID information and photos, which he posted in pairs on a website that invited visitors to rate who was "hot or not." The illicit site—dubbed Facemash—drew 450 visitors and 22,000 views in just its first four hours before administrators shut it down. Building on this idea a few weeks later, Zuckerberg created a web-based study tool to upload 500 images of Roman art with space on each piece for his classmates to add their commentary. Spurred by the sudden success of these two efforts, Zuckerberg and three Harvard College classmates set out to create an electronic version of the printed guides with photos of students and faculty, or face books, that elite schools provided to new students. Launched just weeks later at Harvard, then carried swiftly by word of mouth to other U.S. colleges and schools, Facebook now claims more than half a billion members around the world.[1] Millions of people swept up by a wholly new form of social interaction built on accreting networks of friends are now facebooking nearly every day—that is, visiting one's

Facebook page not only to create one's own content (e.g., by posting short statements called status updates, uploading photos) but also to read others' content and respond with a comment or even a simple thumbs-up gesture to "like" what a friend shared.

Still, even as Facebook envelops the planet, we ought not forget that it was initially born of college students wanting easier ways to swap social information and academic knowledge with classmates. Like cell phones and ringtones, Facebook and college students go together, and although it is clear that college has been good for Facebook's success, what's less clear is whether Facebook and other social media are good for college.

Of course, social networking per se is nothing new to colleges and universities; student clubs and organizations have a long history as gateways to valuable social networks. But social networking sites and other Web 2.0 technologies that harness the potency of the Internet arguably are changing postsecondary education faster, further, and more subtly than any other innovation in recent memory. With Facebook, Twitter, YouTube, Wikipedia, and their like pervading nearly every aspect of U.S. higher education, social media seemingly make themselves indispensible before there's any time to consider the full range of their effects—negative as well as positive—on student learning.

I have no doubt that social technologies when used wisely can greatly enhance college student learning, especially if their use makes what the student is learning personally meaningful and socially relevant. But I argue that using social networking tools also carries significant hidden cognitive costs that when taken into account ought to give students and educators serious pause. This essay first considers the educational merits of social media, then discusses concerns raised by authors of several books, and finally offers suggestions for encouraging the prudent use of social media.

But social networking sites and other Web 2.0 technologies that harness the potency of the Internet arguably are changing postsecondary education faster, further, and more subtly than any other innovation in recent memory.

How Social Media Can Enhance Student Learning Outcomes

Popular social networking sites such as Facebook and MySpace are just a few of the interactive, user-centered applications and tools known collectively as *Web 2.0*, a term first used in 2004 to describe the transition from a read-only Internet (Web 1.0) to one that is read and write for anyone. Generally, Web 2.0 tools provide users with three important capabilities: to establish personalized public profiles, create multimedia content easily, and link content with other users. Web 2.0 thus also comprises media sharing (e.g., YouTube, Flickr, Prezi); social bookmarking (e.g., CiteULike and Delicious); wiki-based knowledge development (e.g., Wikipedia); content creation via podcasts, blogs, and microblogging (e.g., Twitter); content aggregation and tagging (e.g., RSS feeds, Tag2find); and remixing content from various providers into new forms (i.e., mash-ups).[2]

What role do these social media have in college student learning? Research not only shows that students and educators are using Web 2.0 technologies more frequently and extensively but also challenges assumptions about who tends to adopt them. For example, it is commonly assumed that most college students—especially Millennials—are already familiar with social media tools and ready to use them for educational purposes. However, a 2010 survey of University of New Hampshire undergraduates found that although 96% of respondents regularly use social networking sites, they do so primarily for social (89%) and entertainment (79%) purposes; only 26% of students were using social networking for educational reasons.[3] In contrast, a 2010 survey by educational publisher Pearson reported that more than 80% of faculty respondents have social media accounts, and 52% use at least one social networking tool instructionally. Moreover, the Pearson survey found that social media use by older faculty (i.e., those with more than 20 years of experience) is only slightly less than that of their younger colleagues, thereby controverting the notion that older faculty are lagging far behind their younger colleagues in using these tools.[4]

As suggested by these and other findings, current research on social media in postsecondary education has tended to focus on their use—that is, who uses them and for what purposes. Studies that examine their effects on student learning, however, are sparse, typically single-site studies relying only on descriptive statistics and are of limited generalizability. For example, the 2010 University of New Hampshire study compared percentages of heavy and light users of social media to conclude there were no differences between the two groups' grade point averages.[5] More common are studies of social media that have indirect implications for student learning, such as the 2010 study of 200 University of Maryland, College Park undergraduates who, after voluntarily giving up all media for 24 hours, discovered how much they depend on social media for keeping in touch with friends and family.[6] Further, building a knowledge base on social media in higher education is hindered by the fact that changes in these tools, their uses, and their users are occurring so rapidly, studies more than 3 years old already may be of limited validity.

Thus, even as the educational use of social media is accelerating, we really do not know how much they actually enhance or impede student learning in postsecondary contexts. Still, in the absence of specific impact studies, other research on Web 2.0 technologies in education may prove useful for estimating their educational impact on important intellectual and social outcomes of college. Education-technology researchers Christine Greenhow, Beth Robelia, and Joan Hughes have suggested that the salutary effects of Web 2.0 tools on student learning fall into two broad categories.[7]

The first category, which they call *learner participation and creative practices*, focuses on the ways Web 2.0 tools encourage students to engage with each other around certain practical tasks (e.g., solving a problem) or to simply express and share their creative works. The specific activities associated with college students' use of social media that fall into this first category include identifying, analyzing, and evaluating information; gathering data from disparate sources by effectively using searching and filtering tools; learning to classify and organize using tools such as tags; aggregating and integrating digital materials into new forms of expression; collaborating with other members of the network; and using multimedia to present, critique, and defend ideas before unseen audiences.

Here is an example of how learner participation and creative practices can be incorporated into course activities. To foster better instructor-student communication and to encourage more discussion among students, University of Toledo assistant professor of film Kelli Marshall asks students taking her large introductory film course to obtain and use a Twitter account. Before in-class film screenings, Marshall tweets four to five discussion questions that she hopes will shape how the students watch and interpret the assigned movie. She then encourages the students to use their phones or laptops throughout the screening to tweet their reactions to key scenes in real time. For example, during the final scene of *The Silence of the Lambs,* students could tweet their reactions to Marshall's discussion question about the movie's representation of gender.[8]

Even though staring at a computer screen and using a keypad seem like rather passive forms of learner participation, Web 2.0 technologies in fact can be highly engaging and generative and may hold the potential to make learning more personally meaningful, collaborative, and socially relevant. Still, social media may *allow* users to participate and create, but they do not *require* it. That is, users can invest significant quantities of time in using social media, and depending on how that time is spent, may not make appreciable gains in the learning outcomes that Greenhow and her colleagues claim are associated with participation and creation.

The second type of benefit, according to Greenhow and her colleagues, can come from using social media as it pertains to *learners' online identity formation.* Of course, constructing and presenting an integrated identity is a dynamic process that occurs with or without social media. But forming one's identity online involves different risks and rewards. For example, establishing an identity online can, at first, be highly structured by the medium itself—just ask anyone newly signed up for a Facebook account who must decide what photo to post on the profile page or what to write in the text box called "About Me." As a result, constructing one's identity within the constraints and norms of the medium can be an especially self-conscious experience. Some students may resist defining themselves based on the categories of the Facebook profile page, but other students will benefit from a constrained and ordered approach to presenting themselves to a social network. And because identities are more fungible and fluid online than off-line, still other students will embrace the opportunity provided by Web 2.0 to play and experiment with various selves they can create and discard with relatively little risk.

For example, when University of Wisconsin journalism instructor Katy Culver discovered that not everyone in her large lecture course could attend a panel discussion on journalism ethics she had assigned, she had those students who could attend use CoveritLive, a free web-based service for live blogging—sharing short blog posts as an event unfolds. Culver's students not only continually posted descriptions of the event on a website where their classmates could follow along and pose their own questions remotely, but the live bloggers also incorporated links to content, such as websites, documents, and video clips that the lecturers were discussing. Thus, using Web 2.0 tools to report the panel discussion gave Culver's journalism students a singular opportunity to try on the role of being a new-media journalist.[9]

However, if an important educational outcome is establishing what might be called one's face-to-face identity, where (at least for now) the bulk of our human interactions occur, we currently lack the research that could help us understand how who we are *online* shapes who we are *offline*. Nonetheless, engaging in social media often involves activities that may help students better understand themselves, such as learning how much information about themselves to disclose, learning to receive positive and negative feedback, seeing oneself as having the capacities to produce as well as participate and to critique as well as create, and actively adopting different roles in the learning process (e.g., peer teacher, evaluator, investigator, stage manager, coach, promoter).

In addition to the two categories of educational outcomes suggested by Greenhow and her colleagues, I suggest a third category, *community involvement and formation*, which entails a kind of interactivity that differs from the kind of learner participation described in their first category. That is, in contrast to seeing others simply as peer traders of digital content whose significance does not extend beyond an online relationship, community involvement and formation are educational outcomes concerned with establishing enduring relationships with others.

For example, social networking sites not only help students overcome the kind of isolation that otherwise might lead them to leave school, but they also provide shy students with information about others (e.g., neighbors in campus housing, classmates) that actually facilitates face-to-face encounters. Second, social media facilitate how students locate and identify with campus communities of varying scales that range from the institution as a whole to those meeting the needs of niche populations. Third, social networking sites are not only effective at linking people with common interests, but depending on the network, also can provide members with access to people with diverse points of view that may be otherwise unavailable to people from homogeneous backgrounds. Fourth, social media excel at helping members plan the face-to-face interactions (e.g., meetings, meals, athletic matches, service activities, gathering for worship) that are vital to sustaining community. Finally, social networking sites help students develop leadership skills ranging from low-level planning and organizing to forms of activism that promote social change and democratic engagement.

For the past 2 years, DePaul University in downtown Chicago has sponsored a contest called This Is DePaul in which students contribute digital images that best capture specific elements of the DePaul experience (e.g., life on an urban campus, service-learning activities, student diversity). In 2009 contest organizers requested 1- to 3-minute videos that drew nearly 20,000 views on YouTube. Not only did the entry selected by a panel of judges win $2,000, but also the video with the most student votes won $500. In 2010 the contest requirements shifted to still photographs, attracting more than 800 entries that received more than 7,500 student votes on the contest's Flickr site. In addition to helping students find and define campus community, this event gives them a very public role in the formation of institutional identity.[10]

The Drawbacks of Using Social Media

Although the use of social media in higher education is accelerating, even outpacing the education research studies that might inform its appropriate application, a number of books—most notably Nicholas Carr's *The Shallows* and Maggie Jackson's *Distracted*—have drawn greater attention to what these authors claim to be among the unseen and unintended consequences of our growing dependence on the Internet.[11] The scientific evidence they cite and the quality of their arguments suggest there is in fact much to worry about.

According to Jackson, the heavy use of the Internet and social media is exacting a high price from the minds of our youth who, according to various studies, are demonstrating greater impulsivity, less patience, less tenacity, and weaker critical thinking skills. What most worries Jackson is that the cognitive demands of using the Internet—namely, rapidly shifting one's attention from object to object—is silently atrophying an ability all other learning depends on: *self-control*, especially of one's attention. "In a land of distraction," Jackson asks, "can college students become truly reflective citizens [who understand] that ill-structured problems are susceptible to reasoned arguments based on evidence, not just opinion?"[12] In a section that draws upon Pascarella and Terenzini's *How College Affects Students*, Jackson elaborates:

> Minute by minute, self-control blossoms into broader forms of focus and persistence called "engagement" that fuel both academic achievement and

depth of thought. Students who study longer and get more deeply involved in their courses, and their reading and writing, report making greater gains in critical thinking and intellectual development in college, numerous studies show.[13]

In *The Shallows*, which expands on a celebrated *Atlantic Monthly* essay, "Is Google Making Us Stupid?" Carr admits what a boon the Internet can be to someone like himself whose livelihood depends on doing research and gathering information. Yet, Carr warns these benefits come with costs that are largely unseen and potentially huge:

> What the Net seems to be doing is chipping away my capacity for concentration and contemplation. Whether I'm online or not, my mind now expects to take in information the way the Net distributes it: in a swiftly moving stream of particles. Once I was a scuba diver in the sea of words. Now I zip along the surface like a guy on a Jet Ski.[14]

Like Jackson, Carr draws extensively on the research of neuroscientists, psychologists, and others to conclude that what's at stake in our growing reliance on social media is our gray matter. That is, using the Internet exposes one's sensory and cognitive faculties to exactly the kinds of interactive, repetitive, and addictive stimuli that are shown to produce enduring changes in brain structure and functions.[15] The more we use the Internet and social media, the better our brains can skim and scan, but research suggests that these gains come at the expense of our capacity for concentration, reasoning, and reflection. Social media technologies may be, as Greenhow and her colleagues suggest, potent tools for finding information, connecting with others, being creative, and expressing oneself, but we are failing to acknowledge the serious cognitive consequences of their use that may be leading, in Carr's terms, to more Jet Skiers and fewer scuba divers in college. When students immerse themselves in an "ecosystem of interruption technologies," speed trumps depth.[16] Students skip assigned books, favoring screens that can be browsed, 140-character tweets replace sentences and paragraphs, and all of higher education risks becoming a kind of Short Attention Span Theater. A technology that specializes in positively reinforcing its own use, potentially habituating users, like lab rats, to "constantly pressing levers to get tiny pellets of social or intellectual nourishment," reinforces these tendencies.[17] Facebook, e-mail, Google, and other web services that simultaneously seize and fragment our attention tend to subvert higher-order reasoning processes, including the very sort of critical thinking and evidence-based reasoning needed to honestly appraise the full costs of using social media.

Considerations in the Educational Use of Social Media

As we endeavor to weigh the drawbacks and benefits of using social media to further educational aims, I'm reminded of a quotation frequently attributed to St. Thomas Aquinas: "Nothing is either intrinsically good or evil, but its manner of usage may make it so."[18] To help us all think carefully about using social media intentionally and appropriately, I offer three ideas:

Access ≠ Understanding

I realize this statement may seem a little self-evident, but it is essential that students—especially our so-called digital natives—have some explicit assistance with distinguishing the skill of locating information from being able to credibly demonstrate one's understanding of that information (e.g., by explaining the concept to another person, relating it to other concepts). Social media and other Internet technologies excel at piquing, then satisfying the urge to search, leading students to focus only on learning tasks that involve the thrill of the hunt. Using social media to cultivate and demonstrate deep learning is possible but requires overcoming, among other things, the persistence of distraction, the surfeit of irrelevant information, and the temptation to wander.

The Internet Makes Things Easier, Yet Learning Is Always Hard

Bob Pace, University of California, Los Angeles professor emeritus whose work is the foundation for the National Study of Student Engagement instrument, often wrote about the relationship between the quality of a student's effort in educationally purposeful tasks and what she or he actually learned.[19] Learning is a function of effort; no pain, no gain. Yet, technologies are usually adopted because they purportedly reduce effort and increase efficiency. Therefore, does the use of social media in educational settings incorrectly suggest to students and educators that even learning should be easy and quick? If so, then how might we help users of social media see the value of reinvesting the time and effort saved by technology into higher-order tasks that truly matter to their learning, such as putting a complex argument into writing, reading difficult texts, and debating ideas with others?

Using social media to cultivate and demonstrate deep learning is possible but requires overcoming, among other things, the persistence of distraction, the surfeit of irrelevant information, and the temptation to wander.

To Use Social Media Wisely, Students Need Practice With Making Wise Judgments

As Jackson and Carr both suggest, something about the Internet and social technologies eludes close critical examination. Since social technologies are here to stay, it is therefore important to help students learn not only to use social media in an instrumental way—that is, to do stuff—but also to carefully consider when and why social media should be used at all. To cultivate the wise use of social media, teaching students about the dos and don'ts (e.g., rules, expectations, and norms on privacy, propriety, respect for others, and fair use) is necessary—but not sufficient. In the real world, students will undoubtedly find themselves facing a difficult situation involving social media that rules alone cannot resolve and thus requires their best judgment—a kind of practical wisdom that cannot be taught but instead is learned through practice. Helping students develop a capacity for practical reasoning when using social media can occur through various means, such as having multiple, purposeful discussions among educators and students about social media's pros and cons and using realistic case studies of social media in education to help students identify key trade-offs. Exactly how colleges and universities might encourage this type of reasoning is best left to another essay. What matters here is for educators, students, and administrators to recognize that given all the ways social media can enhance and impede student learning, knowing when, where, and with whom to use social media may be the most important learning outcome of all.

The Scope of Social Media in the United States

Since social networking technologies are expanding at rates that defy belief, let's first confirm exactly how pervasive their use is. Here are some provocative figures as of July 2010:

- About 75% of Americans use some kind of social technology. Of worldwide Internet users, the figure is nearly 70%.[20]
- Visiting social networking sites is now the fourth most popular online activity, ahead of checking personal e-mail (searching is first).[21]
- Of the various social networking sites (e.g., Ning, MySpace, Four-Square, Friendster), Facebook is the largest with 500 million members, adding its latest 100 million members in just five and a half months. About 250 million Facebook users log in each day, staying an average of 55 minutes.[22]
- Twitter, the microblogging site, has 75 million user accounts (although only 15 million are regular users) and generates 65 million messages, or tweets, each day.[23]
- YouTube is the world's third most visited site (behind Google and Facebook). Each day, visitors view more than 2 billion video clips, and every hour, users upload to the site an average of 24 hours' worth of video content.[24]
- More than 9 of every 10 college students visits a social networking site each day.[25]
- Women in the 18–34 age range are especially ardent users. More than half (57%) say they communicate through Facebook more than they do face to face. Since about 40% self-identify as Facebook addicts, it is not surprising that 34% of young women make checking Facebook the first thing they do each morning, even before going to the bathroom or brushing their teeth.[26]

Notes

1. Zuckerberg, M. (2010). *500 million stories*. Retrieved from http://blog.facebook.com/blog.php?post = 409753352130; Facebook. *Statistics*. (2011). Retrieved from http://www.facebook.com/press/info.php?statistics

2. Greenhow, C., Robelia, B., & Hughes, J. E. (2009). Learning, teaching, and scholarship in a digital age: Web 2.0 and classroom research: What path should we take *now*? *Educational Researcher, 38*(4), 246.

3. Martin, C. (2010). *Social networking usage and grades among college students.* Retrieved from http://www.unh.edu/news/docs/UNHsocialmedia.pdf

4. Tinti-Kane, H., Seaman, J., & Levy, J. (2011). *Social media in higher education: The survey.* Retrieved from http://www.slideshare.net/PearsonLearningSolutions/pearson-socialmediasurvey2010

5. Martin, *Social networking usage and grades among college students.*

6. Bielski, Z. (2010, April 27). Going cold turkey: Students in study crack without media. *Globe and Mail.* Retrieved from http://www.theglobeandmail.com/life/going-cold-turkey-students-in-study-crack-without-media/article1547473/

7. Greenhow et al., Learning, teaching, and scholarship in a digital age.

8. Marshall. K. (2010). *Twitter and Facebook in the college classroom.* Retrieved from http://kellimarshall.net/unmuzzledthoughts/teaching/twitter-classroom/

9. Edu-tastic. (2009, August 11). Thirteen enlightening case studies of social media in the classroom [blog post]. Retrieved from http://bestonlineuniversities.com/2009/13-enlightening-case-studies-of-social-media-in-the-classroom/

10. *This is DePaul: Student Photo Contest. The votes are in.* (2010). Retrieved from http://icomm.depaul.edu/thisisdepaul/index.aspx

11. Carr, N. (2010). *The shallows: What the Internet is doing to our brains.* New York, NY: Norton; Jackson, M. (2009). *Distracted: The erosion of attention and the coming dark age.* Amherst, NY: Prometheus.

12. Jackson, *Distracted,* p. 229.

13. Ibid.

14. Carr, *The shallows,* p. 7.

15. Ibid. p. 116.

16. Doctorow, C. (2009). Writing in an age of distraction. *Locus, 62*(1), 29.

17. Carr, *The shallows,* p. 117.

18. This quote is probably a modern reformulation of a line from Aquinas's *Summa Theologica*: "But evil is not in things, but in the sinner's use of them, as Augustine says."

19. Pace, C. R. (1980). Measuring the quality of student effort. *Current Issues in Higher Education, 2*(1), 10–16; Pace, C. R. (1990). *The undergraduates: A report of their activities and progress in college in the 1980s.* Los Angeles: Graduate School of Education, University of California.

20. Kagan, M. (2009). *What the f**k is social media? (one year later)?* Retrieved from http://www.slideshare.net/mzkagan/what-the-fk-is-social-media-one-year-later; Nielsen Company. (2009, March). *Global faces and networked places: A Nielsen report on social networking's new global footprint.* Retrieved from http://blog.nielsen.com/nielsenwire/wp-content/uploads/2009/03/nielsen_globalfaces_mar09.pdf

21. Nielsen Company, *Global faces.*

22. Zuckerberg, *500 million stories.*

23. Hird, J. (2010, July 8). *Revised mind-blowing social media statistics revisited . . . and 20+ more.* Retrieved from http://econsultancy.com/blog/6205-revised-mind-blowing-social-media-statistics-revisited-and-20+-more; Alexa Traffic Rank for YouTube (three

month average). *Alexa Internet.* Retrieved from http://www.alexa.com/siteinfo/youtube.com

24. Ibid.

25. Martin, *Social networking usage and grades among college students.*

26. Parr, B. (2010, July 7). *The first thing young women do in the morning: Check Facebook.* Retrieved from http://mashable.com/2010/07/07/oxygen-facebook-study/

Social Media and Learning

A Profile

Ana M. Martínez Alemán, Boston College

In 2004 I noticed an Internet site specifically intended for college students. Students at area colleges were talking about a social network site only for college students, a site they described as engaging and fun. An interactive site, it was indisputably student only. Unlike MySpace, it was an online "walled garden" that restricted use to college campuses. Capitalizing on the sociology of campus culture and the developmental psychology of undergraduates, this Web 2.0 site, Facebook, was fertile ground for student culture and fast becoming the locus of interaction among collegians.[1] Within a year of the site's launching, there were contradictory appraisals: Students sang its praises while adults warned of its dangers. Net generation collegians had become enthusiastic producers of an online campus community while student affairs and campus administrators grew troubled by their inability to direct or supervise this space.[2] These dynamics grasped my attention.

By 2005 Facebook had become a conspicuously intriguing campus phenomenon, especially to researchers like me who are curious about the ways undergraduates create communities, construct identity, and seek cultural relevance. With so many undergraduate students engaged in online social networking, it seemed inevitable that I would examine Facebook use. Katherine Lynk Wartman and I conducted research on social networking use among college students and the emergence of online student culture. Our project culminated in the publication of *Online Social Networking on Campus: Understanding What Matters in Student Culture* (2009).[3] It is from this research that I frame my response to Mark Connolly's essay about social networking and its effects on student learning.

Connolly wonders whether college students' use of Facebook and its online social media cousins can be deleterious to learning in college. He rightly notes that we really do not have extensive empirical proof that a negative causal relationship between college student learning and online social media use exists. Yet, his essay rests on his confidence that "using social networking tools also carries significant hidden cognitive costs, [and that] when taken into account, ought to give students and educators serious pause." Unfortunately, Connolly's argument is mostly unfounded.

By enabling students to move from consumption-only to production-consumption cognition, online social media expanded the range of cognitive skills used, skills that previously were not associated with Internet use. Social media requires students to selectively attend to certain information whether text or image, but admittedly these are not sites that require the type of penetrating analysis essential in literary analysis or other such academic pursuits. But unlike other sites, social media sites engage collegians as producers of social exchanges with peers; its many (and always evolving and increasing) features amplify students' knowledge of networks of associations that compose college culture. Students use Facebook to hone their cognitive skills to create new or alter existing connections of real-life and data that appear in the form of text, video, or still image on a virtual space. Unlike consumption-only sites like online newspapers, social networking sites are interactive spaces where students produce and decipher cultural meaning, generate information, and compose, categorize, and regulate relationships.[4] Online social media cognition also extends to decision making and interconnecting ideas. On these production-consumption sites, students discover the connection between facts, selectively attending to details, and exploit the power of multimedia communication. No longer just text-driven/text-restricted communication, social media sites provide possibilities to create, interpret, classify, compare, contrast, and evaluate communicative forms. Distracted thinking inherent to Internet use (for example, attending to pop-ups, ads, and added windows)—and that appears to have negative effects on cognition—appears less salient in social media precisely because they require user awareness of online and real-world sociocultural contexts to exercise judgment on matters that can have conflicting characteristics.[5] These sites necessitate users to process information that often entails differentiating data within a cultural calculus in which authenticity *and* counterfeiting are valued.[6] Social media is certainly not a site void of complex and nuanced cognitive activity.

Research to determine how the next generation of the web alters thinking processes—whether for good or ill—has to date provided us only with limited causal or relational effects on cognition. In my view, here, Connelly's anxiety is acceptable. We don't really know how Internet use affects learning, nor do we really know much about how online social media affect college learning. The growing body of research on Internet use and brain activity reports mixed conclusions.[7]

Connolly's concerns are understandable given the dearth of evidence on what conditions benefit or do not benefit learning online. How college

---

Unlike consumption-only sites like online newspapers, social networking sites are interactive spaces where students produce and decipher cultural meaning, generate information, and compose, categorize, and regulate relationships.

---

students learn off line has certainly been the focus of much research and scholarly consideration. We can identify with certain confidence many conditions and attributes necessary for successful learning.[8] To optimize learning we know that time on task, rehearsal, and reflection correlate strongly, for example. Learning also requires making connections between the object(s) of knowledge, distinguishing the relationships between events (i.e., are they the same or different?), and making meaningful conceptual maps. The meaning that we make of information has much to do with relevance, individual motivation, and self-regulation.[9] How we experience learning also affects and shapes learning.[10] Collegians learn best when they collaborate and study in groups and get frequent, timely feedback, and in group-focused activities like learning communities.[11]

But as Connolly notes, recent books charting the effects of the Internet on thinking, and by implication on learning, seem to suggest that being online is harmful. In Carr's *The Shallows: What the Internet Is Doing to Our Brains* (2010) and Jackson's *Distracted: The Erosion of Attention and the Coming of Dark Age* (2008) the assertion is that being online negatively alters thinking.[12] These authors contend that because the Internet is a medium based on interruption, users are undermining their capacity to focus, build awareness, and sustain engagement. Internet use decreases users' ability for deep attention, diminishes their capacities to discern details and filter data, and weakens interest in reflection. Information processing is at a fast, fragmented speed that can limit our ability to convert information into knowledge.[13] However, though sites like Facebook contain Internet functions that contribute to user distraction and fragmented thinking, they are distinctive online experiences that may not negatively affect thinking and learning in exactly these ways, a point Connolly overlooks.

My research examined how students manage identities, decipher authenticity, and create student cultures on Facebook. From this research, we learned that students believe that on Facebook they can regulate the presentation or performance of self, that the campus community is broadened and reconfigured, and that online interdependency is increasing. Despite some concerns about using social media to procrastinate, in general the effects of social media on student culture appeared positive.[14]

But how (or if) these media affect learning remains underexplored. For example, a study suggested that Facebook use has no negative effects on grades.[15] European studies have connected social media/Web 2.0 technologies with 21st-century learning outcomes. Researchers conclude that social media "provide easy, fast and efficient ways to access a great diversity of information and situated knowledge"; "provide learners with opportunities to develop their competences in collaboration with other learners"; and "allow individuals to acquire competences in a holistic manner, embedded in real-life contexts; and effectively and efficiently support competence building in a lifelong learning continuum."[16]

If I extrapolate from what is known about the effects of digital technologies on brain function and thinking, what is known about the nature of effective instructional practice and learning, and what is known about Facebook use, I can only put forward the following: Because social networking media are unique interactive sites that rely on user-driven content and real-world associations, if we want to assess their worth in college student learning, we will need to examine whether traditional constructs and norms for learning (and by extension, instruction) are adequate. Like online social media, teaching and learning have never been homogenous nor have they been solitary and strictly autonomous educational interventions. They are by nature simultaneously egocentric and social; they are relational and yet demand some element of separation. Like online social networking, learning is a hybrid event in which the social and the solitary, the relational and the autonomous learner inform each other. The science of learning indicates that the plasticity of our brains enables us to vary cognition and train thinking. Social networking sites certainly present students with opportunities to expand cognition and engage in cognitive skill building their parents never experienced. Consequently, learning may well be delivered and accessed differently. The multidimensional nature of these sites correlates with what we know matters in cognition, and though perhaps these dimensions are (at least for the moment) 2D or 3D, they nonetheless change the process of thinking—but it is still *thinking*. How that thinking becomes the means to learning has yet to be ascertained.

Perhaps the real value of social networking media for learning is the extent to which it can complement, extend, and transform cognitive skill sets trained and drawn out by traditional instruction. In *Natural Born Cyborgs* (2003), Clark argues that as biology and technology grow ever closer, we do much of our thinking and expressive communication through more sophisticated and advanced technologies. But as Clark reminds us, the human brain's plasticity continues to evolve and with it so does technology. The human brain's neuroplasticity is the result of our cognitive ability to develop through and with technology (from tools to cyberspace), not in spite of it.[17]

My anxiety about online social media use in college is that this cognitive space is uncharted. We can't accurately determine the impact of these media on student learning without innovative research on this hybrid environment where "the real and the virtual interact and overlap,"[18] likely making cognition more multifaceted and intricate. Couple that with user developmental and sociocultural generational distinctiveness and the implications for cognition, and it's evident that we are not sufficiently expert enough to judge whether online social media is good for college student learning. Consequently, Connolly can't proclaim whether Facebook is good for college learning. He should delay judgment.

Notes

1. Martínez Alemán, A. M., & Wartman, K. L. (2009). *Online social networking on campus: Understanding what matters in student culture.* New York, NY: Routledge, p. 20.

2. Tapscott, D. (1998). *Growing up digital: The rise of the net generation.* New York, NY: McGraw-Hill.

3. Martínez Alemán & Wartman, *Online social networking on campus.*

4. Ibid.

5. Carr, N. (2010). *The shallows: What the Internet is doing to our brains.* New York, NY: Norton.

6. Martínez Alemán & Wartman, *Online social networking on campus.*

7. Begley, S. (2010, January 8). Your brain online: Does the web change how we think? *Newsweek.* Retrieved from http://www.newsweek.com/2010/01/07/your-brain-online.html

8. Pascarella, E., & Terenzini, P. (2005). *How college affects students* (3rd. ed.). San Francisco, CA: Jossey-Bass.

9. Pintrich, P. (2004). A conceptual framework for assessing motivation and self-regulated learning in college students. *Educational Psychology Review, 16*(4), 385–407.

10. Bransford, J. D., Brown, A. L., & Cocking, R. C. (Eds.) (2000). *How people learn: Brain, mind, experience, and school.* Washington, DC: National Academies Press.

11. Light, R. J. (1992). *The Harvard Assessment Seminars: Explorations with students and faculty about teaching, learning, and student life. Second report.* Cambridge, MA: Harvard University, Graduate School of Education; Kuh, G. D., Kinzie, J., Schuh, J. H., Whitt, E. J. & Associates. (2010). *Student success in college: Creating conditions that matter.* San Francisco, CA: Jossey Bass.

12. Jackson, M. (2008). *Distracted: The erosion of attention and the coming of the dark age.* New York, NY: Prometheus.

13. Carr, *The shallows*; Jackson, *Distracted..*

14. *Martínez Alemán & Wartman, Online social networking on campus.*

15. Truong, K. (2010, July 15). Study finds no link between social-networking sites and academic performance. *Chronicle of Higher Education.* Retrieved from http://chronicle .com/blogPost/Study-Finds-No-Link-Between/25541/

16. Redecker, C., Ala-Mutka, K., & Punie, I. (2010). *Learning 2.0: The impact of social media on learning in Europe.* Retrieved from European Commission Joint Research Centre: http://ftp.jrc.es/EURdoc/JRC56958.pdf, p.8.

17. Clark, A. (2003). *Natural-born cyborgs: Minds, technologies, and the future of human intelligence.* Oxford, UK: Oxford University Press.

18. Martínez Alemán & Wartman, *Online social networking on campus*, p. 50.

Further Reading and Related Blog

Craig Berger, Miami University

Boyd, D. M., & Ellison, N. (2007, October). Social network sites: Definition, history, and scholarship. *Journal of Computer-Mediated Communication, 13*(1), article 11.

This article provides readers with a historical overview of online social networks, defining them and exploring how these sites allow for research on impression management and self-performance. In bringing together scholarship on social network sites, the article also includes a thorough bibliography on this topic.

Carr, N. (2010). *The shallows: What the Internet is doing to our brains.* New York, NY: Norton.

Carr's text concerns itself with the Internet's impact on the human capacity to learn. Carr uses history as a guide, noting that the development of new processes and technologies in the past produced similar, nervous societal reactions. This transition, Carr argues, is worrisome given the Internet's ability to distract us from deep thinking. This text provides readers with an understanding of some red flags that accompany the burgeoning online social networking scene, thereby affecting our students.

Martínez Alemán, A. M., & Wartman, K. L. (2009). *Online social networking on campus: Understanding what matters in student culture.* New York, NY: Routledge.

This book offers professional guidance to administrators and policy makers in higher education, examining students' use of social networking websites and how they contribute to their interpersonal and intrapersonal development. This ethnographic perspective on social networking can assist student affairs administrators and faculty in better understanding the Millennial students on their campuses.

Blog URL: contestedissues.wordpress.com
Corresponding Chapter Post: tinyurl.com/contestedissues07

8

What Is the Relationship Between Changing University Policy and Changing Student Norms?

Where Policy Meets Student Behavior

Jonathan Poullard, University of California, Berkeley

K nowledge of the law is an essential element of the professional practice of any student affairs administrator, for it shapes policies, practices, and decisions on a daily basis. The legal environment of higher
education and student affairs has changed rapidly in the past decades,
and the legal ramifications for student affairs practice have grown even
more pronounced.[1]

Being well versed in laws that shape policies, practices, and decisions of
student affairs practitioners is essential when working on today's college
campuses. Freedom of speech, Family Educational Rights and Privacy Act
(FERPA), federal and state laws that govern the use of race-based aid and
program offerings, and protections for race, sex, sexual orientation, ability status, national origin and religious expression are but a few of the
many issues that influence the daily work of student affairs practitioners.[2]
I refer to *laws* as those federal and state statutes that adhere to the Constitution of the United States and serve as the supreme order for the governance of our country, and to *policies* as those guidelines and rules
established by colleges and universities that are often informed by or

follow the laws of our country. The relationship between university policies and how they affect student behavior and campus norms are as varied as the institutions in higher education. Institutional type (e.g., liberal arts, Research I, Jesuit, or community college) determines how staff members develop and implement policies. While there is a long-standing tradition of student affairs educators supporting the academic mission of the college/university, this commitment has become more challenging because of increased accountability demands, changing student demographics, parental involvement in the lives of students, and the developmental needs of contemporary collegians.[3] Blomley stated:

> critics argue that, far from constituting an autonomous sphere, the legal project is necessarily a social and political project. . . . it is important to contest the abstract neutrality of law because critical legal scholars posit that law is relational, that is, it acquires meaning through social action.[4]

In essence, while laws protect people from acts of discrimination or exclusion, they cannot on their own address how students on the college campus experience such laws and their use in the creation and implementation of policies. The cultural milieu and sociopolitical realities that shape day-to-day interactions of student affairs practitioners with students, faculty, and other administrators must be clearly understood and discussed to assess their ability to address or change student norms. Policies can only go so far in addressing and challenging student beliefs, values, and attitudes, and practitioners should not rely on them solely to produce the learning environments they desire. That said, it is not my intention to make light of the necessity of policies that protect free speech, access to services, and protection from discrimination—however, it is important to consider their limitations in creating safe, open, and respectful communities for learning. Toward this goal, some institutions of higher education have adopted principles of community and respect as a vehicle to express to their members, and particularly students, the value of inclusive, open, and safe environments for learning. The following are two examples of statements that highlight this expectation and desire:

> We, as members of the Brown University community faculty, undergraduates, graduate and medical students, and staff are dedicated to supporting and maintaining a scholarly community in which all share together in the common enterprise of learning. As a central aim, Brown University promotes intellectual inquiry through vigorous discourse, both oral and written. The fundamental principles that must necessarily undergird this aim

include respect for the integrity of the academic process; individual integrity and self-respect; respect for the freedoms and privileges of others; and respect for University resources. In becoming a part of Brown University, we accept the rights and responsibilities of membership in the University's academic and social community, and assume the responsibility to uphold the University's principles: respect for the integrity of the academic process, individual integrity, respect for the freedoms and privileges of others, respect for university resources.

The University's guiding principles are to educate for leadership in the Jesuit tradition; serve as a voice of reason, conscience, and compassion in society; foster academic excellence and a lifelong passion for learning; create a learning environment that integrates rigorous inquiry, creative imagination, reflective engagement with society, and a commitment to fashioning a more humane and just world; encourage innovation, while preserving the best of our traditions, to enhance our learning and living environment; nurture a diverse University community rooted in mutual understanding and respect; promote throughout the University a culture of service that fosters the development of personal responsibility; strive for effective communication and responsible decision making at every level to advance our mission; build a stronger financial base to enhance the quality of the University. It is the responsibility of all members of the Santa Clara University community to work together to achieve the University's purpose according to its guiding principles.[5]

While similar in scope and character, each statement was written in the institution's geographic, historical, political, cultural, and religious context. Practitioners moving from one campus to another must understand not only the extent to which that campus has thoughtfully or intentionally considered the vast complexities of freedom of speech and respect for difference but also how dialogue and debate are practiced on that campus. For example, FERPA provides campus administrators some room to interpret and apply the law. Some campuses adopt a more literal adherence while others opt for a more idiosyncratic interpretation for the disclosure of and access to student information. Campus norms and expectations, past incidents, and current events dictate how a university creates and enacts policy. Similarly, challenges to affirmative action laws across the nation have forced states to reëxamine how they use federal protection in writing admissions policies and developing race-specific programming and services and services for women. No doubt the challenges to affirmative action policies in Michigan with Proposition 2, California with Proposition 209, and the Hopwood case at the University of

Texas—among others, have caused universities, public and private, across the nation to reexamine their existing policies in the application of affirmative action laws and admission-related activities.[6] In addition to laws, student affairs practitioners must also contend with the shifting attitudes, values, and beliefs of their students as they address issues of inclusion, respect, and open dissent. The existence of laws that protect speech, provide for environments free from discrimination, and serve as the basis for the creation of university policies and procedures are insufficient to create campus climates characterized by safety, inclusion, and respect. Likewise, the development of community principles or standards, while laudable and necessary, are insufficient in shifting or changing student norms.

What then accounts for the shift in student's values and beliefs and what influence do university policies and procedures have on these shifts? What roles do student affairs practitioners play in shaping student norms of engagement? In the remainder of this essay I explore these two central questions. Specifically, I examine today's Millennial students and the use of free speech policies, and by extension time, place, and manner policies that affect their interactions on the college campus. I also examine the use of hate crimes law to inform student conduct policies as vehicles for maintaining and creating acceptable student norms of engagement. Finally, I provide a case study that situates this complex issue in the context of how students develop (cognitive, intrapersonal, and interpersonal) using King and Baxter Magolda's developmental model of intercultural maturity.[7]

Campus norms and expectations, past incidents, and current events dictate how a university creates and enacts policy.

Shifting Student Attitudes—How Does Data Inform Policy Development?

It is important to consider the impact policies can have on student norms by first understanding students. Today's college students, often referred to as the Millennial generation, bring with them a set of expectations, challenges, and accepted rules of engagement not seen in past generations. Howe and Strauss noted:

> As we have observed, the Millennials are prone to collective action. While remarkably hardworking, the entrepreneurial spirit will be less congenial to them than it was to Generation X. We suggest that severe economic mismanagement could point them toward communism.[8]

How might a tendency toward collective action inform student activism on campus and thus challenge student affairs practitioners in the construction of useful time, place, and manner restrictions that encourage students to exercise freedom of speech while simultaneously requiring that they not disrupt the normal operations of a university environment? When one considers Millennials' tendency for collective action in a specific campus context, it is easier to gain insight into effective policy development. For example, the University of California (UC) Berkeley campus is the home of the Free Speech Movement, a movement that began during the 1964–65 academic year under the leadership of student Mario Savio, who insisted that the campus lift its ban of on-campus political activity.[9] As an outcome the university designated the steps of Sproul Hall (now Savio Steps) and the surrounding area on Sproul Plaza as a space for political activity and expression and open discussion during certain hours of the day.[10] Today students actively publicize their organizations and reserve Savio Steps for protests and rallies. Working with UC Berkeley Millennial students who are introduced to acts of resistance through protests, rallies, and civil disobedience during campus recruitment events and who witness on a weekly basis spirited debate on Sproul Plaza require a different skill set than one would need at a nearby community college where the vast majority of students commute and work full-time. It is these profound differences in campus culture and not merely the rules that govern student engagement that must be understood and applied effectively by student affairs practitioners. Thus, the development of effective policy must be informed by the sociopolitical context of the campus that students experience on a daily basis.

Millennials' attitudes, beliefs, and values about many of today's contentious issues that often result in protests, rallies, or campus acrimony and that call for the implementation of rules, guidelines, and policies to enforce order are becoming more liberal (liberal as in agreeing to extending rights to U.S. citizens that have been denied on the basis of morality) on some fronts. The Cooperative Institutional Research Program's annual survey to entering first-year students attending 4-year institutions showed a continued climb in support for the question, "Should same sex couples have the right to legal marital status?" About 66% of all respondents beginning their collegiate career in fall 2008 strongly or somewhat agreed with this statement, which was up 2.7% from the previous year, and up almost 7% from the 2002 survey.[11] This trend supporting gay/lesbian rights was also evident when students responded to the question, "How important is it to have laws that prohibit homosexual relationships?" For students beginning their academic career in fall 2008, 23.4% agreed strongly or somewhat agreed that laws should exclude homosexual relationships. This percentage was slightly higher at 24.3% in fall 2007 and still higher at 24.8% in fall 2002.[12] How might these shifts in attitude be affected by the current national sociopolitical landscape in which California, Florida, and Arizona joined 27 other states in passing bans on gay marriage? Two UC campuses experienced an upswing in lesbian, gay, bisexual, and transgender (LGBT) violence and acts of hate. At UC Riverside and Davis, acts of vandalism to their LGBT resource centers were committed during the spring 2010 semester coupled with a reported gay-bashing incident at UC Riverside. These acts came on the heels of the now infamous Compton Cookout party (i.e., a party that encouraged attendees to wear ghetto attire to mock Black History Month) at UC San Diego, and the hanging of nooses on the UC San Diego and Santa Cruz campuses.[13] These acts raised the level of activism by students and necessitated that student affairs practitioners and administrators at the UC Office of the President reexamine the system's policies that provide protection and adjudication for acts of intolerance and hate.

While students report they are more liberal in their attitudes toward LGBT issues, their attitudes about issues of race as captured in the statements "Affirmative Action in college admission should be abolished" and "Undocumented immigrants should be denied access to public education" are more conservative. In the 2009 Cooperative Institutional Research Program study 47.6% of students strongly or somewhat agreed that race should not be used in the college admission processes, down only .2% from the previous year's survey.[14] Regarding the question on immigrant rights to public education almost half, 47.2%, strongly or somewhat agreed that undocumented persons should not be afforded public education: down only .9% from the previous year.[15] As noted earlier, recent court decisions and state laws fuel the growing contest and debate on issues of affirmative action and immigrant rights. In April 2010 Arizona passed a highly controversial law, Support Our Law Enforcement and Safe Neighborhoods Act (SB1070), that grants police officers the authority to question anyone they suspect as being undocumented.[16] The governor signed SB1070 into law and spurred national and international protests including the labeling of the law as misguided by President Obama and prompting a constitutional challenge by the federal government. In California and Arizona mass protests have occurred in response to the signing of SB1070. On the UC Berkeley campus about 20 graduate and undergraduate students staged a 7-day hunger strike to protest the passing of SB1070, to demand that the chancellor publicly denounce the legislation, and to make Berkeley a sanctuary campus.[17] African American students across the UC system sponsored protests to bring attention to the hanging nooses on two UC campuses, the Compton Cookout theme party, and the isolation many students of color feel as a result of their dwindling numbers since the 1996 passage of Proposition 209 against affirmative action.[18] Millennial students' attitudes regarding race are not surprising considering the debate over our society becoming a postracial one, stimulated in large part by the 2008 historic election of Barack Obama as the nation's first African American president. Clearly, these attitudes will require a great deal more than policy development to promote and achieve the campus norms of inclusion that administrators desire. The UC system has changed its code of student conduct to give conduct officers more latitude in increasing the severity of sanctions for code violations that include hate acts or violence. Similar to state and federal laws that allow for stronger sentences for hate crimes and violence, conduct officers have the discretion to impose harsher sanctions when adjudicating student conduct cases involving incidents of hate crimes or violence. Unfortunately, it is rare, if ever, that those who commit acts of hate are identified, thus making the policy change marginally effective. Policy change, while laudable, is not always effective in achieving the intended outcome of values or behavior modification. Policy changes must be accompanied by strong programmatic efforts situated within the specific sociopolitical environment of the campus. Policies often address the what of student behavior and not the how or why. At the University of Arizona, practitioners have implemented the Millennial Student Project that offers a different approach to policy alone and acknowledges that the development of values and institutionally acceptable cultural norms are socially constructed.[19] According to the program objectives:

This study introduces a new way of conceptualizing student perspectives on diversity. Grounded in traditional theories, this study introduces a more comprehensive model of how diversity is perceived. In contrast to diversity models that measure development in a linear fashion, this theory views perspectives as fluid and dynamic, influenced by infinite variables including but not limited to: gender, race, ethnicity, nationality, personal or religious beliefs, culture, socio-economic status, parental influence, peer influence, sexual orientation, first-generation college status, ability, openness to learning/willingness for self-critique, pre-college experiences and college experiences. Student identities and perspectives regarding diversity are socially constructed, multiple rather than singular and shaped by issues of privilege and power.

Policy changes must be accompanied by strong programmatic efforts situated within the specific sociopolitical environment of the campus.

The Millennial Student Project and the UC system policy change offer insights into how student affairs practitioners might not only draft policy but also what tools might be used to better engage students in thoughtful and meaningful dialogue aimed at enriched understanding of these complex and contested issues. The authors of both these initiatives drafted them in the sociopolitical context of the campus environment, ensuring a higher level of success in achieving the expected outcomes of responsible and engaged student behavior. It is also important to consider where students are in their developmental process and to use appropriate theories and concepts as a guide to draft relevant policies and programmatic initiatives. King and Baxter Magolda's developmental model of intercultural maturity offers a comprehensive perspective (centering on cognitive, intrapersonal, and interpersonal development) on how practitioners might use theory to guide their drafting of policies and programs.[20]

Islamo-Facism Awareness Week: Where Policy, Theory, and Student Behavior Meet

From October 22 to 26, 2007, 114 college campuses sponsored Islamo-Facism Awareness Week, a program of the Terrorism Awareness Project of the David Horowitz Freedom Center, to draw attention to the "threat from the Islamic jihad and the oppression of Muslim women."[21] The week received massive attention and prompted protests organized in large part by Muslim and Palestinian students and their supporters. On the UC Berkeley campus, the College Republicans sponsored Islamo-Facism Awareness Week—which prompted counterprogramming and protests by Muslim and Palestinian students and a coalition of 30 student organizations in the form of Peace Not Prejudice Week. Some students from the Jewish Student Union attempted to join the coalition; however, their involvement and inclusion was minimal. The week reignited ongoing tensions between Muslim and Palestinian students and their supporters, and Israeli and Jewish students and their supporters. In years prior several protests and counterprotests had been staged between these two groups. Student leaders from both organizations, who were most active in planning protests, rallies, and counterprotests, fell close to what King and Baxter Magolda characterize as the initial perspective on intercultural maturity—a stage where students find it difficult to relate and build relationships with those of differing beliefs, where their making meaning views difference as wrong and where students lack a clear understanding of their own values and social identity.[22] For these students, there was a right and a wrong—a single truth—and not surprisingly, those student leaders who maintained a more mature perspective on intercultural maturity and who had formed intimate relationships with students with opposing views were often pushed to the margins when they attempted to engage members of their respective organization in dialogue. Students with mature perspectives define their beliefs internally, and not only understand their own values but appreciate and consider the values of those who are different.[23] From an initial perspective, students were unwilling to engage in dialogue and had strong expectations that rules that govern free speech, political expression, and time, place, and manner on the campus be strictly enforced. Student affairs practitioners called on leaders from both sides to discuss the how of their behavior and not merely the what, and attempted to assist students in seeing the perspectives of the other to develop rules of engagement that would build a shared campus ethos, thus reducing the need to enforce campus regulations through university police or student conduct officers. While students met with practitioners they were less willing to do so with students from the opposing perspective, making it difficult for practitioners to build a platform for dialogue and understanding. What to do? Understanding the attitudes and beliefs that drove student behavior, having a clear appreciation of their intercultural perspectives, and situating the decision within the sociopolitical context of the campus, practitioners decided to write more clear guidelines for enforcing protests and counter-protests. Strict adherence to the rules was a must, and students worked with staff and university police to develop acceptable parameters of safe distance to conduct their opposing campaigns of political expression. While far from the optimum, practitioners recognized how much could be accomplished given the realities. And while dialogue could not be achieved between these two groups, practitioners continued to build rela-tionships with those students who maintained a more committed, mature perspective; community partners; and faculty to create programs such as Bears Breaking Bread—a program designed to bring different religious and cultural organizations together around a meal for informal discus-sion and Critical Dialogues Across Difference—an 8-week one-unit course designed to assist students in developing dialogue skills. Recogniz-ing the limitations of policy change alone, practitioners confronted the issue of community norms and acceptable student engagement by modi-fying the existing policy and guidelines that governed political expressive activity and deploying effective ongoing programmatic interventions within a strong conceptual framework.

Conclusion

University policies and procedures can only go so far in fostering and maintaining acceptable norms of student behavior and engagement, and drafting such policies should be framed within the sociopolitical context of the campus. Practitioners should also have a clear understanding of the needs of Millennial students and their campus environment and cul-ture. It is my belief that as practitioners we must recognize the limitations of policy alone in managing student norms and engagement by simulta-neously drafting developmentally appropriate programming that pro-vides students with tools and skills for engaging in open and respectful dialogue.

Notes

1. Barr, M. (2003). Legal foundations of student affairs practice. In S. R. Komives, D. B. Woodard Jr., and Associates (Eds.), *Student services: A handbook for the profession* (pp. 128–150). San Francisco, CA: Jossey-Bass, p. 128.

2. U.S. Department of Education. *Family Educational Rights and Privacy Act (FERPA)*. Retrieved from http://www2.ed.giv/policy/gen/fpco/ferpa/index.html

3. Howe, N., & Strauss, W. (2000). *Millennials rising: The next great generation*. New York, NY: Vintage Books; Nuss, E. M. (2003). The development of student affairs. In S. R. Komives, D. B. Woodard Jr., & Associates (Eds.), *Student services: A handbook for the profession* (pp. 65–88). San Francisco, CA: Jossey-Bass; Thelin, J. R. (2003). Historical overview of American higher education. In S. R. Komives, D. B. Woodard Jr., & Associates (Eds.), *Student services: A handbook for the profession* (pp. 3–20). San Francisco, CA: Jossey-Bass.

4. Vellani, F. (2006). *Law's contexts and scales: Inclusive environments for disabled people*. (Unpublished doctoral dissertation). University of London, UK, p. 112.

5. Dean of the College. *Principles of the Brown University community*. Retrieved from http://brown.edu/Administration/Dean_of_the_College/curriculum/principles.php; Santa Clara University. *Statement of purpose and guiding principles*. Retrieved from http://www.scu.edu/hr/policy/principles.cfm

6. Moore, J. (2004). *Race and college admissions: A case for affirmative action*. Jefferson, NC: McFarland.

7. King, P. M., & Baxter Magolda, M. B. (2005). A developmental model of intercultural maturity. *Journal of College Student Development, 46*(6), 571–592.

8. Howe & Strauss, *Millennials rising*, p. 214.

9. Cohen, R. (2009). *Freedom's orator: Mario Savio and the radical legacy of the 1960s*. New York, NY: Oxford University Press.

10. Goines, D. L. (1993). *The free speech movement: Coming of age in the 1960s*. Berkeley, CA: Ten Speed Press.

11. Pryor, J. H., Hurtado, S., DeAngelo, L., Sharkness, J., Romero, L. C., Korn, W. S., & Tran, S. (2009). *The American freshman: National norms for fall 2008*. Los Angeles, CA: Higher Education Research Institute; Pryor, J. H., Hurtado, S., Sharkness, J., & Korn, W. S. (2008). *The American Freshman: National Norms for Fall 2007*. Los Angeles, CA: Higher Education Research Institute; Sax, L. J., Lindholm, J. A., Astin, A. W., Korn, W. S., & Mahoney, K. M. (2003). *The American freshman: National norms for fall 2002*. Los Angeles, CA: Higher Education Research Institute.

12. Pryor et al., *National norms for fall 2008*; Pryor et al., *National Norms for fall 2007*; Sax et al., *National norms for fall 2002*.

13. Wool, D. (2010, March 2). UCSC officials shocked by noose image. *Santa Cruz News*. Retrieved from http://news.santacruz.com/2010/03/02/ucsc_officials_shocked_by_noose_image; KTLA. (2010, February 18). *Fraternity mocks Black History Month with "Compton Cookout."* Retrieved from http://www.ktla.com/news/landing/ktla-compton-cookout,0,2673438.story

14. Pryor, J. H., Hurtado, S., DeAngelo, L., Palucki Blake, L., & Tran, S. (2010). *The American freshman: National norms for fall 2009*. Los Angeles, CA: Higher Education Research Institute; Pryor et al., *National norms for fall 2008*.

15. Pryor, et al., *National norms for fall 2009*; Pryor et al., *National norms for fall 2008*.

16. Support Our Law Enforcement and Safe Neighborhoods Act. (2010). Retrieved from http://www.azleg.gov/legtext/49leg/2r/bills/sb1070s.pdf

17. Make Chancellor Birgeneau stand up against SB 1070. (2011). Retrieved from Change website: http://www.change.org/petitions/make-chancellor-birgeneau-stand-up-against-sb-1070

18. Hoag, C. (2010, March 3). *Racist incidents, rallies spread at UC campuses.* Retrieved from BlackAmericaweb: http://www.blackamericaweb.com/?q = articles/news/moving_america_news/16811&page = 8

19. University of Arizona. (2005). *Rethinking diversity: The Millennial Student Project.* Retrieved from http://mass.arizona.edu/millennial/modeloverview.html

20. King & Baxter Magolda, A developmental model of intercultural maturity.

21. Terrorism Awareness Project. (2007). *Islamo-Fascism Awareness Week.* Retrieved from the David Horowitz Freedom Center website: http://www.terrorismawareness.org/islamo-fascism-awareness-week/

22. King & Baxter Magolda, A developmental model of intercultural maturity.

23. Ibid.

Using Cultural Theory to Inform Student Affairs Practice

J. Michael Denton, Miami University

In examining the relationship between institutional policy and student culture, Jonathan Poullard rightfully reminds practitioners on p. 146 that "the development of effective policy must be informed by the sociopolitical context of the campus" and that "policy changes must be accompanied by strong programmatic efforts situated within the specific sociopolitical environment of the campus" (p. 148). Poullard uses Millennial generation and student development theory as frames for understanding student culture and cites successful efforts to structure dialogue among students and student organizations on controversial topics. Although understanding characteristics of Millennial students can be helpful, generational theory has severe limitations and often fails to accomplish Poullard's own admonitions. Student development theory can also be extremely useful but often cannot produce a "clear appreciation of . . . intercultural perspectives," as Poullard states on pp. 150–151. Cultural theory provides student affairs practitioners with more robust tools for navigating the sociopolitical environment and intercultural dynamics of a campus.

Lacking the highly visible student activism of the kind Poullard mentions, practitioners might wrongly assume that student culture and activism does not exist on their campus. However, Tierney and Rhoads assert that "to observe student unrest at other institutions but reject any notion of student dissatisfaction at one's own institution is foolhardy."[1] They advocate that universities must be understood as cultures. Indeed, understanding the basics of cultural theory illuminates present yet unobvious student activism, resistance, and invisible subcultures that need attending to as much as the student organizations and activism that draws attention.[2]

Defining Culture

Tierney warns that " 'culture' is one of the most over utilized and misunderstood terms."[3] Tierney and Rhoads define culture as "the informal codes and shared assumptions of individuals participating in the organization."[4] Charon asserts that culture is a "pattern of social organization . . . a perspective on the world that people come to share as they interact."[5] Given these definitions, and based on my understanding of all human interaction as being inherently political, I view *culture* as synonymous with *sociopolitical context*. Culture is neither universal nor unchanging. Culture shapes our lives, but our lives also shape culture.[6] Language informs every aspect of culture. How we communicate, what we communicate about, and what we omit in communication reveal our cultural understandings and values while simultaneously creating them. When individuals create communities in resistance to certain values or norms of the dominant culture, subcultures form.

Subcultures and Hegemony

Magolda and Ebben note that "most of us are confident in our ability to recognize subcultures, so the phenomenon seldom arouses much attention."[7] However, understanding subcultures exposes what "values, beliefs, and practices" the dominant culture considers normal.[8] Subcultures arise in opposition to invisible "dominant discourses about reality, the dominant ideologies."[9] These invisible, dominant ideologies constitute the *hegemony* of a culture. Hegemony makes local and culture-specific values and practices seem normal, universal, "legitimate and natural."[10] For instance, Poullard inquires about the "construction of useful . . . restrictions that encourage students to exercise freedom of speech while . . . not [disrupting] the normal operations of a university" (p. 146). Poullard assumes we share his understanding of what normal operations are and agree with the legitimacy of speech restrictions. These may be correct assumptions, but I seek to expose these usually unquestioned, seemingly legitimate assumptions. Because subcultures arise in resistance to hegemonic ideologies, understanding student subcultures can expose assumptions such as these.[11]

Tierney explains that no student population sees "the world in a particular manner any more than the 'upper class' or 'believers of Islam' act in one, lockstep manner."[12] Although they typically have unifying or organizing principles, a *homology*, subcultures are complex and experience all the politics and conflicts inherent to any community. Poullard alludes to such politics when he recounts that the members of the Muslim, Palestinian, and Jewish student organizations rejected leaders with "a more mature perspective on intercultural maturity" (p. 150). Although student development theory is a valid lens to view these intra- and inter-group tensions, understanding their homology and what these subcultures resist (and why) might better explain these dynamics. For instance, the homology of these subcultures may result in even mature members strictly adhering to and expressing certain beliefs over personally held values. Grasping the homology of a subculture can also assist in making sense of the "infinite variables" that the Millennial Student Project addresses. Identity theories help make sense of individual students; however, cultural theory provides insight into how and why infinitely diverse students interact, collaborate, and bond in resistance to specific ideologies or dominant culture norms.

Resistance as Ritual

While subcultures are one form of resistance, rituals can also express resistance. Rituals constitute an important aspect of culture because they create and transmit values, expectations, and cultural norms.[13] Rituals exist in every facet of society, and in specific contexts (e.g., a student organization, policy and programming committees, student-administrator meetings, etc.).[14] I conceptualize *ritual* as "a formalized, symbolic performance."[15] Rituals convey (i.e., symbolize) specific meanings and values when individuals act (i.e., perform) in certain predetermined ways (i.e., forms).

Many recognize ceremonies like commencement as ritual, but small mundane rituals are often more important.[16] The most powerful rituals are the ones that are "unspectacular, repetitive, and predictable."[17] Student organization meetings, policy development committees or programs may all be rituals. Understanding the ritual aspects of programs can help ensure that programs convey their intended messages. For instance, the Bears Breaking Bread program mentioned by Poullard centers on the ritual of a community meal with "informal discussions" while the Critical Dialogues Across Difference program offers educational ritual in the form of a course that teaches "dialogue skills." These programs employ, intentionally or otherwise, rituals that convey (i.e., symbolize) clear and distinct messages about what participants can expect (i.e., the form) and how those involved will (ideally) interact (i.e., perform). The former suggests a low-pressure, low-structure, and low-commitment opportunity to socialize, while the latter implies more commitment, more structure, and likely required interactions. Educators must decide if these ritual aspects of the program align with and help deliver the outcomes they hope to produce.

Rituals have the potential to transmit new cultural messages or reinforce dominant cultural messages. Rituals of resistance mobilize "hidden grudges and tensions" to rupture dominant messages.[18] Student protests may oppose the ideology of other student groups, but practitioners should consider that these rituals likely oppose institutional messages or practices. Rituals of resistance may be active or passive. A program like Islamo-Fascism Week is likely a passive ritual. Sponsors of such programs may seek less to educate about the "dangers" of Islam than to tacitly subvert certain institutional messages and values. Student demonstrations are types of active rituals of resistance. They overtly resist certain dominant norms, although modern student protests don't usually resist institutional speech restrictions. Rituals of resistance like the Compton Cookout reveal much about student and institutional culture. Administrators and educators should unequivocally denounce such activities and respond through appropriate policy, but, as Poullard states, "policies can only go so far in addressing and challenging student beliefs, values and attitudes " (p. 143). Changing student beliefs must start with understanding student culture and, in this case, student ritual. Although student activities/rituals like these examples are easy to dismiss because of their overt bigotry and racism, only careful exploration of what exactly this ritual resists and what messages the participants seek to convey (rather than just our interpretation) can produce information that may result in a culture change. What institutional messages or practices are student participants resisting or reinforcing and replicating? Given how these students represent, depict or "perform" Blackness, what does Black seem to symbolize for them? Why is Black (instead of other identities) the symbol? These and similar questions, as difficult as they are, can only be answered and addressed by understanding the specifics of the ritual and the subculture of those who participate in the ritual.

Ideology and Policy

Crafting policy, programs, or reexamining policies in response to student resistance represents particular ideologies. *Ideology* is a contested term but broadly refers to the "agreements, expectations, rules, regulations" of a culture.[19] While many conceive of powerful entities imposing ideology on members of society, ideology is "profoundly unconscious" and rarely conveyed explicitly.[20] Rather, we all produce or contribute to ideologies through our every conversation and action, supporting or opposing cultural hegemonic norms. For instance, the method of crafting policy (e.g., to what extent are students involved), the reasons for crafting policy (e.g., allowing greater student expression or reigning in student speech), and the final policy itself all embody ideologies of policy makers and institutional culture. Most institutions, like UC Berkeley, express an ideology that embraces student speech but enact an ideology that successfully co-opts and reassimilates student dissent through free-speech policies. These policies provide opportunity for student expression, but they also work to minimize disruption to the dominant cultural (i.e., institutional) interests. Programs like Bears Breaking Bread and Critical Dialogues can provide positive opportunities to address differing cultural perspectives. They can also provide an institution with the opportunity to avoid addressing deeper, more difficult cultural conflicts that would involve more intensive resources. I am neither impugning these programs nor implying that we should not develop policies or programs. Rather, I suggest that cultural theory allow us to question our unexamined and seemingly legitimate institutional and personal ideologies that unwittingly preserve the status quo, especially in the guise of serving students.

Conclusion

Tierney and Rhoads assert that "it is not merely helpful to *see* organizations as cultures. Instead, organizations *are* in fact cultures, and when we fail to recognize this, we limit our ability to lead academic communities."[21] Understanding culture involves looking at the large, periodic, and noticeable but also the small, daily, and easy to miss. Understanding subcultures, rituals, and ideology requires us to reflect on our seemingly inconsequential and routine actions.

Examining the regular, unspectacular rituals between educators and students (and students with each other) can lead to a better understanding of what students value, to what (or to whom) they are opposed, and to think complexly and intentionally about how to respond. Attending to campus subcultures can unearth unobvious assumptions about what and who constitutes normal. The ability to identify subcultures provides practitioners with an opportunity to engage with seemingly nonnormal or unnoticed student communities. Understanding various campus ideologies can lead administrators to address cultural tensions in ways specific to the institutional culture. In conclusion, understanding culture allows us to investigate whose interests are being served and whose are being ignored.[22]

Notes

1. Rhoads, R. A., & Tierney, W. G. (1992). *Cultural leadership in higher education* (Contract No. R117G10037). University Park, PA: National Center on Postsecondary Teaching. Retrieved from http://www.eric.ed.gov/PDFS/ED357708.pdf, pp. 49–50.

2. Magolda, P. M., & Ebben, K. (2007). Students serving Christ: Understanding the role of student subcultures on a college campus. *Anthropology and Education Quarterly, 38*(2), 138–158.

3. Tierney, W. G. (1994). *Multiculturalism in higher education: An organizational framework for analysis.* (Contract No. R117G10037). University Park, PA: National Center on Postsecondary Teaching. Retrieved from http://www.eric.ed.gov/PDFS/ED371675.pdf, p. 8.

4. Rhoads & Tierney, *Cultural leadership in higher education*, p. 4.

5. Charon, J. M. (2002). *The meaning of sociology.* Upper Saddle River, NJ: Prentice Hall, p. 91.

6. Rhoads & Tierney, *Cultural leadership in higher education*, p. 4.

7. Magolda & Ebben, Students serving Christ, p. 145.

8. Magolda, P. M. (1999). Using ethnographic fieldwork and case studies to guide student affairs practice. *Journal of College Student Development, 40*(1), 10–21, p. 17.

9. Hebdige, D. (1979). *Subculture: The meaning of style.* London, UK: Routledge, p. 15.

10. Ibid.

11. Magolda & Ebben, Students serving Christ, p. 154.

12. Tierney, W. G. (2000). Power, identity, and the dilemma of college student departure. In J. M. Braxton (Ed.), *Reworking the student departure puzzle* (pp. 213–234). Nashville, TN: Vanderbilt University Press, p. 326.

13. Magolda, P. M. (2000). The campus tour ritual: Exploring community discourses in higher education. *Anthropology and Education Quarterly, 31*(1), 24–46.

14. McLaren, P. L. (1985). The ritual dimensions of resistance: Clowning and symbolic inversion. *Journal of Education, 167*(2), 84–97, p. 85.

15. Quantz, R. A. (1999). School ritual as performance: A reconstruction of Durkheim's and Turner's use of ritual. *Educational Theory, 49*(4), 493–513, p. 495.

16. Ibid.

17. Magolda, The campus tour ritual, p. 42.

18. McLaren, The ritual dimensions of resistance, p. 86.
19. Charon, *The meaning of sociology*, p. 53.
20. Althusser, as cited in Hebdige, *Subculture*, p. 12.
21. Rhoads & Tierney, *Cultural leadership in higher education*, p. 6.
22. Ibid.

Further Reading and Related Blog

J. Michael Denton, Miami University

Bailey, G., & Gayle, N. A. (2003). *Ideology: Structuring identities in contemporary life*. Peterborough, Ontario, Canada: Broadview Press.

Bailey and Gayle provide a thorough overview of the different conceptualizations of ideology and how ideology manifests itself. They succinctly present complex information in an accessible manner without sacrificing important details.

Magolda, P. M., & Ebben, K. (2007). Students serving Christ: Understanding the role of student subcultures on a college campus. *Anthropology and Education Quarterly, 38*(2), 138–158.

Magolda and Ebben provide a comprehensive look into student subcultures through their study of a college campus Christian organization. They highlight the complexities of student subcultures and how frequently overlooked student communities provide important information about institutional culture.

Ortiz, A. M., & Rhoads, R. A. (2000). Deconstructing whiteness as part of a multicultural educational framework: From theory to practice. *Journal of College Student Development, 41*(1), 81–93.

This article argues that our construction of whiteness is a crucial element of our ability to understand multiculturalism. The authors describe a developmentally sequenced framework to help people understand the concept of culture, learn about other cultures, recognize and deconstruct whiteness, recognize the legitimacy of other cultures, and develop a multicultural outlook.

Blog URL: contestedissues.wordpress.com
Corresponding Chapter Post: tinyurl.com/contestedissues08

9

If Curbing Alcohol Abuse on College Campuses Is an Impossible Dream, Why Bother With Interventions Aimed at Curbing Abuse?

Navigating the Drinking Culture to Become Productive Citizens

James P. Barber, College of William and Mary

The history of alcohol on college campuses is as long as the history of American higher education. As Eric Burns recounts in *The Spirits of America: A Social History of Alcohol*, Harvard originally built and operated its own brewery that supplied beer for the college's dining hall.[1] The brewery was one of the first buildings at the college, to satisfy early students' expectations for beer.[2] Keep in mind that most students in the early days of Harvard and other colonial American colleges were 14–15 years old, sons of the colonial elite, with many training to be Puritan ministers. The production of the brewery at Harvard could not keep up with demand for alcohol, and students complained they were often deprived of beer between brewings. As a result of this neglect (as well as allegations of beating one of the students), Harvard fired Nathaniel Eaton, the first leader of the institution, after the college's first year in 1639.

Commencement exercises were often rowdy, alcohol-fueled affairs, leading to drunken behavior by town and gown alike. This became such a problem for early colleges that regulations had to be implemented to limit "the Excesses, Immoralities, and Disorders."[3] So how far have we come in over 350 years of higher education in the United States? This essay explores some primary issues related to alcohol use and abuse among American college students, and ponders the challenges associated with confronting a deeply entrenched cultural norm.

Preparing Students to Be Productive Citizens

My core belief about our roles as educators related to college student alcohol use and abuse is the same as my overall perspective on higher education: We should prepare students to be productive citizens in the world they are entering upon graduation. I find this position consistent with the core values of student affairs, and as I began work on this essay I turned to the central texts of our profession, expecting to find specific mention of alcohol as it related to student conduct and health. However, despite the prominence of alcohol and other drugs as perennial challenges to campus leaders, the foundational documents of the student affairs profession offer surprisingly little reference to alcohol use and abuse or interventions to target irresponsible behavior resulting from substance use and abuse.

The original *Student Personnel Point of View* (*SPPV*), published in 1937 just four years after the repeal of Prohibition in the United States, only broadly defines what we today might call health and wellness and student conduct.[4] Likewise, the 1949 update to the *SPPV* does not address alcohol or other drugs directly; it addresses health and wellness, primarily in terms of "an educational program of preventive medicine and personal-hygiene counseling."[5]

"The Student Learning Imperative" and *Principles of Good Practice for Student Affairs* make no mention of alcohol or other drugs, student discipline, or health and wellness.[6] However, both focus heavily on student learning and civic responsibility, two outcomes excessive alcohol use has been shown to diminish.[7] It was not until the 21st century that alcohol is mentioned by name in a foundational document of the profession. In 2004's *Learning Reconsidered: A Campus-Wide Focus on the Student Experience*, a joint publication from the American College Personnel Association and the National Association of Student Personnel Administrators,

"drug and alcohol education" is named as an example of a practical competence in terms of student learning outcomes.[8]

The foundations of the student affairs profession are firmly situated
on educating the whole person; addressing substance abuse and working
to curb alcohol use on campus has been a practical part of this holistic
educational process for decades. However, alcohol education as a functional area or learning outcome per se has appeared relatively recently in
the guiding documents of our profession. This may be because of an
increased demand for accountability in terms of alcohol use and abuse, a
heightened awareness of the consequences of dangerous drinking, or evidence of ongoing specialization in student affairs work.

What Do We Mean by Alcohol Abuse?

The standard definition of a drink according to the National Institute of
Alcoholism and Alcohol Abuse is one 12-ounce bottle of beer or wine
cooler, one 5-ounce glass of wine, or 1.5 ounces of 80-proof distilled
spirits.[9] A blood alcohol content (BAC) level of 0.08% or greater is the
legal limit for driving a motor vehicle in the United States. The Harvard
School of Public Health College Alcohol Study on college student behavior from 1992 to 2006 popularized the term *binge drinking*.[10] This study
was lead by Henry Wechsler, a social psychologist at Harvard University,
who defined binge drinking as five alcoholic drinks in a row for men, or
four drinks in a row for women, on a single occasion in a 2-week time
frame. This definition has provoked controversy, because of the low
threshold of the number of drinks and the vague time frame of "in a
row." Nevertheless, the term has gained widespread acceptance, and
remains linked to the five/four definition based on sex.

Addressing substance abuse and working to curb
alcohol use on campus has been a practical part of
this holistic educational process for decades.

The National Institute of Alcoholism and Alcohol Abuse (NIAAA)
adopted Wechsler's five and four definition of binge drinking in 2004 and

added more specificity to the criteria for a binge. Specifically, NIAAA defined binge drinking as an episode of drinking that brings an individual's BAC to 0.08% or above.[11] For the typical adult this pattern corresponds to a man consuming five or more drinks or a woman consuming four or more drinks in about 2 hours.

The NIAAA distinguishes binge drinking from *risky* drinking, which it characterizes by a slightly lower BAC, between 0.05% and 0.08%, and a *bender*, which it defines as two or more days of sustained heavy drinking.

The Noble Experiment: Alcohol and the Law in the United States

Alcohol use is not only an issue on college and university campuses; it is also embedded in our national culture and shared history. There have been a number of legislative approaches to responding to alcohol not only on college campuses but also in the nation as a whole. Most famously, the United States implemented a prohibition on alcohol in the early 20th century. With the passage of the 18th Amendment to the Constitution, the federal government outlawed the production, distribution, and sale of alcohol from 1920 until 1933. The Noble Experiment, as Prohibition is sometimes called, became increasingly unpopular during the Great Depression and ultimately failed. The federal government passed the 21st Amendment in December 1933, repealing the 18th Amendment and thus ending Prohibition.

Responsibility for regulating the legal age for alcohol consumption transferred to the state legislatures, and policies varied widely. Most states adopted a minimum age of 21 for consumption, but one state, Ohio, was as low as 16 years. During the Vietnam War era of the late 1960s and early 1970s, many states lowered the drinking age to 18 or 19 years of age when the voting age was lowered to 18 with passage of the 26th Amendment in 1971.

The National Minimum Drinking Age Act of 1984 established a federal standard on alcohol consumption for the first time since Prohibition, and set 21 as the minimum legal drinking age for young adults in the United States.[12] Although individual states still technically retained the right to specify a younger age, doing so would result in a 10% decrease in highway and transportation funds from the federal government.

The National Highway Traffic Safety Association estimates that the minimum drinking age of 21 saves nearly 900 lives each year and has saved over 25,000 lives between 1975 and 2006.[13] The nonprofit group Mothers Against Drunk Driving (MADD) was a strong voice advocating for the passage of the minimum drinking age legislation and continues to play a leading role in lobbying for stronger measures against drunk driving in the United States.[14]

An Ingrained Culture of Drinking: Effects of Alcohol Use in Higher Education

There is little debate that alcohol is firmly rooted in college student culture. To contextualize student alcohol use, we must recognize that alcohol is also an integral part of the larger U.S. culture. Here is an experiment for you: Try to keep a tally of how many references to alcohol you encounter in a single day. How many times do you hear a popular song on the radio or on your iPod that mentions drinking? How many beer advertisements do you see on television, billboards, or online? How many drinks are consumed by characters on your favorite TV shows? How many people do you see drinking alcoholic beverages when you go out for dinner? When you keep track, it is astounding the number of times an individual is confronted with images of alcohol in just one day in American society.

The negative effects of alcohol consumption for college students are well documented and widespread. Hingson, Zha, and Weitzman studied the effects of alcohol consumption among college students between 18 and 24 and reported that an estimated 1,825 students died from alcohol-related injuries in 2005, including accidents involving motor vehicles; this represents an increase of 3% per 100,000 from the 1,140 alcohol-related college student deaths in 1998.[15] Additionally, about 600,000 students are injured per year while under the influence of alcohol. Alcohol consumption is also related to violence among students. Nearly 700,000 students are assaulted each year by other students who have been drinking, and about 100,000 college students are victims of alcohol-related date rape or sexual assault.[16] Clearly, the culture of drinking on college campuses has serious repercussions for our students and our society.

Pascarella and colleagues demonstrated that the effects of binge drinking are equal opportunity across gender, race, and educational level.[17]

The negative impact of excessive alcohol consumption on college student achievement, as measured by grade point average, was essentially the same for men and women, White students and non-White students, first-year students and seniors, and for students of varying levels of precollege academic preparation.[18]

In addition to the negative impact of excessive alcohol use on student learning, there are also significant negative effects related to relationships and civic responsibility. Through the Harvard School of Public Health College Alcohol Study, Henry Wechsler and colleagues identified eight major problems associated with binge drinking behaviors, such as interruption of sleep, unwanted sexual advances, and assault.[19] These were termed *secondary binge effects* to reflect that they affected students who were not binge drinkers themselves but lived in residence halls, fraternity or sorority houses, or near peers who were binge drinkers.[20]

Interventions: Approaches to Curbing Alcohol Abuse on College Campuses

A number of approaches to responding to the problem of alcohol abuse on college and university campuses can be grouped into three main theoretical categories: restriction, education, and activism. I highlight one example of each of these types of programs, relating each to the overarching goal of preparing students to be productive citizens.

Restriction: Limiting Access and Corralling Like-Minded People

Restriction involves limiting access to alcoholic beverages for individuals regardless of age. Wechsler et al. found that about one-third of college and university campuses in the United States ban alcohol on campus outright for all students.[21] A larger number (43%), including those that completely banned alcohol, did not allow alcohol in any on-campus residences (regardless of student age), and over three fourths (81%) of all campuses offered an option for alcohol-free residence by choice (either alcohol-free residence hall buildings or floors).[22] Some have argued that alcohol-free residences encourage students to drink elsewhere and drive under the influence to return home. However, Wechsler and his colleagues found that residents of alcohol-free housing were no more likely to drink and drive than residents of unrestricted housing.[23]

The availability of alcohol-free housing undoubtedly offers an environment that many students (and their parents) desire. However, I question
the extent to which alcohol-free housing changes the culture of alcohol
abuse on college campuses or prepares students for the world they will
enter upon graduation. For better or worse, alcohol is present in the
world they will enter; students should be prepared to navigate the complex decisions they may face involving alcohol and other substances. In
this world, individuals are expected to follow the laws or work to change
them; students should learn how to clearly explain their perspective to
others, particularly if it is a dissenting opinion. In this world, individuals
are held accountable for their actions; students should understand that
choosing to break the law may result in sanctions. In this world, students
will interact with individuals from cultures all over the globe, including
people raised in cultures where young adults have much more experience
with alcohol at younger ages than Americans typically do. Students may
live and work in another country, in which alcohol plays a more prominent role or none at all.

Seen in this light, it is a disservice to students to implement policies
that stipulate a complete ban on alcohol even for those over 21. Students
over 21 may benefit from exposure to experiences where they can learn
to drink alcohol responsibly if they choose or politely decline alcohol if
they decide not to drink. Many professional contexts, and in fact many
job interviews, include situations where alcohol is present. In any event,
the message that an institution sends needs to be consistent. It is understandably frustrating to students who see a double standard where alcohol
is not permitted on campus for students over 21 yet is free flowing for a
campus event targeting alumni or donors.

Education: Providing Information to Navigate the Environment

Education includes interventions aimed at providing information for students to navigate collegiate social environments. Additionally, highly visible educational programs serve as a symbol of an institution's
commitment to the health and safety of students. Such educational initiatives can be a means for a college or university to communicate to parents, students, and other stakeholders the behavioral expectations of
membership in the campus community, as well as a strategy for risk management and limiting liability in the event of an alcohol-related incident.

Common curricula are the effects of alcohol on the body, the legal implications for drinking underage, and how to assist a peer who has had too much to drink. Online education programs are a common strategy for institutions to reach a large percentage of students with basic information about the effects of alcohol.

AlcoholEdu is one of the leading programs and is used in 36% of all first-year programs at 4-year higher education institutions in the United States. As a result, AlcoholEdu claims to have the world's largest database on college students and alcohol.[24] Andrew Wall concluded that students who participated in this online education program self-reported fewer negative effects and episodes of binge drinking than a comparison group, as measured 4 to 6 weeks after completion of the online program. Interventions with first-year students appeared most promising in terms of positive effects.[25]

Ideally, an educational program designed to prepare students to become productive citizens would be targeted at the entire student body, as opposed to focusing only on first-year or high-risk students. Such a program would illustrate multiple perspectives about drinking alcohol and employ a variety of teaching methods and points of contact (e.g., online instruction, active learning, and reinforcement in formal curriculum). The challenges of confronting a deeply rooted culture of drinking are substantial but not insurmountable.[26] I describe this ideal type of educational program as *institutional* in nature because the effort can benefit from intentional faculty involvement and crossing contexts between student affairs and academic affairs. I believe that by making punitive measures the primary response to alcohol and other drug issues, without an educational component, undesirable behaviors are pushed further and further into the private domain and away from educators who might help.

Activism: Influencing Policy Change

Activism involves working to change the current context as it relates to alcohol consumption by influencing policy or legal decisions. In 2005 John McCardell, president emeritus of Middlebury College and newly installed president of the University of the South (Sewanee), founded the Amethyst Initiative, a group that advocates lowering the drinking age in the United States, although it does not specify what age. The group's reasoning is that Americans can serve in the military, vote, enter into contracts, and serve on juries before the age of 21, and therefore should be mature enough to have a drink if they choose. One hundred thirty-six college presidents have signed on to the initiative as of early 2011.[27] The cause appears to be having some success influencing policy; the state of Vermont passed a resolution (SR 17) in April 2010 urging the U.S. Congress to grant waivers of federal highway funding penalties to states that would like to explore alternatives to the legal drinking age of 21.

I believe that activist approaches to addressing alcohol abuse are some of the most effective for preparing students to become productive citizens. Without a doubt, policies and practice in working with college students and alcohol must be legal. However, opportunities for questioning the rationale behind the existing laws and their appropriateness in the current climate should be allowed. Accordingly, the Amethyst Initiative is a positive role model for how to engage in substantive dialogue on a controversial topic. The group has expressed its opinion about the drinking age at 21, gathered data to support its position, and recruited supporters in its cause.

The political implications can be substantial for student affairs professionals overseeing alcohol policies. There is a wide array of stakeholders, including students, parents, faculty, upper-level administrators, alumni, community members, and law enforcement—many of whom do not see eye to eye on the issue of alcohol consumption. It is generally not politically correct to speak out against the minimum drinking age of 21; taking this point of view often leads to the erroneous assumption that one supports underage binge drinking or drunk driving.

There are legal implications as well as political ones when dealing with alcohol and college students. We live in an increasingly litigious society, and higher education institutions, student organizations, college administrators, and student leaders are regularly sued for alcohol-related claims. The choices we make (and those we fail to make) as educators or administrators are often under the microscope on campus and in the community. This liability has required a new standard for documentation in the past two decades; meeting minutes, recordings of educational programs, and proof of student participation are all pieces of information that may be requested in the event of legal action.

Why Bother? Considerations for Practice

Curbing alcohol abuse among college students is not an impossible dream. Eliminating alcohol abuse among American college students—

The Amethyst Initiative is a positive role model for how to engage in substantive dialogue on a controversial topic.

that is the impossible dream. Curbing alcohol abuse, however, is an area where progress is well documented. The initiatives discussed here all appear to have incremental success in reducing student alcohol abuse. Despite the many challenges posed by alcohol abuse among college students and its deep roots in university (and American) culture, research shows that individuals who attain a college degree are significantly less likely to experience alcohol abuse or dependency after college as compared to those with only a high school diploma.[28]

Restriction, education, and activism, separately and in combination, offer promising interventions for modifying alcohol-fueled behavior among undergraduates and for preparing students to be productive citizens of the world after graduation. Despite the wealth of well-intentioned approaches to tackling alcohol abuse on college campuses, negative behavior persists. In 350 years, higher education leaders have yet to find an effective recipe for eliminating alcohol abuse.

Alcohol use is pervasive in college and the larger American culture. Since the minimum drinking age is in the middle of the traditional college age distribution, it is extremely challenging to enforce. So why bother? We bother because lives are at stake. Healthy, educated habits and choices learned in college may stay with a person long after graduation (just as unhealthy or abusive habits may linger as well). Developmental research shows that traditional-aged college students are forming their values systems and moral reasoning during the young adult years, and therefore programs aimed at educating students about the responsible use of alcohol, as well as the implications for breaking the law, are important components of an undergraduate (and even high school) education.

Above all, I believe that higher education leaders cannot be afraid to confront inappropriate student behavior and have honest, often difficult, conversations with undergraduates about alcohol use and abuse. Even if interventions do not result in immediate behavioral change, a consistent message is important, and it may click for a student years after graduation.

Notes

1. Burns, E. (2004). *The spirits of America: A social history of alcohol.* Philadelphia, PA: Temple University Press.

2. Furnas, J. C. (1965). *The life and times of the late demon rum.* New York, NY: Putnam.

3. Burns, *The spirits of America,* p. 18.

4. American Council on Education. (1937). *The student personnel point of view.* Washington, DC: Author.

5. American Council on Education. (1949). *The student personnel point of view.* Washington, DC: Author, p. 28.

6. American College Personnel Association. (1996). The student learning imperative: Implications for student affairs. *Journal of College Student Development, 37*(2), 118–122; National Association of Student Personnel Association. (1997). *Principles of good practice for student affairs.* Retrieved from http://www.acpa.nche.edu/pgp/principle.htm

7. Perkins, H. W. (2002). Surveying the damage: A review of research on consequences of alcohol misuse in college populations. *Journal of Studies on Alcohol* (Suppl. 14), 91–100.

8. Keeling, R. P. (Ed.). (2004). *Learning reconsidered: A campus-wide focus on the student experience.* Washington, DC: National Association of Student Personnel Administrators and American College Personnel Association, p. 22.

9. National Institute on Alcohol Abuse and Alcoholism. (2010). *Rethinking drinking: Alcohol and your health.* Retrieved from http://pubs.niaaa.nih.gov/publications/Rethinking Drinking/Rethinking_Drinking.pdf

10. Wechsler, H., & Austin, S. B. (1998). Binge drinking: The five/four measure. *Journal of Studies of Alcohol and Drugs, 59*(1), 122–124.

11. National Institute on Alcohol Abuse and Alcoholism. (2007). *What colleges need to know now: An update on college drinking research.* Retrieved from http://www.collegedrin kingprevention.gov/1College_Bulletin-508_361C4E.pdf

12. National Minimum Drinking Age Act, 23 U.S.C. § 158 (1984).

13. Kindelberger, J. (2005). Calculating lives saved due to minimum drinking age laws. *Traffic Safety Facts Research Note.* Retrieved from http://www-nrd.nhtsa.dot.gov/Pubs/ 809860.PDF; National Highway Traffic Safety Administration. (2006). U.S. Department of Transportation. *Traffic safety facts 2006: A compilation of motor vehicle crash data from the fatality analysis reporting system and the general estimates system.* Retrieved from http:// www-nrd.nhtsa.dot.gov/pubs/tsf2006fe.pdf

14. Davies, L. (2005, Fall). Twenty-five years of saving lives. *Driven Magazine,* 8–17. Retrieved from http://www.madd.org/about-us/history/madd25thhistory.pdf

15. Hingson, R. W., Zha, W., & Weitzman, E. R. (2009). Magnitude of and trends in alcohol-related mortality and morbidity among U. S. college students ages 18–24: Changes from 1998 to 2005. *Journal of Studies on Alcohol and Drugs* (Suppl. 16), 12–20.

16. Hingson, R., Heeren, T., Winter, M., & Wechsler, H. (2005). Magnitude of alcohol-related mortality and morbidity among U. S. college students ages 18–24: Changes from 1998 to 2001. *Annual Review of Public Health, 26,* 259–279.

17. Pascarella, E. T., Goodman, K. M., Seifert, T. A., Tagliapietra-Nicoli, G., Park, S., & Whitt, E. J. (2007). College student binge drinking and academic achievement:

A longitudinal replication and extension. *Journal of College Student Development, 48*(6), 715–727.

18. Ibid.

19. Wechsler, H., Davenport, A., Dowdall, G., Moeykens, B., & Castillo, S. (1994). Health and behavioral consequences of binge drinking in college: A national survey of students at 140 campuses. *Journal of the American Medical Association, 272*(21), 1672–1677.

20. Ibid., p. 1676.

21. Wechsler, H., Seibring, M., Liu, I., Ahl, M. (2004). Colleges respond to student binge drinking: Reducing student demand or limiting access. *Journal of American College Health, 52*(4), 159–168.

22. Ibid.

23. Wechsler, H., Lee, J. E., Nelson, T. F., & Lee, H. (2001). Drinking levels, alcohol problems and second-hand effects in substance-free college residences: Results of a national study. *Journal of Studies on Alcohol, 62*(1), 23–31.

24. Outside the Classroom. (2010). *AlcoholEdu for College.* Retrieved from http://www.outsidetheclassroom.com/solutions/higher-education/alcoholedu-for-college.aspx

25. Wall, A. F. (2007). Evaluating a health education website: The case of AlcoholEdu. *NASPA Journal, 44*(4), 692–714.

26. Bureau, D., & Barber, J. P. (2007). The role of alcohol in student community development: Challenges and recommendations for student affairs practitioners. *NASPA NetResults, March 14, 2007.* Retrieved from http://www.naspa.org/membership/mem/pubs/nr/default.cfm?id = 1577; Pascarella, E. T., & Terenzini, P. T. (2005). *How college affects students: A third decade of research.* San Francisco, CA: Jossey-Bass.

27. Amethyst Initiative. (2011). *Amethyst initiative: Rethink the drinking age.* Retrieved from http://www.amethystinitiative.org/signatories/

28. Pascarella & Terenzini, *How college affects students.*

Curbing Alcohol Abuse on College Campuses: Why Bother, Indeed?

Heidi Levine, Cornell College

James Barber presents a compelling exploration of the long-standing challenges related to student alcohol misuse and the moral imperative to address this problematic behavior. Clearly student alcohol misuse remains one of the most frequently discussed issues among college administrators and other interested constituents.

Barber examines three promising approaches to curbing high-risk drinking among college students—limiting access, education, and activism—and discusses the benefits of "corralling like-minded people" (p. 167). These approaches do indeed show promise in reducing student high-risk alcohol use. However, rather than considering these as discrete, stand-alone initiatives, educators achieve greater efficacy employing these strategies as components of a broader, multifaceted model.

Environmental Management Model

The Higher Education Center for Alcohol and Other Drug Prevention (HEC) offers a campus-based approach to reducing student alcohol misuse adapted from a public health model.[1] This model embraces a comprehensive, community-focused approach to fostering behavior change. As with campaigns related to seatbelt use and smoking, multifaceted approaches (while not eliminating problem behaviors) help moderate individuals' behaviors and their negative influences. Individual education and intervention are still important components, but we recognize they are not silver bullets. This model also incorporates a broad understanding of what constitutes a college or university community, extending its reach beyond the actual campus borders.

The environmental management model targets three spheres of focus and action: the campus, surrounding community, and state or public policy. Within each sphere, advocates can develop strategies that focus on the environment, education, early intervention, and enforcement. I focus primarily on describing campus-based strategies but will also provide brief examples of strategies in the community and public policy spheres.

Campus-Based Strategies

Environmental Change

Campus-based environmental change focuses on multiple aspects of the institutional structure. One facet involves examining students' unstructured free time, particularly on residential campuses. For example, schools might examine their class schedules and pose a series of questions: Are classes typically held on Friday mornings? How are those Friday classes spent—do faculty members avoid scheduling high-stakes activities (such as tests)? Having fewer academic activities on Fridays sends a tacit message that heavy alcohol consumption on Thursday night or Friday afternoon is acceptable, and ensuring that academic activities occur throughout the week is one promising environmental practice.

Another area for environmental change is to identify commonly held beliefs that are prevalent on a campus that suggest alcohol misuse is a normative part of the college experience. These beliefs may be communicated by a wide variety of sources, on campus and in the wider community. On-campus transmitters of these beliefs, surprisingly, may include faculty and administrative staff members who joke about student drinking or share "war stories" from their own college days. Student perceptions about how many students consume alcohol and in what quantity underlie other messages about campus norms. Campus-based public health campaigns that challenge these normative beliefs and replace misperceptions with current, accurate information provide students with new norms to judge their own behavior and subtly shift the institutional culture regarding alcohol use.

A third environmental strategy is for schools to examine the opportunities available for nonalcohol-focused social and recreational activities. Creating and widely marketing a variety of attractive late-night, substance-free programming options provides students with alternatives to drinking.

Education

Barber shares information about the promising practice of using online programs such as AlcoholEdu to provide students with information and feedback about their own behavioral choices.[2] He strongly encourages wide use of these programs rather than focusing solely on higher-risk groups of students. In addition, educational strategies should intentionally provide students with opportunities for personal reflection and engagement. Even the best-designed educational programs will have limited influence on students if they are presented in single-episode formats. A strength of AlcoholEdu is that it incorporates a second module that students complete within 3 months of the initial program. Schools that also build in small-group discussions and personal reflection activities may see even more positive results when implementing such programs.

Early Intervention

Even those campuses with well-developed and integrated environmental and educational strategies will undoubtedly have some students who are at risk for developing alcohol and other substance abuse problems. Schools should have mechanisms in place to provide alcohol (and other drug) screenings and assessments. These may include anonymous, web-based tools that provide students with feedback about their risk level and appropriate resources. Support and treatment services should be easily accessible to students. Providing addictions treatment is beyond the scope of most campus counseling centers, but they typically have information about local resources and can facilitate the referral process. Campus officials should also consider sponsoring programs such as Alcoholics Anonymous on or near campus since students are more likely to use these services if they are convenient and attended by their peers.

Enforcement

The remaining campus-based strategy involves development of clear and widely disseminated policies. A consistent and high level of policy enforcement will contribute to reduced student alcohol misuse on campus. In the next section I discuss ways institutions can form partnerships with their surrounding communities to ensure that alcohol-related problems are not merely driven off campus.

Community Strategies

Three community strategies are particularly effective in curbing high-risk student alcohol use. The first of these is the establishment of campus-community coalitions. The intentional formation of working groups with broad representation from the campus and the extended community can shed light on the impacts of student alcohol use on the broader community and creates a shared sense of responsibility for tackling those issues. Coalitions can be highly effective in addressing issues regarding student groups hosting parties in private residences, a particular concern for neighbors and tavern owners. Good neighbor campaigns can target off-campus students in raising awareness of the impact of their behaviors and of community standards.

Other environmental strategies that can emerge from campus-community coalitions involve agreements between the institution and area tavern owners. Eliminating promotions such as drink specials and Ladies' Night and ceasing sponsorship of or hosting activities like beer pong tournaments challenge social norms about alcohol use and reduce incentives for high-risk drinking. Additionally, agreements can incorporate bar and retail owners' posting social norming and other educational information in visible locations in their establishments.

Finally, the extended community plays a vital role in maintaining clear and consistent enforcement of alcohol-related laws and regulations. The campus can assist business owners with training on how to effectively identify and appropriately limit serving underage patrons. Checking IDs and refusing to serve underage or intoxicated patrons limit students' access to alcohol. Campus officials should develop strong partner relationships with local law enforcement and support local officials in consistently intervening with students who are in violation of public intoxication, underage drinking, and related laws.

Public Policy Strategies

The final sphere of the environmental management model involves advocating for public policy change. Barber discussed public policy initiatives that already exist, including the work of the Amethyst Initiative, as well as political and legal implications of these issues.[3] Additional public policy strategies should include advocating for adequate funding and resources to support early intervention and treatment programs. While individual campus leaders may engage in such advocacy work, these strategies are most effective when conducted in collaboration with other institutions and leaders or in educational systems.

In his discussion of the federal minimum legal drinking age (MLDA), Barber notes that creating alcohol-free housing and campuses minimizes our ability to help prepare students for socially appropriate behavior beyond college. Might the same argument not be made regarding students under 21 years of age? Read, Merrill, and Bytschkow's research concluded that underage students were more likely than their peers to "pregame," or drink to the point of intoxication prior to attending social events.[4] Although students who were 21 and older did occasionally pregame, younger students did so more frequently and excessively, consuming more drinks and reaching a higher BAC level than did older students. While saving money was a motivator for all the students who pregamed, younger students were also motivated by the fact that they might not be able to obtain alcohol at the events to follow.

Interventions most likely to lead to deep, cultural change occur when planned and implemented by task forces with broad institutional representation.

For these students, the current MLDA increases the likelihood that they will engage in faster, more secretive—higher risk—alcohol use. As Barber mentions, the signatories of the Amethyst Initiative are calling for revisiting the MLDA; it is worth considering whether a lower drinking age would create more opportunities to help shape students' use of alcohol over the course of their college careers.

Institutional Leadership

The implementation of an environmental management approach is most effective when leadership is coming from the highest institutional levels. Interventions most likely to lead to deep, cultural change occur when planned and implemented by task forces with broad institutional representation.[5] These task forces should be appointed by and report directly to the institution's president. Such structures reflect an institutional commitment to addressing student alcohol misuse and recognition that this is an issue that involves the entire campus community.

Why Bother, Indeed?

Barber asserts that while we may not be able to eliminate student alcohol abuse, we can curb high-risk behavior and its effects. Existing data do show that a comprehensive and integrated approach can moderate student high-risk drinking. The following are just a few examples of programs that have made an impact:

- At Northern Illinois University, a social norms marketing campaign highlighted the fact that (among those students who consume alcohol) most students drink moderately and do not experience frequent drunkenness. The campaign also provides information about "safer partying," sexual assault prevention, and other safety tips. Over a 10-year period the school saw a 44% reduction in high-risk drinking rates.[6]
- The Penn State–University Park campus has been recognized as a leader in alcohol-free late-night programming. Its LateNight—Penn State program offers live music, dance, comedy, and other entertainment until 2 a.m. on weekend nights.[7] In the first years of this programming, the negative academic effects of alcohol use dropped by 17%.[8]
- The State University of New York developed a systemwide adoption of the environmental management model.[9] Led by a multicampus task force, campuses had access to training, online resources, and state policy makers. Model initiatives include SUNY New Paltz's infusion of alcohol education throughout the curriculum and agreement with community tavern owners to limit high-risk practices, and the University of Albany's Middle Earth peer education program.[10]
- As part of its first-year student environmental management program, Grand Valley State University created engaging peer education programs, a wide range of social activities, and substance-free housing options. In recognition of the fact that some incoming students are already dealing with substance abuse problems Grand Valley's initiatives included the establishment of an on-campus 12-step program and special housing for students in recovery.[11]

So, why bother? Because with intention, collaboration, and understanding that addressing alcohol misuse requires a long-term commitment, we *can* create campuses where high-risk alcohol use is widely understood to be nonnormative, and students can develop socially appropriate behaviors in safe and healthy communities.

Notes

1. DeJong, W. (1998). *Environmental management: A comprehensive strategy for reducing alcohol and other drug use on college campuses.* Washington, DC: U.S. Department of Education's Higher Education Center for Alcohol, and Drug Abuse, and Violence Prevention.

2. Outside the Classroom (2010). *AlcoholEdu for College.* Retrieved from http://www.outsidetheclassroom.com/solutions/higher-education/alcoholedu-for-college.aspx

3. Amethyst Initiative (2010). *Amethyst Initiative: It's time to rethink the drinking age.* Retrieved from http://www.amethystinitiative.org/statement/

4. Read, J. P., Merrill, J. E., & Bytschkow, K. (2010). Before the party starts: Risk factors and reasons for "pregaming" in college students. *Journal of American College Health, 58*(5), 461–472.

5. DeJong, W. (2007). *Experiences in effective prevention: The U.S. Department of Education's alcohol and other drug prevention models on college campuses grants.* Washington, DC: U.S. Department of Education's Higher Education Center for Alcohol, Drug Abuse, and Violence Prevention.

6. National Social Norms Institute at the University of Virginia. (2010). *Northern Illinois University.* Retrieved from http://www.socialnorms.org/CaseStudies/niuinter.php

7. DeJong, *Experiences in effective prevention.*

8. Penn State Office of the President. (1997). *Excessive consumption of alcohol among college students.* Retrieved from http://president.psu.edu/testimony/articles/excessive alcohol.html

9. State University of New York Alcohol and Other Drug Prevention. (2010). Retrieved from http://www.suny.edu/provost/university_life/alcohol_drug.cfm

10. DeJong, *Experiences in effective prevention.*

11. Ibid.

Further Reading and Related Blog

Peter M. Magolda and Marcia B. Baxter Magolda, Miami University

Borsari, B., & Carey, K. B. (2001). Peer influences on college drinking: A review of the research. *Journal of Substance Abuse, 13*(4), 391–424.

The authors review literature on three forms of peer influence: overt offers of alcohol, modeling, and social norms. They conclude that interpersonal processes play an important role in drinking, advocate increased attention to the role of peers in influencing drinking behavior, and provide suggestions for future research that integrates the three forms of peer influence.

Perkins, H. W., Haines, M. P., & Rice, R. (2005). Misperceiving the college drinking norm and related problems: A nationwide study of exposure to prevention information, perceived norms and student alcohol misuse. *Journal of Studies on Alcohol, 66,* 470–478.

This article reports an analysis of the National College Health Assessment Survey responses from over 75,000 college students. Results reveal that students' overestimation of their peers' alcohol consumption influenced their personal alcohol consumption. Lower risk behaviors occurred in settings where preventive information was associated with a more accurate perception of the drinking norm. The authors advocate addressing the misperception of the drinking norm as a prevention method.

Wechsler H., & Nelson T. F. (2008). What we have learned from the Harvard School of Public Health College Alcohol Study: Focusing attention on college student alcohol consumption and the environmental conditions that promote it. *Journal of Studies on Alcohol and Drugs, 69*(4): 481–490.

This article reports findings of this large-scale survey study of more than 50,000 students. The findings include harm to drinkers and those around them, the importance of lowering drink thresholds, and how campus culture, policies, and marketing and promotions of alcohol encourage heavy student drinking.

Blog URL: contestedissues.wordpress.com
Corresponding Chapter Post: tinyurl.com/contestedissues09

10

What Should Universities Do About Overly Involved Parents?

Aiming to Redefine, Not Restrict, Parental Involvement: How to Foster Developmentally Effective Parent-Student Partnerships

Kari B. Taylor, Miami University

To better understand the dynamics between college educators, parents, and students, let's first look at an advising interaction from an adviser's perspective:

"Kari, your four o'clock appointment is here," announces Kris, one of our student workers, as she rounds the corner into my office.

"Great. I'll be right out. I just need to finish this e-mail," I respond as I continue typing. As Kris approaches my desk, I look up to make eye contact.

"You're going to need another chair at your table," she whispers. "M-O-M," she mouths.

Abandoning my e-mail, I begin rearranging my office furniture and reassembling my advising materials. "Miami Bulletin with degree program requirements. Fine. Nothing confidential there," I think to myself. "Student's honors record. Nope. Cannot necessarily show that to Mom." I return confidential materials to a file folder, grab a pen and notebook, and step out of my office to greet Stephen and his mom. "I am ready when you are," I state with a smile. "How's your day going?" I ask. The question falls flat as neither Stephen nor his mom know whom I am speaking to. Finally, Stephen responds, "Not too bad."

Extending my hand to Stephen's mom, I say, "I'm not sure we've met. I'm Kari. I work with honors students who have majors in the School of Fine Arts."

"I'm Sheryl, again. We met at orientation," Stephen's mom states. Her emphasis on *again* signals disappointment. I consider telling her that the fact that I do not remember her indicates that her actions at orientation raised no red flags and thus allowed her to blend in with the other actively involved, occasionally demanding, but ultimately respectful parents. Instead, I move on to my next introductory question.

"Stephen, what brings you to the honors office today?"

"Well," Sheryl begins, even though my gaze remains squarely on Stephen. "We're really frustrated with the honors program requirements, and all the honors courses we wanted for next fall are full."

"OK. I must say I am surprised to hear this. Stephen, what happened between the last time we met and today? When we met a few weeks ago, I did not sense any frustration."

"I don't know," Stephen says as he searches for words. "I just realized that I don't know how I am going to fit honors courses into my schedule. All of us in architecture are really worried."

Sheryl appears to realize that I want to hear Stephen's perspective and remains silent as Stephen and I review the requirements he needs to meet and the various ways he can meet them. As the conversation continues, I notice the look of anxiety on Sheryl's face gradually ease into one of attentive listening, though she occasionally prompts Stephen to ask a question. "Didn't you also want to know about study abroad opportunities?" she interjects at one point. "How will you know if you get honors credit for that experience?" she asks at another point. While I cannot quite tell whether the questions originated from Stephen or Sheryl, I realize the questions uncover important information.

To close the conversation, I say, "Stephen, the next time you're feeling frustrated, please schedule an appointment with me so we can talk. You just need to call our main office and find a time that works for you."

"OK, I will," Stephen says as he rises from his chair.

"Yes, I'll make sure he does," Sheryl adds.

Now, let's look at the same advising interaction from a parent's perspective:

"We have an appointment with Kari Taylor," I explain to the young woman at the front desk of the honors program office.

"OK, I'll let her know," the woman says. "You can have a seat out here," she adds as she motions to two oversized chairs in the lobby.

While my son and I wait in the lobby, I recall our conversation from a few nights ago. During the conversation, when I asked Stephen how course registration for spring semester went, he responded, "Mom, it was awful. I got up at 7:00 a.m. because my registration time was at 7:15 a.m. It was so early! But half the honors courses I wanted to take were already full. There is no way I am going to be able to meet the honors program requirements now."

Remembering that advisers at orientation had encouraged students to have a backup plan in case their first choices were unavailable, I nudged Stephen to explore other course options.

"I did, Mom. But all the other options conflict with the courses I need for architecture."

"OK," I conceded and attempted a different approach. "Well, have you talked to your honors adviser?"

"Uh . . . no. I e-mailed her today, but she hasn't responded."

"Why don't you schedule an appointment with her?" I asked.

"Uh . . . I don't know . . ." Stephen mumbled.

Sensing Stephen's hesitation, I suggested, "Well, we're coming up to visit this weekend. Why don't you schedule an appointment for Friday afternoon, and then I'll come with you to the appointment so we can discuss the situation."

"OK, I guess that'll work. I gotta run." Stephen said as he clicked off his phone.

I know Stephen needs to learn how to meet with advisers on his own, but I have always handled these types of situations in the past. For instance, when Stephen was placed in Mrs. Burns's fifth grade class rather than Mr. Peterson's, I met with the principal to explain that Mr. Peterson would be better able to offer the type of challenge Stephen needed.

Suddenly, the phone in the honors office rings, and I turn my attention back to Stephen. "How'd architecture studio go today?" I ask. "Fine, we have a big project due next week," he says.

Before I have a chance to ask about Stephen's other courses, Kari appears at the front desk and invites us into her office. After some small talk, she asks what brings us in today. As I respond, I sense that she had asked the question to Stephen, not me. As Kari reviews the honors program requirements with Stephen, I fight the urge to take detailed notes and jump into the conversation. But at times, I find myself asking a question I think is important for Stephen to consider. I worry that Stephen will never remember all the details Kari is giving him, but as Kari explains various options, I begin to see it is possible for Stephen to meet the honors program requirements. Also, he appears less anxious about not getting into some of the honors courses and is becoming less shy around Kari. When Kari encourages Stephen to meet with her again if he is frustrated, I realize that Stephen might actually heed her advice. But I make a mental note to follow up with him in a few weeks.

The Millennials: Hovered Over Since Birth

A few years ago Sheryl's mere presence in the honors office would have led me to classify her as a *helicopter parent*—a term that today's journalists and educators alike use to mean, as Deborah Hirsch and Ellen Goldberger have defined it, parents "who 'hover' over their children to shelter them from stress, resolve their problems, and offer unwavering, on-the-spot support and affirmation."[1] Given the negative connotation my colleagues in higher education have assigned to the term, I would have requested that Sheryl wait in the lobby while I met with her son. If she had questioned my request, I would have insisted that I meet with Stephen alone to maintain confidentiality and allow Stephen autonomy. Silently, I would have reasoned that I had successfully completed college less than 10 years ago without such high involvement from my parents and thus had no reason to believe Stephen would need or want his mother involved in our meeting.

Gradually I realized that parents—much like college educators—hope their children develop the capacities necessary to make wise decisions, navigate challenges, build meaningful relationships, and act upon their beliefs and values.

But after multiple occasions in which I ushered a student into my office and left his or her parent in the lobby only to hear the student respond to my first question or two by saying, "Well, I think my mom would want me to . . ." or "I am not sure; I'll have to ask my dad," I realized that physical separation of student and parent proved artificial if not wholly ineffective.

Confidentiality of our conversation became a moot point the minute students left my office because they quickly updated their parents on our conversation. And because parents have been highly involved in each step of students' educational journeys, my goal of granting students autonomy simply could not happen through such superficial and short-term approaches as meeting with a student for 30 minutes without a parent in the room.

In search of more effective approaches, I worked to bring to the surface and then set aside my assumptions about appropriate parental involvement. Rather than immediately interpreting each parent's phone call or visit as a sign of hovering, I began to treat each interaction with parents as an opportunity to better understand their expectations of higher education institutions and their fears and hopes regarding their children's college experience. I also sought out media accounts, conference papers, and journal articles that discussed trends among contemporary parenting practices. Gradually I realized that parents—much like college educators—hope their children develop the capacities necessary to make wise decisions, navigate challenges, build meaningful relationships, and act upon their beliefs and values. As Marcia Baxter Magolda explained in *Learning Partnerships*, developing such capacities—capacities that allow students to meet the complex demands of 21st-century life—requires a transformation in which "adolescent dependence on authorities must be gradually replaced with adult responsibility as a citizen."[2] The vast majority of parents I interact with recognize the necessity of this transformation. Yet, given the unique social and historical contexts that have shaped parenting practices and family dynamics throughout the past 20 years, parents have forged such a close-knit relationship with their children that the process of replacing dependence with responsibility plunges parents and their children into uncharted territory.

Neil Howe and William Strauss have called today's college cohort, students such as Stephen who were born in or after 1982, Millennials; as they explained in *Millennials Rising: The Next Great Generation*, these students place great trust in their parents and tend to accept their parents' authority and values.[3] For example, when scholars Anne Laughlin and Elizabeth Creamer spoke with high school and college women regarding career decisions, they discovered that while the women consulted a variety of individuals such as friends, parents, and advisers, they saw their parents' advice as the most important and influential.[4] Laughlin and Creamer explained, "After asking participants about whose advice was important to them, we asked why they considered opinions from these people important. The most common reply had to do with the participant's sense that the people giving advice (in most cases, parents) cared for her and would know what was best for her."[5] Howe and Strauss explained the basis of this high level of trust among parents and students when they noted that Millennials are "the most watched over generation in memory."[6] Thus, college-age students have grown to expect and rely on a healthy dose of advice from their parents in nearly every arena of their lives. Moreover, during the Millennials' childhoods, youth issues rose to the top of political, media, and commercial agendas as the nation regarded Millennials as special since birth and grew fixated on producing a generation of "better behaved, more achieving, more upbeat, and more civic-spirited" children.[7]

Synthesizing negative as well as positive themes of the Millennial generation's childhood, Howe and Strauss wrote:

> They're kids growing up in houses that contain 50 percent more things (measured by the pound) than houses did twenty years ago. . . . Ten-year-olds who can recite Comedy Central jokes but not the names of presidents. . . . but they're also the Little Leaguers who treat umpires with

more respect than their parents do. Test-tube babies. Babies aboard mini-
vans with childseats, special mirrors, and radar that beeps when something's behind them. Pledgees for True Love Waits.[8]

Ultimately, high societal expectations, widespread technological
advances, relative economic stability, and nonstop political and media
attention regarding child issues have converged to fuel overprotectiveness
and hyper involvement among Millennials' parents—or what is now
commonly referred to as *hovering*.

The Ties That Bind: Fear, Social Class, and Finances

Digging beneath the surface to uncover the roots of why parents hover,
researchers point to psychological as well as social factors. Journalist
Anne-Louise Munroe cited fear as one reason today's parents are prone to
be overprotective.[9] According to psychologist Michael Kieffer, 24-hour-a-
day news coverage can make it seem like we live in a more dangerous
society now than we did in the past. Constant exposure to potentially
dangerous situations tends to amplify parents' natural instincts to protect
their children from harm and erode parents' willingness to trust others
with their children's well-being. Given that teens and young adults face as
many—if not more—dangers than do young children, parents' protective
instincts and struggles to trust others with their children grow over time.
Thus, by the time Millennials reach college, their parents are exceedingly
leery of transferring responsibility to anyone, whether to their own child
or to an experienced educator.

Moreover, high parental involvement—especially the type and degree
that middle-class parents harness—tends to lend social advantages to
children; thus, parents and children alike see high parental involvement
as useful if not essential. When Erin Horvat, Elliot Weininger, and
Annette Lareau conducted interviews with and observations of 88 third
and fourth grade children and their families, they concluded that middle-
class parents' ties to other parents "often enabled them to function as
'guardian angels,' descending on the school en masse and quickly bringing about change."[10] They also found that middle-class parents' networks,
which often involved ties to professionals within the community, "provided resources that made it possible to customize their children's educational careers in important ways—for example, by contesting a placement

decision or obtaining additional resources for a learning-disabled child."[11] In many cases, parents in the study convinced school administrators to reverse decisions they believed to be detrimental to their children or gain additional resources they believed to be beneficial to their children.

According to Horvat et al., high parental involvement in educational settings represented a unique trend among middle-class families. Working-class and poor parents, while intricately connected to family members, lacked ties to other parents in their child's school and to professionals. Horvat et al. noted, "These parents tend to handle the problematic situations that arise in the course of their children's schooling on a purely individual basis, if they don't concede authority to the school altogether" (p. 339).[12] Whereas middle-class parents tend to copiously and collectively work to help their children seize every possible opportunity to achieve academic excellence, working-class and poor parents tend to depend on educational institutions to help their children academically.

Drawing upon a longitudinal ethnography, Annette Lareau found that the trends in parental involvement among middle-class families she and her colleagues identified when interviewing and observing third and fourth graders also appeared as these students applied to and entered college. In a paper she presented at the 2006 annual meeting of the American Sociological Association, she explained:

> Middle-class parents have extensive repertoires of knowledge of higher education systems which they use, often quite effectively, to gain admission for their children. . . . The knowledge appears to come from their own experiences in higher education, their access to social networks or others of a similar class position, who are going [through] the same process, and their use of material resources to procure valuable services for their children.[13]

Lareau noted that working-class and poor parents, in contrast, tend to play a much less active role in the college preparation and transition process. She said these parents "saw their children as autonomous adults . . . and appeared to follow the earlier strategy of managing key aspects of their children's care but leaving responsibility for education with educators and their own children."[14] In essence, working-class and poor parents seem to demonstrate the level of involvement and promote the type of student autonomy that college educators expect. Yet, middle-class parents tend to demonstrate higher than expected (or desired) levels of involvement because of their knowledge, networks, and resources related to the college experience.

Journalist Susan Dominus illustrated how middle-class parents put their knowledge, networks, and resources to use as she described two high school students' college searches:

> The [Devlin] family started thinking about where Maria might apply during her junior year, but the at-home strategy sessions started even before that, around sophomore year. "We'd sit down and have talks together," Maria says. "We were thinking about the recommendations pretty early, because you have to make those relationships before senior year." In classes taught by teachers from whom Maria thought she might request recommendations, she made a point of speaking at least once every day; those were the classes in which she might put in that extra bit of effort for the A-plus.[15]

In Dominus's article, fear also appeared as a motivating factor for parents' hyper involvement. Tracy Rutherfurd—the mother of Win, one of Maria's classmates—stated, "Since the moment these kids were born, we'd been hearing that this was going to be the most competitive year ever."[16] Ultimately, college rejection letters generate more anxiety among parents, who are ever vigilant of events that may cause disappointment for their children, than among the students seeking admission.

Ultimately, when educators step back and leave a need unmet, they give students the vital opportunity to step in and practice how to meet the need on their own.

While natural protective instincts and social trends keep parents and children emotionally connected throughout adolescence and early adulthood, economic trends keep them financially connected as well. In "Understanding Current Trends in Family Involvement," Karla Carney-Hall explained that the shrinking public financial support for higher education means parents are higher education's high-paying customers, which creates a consumer mentality among them. She stated, "Because parents are paying more, they expect better service and higher quality programs and facilities . . . they will not hesitate to pursue the solution they want for any issue, no matter how minor."[17] The consumer mentality hampers the transfer of responsibility from parent to student and makes the question of whose education is it more complex. More significantly, the consumer mentality compels parents to approach financing their children's education in the same way they approach buying material objects such as cars and computers. In other words, they apply a transactional framework in which they seek an even exchange of goods and services to a transformational activity that requires meaningful engagement and intensive effort on students' and educators' part.

A Shift in Position: Allowing Students to Take the Lead

Given the social and historical forces serving to strengthen and lengthen students' dependence on their parents, today's educators must have a clear plan of action for working with parents as well as students to facilitate transformation. Karen Levin Coburn, coauthor of *Letting Go: A Parents' Guide to Understanding the College Years,* notes: "The challenge is to figure out how to enlist these already involved parents in our mutual goal of helping students become engaged learners, competent and creative problem solvers, and responsible and effective citizens—in essence, helping students grow up."[18] To meet this challenge, our field as a whole needs to discuss with consumer-minded parents and students what high-quality learning—the type that allows students to grow into successful adults—entails. Hirsch and Goldberger explained that Millennial students and families tend to believe that "getting their money's worth equals service twenty-four hours a day, seven days a week and accommodation of individual preferences and needs."[19] Yet, researchers, such as Marcia Baxter Magolda, have concluded that significant learning requires students to grapple with uncertainty, make mistakes, and negotiate and uphold community standards.[20] Ultimately, when educators step back and leave a need unmet, they give students the vital opportunity to step in and practice how to meet the need on their own. Transparent discussion regarding the aims of higher education can help parents see the downfalls of their overprotectiveness as well as around-the-clock, on-demand service; such discussions can also ease anxieties and start replacing fear with trust. Coburn argued, "The more successful we are in helping parents understand the normal stages of late adolescent development, the less anxious they are likely to be about their own child's behavior. The less anxious they are, the more likely they are to support their child's growth in appropriate and meaningful ways—and the less likely they are to intervene inappropriately."[21]

So what does appropriate involvement look like? It takes the form of open-ended questions that indicate interest in students' educational journeys yet require students themselves to think through decisions, identify possible resources, and try out solutions. For example, when a student wants to switch his or her major from history to zoology to become a doctor, a parent—rather than immediately extolling the virtues of a medical career or condemning rash decisions—can say something to the effect of, "That's an interesting idea. What has led you to see zoology as a better fit with your interests and talents than history?" Using Baxter Magolda's metaphor of a tandem bicycle, parents can productively support their child's growth by moving to the backseat and encouraging their child to take the front seat.[22] Both individuals need to be on the bike, yet in the journey toward adulthood, students need to be in the position to determine the direction, speed, and destination. Ultimately, appropriate parental involvement in the college experience mirrors appropriate educator involvement; each must leave the front seat open so students grow capable and comfortable taking the lead as they develop authentic identities, build meaningful relationships, and make wise decisions.

Notes

1. Hirsch, D., & Goldberger, E. (2010, January–February). Hovering practices in and outside the classroom: Time to land? *About Campus*, *14*(6), 30–32, p. 30.

2. Baxter Magolda, M. B., & King, P. M. (Eds.). (2004). *Learning partnerships: Theory and models of practice to educate for self-authorship*. Sterling, VA: Stylus, p. xvii.

3. Howe, N., & Strauss, W. (2000). *Millennials rising: The next great generation*. New York, NY: Vintage Books.

4. Laughlin, A., & Creamer, E. G. (2007). Engaging differences: Self-authorship and the decision-making process. *New Directions for Teaching and Learning* (109), 43–51.

5. Ibid., p. 47.

6. Howe & Strauss, *Millennials rising*, p. 9.

7. Ibid., p. 13.

8. Ibid., pp. 20–21.

9. Munroe, Anne-Louise. (2010, January 17). Helicopter parents, experts talk about fine line of overprotection. *The Ledger* (Lakeland, FL), p. D1.

10. Horvat, E. M., Weininger, E. B., & Lareau, A. (2003). From social ties to social capital: Class differences in the relations between schools and parent networks. *American*

Educational Research Journal, *40*(2), 319–351, p. 331. The authors classified a family as middle class when at least one adult was employed in an occupation that entailed managerial, not merely supervisory, authority or required some type of highly credentialed skill. They focus on the effect of social class, rather than race, because they found that Black and White parents exhibited very similar patterns of behavior with regard to "the organization of children's schedules and the propensity for parents to intervene in schooling" (p. 343).

11. Ibid., pp. 331–332.

12. Ibid., p. 339.

13. Lareau, A. (2006, August). *Cultural capital and the transition to college: Unequal childhoods grown up*. Paper presented at the annual meeting of the American Sociological Association, Montreal, Quebec, Canada. Retrieved from http://www.allacademic.com//meta/p_mla_apa_research_citation/1/0/5/0/3/pages105032/p105032-1.php, p. 7.

14. Ibid., p. 2.

15. Dominus, S. (2007, September 30). Tense times at Bronxville High. *New York Times Magazine*, pp. 69–70.

16. Ibid., pp. 69–70.

17. Carney-Hall, K. C. (2008). Understanding current trends in family involvement. *New Directions for Student Services*, *122*, 3–14, p. 4.

18. Coburn, K. L. (2006). Organizing a ground crew for today's helicopter parents. *About Campus*, *11*(3), 9–16, p. 11.

19. Hirsch & Goldberger, Hovering practices in and outside the classroom, p. 30.

20. Baxter Magolda, M. B. (2001). *Making their own way: Narratives for transforming higher education to promote self-development*. Sterling, VA: Stylus.

21. Coburn, Organizing a ground crew for today's helicopter parents, p. 10.

22. Baxter Magolda, *Making their own way*.

Purposefully Partnering With Parents

John Wesley Lowery, Indiana University of Pennsylvania

For the first 325 years in the history of American higher education, college and university administrators understood themselves to be educationally acting in place of the parents, or in loco parentis. As Thelin noted, faculty and ultimately student affairs staff were surrogate parents responsible for the intellectual and moral growth of their charges, who were often much younger than the typical college student today.[1] In 1913 the Kentucky Supreme Court relied on colleges and universities' standing in loco parentis as the legal basis for granting broad power to discipline students, the same authority granted to parents, to side with Berea College in *Gott v. Berea*.[2] During this period, colleges and universities were not just working for parents—they were parents.

This essay examines the evolution of the role of parents in higher education, the parent-student relationship, and legal issues that shape how colleges and universities can work with parents. As Kari Taylor noted, parental involvement in students' lives is not always negative, but overinvolvement can stifle students' development in college. However, she primarily considers this from the perspective of an appropriate relationship between students and parents. This essay seeks to build upon her foundation and examine more meaningfully the institution's role.

This philosophy of in loco parentis is best understood as an educational and distinct legal philosophy. The leaders of the student personnel movement clearly retained aspects of this educational philosophy and recognized the value of forming partnerships with parents. In the 1949 *Student Personnel Point of View*, the authors wrote specifically about working with parents to address some problems students encountered even while acknowledging that parents themselves contributed to other problems through their continued "domination" of their students.[3] In 1959 Melvene Draheim Hardee wrote of the various efforts that colleges and universities were undertaking to foster parents' cooperation to enhance the support provided to students.[4]

The demise of in loco parentis as a legal philosophy began in 1961 when the U.S. Court of Appeals for the Fifth Circuit in *Dixon v. Alabama State Board of Education* rejected this philosophy in higher education and concluded that the relationship between a public institution and students was constitutional, not parental.[5] The legal cases that followed in the 1960s reinforced this conclusion and placed limits on private institutions as well. In 1974 Congress passed the Family Educational Rights and Privacy Act (FERPA) that further influenced partnerships between parents and institutions by placing limits on the information that universities could share with parents without students' consent.[6] While various exceptions allowed information to be shared with parents, FERPA also reinforced the larger message that the courts expected parents to sit on the sidelines when it came to relationships between colleges and students. Kari Taylor described the current nature of parental involvement in higher education, but it is also important to consider the historical context of this involvement.

Parents' and Students' Relationship

The relationship between parents and students has changed over the decades since the end of in loco parentis. As early as 1990 Cline and Fay described the phenomenon of helicopter parents.[7] However, it would be another 10 to 15 years before this term came into wide use in higher education to describe a new and common parental archetype. Over time these concerns about the overinvolvement parents have extended through students' college careers and into their job searches, as Bruno described, and postcollege employment, as Armour observed.[8] As Betsy Hart cautioned, "Helicopter parents do their children no favors by not allowing them to exercise their wings a little before they have to fly on their own."[9] Interestingly these concerns about helicopter parents are not limited to the United States either, as Max Davidson illustrates similar concerns in Britain.[10]

Today's college students—also know as the Millennial generation as described by Howe and Strauss—seem more highly receptive to this parental involvement than collegians during the previous four decades.[11] They contact their parents with what many administrators consider startling frequency. This increased parental involvement is not solely a result of parental desires but is coupled with technology (e.g., cell phones, video conferencing) that facilitates near constant contact with their children. Contemporary college students welcome their parents' involvement in their lives and their parents' willingness to assist them in resolving problems they encounter on campus or simply solving their problems for them. Howe and Strauss warned, "Careful parental management will be one of the most-nerve wracking challenges of the Millennial college era."[12] However, some student affairs professionals argue that college students today are adults, and we should focus our efforts on the students themselves rather than on their parents.

Barbara K. Hofer and Abigail Sullivan Moore, offering advice to parents seeking to find a balance between supporting and smothering their children, warned parents of a number of common mistakes: calling or otherwise contacting their children too often, only listening to their children's side of the story, taking on their children's role, fighting their children's battles, posing as their children online, and "robbing kids of the ability to make decisions."[13] The early response from student affairs professionals when helicopter parents begin to circle the campus is one of significant concern. As Taylor observed, we cannot immediately assume that every communication from parents is evidence of hovering. As Hofer and Moore rightly note, "College administrators do appreciate parents who encourage their children to become independent and who respect what educators are trying to do: give students a good education and prepare them for life after college."[14]

Finding an Optimal Balance

Many student affairs professionals regard in loco parentis as a quaint relic of a bygone time without fully considering what role parents should play in higher education once higher education abandoned this concept. Henning argued that after several decades of floundering, a new model had effectively emerged—*in consortio cum parentibus*—or, in partnership with parents.[15] However, what does that partnership look like in practice? How can colleges and universities develop these partnerships?

As Karen Levine Coburn, coauthor of several editions of popular guides for parents of new college students, *Letting Go: A Parents' Guide to Understanding the College Years*, recommended, it is vital for colleges and universities to effectively educate parents about appropriate ways for them to support their students' development and success in college.[16] However, she warns that without careful planning and coordination, more parental hovering rather than less will be an unintended consequence. Institutions need a campuswide philosophy regarding parental involvement that reflects the messages universities transmit to parents during orientation. This philosophy must be present at all levels, particularly at the top of the institution. Without a message strongly communicated from upper reaches of the institution's administration, many parents will simply assume that if they go up high enough the answer will change. Absent a consistent message, parents will seize upon the perspective that resonates with them most. As Hofer and Moore observed, these overly involved parents are not intentionally setting out to limit their college-aged students' development but are doing what they believe is best.[17]

Like their parents, students need support from their colleges as they forge a new relationship with their parents. Colleges and universities can help parents and students set reasonable expectations for such considerations as the frequency and nature of communication. We can also help equip students to renegotiate this relationship with their parents. Just as we communicate with parents about appropriate relationships, we can assist students in this endeavor as well.

For this partnership between institutions of higher education, students, and parents to work effectively and support student development, institutions and parents must give students the opportunities to make decisions for themselves.

There is another dynamic to the partnership between parents and colleges and universities that must be considered: federal and state laws. FERPA limits the release of information from students' education records without their consent, but there are also multiple exceptions that allow the release of information to parents in a wide variety of situations.[18] These exceptions include releasing information to parents who claim their students as dependents on their tax returns, notifying parents for alcohol and drug violations, and releasing information in health and safety emergency situations. However, federal law does not require colleges and universities to share this information with parents but simply allows its release without violating FERPA.[19] Parents today, it seems, are more knowledgeable than ever before about FERPA and other privacy laws and are quick to correct administrators who mistakenly tell them that federal law prohibits the release of information. Institutions must establish policies and practices that take advantage of this flexibility when desired. There are additional protections regarding students' counseling and health records that prevent the release of these records to parents except in very narrow circumstances. These health-related records typically cannot be shared with parents except in cases of significant, imminent threat.

Kari Taylor built upon Marcia Baxter Magolda's metaphor of the tandem bicycle to suggest that the parents and administrators should move to the backseat and allow students to take the front seat. However, federal and state laws limit the degree to which these backseat passengers can talk specifically about the student. A more productive, and FERPA-appropriate conversation in most cases focuses on students in general rather than on the specific student.

Beyond simply limiting student independence, parental involvement at times runs completely counter to the institution's goals. As institutions implemented policies for parental notification for alcohol violations, many administrators had conversations with parents who considered their underage students' decisions to drink as appropriate and normal. Administrators must be attentive to multiple potential issues related to parental involvement.

For this partnership between institutions of higher education, students, and parents to work effectively and support student development, institutions and parents must give students the opportunities to make decisions for themselves. The most important way parents and institutions can support students is helping them develop the skills to answer these questions from multiple perspectives and, as Kari Taylor noted, help students realize what these questions are. As with institutions of higher education themselves, there will be multiple approaches to managing this relationship. Regardless of approach, the key is for colleges and universities to address the problem directly and seek to develop mission-appropriate responses.

Notes

1. Thelin, J. R. (2004). *A history of American higher education*. Baltimore, MD: Johns Hopkins University Press.

2. Gott v. Berea College, 156 Ky. 376, 161 S.W. 204 (1913).

3. American Council on Education. (1949). *The student personnel point of view*. Washington, DC: Author. Retrieved from http://www.naspa.org/pubs/files/StudAff_1949.pdf

4. Hardee, M. D. (1959). *The faculty in college counseling*. New York, NY: McGraw-Hill.

5. Dixon v. Alabama State Board of Education, 294 F.2d 150 (5th Cir. 1961).

6. Family Educational Rights and Privacy Act, 20 U.S.C. §1232g (1974).

7. Cline, F. W., & Fay, Jim (1990). *Parenting with love and logic: Teaching children responsibility*. Colorado Springs, CO: Pinon Press.

8. Bruno, D. (2008, June 17). Parents, quit the hovering; It's graduation season, and all our 24/7 helicopter parenting has come to fruition, right? Wrong. Many of our kids still have no idea what they want to do, and it's all the parents' fault. *USA Today*, p. 9A; Armour, S. (2007, April 24). More parents hover when kids job hunt: Some employers admit "it hurts" how junior's perceived. *USA Today*, p. 1B.

9. Hart, B. (2006, November 19). Helicopter parents' need to land, walk off. *Desert News* (Salt Lake City, UT). Retrieved from http://www.deseretnews.com/article/650207943/Helicopter-parents-need-to-land-walk-off.html

10. Davidson, M. (2008, March 22). Stop hovering! Just let him go. *Daily Telegraph* (London, UK), p. 11.

11. Howe, N. & Strauss, W. (2000). *Millennials rising: The next great generation*. New York, NY: Vintage Books.

12. Howe, N. & Strauss, W. (2003). *Millennials go to college*. Alexandria, VA: AACRO & LifeCourse Associates, p. 81.

13. Hofer, B. K., & Moore, A. S. (2010). *The iConnected parent: Staying close to your kids in college (and beyond) while letting them grow up*. New York, NY: Free Press, p. 69.

14. Ibid., p. 72.

15. Henning, G. (2007). Is "in consortio cum parentibus" the new "in loco parentis?" *NASPA Journal*, *44*, 538–560.

16. Coburn, K. L. (2006, July–August). Organizing a ground crew for today's helicopter parents. *About Campus*, *11*, 9–16.

17. Hofer & Moore, *The iConnected parent*.

18. Family Educational Rights and Privacy Act, 20 U.S.C. §1232g (1974).

19. Lowery, J. W. (2005). Legal issues regarding partnering with parents: Misunderstood federal laws and potential sources of institutional liability. In K. Keppler, R. H. Mullendore, & A. Carey (Eds.), *Partnering with the parents of today's college students* (pp. 43–51). Washington, DC: NASPA: Student Affairs Administrators in Higher Education.

Further Reading and Related Blog

N. Aminatu Rubango, Loyola University Chicago

Carney-Hall, K. C. (Ed.). (2008). Managing parent partnerships: Maximizing influence, minimizing interference, and focusing on student success. *New Directions for Student Services* (122), 3–14.

This monograph explores the multiple roles parents play in the lives of their children who are attending college. Contributors discuss legal issues, college students' development, crisis management, problem solving, parent outreach, and student success. The monograph also showcases university-sponsored programs and best practices created exclusively for parents.

Coburn, K. L., and Treeger, M. L. (2003). *Letting go: A parents' guide to understanding the college years.* New York: Harper-Collins.

This book provides parents' perspectives on their children's transition to college and advice regarding the physical and emotional process of letting go. It provides practical information and gentle recommendations about ways to constructively alter relationships with children as they pursue higher education. The book provides insights into how collegians change while attending college, campus challenges (e.g., alcohol and drugs, eating disorders, interacting with the other), and available campus services.

Lareau, A. (2003). *Unequal childhoods: Class, race, and family life.* Berkeley, CA: University of California Press.

Based on an ethnographic study of child rearing practices, Lareau illustrates distinctions between natural growth and concerted cultivation and how these approaches relate to social class and race. More importantly, her research reveals that parenting practices sustain and reproduce inequality.

Blog URL: contestedissues.wordpress.com
Corresponding Chapter Post: tinyurl.com/contestedissues10

11

In this Age of Accountability, What Counts as Good and How Do We Know If Student Affairs Educators Really Make a Difference in the Lives of Students?

Student Affairs in the Age of Accountability and Assessment

Jillian Kinzie, Indiana University, Bloomington

O ver the past few years, public debate about higher education has focused on whether colleges and universities can show they make a difference for students. The challenge is usually expressed somewhat rhetorically as: How much do students actually learn in 4 years of college? While this question may simultaneously seem reasonable and unfair, it is emblematic of the current skepticism about quality in undergraduate education and a belief in the need for evidence of educational effectiveness and genuine improvements in student learning and success. Student learning outcomes have essentially taken center stage as a principal gauge of higher education's effectiveness.

Criticism about a lack of accountability for student achievement in institutions of higher education has emerged from evidence that graduation rates have not increased, coupled with a real concern that students are ill prepared for the demands of a 21st-century economy and a cynical view that undergraduate education is an overpriced 4-year sojourn. These concerns have intensified assessment and accountability requirements across every sector of higher education and all units in colleges and universities. Hundreds of public institutions, for example, signed on to the Voluntary System of Accountability (VSA), an initiative to provide basic, comparable information on the undergraduate student experience through a common web report. The Association for American Colleges and Universities (AAC&U) called for data about essential learning outcomes and fundamental changes to help students develop greater intellectual and practical skills. Furthermore, influential publications like *Learning Reconsidered*, which defined learning as an activity that integrates academics and student development, and asserted the accountability that all campus educators have "for identifying and achieving essential student learning outcomes and for making transformative education possible and accessible for all students."[1]

Assessment and accountability for student learning is not new to student affairs. The authors of the 1937 *Student Personnel Point of View* said that personnel workers should evaluate and improve services based on research about students' in- and out-of-class experiences.[2] Many years later, "The Student Learning Imperative," which reaffirmed the profession's commitment to assessment and student learning, refocused student affairs work around student learning and set forth the conditions that constitute a "learning-oriented" division.[3] *Good Practice in Student Affairs* shifted student affairs educators toward a philosophy that embraces student learning.[4] *Learning Reconsidered* expanded these goals by proclaiming that student affairs educators make plain the learning derived from out-of-classroom experiences, commit to assessing the environment for learning, and be more accountable for the contribution their learning experiences make to advancing broad student learning outcomes.[5] These publications established student affairs' focus on student learning.

Student affairs is plainly implicated in the current climate of heightened demands for accountability and increased expectations for evidence of student learning. Demands for accountability amplify the mandate issued in "The Student Learning Imperative." The directive is clear: "If learning is the primary measure of institutional productivity by which the quality of undergraduate education is determined, what and how much students learn also must be the criteria by which the value of student affairs is judged."[6] Thus, the present era of accountability provides an opportune moment to take stock of the extent to which student affairs makes a difference in student learning in college.

Demands for accountability and calls from the field compel student affairs educators to demonstrate their contribution to student learning and to assume greater responsibility for learning outcomes assessment. While student affairs has made strides in these areas, there is little evidence that the field has fully embraced its role regarding learning outcomes. In this essay, I explore this assertion by unpacking some key terms regarding assessment, accountability and learning outcomes. Then I suggest that to respond effectively to current demands, student affairs educators must place student learning at the center of their practice. I close by considering challenges in the current climate.

Assessment, Accountability, and Student Learning Outcomes

The term *assessment* has gained prominence in student affairs, as shown by a growing list of student affairs publications on the topic and the creation of full-time student affairs assessment specialist positions. In contrast, the terms *accountability* and *student learning outcomes* have less standing in the field. Accountability has received little attention in student affairs, in part because it seems external to colleges and universities. Although student affairs educators value outcomes, they have not readily connected these goals to their work, instead surrendering them to faculty. There is little evidence that these terms are understood to be related concepts. Given their significance and status as education buzzwords, it is important to explore definitions.

Assessment is an ongoing process of gathering information regarding the extent to which objectives have been met, evaluating the information against criteria, and applying what has been learned to inform improvement. Although this definition is pretty widely accepted in academia, the topic is contested. Conflicts arise regarding the purpose of assessment and the selection of tools and validity of measures.

A long-standing tension exists between the two purposes of assessment—improvement and accountability. In the former, assessment is an internal matter, in that educators collect evidence about how well students are attaining intended outcomes with the hope this information will improve student performance and institutional practice. In contrast, assessment for accountability is externally focused—results demonstrate the degree to which resources are used to help students learn and graduate. In both cases, assessment is a means for discovering—inside and outside the classroom—what, how, when, and which students achieve an institution's expected learning outcomes. The tension regarding purpose is important because it can stall assessment activities. For example, student affairs unit staff who set out to assess students' perceptions of the quality of student-faculty interactions outside the classroom in organizations and informal opportunities might find their assessment effort and results rejected by faculty if the purpose of the work is not clarified at the outset. If assessment is perceived to be for accountability, faculty might object to results as an unfair judgment of their work. Assessment can serve both purposes so long as the goals are articulated, results are not used to make unfair comparisons or to judge, and the work is conducted in an ethos of quality improvement.

Another important dimension to clarify about assessment is the scope of tools and measures. Assessment is a special kind of evaluation that recognizes a range of data sources, including surveys of students and alumni, exams, portfolios, student work samples, and direct observations, all of which offer evidence to help improve education.[7] Assessments of student learning can include quantitative and qualitative data and should also involve investigations that use multiple sources of information in a mutually reinforcing way. Notably, the instruments commonly used to assess learning include nationally normed measures of general knowledge and skills (e.g., ACT's Collegiate Assessment of Academic Proficiency), portfolios, national or locally developed surveys, and alumni surveys, rubrics, and interviews.[8] Indeed, there are many approaches to assessment, and arguably there should be. However, one important issue related to measures that has emerged in the current emphasis on student learning is that to count as evidence of student learning outcomes, the information collected and presented should go beyond such things as surveys, or measures of satisfaction, to include the actual examination of student performance. Such an assessment can challenge student affairs since commonly used measures including satisfaction surveys or data about student use of services are insufficient.

Accountability in higher education means being a responsible steward of financial resources, institutional productivity, and student performance, and ensuring educational quality. Institutions are accountable to multiple stakeholders, including federal and state governments, students and families, governing boards, and the general public. Accountability

Assessment is a means for discovering—inside and outside the classroom—what, how, when, and which students achieve an institution's expected learning outcomes.

has always been an issue in colleges and universities and is a topic of concern to student affairs administrators. The 2006 report produced by the U.S. secretary of education's Commission on the Future of Higher Education about accountability concluded that "colleges and universities must become more transparent about cost, price, and student success outcomes, and must willingly share this information with students and families."[9] One of the major themes in this new form of accountability is making evidence of student learning outcomes transparent.

The clearest expression of accountability in higher education is the process of accreditation. Since the 1930s, accreditation has been charged with ensuring that higher education meets acceptable levels of quality. Over the last decade, accreditation agencies, along with the federal government and employers, have identified gains in student learning and achievement as the chief accountability goals to ensure societal well-being. Toward these ends, accreditation organizations increased the salience of learning outcomes in their standards and require greater evidence of student learning and how the data have been used to achieve improvement. Increased demands for learning outcomes are something colleges and universities, and particularly student affairs units, should welcome. This emphasis shifts the focus from input measures, such as volumes in the library or student-faculty ratios that have virtually no relationship to educational quality, to meaningful assessments of student learning. However, the value of this emphasis will only be achieved when student affairs takes greater ownership for the accreditation process and, more importantly, fully embraces accountability for student learning.

An *outcome* is broadly defined as something that happens to a student (hopefully for the better) as a result of participating in higher education.[10] Student learning outcomes are a special form of outcome attained as a result of engaging in particular collegiate experiences. Learning outcomes can be further defined as specific levels of attainment of knowledge outcomes, skills outcomes include the capacity to do something such as communicate effectively, and affective outcomes, involving changes in beliefs, for example, increase one's commitment to the welfare of the community. Learning outcomes are specific statements derived from educational goals about what students gain from college. Although most college educators would claim chief responsibility for learning outcomes, what garners attention on many campuses does not always align with student learning. For example, outcomes such as student persistence, while important, can capture more attention than student learning outcomes.

According to a 2009 report, *More Than You Think, Less Than We Need: Learning Outcomes Assessment in American Higher Education*, which summarized what universities are doing to measure student learning, about 75% of all institutions have adopted common learning outcomes for all undergraduate students, an essential first step in assuring campuswide efforts to assess learning outcomes.[11] In the late 1990s, for example, Indiana University-Purdue University Indianapolis (IUPUI) established Principles of Undergraduate Learning (PULs), six institution-wide learning outcomes that are explicitly integrated and assessed throughout the undergraduate program. The PULs orient the entire community through shared goals for student learning. They prompted student affairs educators to examine the extent to which student activities and programs align with these goals and to rethink administrative structures for increased intentional collaboration between academic and student affairs. As student affairs educators at IUPUI shifted the focus in student affairs to support PULs and the academic mission of the institution, they found greater opportunities for partnership with academic affairs. Most importantly, real improvements in student learning and success resulted.

Student Affairs in the Age of Accountability: Fundamental Principles

In this age of accountability, student affairs educators have a professional responsibility and a moral imperative to take greater responsibility for assessment and accountability for student learning. This assertion is grounded in four principles that originate from my observations of student affairs practice and the assessment and accountability literature.

First, and foremost, like all units in undergraduate education in this era of accountability, student affairs educators must make plain their role in the intentional promotion of student learning. This commitment requires student affairs educators to be explicit about the student learning outcomes they seek to foster. For example, student affairs staff at the College of St. Scholastica identified how all its units and programs addressed learning outcomes deemed important to the institution, including holistic growth such as critical thinking, problem solving and conflict resolution; intercultural competence; and responsibility to community. Residential life educators specified how through the process of resolving aspects of community living, including roommate conflicts, students in residential life develop a style of critical thinking that allows them to understand the complexities of a situation rather than perceive difficulties in simple terms.

Second, student affairs educators must assess the extent to which students are making gains on specific learning outcomes. This requires that assessments focus on evidence of what students know and can demonstrate when they have completed or participated in a program or project. For example, California State University Fullerton assessed how much students who participated in student activities programs gained in three areas of effective communication, including teamwork and working with students from diverse backgrounds. A variety of measures, including reflection papers following programs and evaluation of student performance in teams, can be used to assess these outcomes. Greater attention to assessing student learning rather than satisfaction or program participation is a clear expression of the directive that student learning be taken seriously in student affairs.

Third, the motivation for assessment should emerge from a desire to understand as fully as possible the strengths and shortcomings of students' experience and learning, and to use this information to determine if good work is being done and where changes need to be made. For example, educators in career services have an unequivocal stake in fostering students' preparation for the world of work. Assessment efforts should focus on key preparation experiences such as internships, and the extent to which all students have access to and participate in these activities, as well as the quality of learning in these experiences. Assessment results, including questionnaires about students' awareness of internships, interns' self-assessments, and employer surveys about knowledge and skill development, could provide career services educators with an array of information to inform improvements in the quality of internships. To know that student affairs is providing the best in the service of all students, student affairs educators must have assessment data and act on these results to enhance the conditions for learning.

Finally, learning outcomes should be emphasized, assessment should be undertaken, and accountability should be demonstrated, because they are the *right things to do*. Student affairs educators must measure educational outcomes and identify and implement effective practices as part of a commitment to improvement, and demonstrate accountability and stewardship to students, families, and the broader public. This reflects the best of professional and ethical practice. It is taking leadership in ensuring quality in undergraduate education and advancing a learning outcomes agenda in student affairs.

Assessment, Accountability, and Student Affairs

Just as all university officials are being asked tough questions about student learning, student affairs educators have also responded to the accountability challenge. John Schuh and Lee Upcraft argued that student affairs units must demonstrate the effectiveness and worth of services and programs, show positive relationships between students' out-of-class experiences and learning gains, and respond to pressures for accountability by providing evidence of program worth.[12] Various publications now provide guidance for student affairs educators to integrate assessment into practice.

Student affairs has made advances in terms of the practice of outcomes assessment. How-to workshops draw crowds at national meetings, more resources about assessing student learning in student affairs have been produced, and student affairs is more public about assessment results. Student affairs educators are more practiced at the creation of learning outcomes, and more student affairs professionals can answer the basic outcomes assessment question, What do I hope students will be like or be able to do after having participated in this program? or, more specifically, "As a result of participation in this program, students will . . ." For example, California State University Chico has employed a basic approach to student learning outcomes assessment by asking staff from each student affairs unit to describe the learning that should occur from participation in their programs and post it in their website.[13] Student affairs staff created statements in response to two questions: What are the learning objectives that your program has (explicit or implicit) for students using your services? What are the indicators by which you estimate the extent to which students are learning each of those things your program intends for them to learn? These straightforward questions orient practice, direct action, and help unit staff reflect on their contribution to student learning.

Another indication of advancements in assessment in student affairs is the growing expertise in measurement. Although the identification of evidence still tends to include simple measures of student use of or satisfaction with services, more student affairs units have adopted locally developed surveys to explore student perceptions of learning gains, or rubrics to assess whether students have achieved specific outcomes. Still others have connected their assessment activities to institution-wide assessment approaches, such as the National Survey of Student Engagement (NSSE), to more broadly determine the extent to which participation in programs, such as service-learning, are associated with higher levels of student engagement and to benchmark the data with comparable institutions.[14] The dedication of resources to assessment and the expansion of centralized student affairs assessment activities are also expressions of a commitment to outcomes assessment.

Yet the profession needs more systematic and comprehensive approaches to assessing outcomes of student affairs services, programs, and facilities to address persistent accountability demands. These approaches require moving from the mechanics of assessment and the basic description of student learning outcomes to a learning-centered student affairs practice.

Placing Student Learning at the Center of Practice

The sharper focus on assessment in student affairs is an important step toward being more responsive to the ubiquitous demands for student learning assessment and accountability. However, one critical next step is to expand the extent to which student learning is the epicenter of student affairs practice. When learning is at the center, student affairs educators identify with student learning processes and the results. They have a clear understanding and evidence of what they do to promote student learning and the impact it has on student learning.

The suggestion to situate student learning at the center of student affairs practice is evocative of the learning-oriented focus for student affairs advocated in "The Student Learning Imperative" and the conditions at educationally engaging institutions outlined in Kuh, Kinzie, Schuh, Whitt, & Associates" (2005/2010) *Student Success in College.*[15] The idea also follows from Peggy Maki's work advocating for the need to build commitments across the institution that rely on evidence of student learning to inform institutional actions.[16] In a learning-oriented model, the mission of the unit is student learning, and work is oriented around explicit statements about what students are expected to accomplish.

One critical next step is to expand the extent to which student learning is the epicenter of student affairs practice.

The learning-oriented characteristics highlighted in the "Student Learning Imperative" provide a useful frame for enacting a commitment to student learning outcomes. Three characteristics are particularly relevant to advancing a student learning outcome agenda in student affairs.

Complementary alignment between student affairs' and the institution's mission. Student affairs staff must make explicit their division's alignment with the educational mission and specifically its contribution to student learning. This should be articulated in the mission statement, such as, "The division of student affairs exists to advance student learning," and the declaration must be followed by learning outcome objectives. The division of student affairs at California State University Northridge, for example, established a one-sentence mission statement asserting their commitment to learning, and they specified department-level outcomes related to five common learning themes that complement the university's defined outcomes for its graduates.[17] One resource for establishing learning goals is the Council for the Advancement of Standards in Higher Education (CAS). The CAS standards describe desirable outcomes that colleges and universities should develop in students, specify indicators across functional areas in student affairs, and provide a series of self-assessment guides for assessing student learning. Aligning missions and demonstrating that the enhancement of student learning is central to practice makes student affairs accountable for learning and provides greater potential for collaboration with academic affairs.[18]

Resources allocated to programs that demonstrate contributions to student learning. Allocating resources to programs and practices that demonstrate contributions to student learning signals a commitment to learning outcomes. The investment of resources sends important messages about priorities, and such decisions should be guided by evidence of educational effectiveness. The high-performing colleges and universities featured in *Student Success in College* used data to make decisions and allocated funds to what matters most: effective education of students.[19]

Collaborate to foster student learning and personal development. The emphasis on campus collaboration in support of student learning and success has been a long-standing theme in student affairs. Trudy Banta emphasized that because student learning takes place inside and outside the classroom, some of the best work in assessment involves collaboration among faculty and student affairs professionals.[20] In addition, because student affairs educators are experts on students, their environments, and learning, they have specific contributions to bring to assessment conversations. Collaboration is particularly important and should be nurtured by campus leadership.[21]

Student affairs policies and practices are based in research on student learning and informed by institution-specific assessment data. Applying research about what matters to student learning and institutional evidence of effectiveness to guide practice is central to ensuring greater levels of student learning. Student learning outcomes information is essential to designing educational practice. Student affairs educators must use a combination of theory, research, and information from student learning outcomes assessment to guide practice and strategies to improve institutional and student achievement.

The extent to which student affairs educators can focus on these characteristics is key to furthering efforts to advance student learning. Indeed, student affairs professionals have achieved notable levels of learning-oriented practice and did so by intentionally orienting their work toward student learning outcomes, aligning practice with the educational mission, collaborating across campus, and maintaining a laser focus on what matters for student learning.

Lingering Challenges

Although student affairs has advanced learning-oriented practice, the reality is that student affairs educators have had difficulty shifting to learning outcomes. Lessons about how to proceed can be found in resources such as Peggy Maki's *Assessing for Learning.*[22] Terry Piper chronicled the shift to learning outcomes assessment in student affairs at California State University Northridge, providing an informative, candid, and cautionary tale about the challenges associated with the process.[23] However, the end product—a strong student affairs unit with a clear mission, boundary-spanning collaborations, practice anchored in a shared educational mission, and improved student learning and success—demonstrates the power of this work.

The focus on ensuring quality in student learning can be thwarted by a preoccupation with the technology of assessment. The search for the perfect tool, for example, the test with impeccable psychometric properties or the indisputable research design is often at the expense of using the reasonably good evidence on hand to influence action. The pursuit for more robust measures or control group designs preoccupies our attention and immobilizes efforts to act on available information. Correspondingly, we should also not reach for simple measures, such as the convenient online survey, rather than investigating the rich, authentic assessment rubrics or multiple methods that characterize good assessment practice.

Finally, assessment of student learning must have additional support from all educators on campus but particularly from top-level administrators and governing boards. Effective and enduring assessment programs are characterized by top-level support, multiple opportunities for collaboration, and by linking assessments to the departmental, divisional, and institutional planning processes.[24]

Conclusion

In this age of accountability, student affairs educators must provide greater evidence of their contributions to student learning. However, this work should be motivated by a commitment to learning-oriented and ethical practice and a curiosity about student learning. Attention to student learning outcomes is the key to designing effective educational practice and is essential to responding to the persistent demands for improved student learning and quality in undergraduate education.

Notes

1. Keeling, R. P. (Ed.). (2004). *Learning reconsidered: A campus-wide focus on the student experience.* Washington, DC: National Association of Student Personnel Administrators and American College Personnel Association, p. 1.

2. American Council on Education. (1937). *The student personnel point of view.* Washington, DC: Author.

3. American College Personnel Association. (1996). The student learning imperative: Implications for Student Affairs. *Journal of College Student Development, 37*(2), 118–122.

4. Blimling, G. S., Whitt, E. J., & Associates. (1999). *Good practice in student affairs: Principles to foster student learning.* San Francisco, CA: Jossey-Bass.

5. Keeling, *Learning reconsidered.*

6. American College Personnel Association. The student learning imperative.

7. Ewell, P. T. (2002). An emerging scholarship: A brief history of assessment. In T. W. Banta (Ed.), *Building a scholarship of assessment* (pp. 3–25). San Francisco, CA: Jossey-Bass.

8. Kuh, G. D., & Ikenberry, S. (2009). *More than you think, less than we need: Learning outcomes assessment in American higher education.* Urbana, IL: University of Illinois and Indiana University, National Institute for Learning Outcomes Assessment.

9. Spellings Commission on the Future of Higher Education. (2006). *A test of leadership: Charting the future of U.S. higher education.* Washington, DC: U.S. Department of Education.

10. Ewell, P. T. (2001). *Accreditation and student learning outcomes: A proposed point of departure.* Washington, DC: Council for Higher Education Accreditation.

11. Kuh & Ikenberry, *More than you think.*

12. Schuh, J. H., Upcraft, M. L., & Associates (2001). *Assessment practice in student affairs: An application manual.* San Francisco, CA: Jossey-Bass; Upcraft, L. M., & Schuh, J. H. (1996). *Assessment in student affairs: A guide for practitioners.* San Francisco, CA: Jossey-Bass.

13. See http://www.csuchico.edu/sa/assessment/index.shtml

14. National Survey of Student Engagement. (2007). *Experiences that matter: Enhancing student learning and success.* Bloomington, IN: Indiana University Center for Postsecondary Research.

15. American College Personnel Association. The student learning imperative; Kuh, G. D., Kinzie, J., Schuh, J. H., Whitt, E. J., & Associates. (2005/2010). *Student success in college: Creating conditions that matter.* San Francisco, CA: Jossey-Bass.

16. Maki, P. (2004). *Assessing for learning: Building a sustainable commitment across the institution.* Sterling, VA: Stylus.

17. See http://www.csun.edu/studentaffairs/pdfs/clt_o_composite.pdf and http://www.csun.edu/studentaffairs/about/mission.htm

18. Council for the Advancement of Standards in Higher Education. (2003). *The book of professional standards for higher education.* Washington, DC: Author.

19. Kuh et al., *Student success in college.*

20. Banta, T. W. (2002). Characteristics of effective outcomes assessment: Foundations and examples. In T. W. Banta & Associates, *Building a scholarship of assessment* (pp. 261–283). San Francisco, CA: Jossey-Bass.

21. Koester, J., Hellenbrand, H., & Piper, T. D. (2008). The challenge of collaboration: Organizational structure and professional identity. *About Campus, 13*(5), 12–19.

22. Maki, *Assessing for learning.*

23. Piper, T. D. (2007). In search of the wizard of assessment. *About Campus, 12*(5), 24–27.

24. Smith, K. M., & Mather, P. C. (2000). Best practices in student affairs research. In *New Directions for Institutional Research* (108), pp. 63–78.

Engaging the Professed Good of Learning as Contested Terrain

Andrew F. Wall, University of Rochester

The question of what counts as good in student affairs practice is a moral and ethical one situated in time and within a specific social context. What is good practice and what evidence constitutes knowing that student affairs educators' efforts are making a difference; have persistent elements; but also change as people, knowledge, technology, and social, political, and economic conditions change?[1]

The 1970s' developmental view of good student affairs practice was once the state of the profession.[2] Today this has given way, as shown in Jillian Kinzie's essay, to the commitment to learning and assessment of learning outcomes as a central tenet of student affairs practice.

In this response, I expand Kinzie's view of learning as situated primarily in the service of the institutional mission and offer an alternative positioning of assessment away from measuring intended learning outcomes and toward a process of dialogue. In my response, I develop three main points: First, while Kinzie has positioned learning in the service of the institutional mission, I situate what counts as learning as contested terrain shaped by moral commitments along with social, political, and economic forces; second, I see the highest form of accountability in determining what is good as personal accountability and advocate for reflective and competent practice that orients student affairs educators on a trajectory toward expertise; and third, I propose a view of student affairs assessment as a process of dialogue about what type of learning should be and is counted as good in an era of accountability.

The Context of Learning as a Professed Good

A commitment to learning as professed good in student affairs practice places educators into moral and ethical terrain associated with navigating varying interests and professional commitments. Determining what counts as good learning engages our value commitments along with the pressures from the market, government, our institutions, and our profession over the content and emphasis of learning. Professionals are simultaneously pulled by a national discussion advancing technical knowledge and skills as preparation for a global marketplace, institutional commitments to liberal learning, and student desires to ensure their educational investment prepares them to be competitive in the job market. Concomitantly, professional commitments in student affairs also advance a knowledge base, ethical guidelines, and ethos of practice. Professional guidance, government interest, institutional mission and culture, and students have vested interests and exert influence on what learning is valued as do persistent moral commitments of our democracy, such as the pursuit of equity, an informed citizenry, and deliberative dialogue.

Learning as a professed good should be contested rather than settled terrain, open to interrogation, revision, and ongoing dialogue as a reflection of our deliberative democratic society.

Holding tension between moral, ethical, and social professional commitments is a means of ensuring that student affairs educators are responsive to contemporary concerns and address broader questions of how student affairs educators serve society. Professional discussion of seven domains of desired learning as described in *Learning Reconsidered*, such as cognitive complexity, knowledge acquisition, and humanitarianism, can serve to fuel dialogue about what learning is valued across diverse institutional contexts.[3] Student affairs educators' commitment to core professional and moral beliefs can ensure that the pressures of the admission cycle, economic realities, institutional drive for prestige, leadership direction, or social trends do not obscure the value of learning which has a less immediate, tangible, or popular appeal. For example, commitments to social justice by providing educational access, supports for student success, and safe spaces on campus for marginalized groups are a part of the ethos of student affairs and function to emphasize humanitarian learning outcomes, even when they are viewed locally or nationally as a contested good.

Learning as a professed good should be contested rather than settled terrain, open to interrogation, revision, and ongoing dialogue as a reflection of our deliberative democratic society. The broad social context of global competition, student concerns about the value of their education, local institutional direction, professional knowledge, and moral and ethical commitments are all examples of the pressures that should shape an ongoing dialogue about what counts as good in student affairs practice. Entering the contested terrain of what type of learning should be valued extends Kinzie's definition of learning as a professed good and facilitates dialogue about what types of learning outcomes are valued most in daily practice.

Developing a Professional Commitment to Competence

The act of reconciling conflicting pressures and value commitments demands that student affairs educators be competent professionals capable of integrating personal skills with knowledge and values to respond to complex campus problems. Competence, as "politically negotiated and socially situated" requires professionals to have the "ability to perform the tasks and roles to an accepted standard."[4] Being competent requires professionals to engage in ongoing reflection, growth, and personal accountability, key elements of practice in the age of accountability. In student affairs, the emerging 10 competency areas identified by the Joint Committee on Professional Competency of the National Association of Student Personnel Administrators and the American College Personnel Association can inform what counts as good by setting standards for practice and personal accountability.[5] The competency areas are a politically negotiated reflection of professional values commitments, ethical standards, and desired content knowledge. The implementation of these standards in an integrated manner in the complex environment of practice provides a description of the emerging standard for personal professional accountability.

Competent practice is a minimum threshold and a developmental trajectory toward expertise.[6] The trajectory of competence, and the need to know if one's practice is really making a difference should be advanced by the act of reflecting on practice. Donald Schön defines reflective practice as "reflection on action," and "reflection on reflection on action."[7] Reflection on action asks student affairs educators to consider how students receive these educational efforts and asks for educators to make adjustments based on what is and is not working along the way. Reflection on reflection on action asks educators to explicitly verbalize their emerging *in-practice* theories as a means to facilitate ongoing learning about practice. What counts as good in an age of accountability begins with the development and evolution of competent practice, grounded in an integration of value commitments, knowledge, and the activity of reflection that leaves professionals open to constantly evolve to fit new learners, learning demands, and situations.

The Special Role of Assessment as Dialogue

Assessment in student affairs has a special role as a form of evaluation in creating a democratic, deliberative dialogue about what is valued and therefore counted as good.[8] My view differs from Kinzie's in that while measurement of intended learning is a part of assessment, the focus of the assessment is not on gathering data but a process of dialogue.[9] Assessment then is not simply a technical process of data collection and analysis by which the person conducting assessment determines what is good or real but a moral and ethical process that should create credible and actionable evidence that facilitates dialogue and reflection for individuals with varying interests.[10] The process of assessment, and the related collection of credible and actionable evidence, should be an inclusive process guided by six critical elements. Assessment processes should be entered into by practitioners with a willingness to change, foster democratic deliberative dialogue, intentionally engage multiple stakeholders, attend to issues of power, strive to collect credible and actionable evidence, and ask questions of what is in the interest of society.[11]

Just as engaging in reflective practice requires individual willingness to learn, evolve, and change, so too does formal assessment of student affairs. Assessment can be a process of individual and organizational transformation and accountability through dialogue and discovery, but only when individuals have the courage to authentically examine their work and the related learning of students. Assessment should be entered into with humility and hope; humility of what one does not know and hope of a journey of new discovery.[12] Assessment processes are about democratic deliberative dialogue, the type of dialogue that requires meaningful investment, openness to hearing contested points of view, and space to engage in deliberation of contested views of what should be counted as good and real. Assessment is not a process to be rushed for the sake of reaching the end; instead, it is an authentic dialogue where multiple voices and perspectives are valued. One can envision a collection of students, faculty, staff, and alumni of differing backgrounds meeting as a means to discuss an assessment process, akin to a community dialogue session. The related dialogue addresses questions of social reality, as in what is valued, has value and should be valued through data collection. Multiple voices must be given space, specifically those who are often excluded in assessment processes, be they students, community members, parents, faculty, entry-level professionals, or traditionally marginalized communities.

Assessment concerns itself with issues of power and intentionally seeks to hear and then negotiate different views of what counts as good or real. People conducting assessment in student affairs must recognize their own position in the organization and how that limits or facilitates their own contributions to a deliberative, democratic process of dialogue. Data collection, analysis, and use as an extension of a process of dialogue should be concerned with collecting data that is credible and actionable. Credible data must be developed in a manner respectful of quantitative and qualitative method traditions of reliability, validity, and trustworthiness but also responsive to the deliberated views of what different parties see as good (including those with accountability interests). Credible data create information that is actionable, as data should be generated with an aim to be used by specific individuals participating in an assessment process.[13] Finally, individuals who involve themselves in leading assessment processes in student affairs should have a special commitment to go beyond asking whether a particular program is meeting student learning outcome objectives that fit with departmental and institutional mission, and deliberate questions of whether a program is good for society.

Conclusion

Determining what counts as good and knowing if our work in student affairs is really making a difference should not be taken up as a response to an accountability mandate, to ensure programmatic survival in a challenging fiscal climate, or be left to some group of amorphous others to determine. Rather, negotiating what is good and what counts as evidence of making a difference must be a "socially situated, and politically negotiated" component of everyone's practice that is respectful of competing interests, viewpoints, and professional values.[14]

Notes

1. Rawls, J. (1971). *A theory of justice.* Cambridge, MA: Belknap Press of Harvard University Press.

2. Council of Student Personnel Associations. (1994). Student development services in postsecondary education. In A. L. Rentz & G. L. Saddlemier (Eds.), *Student affairs: A profession's heritage* (2nd ed., pp. 150–197). Lanham, MD: University Press of America.

3. Keeling, R. P. (Ed.). (2004). *Learning reconsidered: A campus-wide focus on the student experience.* Washington, DC: National Association of Student Personnel Administrators and American College Personnel Association, pp. 22–23.

4. Eraut, M. (1998). Concepts of competence. *Journal of Interprofessional Care, 12*(2), 127–139, p. 129.

5. National Association of Student Personnel Administrators & American College Personnel Association. (2010, March 2). *Professional competency areas for student affairs practitioners: Informing intentional professional development design and selection* [Working draft]. Washington DC. Author. Retrieved from http://www.naspa.org/DraftCompetency Areas3210.pdf

6. Moulton, C. E., Regehr, G., Mylopoulos, M., & MacRae, H. M. (2007). Slowing down when you should: A new model of expert judgment. *Academic Medicine, 82*(10), S109–S116.

7. Schön, D. (1987). *Educating the reflective practitioner.* San Francisco, CA: Jossey-Bass.

8. House, E. R., & Howe, K. R. (2000). Deliberative democratic evaluation. *New Directions in Evaluation* (85), 3–12. San Francisco, CA: Jossey-Bass.

9. Freire, P. (1972). *The pedagogy of the oppressed.* Harmondsworth, UK: Penguin.

10. Guba, E., & Lincoln, Y. (1989). *Fourth generation evaluation.* Thousand Oaks, CA: Sage.

11. Schwandt, T. A. (2002). *Evaluation practice reconsidered.* New York, NY: Peter Lang; Freire, *Pedagogy of the oppressed*; House & Howe, Deliberative democratic evaluation; Guba & Lincoln, *Fourth generation evaluation.*

12. Freire, *Pedagogy of the oppressed.*

13. Patton, L. (1997). *Utilization focused evaluation.* Thousand Oaks CA: Sage.

14. Eraut, Concepts of competence, p. 129.

Further Reading and Related Blog

Ashya Majied, Miami University

Bresciani, M. J., Zelna, C. L. & Anderson, J. A. (2004). *Assessing student learning and development: A handbook for practitioners.* Washington DC: National Association of Student Personnel Administrators.

This handbook explicitly discusses the importance of student learning assessment in higher education and provides specific examples of how to conceptualize and implement assessment. This guide also synthesizes past research about assessment in student affairs.

Kuh, G. D., & Banta, T. W. (2000). Faculty-student affairs collaboration on assessment: Lessons from the field. *About Campus, 4*(6), 4–11.

This article identifies learning practices in student affairs aimed at enhancing student learning. This work also acknowledges the dichotomy in higher education between academic and student affairs and calls for student affairs professionals to bridge the gap, leading to greater respect and cooperation with faculty.

Schuh, J. H., Upcraft, M. L., & Associates (2001). *Assessment practice in student affairs: An application manual.* San Francisco, CA: Jossey-Bass.

The manual provides specific examples of assessment in student affairs. Schuh and Upcraft focus on qualitative assessment and introduce various assessment studies.

Smith, K. M., & Mather, P. C. (2001). Best practices in student affairs research. *New Directions for Institutional Research* (108), 63–78.

This work emphasizes the importance of the collaboration involving student affairs professionals and institutional researchers. The authors' article on best practices provides specific examples, strategies, and techniques to apply to student affairs research and practice.

Blog URL: contestedissues.wordpress.com
Corresponding Chapter Post: tinyurl.com/contestedissues11

PART THREE

Achieving Inclusive and Equitable Learning Environments

12

Why Is It So Challenging for Collegians and Student Affairs Educators to Talk About Race?

The Elephant in the Room—Race

Julie J. Park, University of Maryland, College Park

In 2009 an issue of *Newsweek* featured a close-up shot of a baby accompanied by the provocative title "Are Babies Racist?" in big bold letters. Once I got over the shock, I found a fairly nuanced article by Po Bronson and Ashley Merriman on how good intentions to raise children as color-blind can backfire.[1] The authors explained how they thought that the best way to pass on the values of equality and multiculturalism to their children would be to expose them to diversity in a variety of ways: attending racially diverse schools, playing with racially diverse kids, and attending dinner parties with their parents' racially diverse friends. Tolerance would just be a way of life. But talk about race? There was no need to. In fact, talking about race was dangerous, because recognizing race would just open the door to racism.

Despite this attempt to communicate that race was irrelevant, Bronson and Merriman found their children were already noticing skin color and formulating their own hypotheses about why it differed among people. In the meantime the authors became more versed on social science research that explains how children tend to develop in-group prefer-ences—favoritism toward those who share a common attribute like skin color. They realized that a collective silence about race discourages con-versation that could help their children make sense of the role race plays in society. Bronson wrote, "Katz's work helped me to realize that Luke was never actually color-blind. He didn't talk about race in his first five years because our silence had unwittingly communicated that race was something he could not ask about."[2]

After I put down the magazine, I thought, "Well, this explains a lot."

Time after time, students have told me that race doesn't matter. I've heard it most often from White students, but I've also heard it from students of color. Reading the *Newsweek* article made me realize that this hesitance to talk about race stems from experiences and encounters that happen years before students even step foot on a college campus. Like Bronson's child, many students and student affairs educators alike have been implicitly or explicitly socialized to the idea that race is something we cannot talk about. Thus, we tend to see race as a problem of the past, and we pay tribute to people like Martin Luther King Jr. who put their lives on the line so we could live in a more progressive society. After all, wasn't the whole point to be able to see people for the content of their character and not the color of their skin?

This color-blind perspective is usually well intentioned. Unfortunately, it ill equips us to respond to today's realities. When people feel they cannot talk about race, how can they begin to explain or understand concepts like the fact that 90% of American Protestant churches are racially homogeneous, as Michael Emerson and colleagues' research has shown?[3] How do they explain the racial profiling phenomenon of driving while Black or flying while Brown? How do they explain the underrepre-sentation of Asian Americans in leadership and management positions? How do they explain that over 50 years after *Brown v. Board of Education* a large proportion of Black, Latino/Latina, and White students still attend intensely segregated schools, as Gary Orfield and the Civil Rights Project have found time and time again?[4] And I could go on and on.

Why is it so challenging for collegians and student affairs educators to talk about race? While I cannot pinpoint a single explanation, in this essay I highlight several reasons that contribute to our society's general hesitation to talk frankly and constructively about race, all of which have major implications for the ability of collegians and student affairs educa-tors to engage in dialogue about race. First, the idea that color blindness is the appropriate way to promote equity hinders people's efforts to talk about race. Second, people have a tendency to associate race with blatant acts of racism but have trouble recognizing the subtler ways race affects society and daily interactions. Third, racist acts result in a climate where not only discussions about race are stifled, but people have difficulty validating one another as knowers on issues of race, a concept that I explain in more detail later.

Color Blindness: Well Intentioned But Inadequate

The first issue that makes talking about race difficult is the widespread idea that color blindness is the best way to promote equity, fairness, and justice. By color blindness, I refer to the desire to downplay or disregard talking about or recognizing race. Anything from a comment (e.g., "I don't see you as Asian, I see you as being like everybody else.") to a policy (e.g., anti-affirmative action ordinances) can reflect color-blind values. As Bronson and Merriman showed, color blindness usually comes from good intentions.[5] Where does the idea come from that being silent about race is actually beneficial to society? In the not-so-distant past, when people were conscious of color and paid attention to race, they did so because they wanted to use race as a justification to discriminate against people of color. There is a reason Martin Luther King Jr. wanted people to judge his children not for the color of their skin but for the content of their character—judging people by their skin color only resulted in bigotry and malice. So once people finally saw the light of day and realized the ignorance inherent in, say, refusing to let Black people eat at the same restaurants as White people, they veered to the other extreme and decided that any sort of mention of race was opening the door to racism. The best solution was to just be silent on race and assume that because civil rights legislation had been passed, the race problem in America was over.

Oftentimes people who promote a color-blind approach to race relations also promote the idea that we are living in a postracial society in which race is an irrelevant construct and racism is a thing of the past. With this line of thinking we are beyond needing to recognize race. After all, Americans elected a Black man, Barack Obama, as president. As the logic goes, anything is possible, and talking about race will only hold people back. Many individuals point to the election of Obama as America's first Black president to argue that America has finally gotten beyond issues of race.

The problem with color blindness, well intentioned as it may be, is that it leaves us without language to talk about the many ways race continues to affect people's lives here and now in the 21st century. As President Obama recognized in his historic speech on race:

> But race is an issue that I believe this nation cannot afford to ignore right now. . . . Understanding this reality requires a reminder of how we arrived at this point. As William Faulkner once wrote, "The past isn't dead and buried. In fact, it isn't even past." We do not need to recite here the history of racial injustice in this country. But we do need to remind ourselves that so many of the disparities that exist in the African American community today can be directly traced to inequalities passed on from an earlier generation that suffered under the brutal legacy of slavery and Jim Crow.[6]

In the same speech, Obama referred to slavery as our nation's "original sin." Original sin is an appropriate metaphor to understand how past racial injustices and inequities continue to affect us today. Some members of the Christian tradition use the term *original sin* to explain how one sin at the beginning of creation (i.e., Adam and Eve disobeying God in the Garden of Eden) has continued to affect people to this very day. Even though people living today obviously had no direct role in what happened, they still have to live with the legacy of a broken world, a brokenness that some believe can be traced to that original sin. Likewise, none of us were alive when the first Americans decided to enslave Black people (or take the land of Native Americans or deny citizenship to Chinese Americans) and perpetuate systemic, institutionalized oppression and discrimination against an entire people. Still, we live with the repercussions today, whether we know it or not. It is our country's original sin, and we are ill equipped to understand how its aftermath affects us today unless we can openly talk about the continuing significance of race in our lives and in society.

The problem with color blindness, well intentioned as it may be, is that it leaves us without language to talk about the many ways race continues to affect people's lives here and now in the 21st century.

One example of how color blindness leaves us unprepared to diagnose and address how race affects our everyday lives on college campuses is Greek life. The continuing racial divide in Greek life is an excellent example of how past racial injustices affect contemporary racial dynamics. From their inception, many Greek letter organizations had explicit exclusionary policies that barred the admission of Black members, and many explicitly barred other non-Whites and Jews. As a result, Black students founded the National Pan-Hellenic Council because they were officially banned from joining groups in the National Panhellenic Conference (NPC) and North-American Interfraternity Council (IFC). As Alfred McClung Lee explained in his book documenting racial divides in Greek life, 10 IFC groups in 1955 still had official exclusionary policies, and 9 others still used language in their by-laws that achieved similar goals, but only one NPC sorority still had a formal ban against students of color.[7] While the lack of exclusionary policies in the NPC may have conveyed the perception that it was more integrated than the IFC, the NPC remained just as homogeneous as its male counterpart during the time. Lee commented, "Although [exclusionary policy] has disappeared from formal documents, Aryanism has not died out; in most cases it is very much alive even though underground."[8]

Fast-forward to contemporary times. While Greek life has made some progress toward diversifying, at many campuses—NPC and IFC groups are as racially homogeneous as they were 50 years ago. A color-blind perspective has little to offer in terms of remedying the situation, because a person holding that perspective believes that while there were troubling exclusionary policies in the past, Greek life is totally open to whomever wants to join today. With this line of logic, there is no race problem in Greek life, and no one is responsible for the lack of diversity in these groups. If anything, the blame lies on people of color for not wanting to join the groups in the first place. As I explained in an article, this color-blind perspective is an overly simple explanation of why racial divides persist in Greek life.[9] Instead, subtler issues, such as students of color feeling unwelcome by Greek life and Greek organizations' resistance to recognizing the relevance of race in the system, perpetuate a culture that does little to break the cycle of homogeneity.

Color blindness leaves student affairs educators without the tools they need to understand why racial divides and inequities persist in higher education. Critical race theory (CRT) is a powerful theoretical tool that provides insight into the issue of color blindness. By emphasizing how race continues to affect everyday life and challenging the idea of a color-blind society, CRT can help student affairs educators diagnose how race may be affecting a situation even in the absence of explicit racism or overt exclusion.

Overt Is Less Common, Subtle Is In

A second key reason student affairs educators and collegians may struggle to converse about race is our tendency to only see race as relevant when overt, blatant acts of racism occur. We are unprepared to recognize and understand how in today's society racial bias is much more likely to be characterized by subtler actions and attitudes. Terms like *symbolic racism*, *subtle racism*, and *aversive racism* all attempt to capture how blatant racism is socially unacceptable in today's society; thus, racial bias manifests itself through different forms besides overt discrimination against or hatred toward people of color.[10] For example, John Gaertner and Samuel Dovidio use aversive racism to explain how most Whites believe racial equality is an important and worthy cause, but they still carry subtle, negative attitudes toward Black people and other people of color.[11] Because it is not socially acceptable to directly express these negative attitudes, individuals will use nonracial terms instead. An example of aversive racism might be the comment, "Of course I'm not prejudiced, I just wouldn't send my children to the neighborhood school because the test scores are so low." Untangling the relevance of race in such a statement is a lot more difficult than in past decades, when people were more forthcoming about their racial bias.

Another example of how race and racial bias are more subtly expressed in current times is the concept of racial microaggressions, which scholars like Chester Pierce, Derald Sue, and Daniel Solórzano have advanced in the literature.[12] Racial microaggressions are subtle, slight comments that remind people of color of their marginalization. They can have a cumulative and fatiguing effect. While teaching at a predominantly White institution located in a rural area, I was never stopped in the street and called "chink" or "gook," nor did I expect anyone to do so. However, on a day-to-day basis I received compliments on my English (perhaps because it's my native and only tongue); questions like, "Where are you from?" (and an accompanying look of confusion when I answer "Dayton, Ohio"); and even once, the befuddling question of "What's your real name?" when I introduced myself as Julie. On an individual basis, these slights are annoying and just something to roll my eyes at. On a cumulative basis, they make me less willing to want to be gracious and patient with others' ignorance. When I read accounts of faculty of color who have left the academy, it is rarely because of a dramatic incident where someone wrote racial slurs outside their door, although these incidents still happen in 21st-century America. Instead, it is the day-to-day strain of being reminded that they are somehow unwelcome and that their voices are not valued. Little things add up, but we sometimes have difficulty engaging in conversations around these subtle dynamics.

Concepts like aversive racism and racial microaggressions highlight some of the complexity behind understanding how race and racial bias have evolved over the years. It is much easier to recognize and address racial prejudice when it is overt and blatant. For instance, in Spring 2009, the University of California, San Diego (UCSD) campus reacted in anger when an off-campus group of students held a ghetto-themed party called the "Compton Cookout," named after an area ghetto, that displayed crude and hurtful stereotypes meant to caricature inner-city life. All of a sudden, UCSD was a center of attention in the national media for the incident, and deservedly so. However, it was much easier for the Compton Cookout to get a response from UCSD administrators than it was for another troubling issue that had been simmering at the school for well over a decade: the continuous low enrollment of Black students and the unsupportive campus climate for Black students at UCSD. Sadly, it took an incident like the Compton Cookout to force UCSD administrators to realize their campus had been an unfriendly environment for Black students even prior to the Compton Cookout.

Similarly, during my undergraduate years, someone vandalized a residence hall bathroom with ugly slurs that targeted multiple racial groups. We mobilized the campus community to speak out against the incident. While it was relatively easy to get people to express outrage against explicit acts of prejudice, it was much more difficult to get people to care about long-term issues such as recruiting and retaining faculty of color and the paucity of staff working on diversity issues. Addressing the bathroom incident was easier because everyone could collectively condemn the anonymous racist cowards who committed the act and then pat themselves on the back for being so enlightened and educated. Addressing an issue like the general chilly campus climate that students of color encountered even when explicit acts of racism were not being committed was a lot riskier.

Perhaps part of the reason talking about race in subtler, nuanced ways is difficult is because doing so requires an ability to recognize individual and institutional/structural responsibility for racial inequities. Racism is easier when we can trace it to deviant individuals. With the Compton Cookout and the bathroom vandalism, there were people to blame, and thus the general response was to educate the ignorant individuals on the hurtful implications of their actions. While I recognize the good intentions behind this response, I question the long-term effectiveness. Things like the Compton Cookout are connected to broader, systemic inequities in society. For instance, Proposition 209 banned affirmative action in the state of California, which is partially responsible for why UCSD only has a 2% Black student population. This lack of structural diversity means there is a very, very small chance that students involved in organizing the Compton Cookout party would ever have a chance to sit in a class with, let alone befriend, a Black student at UCSD. The racial and socioeconomic stratification of California public schools makes it very unlikely that a student from Compton would ever attend UCSD in the first place. And UCSD as an institution is also responsible for having done little in past years to foster a supportive campus racial climate, further exacerbating its enrollment problem. Looking at the role that structural inequities and institutions play in setting the stage for something like the Compton Cookout to happen is a lot more complicated than addressing the immediate problem of how to deal with the students who threw the party. However, if student affairs educators want to challenge students to think about long-term solutions and institutional change, just exhorting individual students to reject racism will do little to change problems that go much deeper.

Seeking Students as Knowers About Race: A Risky But Valuable Proposition

Finally, the last reason that I offer why conversations about race in campus communities are difficult to have is related to Marcia Baxter Magolda's learning partnerships model.[13] Baxter Magolda stipulates that learning partnerships support self-authorship, an internally coordinated belief and values system, through validating students as knowers, situating learning in students' own experiences, and defining learning as mutually constructed meaning. When it comes to discussing race, I suggest that one reason White students in particular often falter is because they generally do not feel validated as knowers on the subject of race or feel capable of having anything to contribute to the conversation. This is an ironic dynamic considering that students at times overestimate their knowledge and understanding of issues of race and thus come into dialogues unwilling to validate others' knowledge and experiences. Furthermore, when some students participate in dialogues on race, it is easy to not want to validate their capacity as knowers when they espouse problematic viewpoints. In *Creating Contexts for Learning and Self-Authorship*, Baxter Magolda wrote, "validating students as knowers validates their capability to think and construct knowledge, it does not validate misunderstanding of concepts under study or interpretations that lack foundation."[14] Validating students as knowers about the issue of race does not mean that everything goes and that any viewpoint is legitimate. However, honoring the capacity of students and student affairs educators to know is a valuable foundation for entering conversations on race.

"Why do you think that?" can be a simple, but disarming question that makes students take a step back, go off autopilot, and reflect on why they believe what they believe.

One way we can validate students as potential knowers regarding issues of race is by inviting them to coconstruct meaning and understanding on issues of race. Too often I see students, particularly White students, talk about a diversity workshop or class where they seem to have appreciated the knowledge they gained from a facilitator or professor but had little room to add their own voice to the conversation. At other times they may express resentment at being preached at. At one institution I heard students refer to a certain class as the "White Guilt" class. In such scenarios, political correctness about race becomes what Baxter Magolda would call an "external formula." Students come to see racial sensitivity as important because someone in authority told them they needed to, but they lack an internal foundation for independently understanding why we want them to care about issues of race and diversity. Inviting students to coconstruct meaning on issues of race is a somewhat scary and risky concept to me as a faculty member of color. It is tempting for me to not want to give students space to grapple, sometimes awkwardly, with issues that are so personal to me. I am also cognizant of how giving students space to say what they really think opens the possibility of them saying things that may grieve other students in the classroom.

When a student says something that I see as problematic, I am tempted to draw from my arsenal of statistics and academic language to offer an authoritative-sounding counterpoint. I am still learning how to take a second, breathe, and ask a question that can challenge a student to go deeper or consider the issue from a different perspective. Sometimes, "Why do you think that?" can be a simple, but disarming question that makes students take a step back, go off autopilot, and reflect on why they believe what they believe. These are hard things to do, and thus I am not surprised that students and student affairs educators alike have difficulty having honest and authentic conversations about race. Still, the learning partnerships model provides a helpful pedagogical tool to encourage students and educators alike to enter into conversations about race with a posture of learning.

In summary, there is no single reason that having conversations on race is so difficult for students and student affairs educators, but I hope that my analysis of these three topics sheds light on some of the barriers to talking about race. Bronson and Merriman's article also reminded me that it is unsurprising that students come into college so hesitant to use color-conscious language and often have difficulty recognizing and articulating the many complexities and nuances that surround issues of race.[15] After all, many of our students have experienced a minimum of 18 years of socialization that basically runs in the opposite direction of what we are trying to do as student affairs educators. No wonder these conversations are difficult! However, student affairs educators can play a powerful role in expanding students' horizons to different ways of understanding the complicated world around them.

Notes

1. Bronson, P., & Merriman, A. (2009). See baby discriminate. *Newsweek*. Retrieved from http://www.newsweek.com/2009/09/04/see-baby-discriminate.html

2. Bronson & Merriman, See baby discriminate., p. 5.

3. Emerson, M. O., & Chai Kim, K. (2003). Multiracial congregations: An analysis of their development and a typology. *Journal for the Scientific Study of Religion, 42*(2), 217–227.

4. Orfield, G. (2009). *Reviving the goal of an integrated society: A 21st century challenge.* Los Angeles, CA: Civil Rights Project/Proyecto Derechos Civiles at UCLA.

5. Bronson & Merriman, See baby discriminate.

6. Obama, B. (2008). *Transcript: Barack Obama's speech on race.* Retrieved from http://www.npr.org/templates/story/story.php?storyId = 88478467

7. Lee, A. M. (1955). *Fraternities without brotherhood: A campus report on racial and religious prejudice.* Boston, MA: Beacon.

8. Ibid., p. 78.

9. Park, J. J. (2008). Race and the Greek system in the 21st century: Centering the voices of Asian American women. *NASPA Journal, 45*(1), 103–132.

10. Researched extensively by David Sears, symbolic racism is expressed through ideas such as thinking societal inequities persist because Black people are unable to take responsibility for their own lives, or that racial discrimination is no longer a major factor in people's lives. Subtle racism is based on the work of Thomas Pettigrew in Pettigrew, T. F., & Meertens, R. W. (1995). Subtle and blatant prejudice in Western Europe. *European Journal of Social Psychology, 25,* 57–75.

11. Dovidio, J. F., & Gaertner, S. L. (2000). Aversive racism and selection decisions: 1989 and 1999. *Psychological Science, 11*(4), 315–319.

12. Sears, D. (1988). Symbolic racism. In P. A. Katz & D. A. Taylor (Eds.), *Eliminating racism: Profiles in controversy* (pp. 53–84). New York, NY: Plenum; Solórzano, D., Ceja, M., Yosso, T. (2000). Critical race theory, racial microaggressions, and the campus racial climate: The experiences of African American college students. *Journal of Negro Education, 69*(1–2), 60–73; Sue, D. (2010). *Microaggressions in everyday life: Race, gender, and sexual orientation.* Hoboken, NJ: Wiley.

13. Baxter Magolda, M. B. (1999). *Creating contexts for learning and self-authorship: Constructive-developmental pedagogy.* Nashville, TN: Vanderbilt University Press.

14. Ibid., p. 73.

15. Bronson & Merriman, See baby discriminate.

Far From Perfection, Closer Than Ever Before

Employing New Forums to Facilitate Dialogues About Race

Chris Mundell, Columbus College of Art and Design

As a relatively new student affairs practitioner, I recall vividly the moment when I realized the level of complexity and challenge that comes with engaging today's college students in meaningful dialogues about race. It was the summer of 2007, and I had been on the job for just a few weeks. I entered a computer lab on campus one afternoon to find a group of students gathered as a YouTube music video played on the screen in front of them. Nothing stood out about the group aside from the fact that their racial diversity would have made a dream photo-op for any college admissions office. They laughed together and shared expressions of apparent bemusement. As I sat down at a computer station near them, I noticed that the laughter had shifted to conversation and one of the students remarked about the "random" and "lame" nature of the video. Another student then abruptly said, "Actually, I think the song's about being Black." The reaction to his statement was complete and utter silence among the group. The fun had ended, and facial expressions changed from smiles to puzzlement as the students struggled with how to react. Finally, a student in the group filled the void. "I really don't think it's a racial thing. Don't take things so seriously. The video was just a joke." As quickly as the conversation started it was now over, and the group shifted its attention—most likely to another Internet site. An opportunity for an honest dialogue about race had been lost, but why?

As it turns out, the students were watching the soon-to-be infamous viral music video *Chocolate Rain* posted on YouTube in April 2007 by the artist Tay Zonday.[1] The video features an African American teenager performing a song with oblique, but deceptively insightful, lyrics about the state of race relations in America. The video went on to attain Internet sensation status as it was played repeatedly on college campuses across the country. However, the song's allegory about modern-day racism rarely entered into the collective discussion.

In Julie Park's essay, she identifies three distinct barriers that keep collegians and student affairs professionals from engaging in meaningful dialogues about race: the misguided ideal of a color-blind society, the lack of awareness about subtler forms of racism, and our collective difficulty validating each other as knowers on the subject of race. The uncomfortable exchange I witnessed about the racial video is yet another example of how these barriers prevent authentic dialogue from occurring among college students. More specifically, this casual conversation among students exemplified what Park describes as "our society's general hesitation to talk frankly and constructively about race" (p. 226). While I agree with the notion that early childhood socialization steers students away from discussing race, I also believe there is value in further examining and, perhaps, challenging that explanation. Specifically, I suggest that dialogues about race do occur among college students and within the broader society—but they often happen within nontraditional forums that can make them difficult to recognize. These conversations take place on the Internet via discussion boards, blogs, social networking websites, and the various other forms of instantaneous public exchange provided by the expanding reach of digital technology. The structure of the Internet as a medium, including its capacity for anonymity, poses challenges and opportunities for student affairs professionals. As educators, our main challenge will be to find ways of harnessing these new forums to inform and elevate the dialogue.

A second point of contention centers on Park's belief that people "have trouble recognizing the subtler ways race affects society and daily interactions" (p. 227). That some people are unable to recognize or confront subtle racist behavior can only partially explain the pushing back that student affairs professionals receive when we ask students to consider issues from the perspective of race. Another interpretation is to consider we may be witnessing the emergence of a generation that acknowledges the continued existence of racism but at the same time seeks to challenge the degree to which it actually preserves inequalities and the degree to which it matters in their daily lives. Evidence exists to support the notion that America's young people have developed postracial attitudes, but they are still conflicted about matters of race in other key areas. For example, a 2010 Pew Research Center study of the millennial generation finds broad support among 18- to 29-year-olds for interracial marriage.[2] Roughly 9 in 10 respondents say they would be fine with a family member's marriage to someone of a different racial or ethnic group. In this area, it seems that race matters less to college students now, when compared to the callused ways it did in the not so distant past. However, the same Pew Center study indicates a growing gap between African Americans and

Whites in regard to perceptions of racial discrimination and the degree to which it still affects society.[3] What remains is a complex paradox that illustrates why it's so difficult to get students to talk about race. They are over this conversation in important ways we need to recognize and honor. However, the need for more dialogue is clear on other matters pertaining to race, which reinforces the notion that student affairs professionals must be intentional and nuanced in our approach to these discussions.

Recognize the Forum, Change the Dialogue

In his 1985 book, *Amusing Ourselves to Death*, Neil Postman laments what he viewed as a gradual decline in public discourse in America because of the rising influence of electronic media—at that time mainly television. Postman's work uses a sociological and philosophical lens to suggest that "all public discourse increasingly takes the form of entertainment" and therefore fundamentally changes how people understand their world and enter into meaningful dialogue with each other.[4] To take the idea further, he asserted that the medium used to communicate information has a vast influence on the ideas individuals can express. For example, think about how the traditional format of the nightly television news (each story told in under 2 minutes arranged around brief interview sound bites and video footage) influences the way many Americans obtain the news and understand the world. What does this mean for student affairs educators seeking to engage students in meaningful discussions about race? I believe it calls us to consider the forum (i.e., the Internet) where many important dialogues happen among our students and how this medium presents opportunities and challenges to extending the dialogue.

A prime example of digital media as the forum for discussions about race surfaced in November 2008 when a student athlete at the University of Texas (UT) posted a message about the election of Barack Obama as president on his personal Facebook page.[5] His comments read, "All the hunters gather up, we have a [racial slur] in the White House." The incident resulted in a flurry of media attention and the swift dismissal of the student from the university's football team. Upon further reflection, the exact words this student chose are of less significance than what his decision to post them communicates about where and how racial dialogues occur among college students. Before the UT student's post was taken down, several of his friends had posted their own comments in response, and once the story reached the national news media it became fodder for even more discussions among college students on Facebook, Twitter, and elsewhere. In this instance, it is difficult to determine whether the student's post about the president was an offensive joke or an example of his grappling with his feelings about race in a very public way. Regardless, it is a prime example of where contemporary dialogues about race happen and the manner in which they take place. Although students may hesitate to speak up at campus-sponsored diversity programs or when class discussions turn to race, they are not always silent on these issues.

Today's college students reside in a world that expects random access to connected information in an environment that blurs the lines between entertainment, stimulation, and authentic dialogue. Dialogues about race are bound to take shape in this medium and in a similar format.

Overall, many educational and social science researchers have noted that young people are increasingly more likely to make provocative comments and invite contested dialogue within the realm of their digital social networks. Palfrey and Gasser use the term *digital native* to define the freewheeling online identity displayed by young people who are "native speakers" of the digital language of computers, video games, and the Internet.[6] To describe how digital natives gather information and participate in public discourses, Palfrey and Gasser outline "a multi-step process that involves grazing, a deep dive, and a feedback loop."[7] These authors illustrate what this process looks like by using the example of a first-year collegian interested in learning about the Middle East who begins her search online:

> With some of the stories she sees, she decides she wants to go beyond the headline, to learn more about a topic or event—to take a deep dive. In this

way, she is searching for what's behind the headline, what the facts are, what it might mean for her, what the people involved looked like, and so forth. It might mean clicking on a hypertext link, loading up a video, or downloading a pod cast to listen to on the train. The deep dive helps her to make sense of the news, to put it into a frame or better context, to offer an analysis of it, to introduce relevant other voices.[8]

As student affairs educators, we are well aware of how college students use digital media to conceptualize their identity, make social commentary, and share information for their friends or followers to graze. Many of these digital exchanges are mundane, but sometimes they can be quite profound. In the context of dialogues about race, it is not unusual for race to enter the conversation during the grazing phase. I can personally attest to observing many exchanges not unlike the one described at the start of this essay about the controversial YouTube video. Today's college students reside in a world that expects random access to connected information in an environment that blurs the lines between entertainment, stimulation, and authentic dialogue. Dialogues about race are bound to take shape in this medium and in a similar format. Our challenge, therefore, is to engage students in taking the deep dive into what their friend's comment really meant or what may be behind the provocative news headline. How do we engage students in deeper and more thoughtful discussions in these forums? I have no formula or road map, but I know that it starts with educators who are willing to take intentional risks to achieve the rewards of authentic dialogue. For example, many in our field use social networking sites such as Facebook to connect with our students. Fewer have likely been willing to use that medium as a way to publicly examine their own thoughts about race relations or to invite students to do the same. Furthermore, if today's students respond best to information that is instantaneous and entertaining, the best way to engage them may be through the creation of our own multimedia content using humor, sarcasm, or provocation to kick-start the conversation.

Concluding Thoughts—Engaging a New Generation

Another key barrier to dialogue Park identified is society's general lack of awareness about subtler forms of racism. As an African American male, I can easily relate to her frustration about the hidden impact of subtle yet insulting comments or stereotypes based on skin color. For example, I am keenly aware of the subtext behind compliments I receive about my eloquence or ability to draft a persuasive e-mail (i.e., "I have low expectations for the articulateness of Black males."). Even among my student affairs colleagues it is frequently assumed that I must be in a minority affairs/support role on my campus (i.e., "Why else would *he* enter this field?").

Given that these microaggressions are the most common form of racism directed toward and perpetrated by students, it would make sense to use critical race theory as a construct to expose these problems and move toward authentic dialogue as Park suggests. However, in doing so we must be careful to not unwittingly communicate that students (especially White students) are all ignorant to the ongoing existence of racism. In Park's essay she asserts that White students "generally do not feel validated as knowers on the subject of race or feel capable of having anything to contribute to the conversation" (p. 233). I certainly recognize this as a common mentality among students. However, I have also encountered (in equal measure) students who get turned off to discussing matters of race because educators have assumed they did not understand the subtle and complex ways racial prejudices continue in our society. Many students today do recognize the existence of racism and its ongoing impact, but they genuinely disagree with the necessity of continuing to discuss it. In the eyes of these individuals, they get that institutionalized racism still exists—but also believe it is slowly but surely fading away. And if slavery stands as our country's original sin (as our president has suggested), these students believe it is a fair question to ask when we will know that redemption has been achieved.

Clearly, many challenges exist to engaging students in authentic and learning-oriented discussions about race. Park illuminates the key barriers that inhibit dialogue while also offering theoretical tools (e.g., critical race theory and the learning partnerships model) that can help student affairs educators to overcome these barriers. My reflections here seek to further our understanding of how to use these tools to infiltrate a medium (the Internet/digital media) that holds many possibilities as an incubator for dialogues about race. Furthermore, I also challenge student affairs practitioners to consider new strategies for engaging a contemporary generation of students who may be more prepared than we think to take these discussions to a higher plane.

Notes

1. Zonday, T. (2007, April 22). *Chocolate rain* [Music video]. Retrieved from http://www.youtube.com/watch?v = EwTZ2xpQwpA

2. Pew Research Center. (2010). *Millennials: A Portrait of Generation Next.* Retrieved from http://pewresearch.org/millennials/

3. Ibid., p. 13.

4. Postman, N. (1985). *Amusing ourselves to death: Public discourse in the age of show business.* New York, NY: Penguin Books, p. 3.

5. Read, B. (2008). *U. of Texas Kicks Football Player Off Team for Anti-Obama Comment on Facebook.* Retrieved from http://chronicle.com/blogs/wiredcampus/u-of-texas-kicks-football-player-off-team-for-anti-obama-comment-on-facebook/4371

6. Palfrey, J., & Gasser, U. (2008). *Born digital: Understanding the first generation of digital natives.* New York, NY: Basic Books.

7. Ibid., p. 241.

8. Ibid., p. 242.

Further Reading and Related Blog

Sue Ann Huang, University of Washington

Emerson, M. O., & Yancey, G. (2010). *Transcending racial barriers: Toward a mutual obligations approach.* New York, NY: Oxford University Press.

Emerson and Yancey trace racism in American society from the perspectives of the White majority and people of color, examining the historical views both sides take in pushing responsibility away from their groups. Emerson and Yancey provide approaches that take into account perspectives of both groups and their mutual values and goals in dealing with racial tensions in American society. This book is a good primer for understanding racism in American society and higher education.

Hurtado, S., Clayton-Pedersen, A. R., Allen, W. R., & Millem, J. F. (1998). Enhancing campus climates for racial/ethnic diversity: Educational policy and practice. *The Review of Higher Education, 21*(3), 279–302.

The authors summarize current and past research on campus climates according to a four-dimensional model: an institution's history of inclusion/exclusion of various ethnic/racial groups, structural diversity or numbers of various ethnic/racial groups, psychological climate between and among groups, and campus intergroup relations and behavior. The authors provide suggestions for changing and improving educational policies.

Smith, D. G. (2009). *Diversity's promise for higher education: Making it work.* Baltimore, MD: Johns Hopkins University Press.

Smith's book provides a comprehensive look at diversity in higher education over the past 40 years. She asserts that just as technology is crucial for higher education institutions to address, institutions need to view diversity in the same light. Whereas diversity work was for individuals in the past, Smith suggests that now it needs to be the work of institutions.

Blog URL: contestedissues.wordpress.com
Corresponding Chapter Post: tinyurl.com/contestedissues12

13

Do Identity Centers (e.g., Women's Centers, Ethnic Centers, LGBT Centers) Divide Rather Than Unite Higher Education Faculty, Students, and Administrators? If So, Why Are They So Prevalent on College Campuses?

Identity Centers: An Idea Whose Time Has Come . . . and Gone?

Kristen A. Renn, Michigan State University

The answer to the question posed in the title of this essay depends in part on which faculty, students, or administrators one is concerned about dividing or uniting. Historically, identity centers have brought together faculty, students, and administrators within the communities represented in the centers, but they have also become lightning rods for accusations of self-segregation or campus balkanization and locations for in-group discrimination (e.g., racism in lesbian, gay, bisexual, and transgender [LGBT] centers, sexism in ethnic centers). Identity centers are one institutional response to helping students cope with campus climates characterized by outright hostility and subtler, but no less harmful, microaggressions. They are also sites of positive, strengths-based identity development. Yet, the idea persists that women or students of color or LGBT students who get together in their own centers are practicing reverse sexism, racism, or heterosexism; a common criticism is that identity centers create spaces that deprive majority students of opportunities to meet the other. I propose four reasons these centers exist and should remain: (a) they respond to noninclusive campus climates, (b) they are part of the ecology of identity groups on campus, (c) some centers play a role in bridging academic and student affairs, and (d) they carry on traditions and have a symbolic function. First, however, I define identity centers and present the case for centers as dividing, rather than uniting, forces.

Identity Centers in Higher Education

So-called identity centers are institutionally supported locations for the provision of programs and services related to members of one or more historically underrepresented groups in higher education. They often but not always have a designated space—sometimes a building, a room, or part of a larger room. Centers may be based on ethnic, racial, gender, religious, ability, or sexual orientation identities, among others. In some cases, individual groups (e.g., Black, Asian American, Latino/Latina, American Indian) have separate centers or spaces within a shared center. In other cases, such as at Spokane Community College, all underrepresented racial and ethnic groups exist under the umbrella of multicultural student services. A few campuses, such as The Ohio State University, include gender and sexual orientation under the multicultural center umbrella, though most often a women's center or LGBT center stands apart from the racial and ethnic identity groups. Students of faith-based identities are typically served by religious staff (e.g., clergy, chaplains), and students with disabilities may find identity-related programs in a campus office primarily focused on assessment and accommodation of disabilities. But at Bryn Mawr College, for example, these students are included in the Office of Intercultural Affairs/Multicultural Center with gender, sexuality, race, and ethnicity.

On some campuses identity centers are staffed by a full-time or part-time professional or a graduate assistant; elsewhere they are run by students, volunteers, or paid paraprofessionals. Occasionally, they are led by faculty members who may have release time from other professional responsibilities. Educators who work in identity centers have formed organizations for professional networking and development (e.g., Association for Black Culture Centers, http://www.abcc.net; Consortium of Higher Education LGBT Resource Professionals, http://www.lgbtcampus.org). They are also represented in student affairs professional associations in commissions (e.g., American College Personnel Association) or knowledge communities (e.g., National Association for Student Personnel Administrators). No matter what their configuration and staffing, identity centers as a whole polarize supporters and critics in academe.

Identity Centers as Spaces That Separate

Identity centers are typically designed to promote learning and development of students defined as disempowered, underrepresented, or otherwise in need of designated support programs and services. Often universities created these centers in response to student activism or a significant discriminatory act. Although it is rare for centers to actively exclude students from other backgrounds (e.g., men, White students, heterosexuals), campus cultures often dictate that identity centers belong to the group whose interests they represent.

Many outsiders to these groups are afraid to challenge these norms or even to explore activities they would be openly welcome to participate in. They may feel excluded, confused, or resentful that minority students have their own center; there could never be, for example, a White student center. They may also feel deprived of interaction with diverse others, running counter to the goal of "helping to promote racial understanding," which John Pryor and colleagues at the Cooperative Institutional Research Program reported 33.1% of entering students nationwide shared in 2009.[1] Beverly Daniels Tatum addressed this intergroup dynamic in *"Why Are All the Black Kids Sitting Together in the Cafeteria?" And Other Conversations About Race.*[2] As Tatum pointed out in the context of race, students who live with unearned privilege are not always prepared to understand why others might want or need a space of their own, away from real or perceived scrutiny.

In an *About Campus* article in which she debunked several myths about cultural centers, Lori Patton outlined arguments of campus constituents who believe identity centers are divisive.[3] This camp points to cultural center staff not collaborating with campus colleagues, and minority students being encouraged to depend only on one another rather than use campus programs and services designed for all students. A third argument is that cultural centers actively discourage students from reaching out beyond their own group, hampering their development and that of students from other groups.

Students who live with unearned privilege are not always prepared to understand why others might want or need a space of their own, away from real or perceived scrutiny.

Patton provides counterevidence for each of these claims, although cultural centers do in fact separate people on the basis of identity. They bring attention to differences between groups, not the commonalities they share as members of a campus community. They point out a paradox of the Millennial generation, the most demographically diverse to date in U.S. history, yet Millennials have been raised in the most segregated public schools in decades. This is a generation of students who want to believe differences have been overcome, but they lack the intercultural skills necessary to level the playing field. Identity centers are physical representations of this paradox. Millennial students unhappy with what they perceive as the divisive effects of identity centers may find allies in faculty and administrators who are veterans of the multicultural battles of the 1990s when they argued against the balkanization of the curriculum into ever narrower slices of knowledge rooted in marginalized histories and cultures. According to this group, identity centers are another representation of intellectual and interpersonal self-segregation. Yet they persist. Why?

Campus Climate and Student Success

The first reason I advocate for the persistence of identity centers is that campus climate for members of all groups is not yet equally inclusive and supportive. Sylvia Hurtado and colleagues described a framework for understanding campus climate, which includes four factors: historical legacy of inclusion or exclusion, structural diversity, psychological dimension, and behavioral dimension.[4] In assessing these four components, few if any institutions can claim to have created inclusive climates for members of all racial, ethnic, gender, and sexual orientation groups, to say nothing of faith tradition, ability, age, and veteran status. Even on campuses with well-intentioned faculty, students, and staff, students from underrepresented groups experience what Daniel Solórzano, Tara Yosso, and Miguel Ceja called microaggressions—the day-to-day messages that these students do not completely belong at the institution.[5] These hostile campus climates—or hostile subclimates, such as those for women and students of color in science, technology, and engineering—contribute to differential outcomes in student success.

As Lori Patton pointed out in a second article on Black culture centers, identity centers create buffers against microaggressions and other negative aspects of the campus climate.[6] They form counterspaces for and by students who share identities that are not reflected positively across Hurtado and colleagues' four components. Identity centers help students from similar backgrounds find one another, and they create a sense of critical mass. They may also represent a physical refuge—a place where students can express themselves freely without worrying about the omnipresent scrutiny they feel elsewhere on campus.

Some identity centers offer extensive academic support programs conducted by professionals and peers. At Portland State University, Minnesota's Century College, and South Dakota State University, academic support is woven into the fabric of the multicultural centers, which also provide programs and services common to identity centers. Utah Valley University includes an Educational Opportunity Center with Federal TRIO Programs in its multicultural center. To be clear, not all students who might find themselves represented in an identity center need academic support beyond what is available to students in general, but for those who do need some assistance, having access to it in a context that is culturally comfortable is valuable.

Identity centers also create positive locations for strengths-based development of intellectual and psychosocial domains. Leadership programs, for example, in identity centers provide valuable opportunities for students to develop skills and confidence to use in the general campus environment. Identity centers sometimes house resources (e.g., library, media collection) students can access for academic purposes. Centers also bring together students across the academic years, providing opportunities for younger students to find role models and mentors among their more senior peers. Rather than being seen as a center where students from nonprivileged groups go for support in assimilating to campus norms (a deficiency approach), a strengths-based perspective illuminates the ways centers can capitalize on students' experiences and identities to motivate success in a number of domains. This perspective partially explains the persistence of identity centers in the face of criticisms previously mentioned.

Identity centers help students from similar backgrounds find one another, and they create a sense of critical mass.

Ecology of Identity Groups

As I described in an article on biracial students at predominantly White institutions, identity-based groups may operate on campus in an ecology of peer culture that promotes or inhibits cross-group permeability based on factors such as critical mass and the overall campus climate for diversity.[7] Identity centers create physical space that can be claimed by students who share that identity. This sense of ownership may lead to the persistence of identity centers, but it does not necessarily lead to excluding students from other groups. For example, biracial students on one campus I studied described a climate that encouraged students from different groups to interact and create friendships across identities. They attributed this climate in part to the small size of the campus (1,400 students) and the small number of students of color (140), a situation that led groups to open their spaces and organizations beyond those individuals who shared an identity. The multicultural center on this campus included issues of race, ethnicity, gender, and sexual orientation among its charges.[8]

In the same article, I described two other campuses where the peer cultures led to rigid boundaries around groups and clear—though often tacit—rules about who was authentic or legitimate enough to belong. On these campuses, biracial students saw identity centers based on race and ethnicity as spaces exclusively for students of color, and particularly for students of color who identified strongly with their race or ethnicity. Historical and contemporary forces in the overall campus culture acted against any impulse groups might have had to be more inclusive. Membership in student groups based on race, ethnicity, and nationality (e.g., Black Student Union, Latino/Latina Alliance, Korean Student Organization) were a sign of one's legitimate claim to that identity; conversely, being seen as authentic in one's identity (e.g., speaking a language, eating ethnic foods, wearing ethnic clothing/symbols) was an unspoken requirement for acceptance by the group.[9] In these contexts, multicultural centers focused exclusively on race and ethnicity, operating as administrative structures in tandem with student cultures to celebrate the uniqueness and contributions of discrete groups. A decade later, in her article on biracial students and race-oriented student services, Patricia Literte noted that a similar "left-liberal racial project," still left out students who did not identify monoracially.[10]

Of course, campuses may blend the two approaches I observed on these three campuses. Student identity politics have evolved over time, and student affairs professionals have learned new ways to promote the dual goals of supporting individual identity communities and cultivating commitment to shared community values. Wherever identity centers fall in this mix of support for individual and community development, attention to the ecology of peer culture is warranted. How does peer culture promote or inhibit student mobility across identity groups? How do biases that may exist within one identity center (e.g., a predominantly White LGBT center or a male-dominated ethnic organization) affect students whose identities span multiple nonprivileged groups? It is critical for professionals to understand the role of peer culture in students' experience within, across, and outside identity centers. This understanding helps to answer, in part, the question of the utility of the identity center model in the 21st-century campus context.

Bridging Academic and Student Affairs

Student affairs professionals may first think of identity centers as part of the cocurriculum, places where students gather for programs, networking, and support. But some identity centers emerged from efforts to broaden the curriculum to include women's studies, gay and lesbian studies (now queer studies), and ethnic studies. Located first within academic programs, these centers evolved to include educational programming and support for identity-based student organizations. The Sarah Doyle Women's Center at Brown University and the Center for Black Culture and Research at West Virginia University are examples.

Conversely, students have sometimes used the leadership and organizing resources of identity centers to mobilize for the creation of academic programs. For example, as reported online by the Committee on Institutional Cooperation, Asian American student organizations and faculty at the University of Illinois at Urbana-Champaign came together to demand an Asian American studies interdisciplinary academic program.[11]

Student affairs professionals often lament the gap between their work and that of their faculty colleagues, but identity centers provide a point of connection that goes both ways, from curriculum to cocurriculum and back. Faculty—who may be seen as more permanent members of the campus community than students or student affairs professionals—may be one reason for the persistence of identity centers. Those faculty members who teach in areas related to race, ethnicity, gender, and sexuality may have an interest in supporting the visibility of identity centers and the student populations they serve. This academic–student affairs connection is another reason these centers persist—faculty have an interest in perpetuating resources on campus for students from underrepresented groups and for pursuing their own work in identity-related scholarship.

Tradition, Symbolism, and Identity Politics

Higher education in the United States is bound by tradition, symbolism, and identity politics. These forces combine in institutions to create powerful motives to maintain the status quo, whatever it is. Although on many campuses it took a substantial effort to overcome this inertia to establish identity centers, now that they are in place, the effort and political cost to transform or close them would be even greater.

Undergraduate students move through an institution on 4- to 6-year cycles. It therefore takes very little time for a new identity center to be seen as a tradition that was always part of campus life. Says the sophomore of a 3-year-old office: "We've *always* had an LGBT Resource Center!"—and she is correct that in her experience, the office has always been there. As George Kuh and Elizabeth Whitt pointed out in their foundational work on student culture, "Institutional policies and practices are culture driven and culture bound."[12] Traditions are a vital component of campus culture. Messing with a campus tradition is a dangerous business for administrators, no matter how well meaning their intentions.

Identity centers are also powerful symbols of the institution's commitment to diversity and support for students from a certain identity group. They signify an investment of resources (e.g., space, staff, budget) and a recognition that the group belongs to the campus community. Beyond the individual campus level, experts who study campus climate consider the presence of an identity center to be a valuable symbol of institutional commitment to the group. For example, when Brett Genny Beemyn, Sue Rankin, and Shane Windmeyer designed an online index to assess LGBT campus climates, they included questions about the presence and activities of an LGBT resource center.[13]

Even if campus leaders determined they wanted to close an identity center, the forces acting against them would be difficult to overcome. Who wants to be the vice president of student affairs who closed the Women's Center or the Queer Resource Office or the Multicultural Center? What kind of message would such an action send to women, LGBT people, and people of color on campus? Even in a context where the campus climate was supportive of all students, the political deck would be stacked against taking such an action. Indeed, closing a center could be seen as creating a less welcoming climate, particularly if the person doing the closing is not a member of the identity group. Reorganization and renaming of centers have happened on some campuses, such as at Michigan State University, in response to external political forces (in Michigan State's case, the passage of a statewide ballot initiative that forbids public educational institutions to, as the League of Women Voters documented, "discriminate against, or grant preferential treatment to, any individual or group on the basis of race, sex, color, ethnicity, or national origin") or to budget reallocation.[14] But for the most part, identity centers persist in some format across a range of institutional types, and traditions, symbolism, and politics contribute to their persistence.

Conclusion

Although identity centers can be seen as divisive, they continue to exist because they serve critical functions that support student learning and success. They operate within a system of campus politics and symbols that reinforces their importance in supporting students from diverse identity categories. They link academic and student affairs in mutually supportive ways. Identity centers clearly have a place in higher education at the beginning of the 21st century.

Do they have a place in the university of the future? Certainly the financial constraints facing higher education are not going to improve, and supporting multiple identity centers on a campus could be seen to draw resources away from the central academic mission. I argue that until all students can partake equitably in that central academic mission, with equitable outcomes, the need for identity-based support for students remains. In an age of increasing diversity yet inequitable student outcomes, I suggest an emphasis on supporting centers as providing separate, but not separatist, resources that support success for marginalized students.

Notes

1. Pryor, J. H., Hurtado, S., DeAngelo, L., Palucki Blake, L., & Tran, S. (2009). *The American freshman: National norms fall 2009.* Los Angeles, CA: Higher Education Research Institute, University of California, Los Angeles.

2. Tatum, B. D. (2003). *"Why are all the Black kids sitting together in the cafeteria?" And other conversations about race.* New York, NY: Basic Books.

3. Patton, L. D. (2006). Black culture centers: Still central to student learning. *About Campus, 11*(2), 2–8.

4. Hurtado, S., Milem, J. F., Clayton-Pederson, A. R., & Allen, W. R. (1998). Enhancing campus climates for racial/ethnic diversity: Policy and practice. *Review of Higher Education, 21*(3), 279–302.

5. Solórzano, D., Yosso, T., & Ceja, M. (2000). Critical race theory, racial microaggressions, and campus racial climate: The experiences of African American college students. *Journal of Negro Education, 69*(1–2), 60–73.

6. Patton, L. D. (2006). The voice of reason: A qualitative examination of Black student perceptions of Black culture centers. *Journal of College Student Development, 47*(6), 628–646.

7. Renn, K. A. (2000). Patterns of situational identity among biracial and multiracial college students. *Review of Higher Education, 23*(4), 399–420.

8. Renn, Patterns of situational identity.

9. Ibid.

10. Literte, P. E. (2010). Revising race: How biracial students are changing and challenging student services. *Journal of College Student Development, 51*(2), 115–134, p. 125. doi: 10.1353/csd.0.0122

11. Committee on Institutional Cooperation. (2010). Asian American studies in the Big Ten universities: An overview of the field's development in the Midwest, with contacts for information about AAS. Retrieved from the IMDiversity.com website: http://www.imdiversity.com/villages/asian/education_academia_study/midwest_asian_american_studies.asp

12. Kuh, G. D., & Whitt, E. J. (1988). *The invisible tapestry: Culture in American colleges and universities.* (ASHE-ERIC Higher Education Report No. 1). Washington, DC: Association for the Study of Higher Education.

13. Beemyn, B. G., Rankin, S. R., & Windmeyer, S. L. (2006–07). *Overall campus climate score: LGBT-friendly campus climate score national assessment tool questions.* Retrieved from http://www.campusclimateindex.org/details/overall.aspx

14. Constitution of the State of Michigan, Article I, Sec. 26(1). Retrieved from http://www.legislature.mi.gov/documents/publications/constitution.pdf

Promoting Critical Conversations
About Identity Centers

Lori D. Patton, University of Denver

In this response I offer a few original considerations for identity centers and extend some of the valuable arguments raised by Kris Renn, who contends that identity centers play a vital role on campus but face tremendous scrutiny, particularly accusations of separatism. Renn acknowledges the strengths and justifies the continued existence of identity centers, yet argues they pose challenges for Millennial generation students because of a stringent focus on identity categories. I extend and complicate Renn's insights on issues of belongingness associated with identity centers and rethink how one frames critical questions surrounding identity centers. Questions of how identity centers contribute to or dissuade unity become irrelevant without a larger dialogue regarding institutional (ir)responsibility for historically and consistently promoting inequitable campus environments. I suggest that identity centers can enhance their mission by serving as spaces to disrupt privilege and address identity intersectionality. Finally, I discuss what's at stake when we focus on commonalities only, and the contentious position of identity centers as symbols of a commitment to diversity and scapegoats during institutional financial crises.

In her essay Renn notes, "A common criticism of identity centers is that they deprive majority students of opportunities to meet the other." This criticism, though prevalent, troubles me for two reasons. At its core, this argument decenters the experiences of minoritized groups and reinscribes the privilege that majority students already possess by making their concerns about being deprived the central focus. This critique of identity centers mirrors some existing discourses regarding the rationale for diversity in higher education. The dominant and prevailing thinking suggests that diverse campus settings are important for the education of majority groups, White students in particular, because they gain benefits from cross-cultural interactions.[1] This perspective places the onus upon minoritized groups to educate and initiate diverse interactions. Yet rarely does such discourse account for what benefits might accrue for minoritized populations.

This criticism is also problematic because it erroneously situates majority students as deprived by the other. The statement assumes that minoritized groups wield power to prevent majority students from access and opportunities to engage cross-culturally but fails to address the many majority students who deprive themselves of these opportunities because of their lack of interest and awareness, feelings of discomfort around those deemed different, or the belief that identity centers belong to particular groups. However, identity centers do not belong to any designated group nor have there been institutional policies that dictate ownership or communicate that majority students are not welcome. Conversely, from its inception until the 1960s, higher education has a long history of explicit discrimination against minoritized groups as space controlled solely by White men. Despite legislation to dismantle this discrimination, higher education institutions still create or refuse to remove barriers that prohibit full access and equal opportunity.

Many of these barriers, though considerably less visible, are still in place and send unambiguous messages about to whom the campus does or does not belong. Renn says that campus cultures dictate that identity centers belong to particular groups and that there could never be a White student center. She also notes that identity centers "create physical space that can be claimed by students who share that identity" (p. 249). To counter, I challenge readers to visit any predominantly White institution and conduct a mini campus audit beginning with a visit to the student union. The artwork, photography, history, programming, behavioral cues, and overall ambience would likely symbolically communicate to minoritized students that they do not belong or that the union does not belong to them. In other words, students of color could not necessarily claim anything, while their White counterparts could because the student union on many campuses serves as a White identity center in several respects. The same observations could be made in an analysis of the curriculum, athletics, and larger traditional campus celebrations that have historically and continue to marginalize the voices of minoritized groups. Thus the prevailing question is not, Do identity centers divide rather than unite? A more critical and accurate question is, How do the majority of the campuses in the United States consistently maintain practices and policies that separate students and reproduce inequitable structures in ways that ensure the continued need for identity centers? Moreover, how can universities engage majority students in ways that make them recognize and understand the unearned privileges they solely possess?

To address the first question, I refer to Bettina Shuford and Carolyn Palmer who described the history of multicultural student services and centers. They contend these departments, for all intents and purposes, served as "mini student affairs divisions."[2] This historical reality is not significantly different in the present context of higher education. In other words, many identity centers function as one-stop shops for advising, counseling, programming, involvement opportunities, orientation, retention, and mentoring. Unfortunately, American higher education, student affairs in particular, organizes itself in ways that require identity centers to oversee all these responsibilities. Frances Stage and Florence Hamrick said that when identity centers and similar services exist on college campuses, other departments exempt themselves from sharing any substantive responsibility for ensuring the implementation of diversity initiatives.[3] An example of this often exists in Greek affairs when the multicultural center staff—not Greek life staff—advise historically Black and Latino groups.[4]

Given their history of serving as political and critical spaces of engagement, identity centers are appropriate for examining whiteness (and other forms of privilege) because they provide the venue for White students to engage in the complicated deconstruction of whiteness.

If the mission of student affairs divisions is to serve all students, then all student affairs divisions should be grounded in practices that value diversity of all students and be geared toward producing equitable and safe environments for all students. Unfortunately, this is the exception, not the rule in American higher education. The expectation persists that identity centers, despite inequities, do the work of entire student affairs divisions with only a fraction of the budget, staff, and resources.

If student affairs divisions fail at modeling behaviors that value diverse identities, privileged students will likely follow in a similar path. This is unfortunate given that "Student affairs departments shape, manage, and influence significant aspects of the university environment. . . . [and] can directly influence the formation of a multicultural environment, build an inclusive campus environment, and transform institutional structures," according to Kathleen Manning and Patrice Coleman-Boatright.[5]

However, identity centers can play a significant role in engaging students in opportunities that can promote the development of socially just attitudes and actions. For example, Michael Benitez contends that culture centers should and can reposition their missions in ways to counter the assumption that White students are not welcome.[6] Given their history of serving as political and critical spaces of engagement, identity centers are appropriate for examining whiteness (and other forms of privilege) because they provide the venue for White students to engage in the complicated deconstruction of whiteness. Identity centers are also optimal spaces for this type of work because it is less likely to occur elsewhere on campus.

Renn also notes that one of the realities of identity centers is that they do indeed separate based on identity categories rather than focusing on commonalities. While I understand this assertion to some extent, I am not totally persuaded that recognizing differences is a negative outcome. One of the ideas I mention in a 2006 essay is that at times the overwhelming focus on commonalities can contribute to a melting-pot phenomenon.[7] Consequently, all identities are melded, become seemingly unrecognizable, and strip individuals of their unique contributions and histories. The result is the creation of a group identity that largely resembles the majority.

This observation, however, does not alleviate the paradox that identity centers pose for the Millennial generation. Millennial generation students—particularly those occupying multiple locations of oppression—are not content with identifying themselves in simple, one-dimensional ways. Thus identity center administrators will need to shift their mission and programming to move beyond a single identity and address the overlapping, intersecting nature of identities. This is particularly true, for example, for biracial, multiracial, and transgender students who do not fit neatly into race, gender, and sexual orientation binaries.

Renn also notes that identity centers should be situated through a strengths-based lens. In discussing Black culture centers (as well as other identity centers), I raise the point that they are subject to deficit discourses and characterized as no longer relevant, removed from their historical foundations and original mission, and incapable of serving diverse students.[8] While it is important to understand the challenges identity centers endure, it is equally valuable to disrupt deficit thinking by identifying their successes. One strength that Renn identifies is the role they play in bridging divisions of student affairs and academic affairs. I concur, yet it is important to note that faculty as a whole are not supportive of identity centers.[9] As Renn noted, it is typically faculty who teach courses that deal with social identities and related issues who collaborate with identity centers. To clarify, the majority of faculty who are involved not only teach these types of courses but also identify as a member of minoritized groups. Such engagement with identity centers is mutually beneficial for students and faculty who meet and interact with one another to provide support, as well as social and intellectual engagement. Moreover, faculty can foster relationships they may not have in their departments, especially when they are disproportionately underrepresented in the ranks.

The final point that resonated with me was Renn's assertion that because of challenging fiscal climates in higher education, "Supporting multiple identity centers . . . could be seen to draw resources away from the central academic mission" (p. 253). Though higher education is facing tough financial times, news reports these days indicate that when budgets need to be reduced, identity centers are typically on, if not at the top of, the chopping block.[10] Unfortunately, Renn's statement implies that universities collectively conclude that identity centers are antithetical to the academic mission of higher education institutions and provides further leverage for these centers to be dismantled. It is commonplace for postsecondary institutions to espouse diversity and inclusion within or in tandem with their mission statement. Such statements point to desired outcomes for students to be able to interact in a diverse and changing world. Identity centers serve as physical evidence of an institution's commitment to diversity and represent the space where such outcomes are fostered. They should be seen as facilities that bolster and breathe life into the academic mission rather than compete with it. Therefore, in difficult fiscal times, campus administrators should not view identity centers as a strain but instead as critical to maintaining the integrity of institutional missions and academic goals.

As the title of this essay indicates, critical conversations pertaining to identity centers are not simply important but essential to addressing diversity and equity at colleges and universities. How we approach such conversations requires the incorporation of multiple perspectives that address strengths and issues of concern. Moreover, these conversations should be situated in historical and contemporary contexts that acknowledge institutional accountability (or lack thereof) and the maintenance of inequitable structures and practices that make identity centers necessary.

Notes

1. Hudson Banks, K. (2009). A qualitative investigation of White students' perceptions of diversity. *Journal of Diversity in Higher Education, 2*(3), 149–155.

2. Shuford, B. C., & Palmer, C. J. (2004). Multicultural affairs. In F. J. MacKinnon & Associates (Eds.), *Rentz's student affairs practice in higher education* (pp. 218–238), p. 226. Springfield, IL: Charles C Thomas.

3. Stage, F. K., & Hamrick, F. A. (1994). Diversity issues: Fostering campuswide development of multiculturalism. *Journal of College Student Development, 35*(5), 331–336.

4. Patton, L. D., Ranero, J., & Everett, K. (in press). Multicultural student services through a different lens: A critical race perspective. In D. Stewart (Ed.), *Building bridges, re-visioning community: Multicultural student services on campus.* Sterling, VA: Stylus.

5. Manning, K., & Coleman-Boatwright, P. (1991). Student affairs initiatives toward a multicultural university. *Journal of College Student Development, 32*(4), 367–374, p. 367.

6. Benitez, M. (2010). Resituating culture centers within a social justice framework: Is there room for examining whiteness? In L. D. Patton (Ed.), *Culture centers in higher education: Perspectives on identity, theory and practice* (pp. 119–134). Sterling, VA: Stylus.

7. Patton, L. D. (2006). The voice of reason: A qualitative examination of Black student perceptions of the Black culture center. *Journal of College Student Development, 47*(6), 628–646.

8. Patton, L. D. (2010). On solid ground: An examination of successful strategies and positive student outcomes of two Black culture centers. In L. D. Patton (Ed.), *Culture centers in higher education: Perspectives on identity, theory and practice* (pp. 63–79). Sterling, VA: Stylus.

9. Patton, L. D., & Hannon, M. D. (2008). Collaborating with cultural centers and multicultural affairs offices. In S. Harper (Ed.), *Creating inclusive environments for cross-cultural learning and engagement* (pp. 139–154). Washington, DC: National Association of Student Personnel Administrators.

10. Hernandez, A. (2009, October 28). Temple University's commitment to diversity questioned, *Diverse Issues in Higher Education.* Retrieved from http://diverseeducation.com/article/13160/templeuniversity-s-commitment-to-diversity-questioned.html; de Vise, D. (2009, November 6). U-Md. students protest official's firing. *Washington Post.* Retrieved from http://www.washingtonpost.com/wp-dyn/content/article/2009/11/05/AR200911050 2997.html

Further Reading and Related Blog

Kerry Thomas, Oregon State University

Davie, S. L. (Ed.) (2002). *University and college women's centers: A journey toward equity*. Westport, CT: Greenwood Press.

This handbook provides details from directors of women's centers across the country about implementing and expanding a women's center. Women's centers provide opportunities for transforming individuals and institutions through education and collaboration. This volume contains practical information on developing programs, structural issues, social identity, advocacy, improving campus environments, and responding to gender issues at diverse types of higher education institutions from community colleges to private colleges to large research institutions.

Patton, L. D. (Ed.) (2010). *Culture centers in higher education: Perspectives on identity, theory and practice*. Sterling, VA: Stylus.

This book underlines the importance of having cultural centers at predominantly White institutions to provide spaces of refuge and rejuvenation to students with marginalized identities. Book sections focusing on identity, theory, and practice allow for a broad understanding of various cultural centers, historic and current developments, and implications for the future. The information contained in each chapter focuses on the larger mission of identity centers—to provide support to underrepresented populations—to dispel the myth that cultural centers promote segregation from the larger campus community.

Sanlo, R. L., Rankin, S., & Schoenberg, R. (Eds.) (2006). *Our place on campus: Lesbian, gay, bisexual, transgender services and programs in higher education*. Westport, CT: Greenwood Press.

This book describes the nature of lesbian, gay, bisexual, and transgender (LGBT) centers and provides information on how to start an LGBT center, how to develop programs and services, and how to maintain an LGBT center. These centers provide a space for students to feel safe, engage in social justice, explore identity development, and have their voices heard in the face of homophobia. LGBT centers not only serve LGBT students but also the greater campus community by creating an equitable and welcoming environment.

Blog URL: contestedissues.wordpress.com
Corresponding Chapter Post: tinyurl.com/contestedissues13

14

What Does It Mean to Act Affirmatively in Hiring Processes?

Diversity as a Strategic Imperative in Higher Education

Karen L. Miller and J. Douglas Toma, Institute of Higher Education, University of Georgia

In a democratic society, higher education can only remain credible if proportions of those enrolled and employed align to a reasonable extent with the demographic composition of the broader community. The United States is only becoming more diverse, with the trend likely to accelerate, as Hispanic, Asian American, and African American populations are increasing more rapidly than non-Hispanic White ones.[1] Our premise is that traditional values and strategic interests drive universities and colleges. Values influence administrators of institutions to want to reflect the overall U.S. society in whom they admit or hire. Strategic interests compel them to pursue enhanced prestige, which they perceive will be accompanied by obtaining additional resources.[2] The essential means to obtaining these resources is the recruitment and retention of the most desirable students, faculty members, and administrators—and accomplished people from underrepresented groups are often particularly sought after.

Diversity in higher education is not only reflective of our values but is also a strategic imperative for universities and colleges. The most prestigious American institutions, which are also usually the wealthiest, tend to enroll the students and hire the people they want. They can more readily approach, or even attain, goals in diversity. As a result, although not commonly recognized, diversity is directly associated with perceptions about prestige and resources. Officials of universities and colleges not only pursue diversity, such as investing in scholarships, because it is right. The desired outcome also contributes to their overall ambitions in becoming more prestigious and therefore more prosperous.

We begin by exploring what is possible as administrators attempt to increase diversity in admissions under the 2003 decision in *Grutter v. Bollinger* as well as in employment, an issue the U.S. Supreme Court has not addressed directly.[3] Drawing from writings about corporate strategy, we then connect enhancing diversity and strategic advantage, applying three perspectives: creating value in organizations for those connected with them; external positioning, as for enhanced prestige; and internal resources alignment. We contend that administrators of universities and colleges are most effective in enhancing values such as learning when they develop strategies particular to them, as opposed to the generic ones they tend to default to in the interest of achieving or maintaining legitimacy.

What Is Legally Possible?

Voluntary programs to increase student diversity initially relied upon establishing numerical quotas related to the admission of minority students. In 1978 a White plaintiff who was denied admission to medical school at the University of California, Davis successfully challenged the school's program in *Regents of the University of California v. Bakke.*[4] In deciding Bakke, the U.S. Supreme Court did recognize diversity in public higher education institutions as a compelling governmental interest, deeming voluntary affirmative action admissions programs as an acceptable means to achieve these ends, provided they are narrowly tailored to meet the desired objectives. Institutions could meet the narrowly tailored standard by considering race as one of several factors in an admission decision, with committees prohibited from segregating applications from underrepresented groups from the overall pool of candidates.

But how to interpret the plurality opinion by Justice Lewis F. Powell remained contested for the next 25 years, with various appellate courts reaching contrary decisions on the applicability of affirmative action to selective admissions. In some circuits, the U.S. Court of Appeals emphasized the compelling governmental interest in educational diversity, as did the Ninth Circuit in *Smith v. University of Washington School of Law* in 2001.[5] Other courts either disputed it or simply ignored the question. In *Hopwood v. Texas* in 1996, the Fifth Circuit denied that diversity played any role in the educational process: "The use of race, in and of itself, to choose students simply achieves a student body that looks different. Such a criterion is no more rational on its own terms than would be choices based upon the physical size or blood type of applicants."[6] The 11th Circuit meanwhile did not address the compelling interest question in its 2001 decision in *Johnson v. Board of Regents of the University of Georgia*, ruling the program failed because it was not sufficiently narrowly tailored.[7]

Traditional values and strategic interests drive universities and colleges.

In 2003 the U.S. Supreme Court resolved the conflict among the circuit courts when it rendered its decision in *Grutter v. Bollinger*, which addressed the use of affirmative action in admissions at the University of Michigan Law School.[8] The court affirmed that student diversity is a sufficiently compelling state interest to justify the use of race in selective admissions, provided that practices are narrowly enough tailored. As in Bakke, race could be a factor in an admissions decision but not the overriding factor—and institutions needed to read applications holistically. Writing for the majority in Grutter, Justice Sandra Day O'Connor emphasized the importance of diversity in American higher education:

> The concept of critical mass is defined by reference to the educational benefits that diversity is designed to produce . . . [such as] cross-racial understanding [that] helps to break down racial stereotypes and enables [students] to better understand persons of different races. These benefits are "important and laudable" because "classroom discussion is livelier, more spirited, and simply more enlightening and interesting."[9]

The court found social science evidence of the educational benefits of diversity to be persuasive.[10] But programs must be as narrow as possible. In *Gratz v. Bollinger*, the companion case to Grutter, the court held that a points system used to determine undergraduate admissions at the University of Michigan was invalid, because certain candidates, such as those receiving a set number of points for being from an underrepresented race, had more of an advantage than other applicants.[11]

Perhaps the next question is whether the educational benefits of diversity that O'Connor acknowledged can be obtained without also diversifying the higher education workplace. Diversity likely has positive effects on productivity and other important objectives in organizations, particularly given the increasingly diverse American workforce and competition in global markets. But unlike the educational benefits of diversity, whether such interests are sufficient to be deemed a compelling state interest is an open-ended question.[12] Universities and colleges do have the advantage of being understood by courts to occupy a special niche in society and have traditionally been given deference in questions of academic importance.[13] Framing the diversifying of the institutional workforce as linked to educational purposes would thus be crucial.

Finally, private institutions, which are governed by Title VII of the Civil Rights Act of 1964 and not the Equal Protection Clause of the Fourteenth Amendment, which applies only to public universities and colleges as state actors, are not obligated to engage in affirmative action.[14] But they may—and certainly do—initiate voluntary programs. There must be a sufficiently strong justification, such as the demonstrated present effects of past discrimination, and the efforts cannot unduly burden any group. For instance, a voluntary effort by a corporation and labor union to address a manifest racial imbalance in the labor market in a traditionally segregated field was held permissible provided it neither unnecessarily trampled the rights of White employees nor established explicit quotas.[15] Direct discrimination can be allowed in the case of a bona fide occupational qualification, as in the necessity of hiring a priest to serve as a chaplain at a Catholic university.

Diversity as a Strategic Imperative

Aside from the educational values associated with structural diversity among students, we contend that diversity efforts have strategic importance for universities and colleges. Diversity is an increasingly important criterion by which society recognizes higher education institutions as legitimate and measures them as exemplary. At a minimum, the increasing diversity of college-going populations suggests to university officials that they must pay attention to diversity to compete successfully for students and resources Additionally, reputational risk is associated with insufficient attention to diversity. For instance, a leading university or college with proportions of underrepresented students seen to be lagging would rightly be exposed to intense criticism. The opposite situation—success in diversity—is likely to provide a strategic advantage.

But mere structural diversity through numerical representation among students is likely insufficient in higher education. The diversity in climate and values that supports positive outcomes in learning and citizenship among students can realistically only be accomplished with a diverse faculty making curricular decisions, a diverse student affairs division focusing on student development, and diverse senior management providing leadership through direct and symbolic means. Extending the justification in Grutter to workforce diversity may thus be necessary. In doing so, connecting the broader strategic interests of institutions with various educational and societal benefits may prove advantageous.

Any strategic approach sets a direction for the institution that enables it to maneuver through the environment, focuses efforts and promotes coordination of activities, defines the organization, and reduces uncertainty and provides consistency.[16] Using Collis's framework, we examine the strategic advantages of diversity in higher education from three core strategic perspectives: as value creation for those connected with an organization, as an external focus by an organization, and from an internal, resource-based focus on the coordination of activities in an organization.[17]

Diversity as Environmental Focus

In an external perspective, strategy relates to the positioning of the organization in its environment in a manner that yields some sort of competitive advantage. Such an approach to strategy is most often defined as a specific plan or ploy intended to outwit or outmaneuver an opponent or competitor, usually through positioning products and services based on market niches, customer need, or geographical location.[18] The main idea is appreciating the organization in its environment.[19] Strategy developed from an external perspective has the appearance of being a choice—an organization deciding how to exploit strengths and opportunities and overcome weaknesses and threats in the environment. But the environment is usually more deterministic in actuality, proscribing what strategic approaches are permissible for the organization.[20] There may be actual limits on how a university or college can position itself, such as with desiring to be highly selective in admissions but is constrained by its available resources and existing reputation.

But institutional theory may more completely explain why universities and colleges tend to be so limited in their approaches. Organizations tend to crave legitimacy, engaging in isomorphic behavior because acting in standard ways provides the comfort that comes with the perceived safety of the herd. Copying other organizations, especially those recognized as leaders, reduces uncertainty in the appropriateness of a strategy. Coercive pressures are also associated with exogenous providers organizations depend upon for resources, pushing institutions toward norms.[21] New logics may come into being, but only when they achieve moral or pragmatic legitimacy that becomes widely diffused in the environment.[22]

Administrators of universities and colleges tend to perceive a deterministic causal relationship with the broader environment, essentially settling for legitimacy as the only realistic option. Accordingly, they rarely differentiate by developing their own particular strategies. Institutions instead default to generic strategies, which are reassuring but also limiting because they stunt creativity. These standard visions and generic approaches tend toward administrators' being content with the default strategy to aspire to the next level of prestige.[23] Strategies related to enhancing diversity are no different, with officials of universities and colleges essentially acting in expected and undifferentiated ways, competing with one another for attractive applicants among diverse populations. In this sense, diversity has evolved into a new logic, a shared meaning by which we know higher education. It is something that all institutions are expected to emphasize—to do otherwise would threaten legitimacy.

But diversity as a strategy is then driven by environmental factors and essentially divorced from institutional factors. But can mimicry of best practices or capitulation to coercive pressures really amount to the compelling interest necessary to withstand the scrutiny of a constitutional or Title VII challenge? It may well be an insufficient justification for extending the Grutter argument about the importance of diversity to the workforce—or perhaps even endanger its basis in enabling affirmative action in student admissions. Embedding student and workforce diversity more specifically in institutional contexts, as opposed to being connected with playing it safe in the external environment, ensures the vitality and essential standing of an institution's diversity strategy.

Diversity as Value Creation

A strategic goal in any corporate setting should be based on the creation of value for customers, employees, and investors. This simple statement means two foundational strategic abilities are necessary for any successful firm: the ability to articulate clear value statements for each constituency and the ability to align and balance those interests as much as possible.[24] No head of a corporation wants to invest significant funds in the development of a product or service only to discover that it brings minimal value to customers. Neither does management want to produce a value that does not have benefits for the corporation.

Diversity likely has positive effects on productivity and other important objectives in organizations, particularly given the increasingly diverse American workforce and competition in global markets.

Translating this concept to higher education, value creation should focus on multiple constituents, not only students but also society as a whole, given traditional public purposes. Administrators of universities and colleges must clearly state, developing the ability to do so persuasively, not only the value that diversity brings to students and society but also that educational and societal interests are inextricably linked. In Grutter the University of Michigan did just that in justifying affirmative action in admissions, offering empirical evidence of the value of diversity to students and society as constituencies.[25] In defending the case, Michigan featured the demonstrated positive educational benefits from students interacting formally and informally with diverse peers, such as higher levels of self-assessed intellectual engagement.[26] The university underscored the alignment of such ends with the societal benefits of student diversity that have also been demonstrated empirically, as with enhanced academic outcomes, career success, and civic engagement among minority students who attended highly selective institutions.[27]

In opting to expand affirmative action to the workplace, universities would have to similarly express such diversity as crucial in realizing various essential purposes. Diversifying the ranks of faculty members and student affairs professionals who shape the experience of students would have to be framed as indispensable—as necessarily aligned with the most important outcomes in and beyond institutions. More ordinary goals associated with building structural diversity in the higher education workforce would be less likely to meet the compelling state interest standard, such as mirroring student body diversity, providing role models for students, or enhancing the experience of employees themselves. The necessary argument would be that the educational and societal benefits of diversity among students are unlikely to be fully realized without a properly diversified workforce and the campus environment that is essential for the benefits of diversity to be realized.

It may also prove sensible in value creation to consider diversity not only in terms of academic values but also the strategic interests they need to be aligned with. People across constituencies reap benefits through improving the strategic position of an institution and increasing its capacity for revenue generation. Diversity is a necessary component in realizing aspirations. It can be a strategic advantage if attained—and a liability in positioning an institution to advance if efforts lag.

Diversity From a Resource-Based Perspective

In a resource-based view, managers of the organization focus on strategic resources, developing a set of particular and connected activities they can employ in innovative ways in a changing environment to create value that competitors cannot match.[28] While an external perspective tends to result in commonalities among organizations, no one organization replicates any other from a resource-based perspective, as none has the same set of experiences, assets, skills, or culture. Resource-based strategies focus upon creating *fit* by combining internal resources to maximize alignment. When resources complement one another in ways that create real economic value, the whole becomes greater than the sum of its parts. At its most basic level, according to Porter, fit is a simple consistency between each activity and function and the overall strategy (first-order fit). When an organization focuses on more complicated orders of fit, the activities become reinforcing (second-order fit), and then move to optimization of effort (third-order fit).[29]

Contrary to the generic strategies that position various institutions so similarly, a resource-based perspective encourages universities and colleges to develop unique internal competencies. One of these could be framing diversity in ways particular to their own advantages. For instance, administrators of an institution might emphasize the racial and ethnic characteristics of the surrounding community. When such diversity becomes more aligned with other institutional advantages, administrators can achieve the advantages that fit provides. Such a prospect is more likely when diversity is not just numbers but instead becomes associated with the values and climate that permeate an organization. This requires an investment across a community, arguing not only for advancing diversity among student populations but also throughout an institutional workforce. The result of viewing diversity as complementary and reinforcing relative to other institutional advantages can make the whole greater than the sum of its parts, thus creating value and advantage for a university or college.

But institution administrators cannot simply declare their university or college diverse or aligned. They need to work to understand how real diversity occurs and what resources are required—and how to demonstrate outcomes empirically.[30] Given that the resulting diversity becomes so integral to the whole of the institution, resource-based strategies may ultimately offer universities and colleges the most promising opportunity to build an effective case for affirmative action hiring and retention practices, as well as buttressing established ones in student admissions.

Conclusion

Along with being a core value in higher education, diversity is a strategic imperative for institutions, not only because of its demonstrated contributions to learning but also because of the need to attract students and workers from increasingly diverse and competitive markets. Institutions are likely to profess the importance of diversity, embedding it in mission statements and strategic plans most commonly focusing on structural diversity among students. We contend that workforce diversity is equally crucial, especially in working toward the advantages that can accompany the more holistic approach of a resource-based perspective and the articulation of values and alignment of constituencies central to a value creation perspective. Given the societal and individual benefits of educational diversity, higher education administrators owe it not only to themselves but also to the broader public to move beyond self-limiting environmental perspectives.

Notes

1. U.S. Census Bureau. (2007). *An older and more diverse nation by midcentury.* Washington, DC: Author. Retrieved from http://www.census.gov/newsroom/releases/archives/population/cb08–123.html

2. Toma, J. D. (In press). Strategy and higher education: Differentiation and legitimacy in positioning for prestige. In M. Bastedo (Ed.), *Organizing higher education.* Baltimore, MD: Johns Hopkins University Press.

3. Grutter v. Bollinger, 539 U.S. 306 (2003).

4. Regents of the University of California v. Bakke, 438 U.S. 312 (1978).

5. Smith v. University of Washington Law School, 233 F.3d 1188 (9th Cir. 2000) cert. denied 532 U.S. 1051 (2001).

6. Hopwood v. Texas, 78 F.3d 932 (5th Cir. 1996), p. 945.

7. Johnson v. Board of Regents of the University of Georgia, 263 F.3d. 1234 (11th Cir. 2001).

8. Grutter v. Bollinger.

9. Grutter v. Bollinger, 539 U.S. 306, 330 (2003).

10. Gurin, P., Dey, E. L., Hurtado, S., & Gurin, G. (2002). Diversity and higher education: Theory and impact on educational outcomes. *Harvard Educational Review, 72*(3), 330–336.

11. Gratz v. Bollinger, 539 U.S. 244, (2003).

12. Appel, R. N., Gray, A. L., & Loy, N. (2005). Affirmative action in the workplace: Forty years later. *Hofstra Labor and Employment Law Journal, 22,* 549–574.

13. Grutter v. Bollinger.

14. Civil Rights Act of 1964 § 7, 42 U.S.C. §2000e et seq; U.S. Constitution, amend. XIV.

15. United Steelworkers of America v. Weber, 443 U.S. 193 (1979).

16. Mintzberg, H. (1987). The strategy concept II: Another look at why organizations need strategies. *California Management Review, 30*(1), 25–32.

17. Collis, D. J. (1998). *Corporate strategy: A resource-based approach.* Boston, MA: McGraw-Hill.

18. Mintzberg, H. (1987). Crafting strategy. *Harvard Business Review, 65*(July–August), 66–75; Porter, M. (1996). What is strategy? *Harvard Business Review, 74*(November–December), 61–78.

19. Keller, G. (1983). *Academic strategy: The management revolution in American higher education*. Baltimore, MD: Johns Hopkins University Press; Chaffee, E. E. (1985). The concept of strategy: From business to higher education. In J. C. Smart (Ed.), *Higher education: Handbook of theory and research* (Vol. 1, pp. 133–171). New York, NY: Agathon Press.

20. Astley, G. W. (1984). Towards an appreciation of collective strategy. *Academy of Management Review, 9*(3), 526–535.

21. Friedland, R., & Alford, R. R. (1991). Bringing society back in: Symbols, practices, and institutional contradictions. In W. W. Powell and P. J. DiMaggio (Eds.), *The new institutionalism in organizational analysis* (pp. 232–266). Chicago, IL: University of Chicago Press; DiMaggio, P. J., & Powell, W. W. (1983). The iron cage revisited: Institutional isomorphism and collective rationality in organizational fields. *American Sociological Review, 48*, 147–160.

22. Greenwood, R., Suddaby, R., & Hinings, C. R. (2002). Theorizing change: The role of professional associations in the transformation of institutionalized fields. *Academy of Management Journal, 45*(1), 58–80.

23. Toma, Strategy and higher education.

24. Ibid.

25. Grutter v. Bollinger.

26. Orfield, G., & Whitla, D. (2001). Diversity and legal education: Student experiences in leading law schools. In G. Orfield (Ed.), *Diversity challenged: Evidence on the impact of affirmative action* (pp. 143–174). Cambridge, MA: Harvard Education Publishing Group; Gurin, Dey, Hurtado, & Gurin, Diversity and higher education; Maruyama, G., Moreno, J., Gudeman, R., & Marin, P. (2000). *Does diversity make a difference: Three research studies on diversity in college classrooms*. Washington, DC: American Council on Education.

27. Bowen, W., & Bok, D. (1998). *The shape of the river: Long-term consequences of considering race in college and university admissions*. Princeton, NJ: Princeton University Press.

28. Prahalad, C. K., & Hamel, G. (1990). The core competence of the corporation. *Harvard Business Review, 68*(May–June), 79–91.

29. Porter, What is strategy?

30. Archibong, U., & Buford, B. (2007). The cultural understanding in leadership and management (CULM) project. In S. Marshall (Ed.), *Strategic leadership of change in higher education: What's new?* (pp. 93–101). New York, NY: Routledge.

Acting Affirmatively

Patricia M. King, University of Michigan

Personally, I like the word *affirmative*. It's positive, indicates agreement, and can be used to mean optimistic; further, intentionally affirmative actions require consideration of one's options and conscious decision making. These attributes appeal to me. So too does the fact that when we use the word affirmative in the context of a proposition (e.g., when one votes yes, meaning in the affirmative), it conveys forward movement toward a goal. I like being associated with positive, optimistic, goal-directed people. I like working in organizations with these characteristics, and I try to be affirmative in my own life. So what is the source of educators' and employers' hesitance to act this way—that is, affirmatively? I believe this uneasiness stems in part from the fact that the word is strongly associated with affirmative action policies and the debate about how to be fair while redressing historical wrongs and contemporary social dilemmas. Although I believe this word has much broader applicability, like Karen Miller and J. Douglas Toma, I frame my response to the question, "What does it mean to act affirmatively in hiring processes?" by putting it in the context of affirmative action policies.

The phrase *affirmative action* refers to steps actively taken to provide educational and occupational opportunities to women and minorities and has been used widely since the mid-1960s, following passage of the Civil Rights Act of 1964.[1] This landmark legislation forbids discrimination based on race, color, religion, sex, or national origin, opening access to many rights of citizenship based on these characteristics. Americans also use affirmative action to refer to mandatory and voluntary programs intended to ensure full participation in education and employment among those who have been historically excluded. The rationale for such steps was to address past discrimination. As Earl Lewis argued in "Why History Remains a Factor in the Search for Racial Equality," the legacy of race in the United States has very deep historical roots, legislatively and socially.[2] Administrators and policy makers in higher education also use affirmative action plans to address contemporary social quandaries, such as the underrepresentation of those from ethnic minority groups in postsecondary education.

The opening comment of Miller and Toma's essay reflects the proportional representation approach. They claimed that institutional credibility will be lost if students and employees are not represented in higher education in numbers proportionate to their composition in the broader community. Using this criterion to judge whether universities fairly hire students or staff, a sign of fairness (and presumably, the result of acting affirmatively) would be whether the university hires staff at levels that are proportionate to the demographic composition of the population.

The aspect of this issue that I discuss in the remainder of this essay is the selection and definition of these demographic factors. This may sound odd given that demographic categories such as race and gender are so prevalent and are sometimes treated like fixed entities rather than social constructions. As C. Matthew Snipp chronicled in "Defining Race and Ethnicity: The Constitution, The Supreme Court, and the Census," definitions of race and ethnicity have changed greatly over time, and often political agendas drive these conceptualizations.[3] Many demographic categories remain a problem, so continuing to use them without due consideration of intended and unintended consequences is also a problem. Thus, I advise those who choose to promote diversity using the proportionality criterion to carefully consider the selection and definition of the demographic categories they use. For example, until the 2010 census U.S. residents could not indicate a multiracial heritage; options for bi- or multiracial individuals are few or nonexistent in many demographic surveys and databases. In light of trends in interracial and interethnic marriages reported by the Pew Research Center, there is a high likelihood of even more individuals coming from ethnically or racially mixed groups in the future.[4] Thus, attempts to achieve proportional hiring goals based on categories that exclude multiethnic individuals are misguided. A second important example of demographic categories that pose problems is the Hispanic category. As Bernardo Ferdman and Plácida Gallegos said, this is a broad category containing many ethnicities and cultural histories that are quite distinct across groups (those with roots in Mexico, Puerto Rico, Cuba, Central America, South America, and the much broader category of those from countries colonized by Spain).[5] The use of such expansive categories will also result in poor data on representation. A similar issue is readily apparent with the Asian American category, which is also overly broad given distinct differences in nationality and socioeconomic and immigrant status among Americans of Asian descent. This is carefully detailed across educational levels in two reports, one by the National Commission on Asian American and Pacific Islander Research in Education and the second by the Higher Education Research Institute.[6] The use of such sweeping categories can mask relevant socioeconomic differences. For example, high-income Korean Americans may be represented well on campus or in a hiring pool, and low-income Hmong in the same community may be represented poorly; the demographic category Asian American would mask this difference. Issues like these that challenge the composition of the major ethnic group categories in common usage contribute to the complexity of determining whether members of any demographic group are proportionately represented.

Although the perceived risk to an institution's reputation is a relevant factor to weigh when making institutional decisions, it should not be used as a guiding principle.

In their discussion of promoting diversity as a strategic imperative, Miller and Toma state: "Diversity is increasingly an important criterion by which society recognizes higher education institutions as legitimate and measures them as exemplary. . . . Additionally, reputational risk is associated with insufficient attention to diversity" (p. 265–266). I agree these propositions are true to the extent that they reflect existing societal values, here, that prospective students and others involved in the college selection process value diversity as an important and attractive institutional quality, and that insufficient attention negatively affects an institution's reputation. Given that the societal value placed on institutional diversity has changed rather dramatically since the 1950s when segregation was the norm, it is important to note that universities have used reputational risk to deny access. The accuracy and utility of these propositions depend on the cultural and historical context of societal values. Thus, whether institutions are likely to profess the importance of diversity and embed it in mission statements and strategic plans (as Miller and Toma contend in the concluding paragraph of their essay) depends on the times.

The significance of the role of diversity in higher education is particularly salient at the University of Michigan, which vigorously defended the use of race as a factor in undergraduate admissions that was decided by the U.S. Supreme Court in 2003 in *Gratz v. Bollinger*.[7] It also successfully argued in a related case, *Grutter v. Bollinger*, that having diverse student bodies enrolled in higher education is a compelling national interest.[8] In the undergraduate admissions case, University of Michigan's argument was based in part on the demonstrated beneficial educational effects of learning with diverse peers. At Michigan, faculty and administrators frequently affirm diversity as a guiding institutional value, and many such affirmations include the reminder that diversity must not only be stated and defended in public, (such as the University of Michigan's 2010 Accreditation Report) but also enacted in daily pursuits.[9] I point this out to acknowledge that working in a context that emphasizes the need to shape public opinion and not only respond to it has in part shaped my views on this topic. Many applicants to our higher education graduate programs are keenly aware of University of Michigan's willingness to take a public stance in defense of affirmative action and seek to address disparities in educational access and success themselves. As a result, students enter with high expectations for individual and institutional commitments to acting affirmatively and in ways that are aligned with institutional mission and values. Although the perceived risk to an institution's reputation is a relevant factor to weigh when making institutional decisions, it should not be used as a guiding principle. To provide equal opportunity and to create rich environments for learning and working is a stronger rationale for universities to give sufficient attention to diversity. In *Defending Diversity: Affirmative Action at the University of Michigan*, Patricia Gurin and her colleagues present a summary of the rationale and data that were successfully used to frame this portion of the Michigan case in the affirmative action cases before the Supreme Court.[10] They provide compelling evidence that having opportunities for sustained experiences in diverse learning environments improves student outcomes during and after college.

Although educational and employment opportunities are now somewhat more equally distributed than during some previous decades, evidence persists that universities continue to use race as an organizing framework for perceptions of and interactions with racially different others in the United States, and they use it in ways that often benefit those with more power and influence. Hazel Markus and Paula Moya provide extensive evidence of this from across many disciplines in their book *Doing Race: 21 Essays for the 21st Century*.[11] Thus, despite the complexities noted previously, race continues to be a salient factor affecting educational access and occupational success, and thus a relevant factor to take into account in decisions about how to act affirmatively. As Earl Lewis noted when discussing the challenges of recruiting a diverse class of students, "After all, how do you achieve sufficient numbers of students from various backgrounds if you are asked to ignore the entire person?"[12]

Having concluded that race is a relevant factor in college admissions and hiring, it is nevertheless an insufficient basis for framing and organizing one's approach to acting affirmatively. That requires other knowledge and skills, starting with the ability to place issues of affirmative action in historical, legal, social, local, and institutional contexts. Making determinations about issues of fairness in these contexts is complicated, especially when they involve attempts to fairly distribute resources (e.g., college admissions and employment opportunities), and many people are understandably uncertain about how to do it. Miller and Toma remind us that much is at stake for colleges and universities that do not effectively address diversity issues. And as demonstrated in the University of Michigan affirmative action cases, another reason for working hard to recruit and retain diverse students is because a diverse student body often results in greater gains in learning, especially for social outcomes such as citizenship and working well with people from different backgrounds. For those in underrepresented groups, having a critical mass of students from different groups helps lessen the impact of being underrepresented in an institution and the associated educational and psychological costs this carries; for those in majority groups, this increases the likelihood they will have occasion to interact with students from backgrounds different from their own and to develop broader perspectives and skills. There are many ways individuals and institutions can act upon their commitments to being a positive force for social good that are consistent with higher education's civic purposes; acting affirmatively is one of those.

Notes

1. *Teaching with documents: The Civil Rights Act of 1964 and the Equal Employment Opportunity Commission.* Retrieved from the National Archives website: http://www.archives.gov/education/lessons/civil-rights-act

2. Lewis, E. (2004). Why history remains a factor in the search for racial equality. In P. Gurin, J. S. Lehman, & E. Lewis, with E. Dey, G. Gurin & S. Hurtado. *Defending diversity: Affirmative action at the University of Michigan* (pp. 17–59). Ann Arbor: University of Michigan Press.

3. Snipp, C. M. (2010). Defining race and ethnicity: The Constitution, the Supreme Court, and the census. In H. R. Markus & P. M. L. Moya, *Doing race: 21 essays for the 21st century* (pp. 105–122). New York, NY: Norton.

4. Passel, J. S., Wang, W., & Taylor, P. (2010). *One-in-seven new U.S. marriages is interracial or interethnic.* Pew Research Center. Retrieved from the Pew Research Center website: http://pewresearch.org/pubs/1616/american-marriage-interracial-interethnic

5. Ferdman, B. M., & Gallegos, P. I. (2001). Racial identity development and Latinos in the United States. In C. L. Wijeyesinghe & B. W. Jackson (Eds.), *New perspectives on racial identity development: A theoretical and practical anthology* (pp. 32–66). New York: New York University Press.

6. National Commission on Asian American and Pacific Islander Research in Education. (2008). *Asian Americans and Pacific Islanders: Facts not fiction: Setting the record straight.* Retrieved from http://professionals.collegeboard.com/profdownload/08–0608 -AAPI.pdf; Chang, M. J., Park, J. J., Lin, M. H., Poon, O. A., & Nakanishi, D. T. (2007). *Beyond myths: The growth and diversity of Asian American freshman, 1971–2005.* Los Angeles: Higher Education Research Institute, University of California, Los Angeles.

7. Gratz v. Bollinger 539 U.S. 244 (2003).

8. Grutter v. Bollinger, 539 U.S. 306 (2003).

9. Regents of the University of Michigan. (2010). *Accreditation 2010.* Ann Arbor, MI: Author.

10. Gurin et al., *Defending diversity.*

11. Markus & Moya, *Doing race.*

12. Lewis, Why history remains a factor, p. 55.

Further Reading and Related Blog

Amanda Wilson, University of Iowa

Gurin, P., Lehman, J. S., & Lewis, E. with E. Dey, G. Gurin, & S. Hurtado (2004). *Defending diversity: Affirmative action at the University of Michigan.* Ann Arbor: University of Michigan Press.

Gurin et al. lay out several key arguments about the value of diversity for student learning that were used in the University of Michigan affirmative action cases considered by the U.S. Supreme Court. This book has been widely cited and is considered a seminal work that moved the conversation about the role of affirmative action beyond redressing historical wrongs to contemporary learning environments on campus.

Hogan & Hartson, L. L. P. (2003). *The Supreme Court decisions in Grutter V. Bollinger and Gratz V. Bollinger.* Retrieved from http://www.college board.com/prod_downloads/highered/ad/mich_white_paper.pdf

This paper provides a useful summary of *Grutter v. Bollinger* and *Gratz. v. Bollinger*, two landmark U.S. Supreme Court cases that addressed affirmative action in college and university admissions.

Markus, H. R., & Moya, P. M. L. (2010). *Doing race: 21 essays for the 21st century.* New York, NY: Norton.

Markus and Moya explore scholarship on race from the perspective of many disciplines. The authors apply these perspectives to scholarship on race, and the weight of the convergent evidence demonstrates the importance of examining race as a factor affecting many issues in the United States today, including affirmative action.

Blog URL: contestedissues.wordpress.com
Corresponding Chapter Post: tinyurl.com/contestedissues14

15

Girl or Woman? Dorm or Residence Hall? What's the Big Deal About Language?

The Power of Language

Stephen John Quaye, University of Maryland, College Park

ovies and television shows frequently depict college life. For example, *Dorm Life* is a fictional Web series in which the characters endeavor to portray life in college dorms. A perusal of some viewers' reactions to the show on its website reveals several comments indicating the show is quite believable to past and current dorm residents. When the media portrays postsecondary education, consumers often take the term *dorm* to refer to students' living spaces. Yet many student affairs educators cringe when they hear dorm and quickly chide users, informing them that the preferred descriptor is *residence hall*. I vividly remember being corrected during my first semester as a resident adviser at James Madison University and not fully understanding the offense. However, after being corrected by a member of the residence life staff, I purged dorm from my vocabulary.

Students on college campuses also frequently debate the use of *Redskin* or other words purported to describe Native Americans, often arguing that Redskin is simply a mascot and does not convey anything more beyond a name. In addition, student affairs educators have consistently favored *cocurricular* instead of *extracurricular* to demonstrate the importance of the cocurriculum to student achievement, and they have also advocated for the use of *first-year student* as opposed to *freshman* to be more inclusive of women. I frequently tell the graduate students I work with to use *student affairs educator* as opposed to *student affairs practitioner* to emphasize the learning-centered focus of the work that we do.

What's the big deal anyway? Why should one care about using certain words instead of others? My answer to this question in a residence life context, when I myself began correcting students, was that a dorm is where one sleeps; however, a residence hall is where one builds community. Now reflecting on this answer, I realize how vague, silly, and meaningless my response must have sounded. For most collegians, dorm was just fine. Simply scolding students for using dorm is insufficient and counterproductive. Given the widespread use of dorm in non–student affairs contexts, it is no surprise many students remain confused by these semantic demands. Rather than offering students a rote and seemingly petty response, it is important to possess and communicate a clearer understanding of the meaning and power that words convey. This essay explores the implications of language and why language is such a big deal. I first offer examples of the significance of language followed by implications for student affairs practice.

Understanding Language

Before making my argument for why language is important, I offer a primer on linguistics that serves as the backdrop for this essay. As linguistic theorist Norman Fairclough said, language is meaningful because people use language through writing and speaking in social contexts.[1] Therefore, language does not exist in a vacuum but exists instead in social relations that add meaning and significance to language. As an example, Fairclough discusses disputes over words like *terrorism* and *democracy* in U.S. society. Politicians use these words in starkly different ways, despite that they are using the same words. As Fairclough wrote: "Politics partly consists in the disputes and struggles which occur in language and over language."[2] Language is a big deal because users of language struggle over the meaning behind words in an effort to shape reality. As illustrated in the following essay, this struggle occurs not only in politics but also in postsecondary settings.

The Symbolic Nature of Language

Many mascots in professional sports and college athletics are images of Native Americans. For example, the Washington Redskins, Atlanta Braves, Cleveland Indians, Kansas City Chiefs, and Chicago Blackhawks are names of professional sports teams. In higher education, Miami University abandoned its Redskins mascot following a lengthy debate about its implications. Similarly, the University of North Dakota abandoned their use of the Fighting Sioux as a mascot at the end of 2010.[3] The Florida State University Seminoles have kept their mascot by gaining approval from the Seminole tribe.[4]

A perusal of comments by readers on articles about these mascots reveals strong confusion about the problem with using Native American imagery and symbols as mascots. Many readers see these mascots as trivial and identify strongly with their college and university mascots. The common argument against these mascots is that they portray Native Americans in stereotypical ways. Hence, these mascots symbolize one representation of Native Americans and invoke images in the minds of viewers about what Native Americans are like. The challenge with the symbolic nature of language is that when there are few alternative images or messages conveyed through language, people will regard the symbols provided by language as the one and only true representation of a group. The darker skin, lack of clothing, and red feathers commonly seen in Native American mascot images cast all Native Americans in stereotypical ways because there are few other images of Native Americans in popular culture that symbolize something different about this group. Proponents of these mascots often argue that they are meaningless and not a big deal; yet the reason these mascot images are a big deal is because of the powerful way one can use language (in this case an image) to create meaning. Language conveys meaning through the symbols it invokes and reinforces.

Philosopher Michel Foucault explained the symbolism embedded in language in *Power/Knowledge: Selected Interviews and Other Writings 1972–1977*:

> Each society has its regime of truth, its "general politics" of truth: that is, the types of discourse which it accepts and makes function as true; the mechanisms and instances which enable one to distinguish true and false statements, the means by which each is sanctioned; the techniques and procedures accorded value in the acquisition of truth; the status of those who are charged with saying what counts as true.[5]

As Foucault helps make clear, United States society, like any other society, has its own forms of what counts as true. Therefore, when one speaks, others make judgments about the truth of the person's claim. A Native American mascot maintains its significance because it connotes some version of truth in the mind of the listener. This is part of what makes language so powerful—because of what it signifies. Even if supporters of Native American mascots remain unclear about why they adamantly support these mascots, they can use imagery to incite fear, anxiety, stereotypes, and lack of understanding about Native Americans since *Native American* now has a regime of truth, to use Foucault's phrasing, that is based on a lack of understanding about this particular group of people. Hence, language becomes a powerful tool to create symbols that one uses to fashion meaning among a group of people in a particular society.

Likewise, residence life staff members want their colleagues and students to use residence hall because of their desire to reinscribe in the minds of colleagues and students a different understanding of one's living space. When residence hall staff members insist on not using dorm, they intend to convey that residence hall is the preferred word choice because a residence hall symbolizes something dramatically different from a dorm. The seemingly trite response of "one builds community in a residence hall" actually (although ineffectively) conveys a larger message that residence life staff desire to promote learning and development in students' living space—their residence hall. Student development researchers such as Marcia Baxter Magolda and Patricia King, and student outcomes researchers Patrick Terenzini and Ernest Pascarella, have consistently shown that the kinds of peer interactions residence hall environments encourage can promote important learning and development outcomes, such as cross-cultural learning and intellectual growth.[6] Not surprisingly, it makes sense that student affairs educators would want to use residence hall to describe the kind of unique and value-added outcomes they hope to promote in these environments. Thus, words like dorm and residence hall become meaningful because of the truth these words convey and the symbolic nature of what they signify. The problem, however, is that often those who insist on particular language choices do not know why they prefer these terms nor offer a clear and persuasive rationale for these word choices, thus leaving students wondering why they should use certain terms.

The Internalization of Language

In *Rock My Soul*, bell hooks explored the struggle of self-esteem among many Black people that is predicated on experiencing racism.[7] Over time, hooks argued, labels used to refer to Black people as inferior have led them to internalize these messages about their self-worth and intelligence. Thus, another reason language is such a big deal is because of the messages it can enable persons to internalize. Just like racist epithets and insults can cause harm, as explained in *Words That Wound*, language can reinforce certain images in people, which they then internalize as the truth to describe them.[8] Individuals privileging only one version of the truth to the exclusion of alternative messages through language exacerbates the problem.

To illuminate this argument, I turn to the use of *girl* and *woman* or *boy* and *man*. In the United States, the terms girl and boy normally refer to people who are not yet adults. Thus, parents or guardians viewed them as incapable of making their own decisions. Black male slaves were referred to as boy by White men to signify their lack of status in society and the fact that they could not control their own bodies but were forced to serve their masters. Boy signified Black men's inferior positions and that they were incapable of making their own decisions, akin to children. Even in today's society, when a Black man is called boy, symbolic messages of slavery arise and create a situation in which the Black man is made to feel powerless and less than a person. The use of boy only works because of the symbolic messages it conveys and the history and context it is used in. What becomes more of a problem, however, is that some Black men have internalized this perception of inferior status and thus do not see themselves as worthy of having the same place in life as White men. As hooks wrote:

A dangerous form of psychological splitting had to have taken place, and it continues to take place, in the psyches of many African Americans who can on one hand oppose racism, and then on the other hand passively absorb ways of thinking about beauty that are rooted in white supremacist thought.[9]

Language is important because it conveys messages to people about their worth, which they then internalize as truth. For instance, the internalization of language about whose skin color is more beautiful underscores the ways we use language as a tool of oppression.

Similarly, girl and woman have different meanings. Both men and women refer to women more frequently as girls than men as boys. The problem with using girl as opposed to woman is when the user says men and girls in the same breath. In this tandem, man is often positioned with girl; whereas, boy is seldom used with woman. Calling women girls positions them as less than men, particularly when the equivalent of boys is not used. An examination of television shows and conversations on college campuses reveals that even women refer to themselves as girls. This usage often begs the question, Who decides what a woman should call herself? Although it is difficult to say whether those who refer to themselves as girls are internalizing messages of their inferiority, feminist authors, such as Patricia Hill Collins, discussed the lack of status of women in society and how over time women can begin to internalize their low place in society.[10] Consequently, when a student queries, "What's the big deal about using the word girl anyway?" a reasonable response can be, "Because of the internalized messages that women might receive about their lack of worth in society." In instances where a woman chooses to call herself a girl, the goal of engaging in conversation with this person is not to convince her why using girl is wrong but instead to raise questions about what girl connotes. This strategy is more productive given the various ways different people interpret the same words.

Implications for Student Affairs Educators

What do my arguments mean for student affairs educators? What does it mean to become cognizant of the symbolic nature of language and the internalized messages language can convey? Thus far in this essay, I focus

Those who control language have the means to set standards for what counts as knowledge and discourse.

almost exclusively on how language can be used negatively to marginalize and exclude others and can be used as a source of fear, internalized oppression, and powerlessness. However, power is not always negative. Language can be used productively and as a tool of agency and resistance.

Productive Means of Language

According to Foucault,

> What makes power hold good, what makes it accepted, is simply the fact that it doesn't only weigh on us as a force that says no, but that it traverses and produces things, it induces pleasure, forms knowledge, produces discourse. It needs to be considered as a productive network which runs through the whole social body, much more than as a negative instance whose function is repression.[11]

Just as language can be used to implant negative images in the minds of listeners through, for example, girl, Native American, or dorm, users of language can also convey positive messages. As Foucault noted, power produces and forms knowledge and discourse. A key component in knowledge and discourse is language. Those who control language have the means to set standards for what counts as knowledge and discourse. In teaching students why student affairs educators prefer the term residence hall, student affairs educators can help students understand notions of community and learning they try to foster in the residence hall rather than merely scolding students for using inappropriate language. In addition, they can help students contemplate gendered relationships in society through the ways they refer to women and men. When students are able to understand the assumptions that undergird certain words, they are better positioned to use language that promotes agency and equality rather than marginalization and exclusion. The words girl or dorm are not bad in and of themselves, but rather it's the messages they could convey as compared to what woman and residence hall suggest— the former maturity and adulthood and the latter community.

Agency and Resistance in Language

In "Age, Race, Class, and Sex: Women Redefining Difference," Audre Lorde wrote about the relationship between oppressed groups and their oppressors and the significance of language in the process:

> For in order to survive, those of us for whom oppression is as american [sic] as apple pie have always had to be watchers, to become familiar with the language and manners of the oppressor, even sometimes adopting them for some illusion of protection.[12]

Lorde also noted that oppressed people consistently have to teach the oppressors about their oppressed lives.[13] For instance, women teach men about what it means to be women, and lesbians and gay people educate heterosexual persons about sexuality. Although this process can help educate privileged people through understanding different language, Lorde insisted that it could also be draining to the oppressed and could take energy and time away from oppressed people who are redefining themselves and changing the situations that lead to their oppression. Lorde noted the role of agency in the process of defining oneself.[14] This argument is a consistent theme in the notion of culture, wherein culture can act as an organizing and dominating force but there is always some element of agency in culture where people have the means to shape and define culture just as it influences those who participate in the culture. MacLeod demonstrated this point in his ethnography where he revealed that those who seemed to have the least power in society found ways to assert their agency even in the most difficult of circumstances.[15]

Subordinate groups have consistently sought ways to use the oppressor's terms and language, as well as their own language, to redefine themselves in more powerful ways. One example of this is when gay and lesbian folks use *queer* to gain power and take away the negative meaning of this term from their oppressors. Robert Rhoads discussed this point in his book *Coming Out in College: The Struggle for a Queer Identity*.[16] He found that gay students in his study identified with the term queer as a political identity and to demonstrate their lack of shame for being gay.

When students are able to understand the assumptions that undergird certain words, they are better positioned to use language that promotes agency and equality rather than marginalization and exclusion.

Even though several participants identified with this term, some still viewed queer as a problem, demonstrating the various ways people interpret language.

This notion of cultural agency is critical to student affairs practice in that it represents a form of resistance to the labels inscribed by others on certain people. Merely resisting is not where the agency lies; rather, the agency is found in whether the resister understands why she or he is resisting. When students refer to themselves as queer and can convey their rationale for labeling themselves as an act of resistance toward the oppressor, this represents the kind of struggle Norman Fairclough wrote about. He said those who do not hold power are "always liable to make a bid for power" in the struggle to assert themselves.[17] Student affairs educators must work to better understand students' reasons for the language they use. Inviting students to discuss what certain terms mean to them and the ways they label themselves and their peers would enable student affairs educators and students to understand the symbolic nature of the language students use.

Conclusion

In *How the Way We Talk Can Change the Way We Work*, Robert Kegan and Lisa Laskow Lahey wrote about *big assumptions* as those "we do not actually take as an assumption but instead as the truth."[18] To return to the mascot example, if we view Native American mascots as trivial entities simply used to represent sports teams, why would we bother to even look at alternative understandings of these mascots? Similarly, if we think girl is just a word, then there is no reason to think any differently. Why challenge our big assumption when we see that assumption as the truth?

However, assumptions are just that—they may have some elements of truth but may also be false beliefs. The implication of Kegan and Lahey's work for the discussion on language is that the words we use are a big deal because we operate from our own big assumptions or various truths.

Student affairs educators should examine their big assumptions about various groups and question their colleagues and students about how they developed their big assumptions. Simply correcting one's language more often results in arguments about political correctness instead of a conversation about the real issues that underlie certain words. Consequently, rather than quickly labeling someone else's assumption as wrong or untrue, I propose that we instead seek to understand how the person developed her or his big assumption or version of truth. Doing so would lead to a more productive understanding of the various ways colleagues and students come to develop their truths. Equally important, inviting students to consider the language they use could lead to dialogue in which students and student affairs educators explore the meaning of language and negotiate more productive ways to use it. Dorm, American Indian mascots, girl, and student affairs practitioner only gain significance because of the social context people use them in and the underlying assumptions of these word choices. The point is that the words we use are a big deal and implicitly convey our values, beliefs, and assumptions. Because words have different interpretations, participating in numerous, sustained dialogues about the various ways students and student affairs educators interpret the words they use can lead to newfound learning and understanding. We learn more about ourselves, our colleagues, and our students when we examine the underlying reasons for the words we use.

Notes

1. Fairclough, N. (1989). *Language and power.* New York, NY: Longman.
2. Ibid., p. 23.
3. Fuhrman, Z. (2010, April 9). *North Dakota Fighting Sioux to change school nick-name.* Retrieved from http://bleacherreport.com/articles/375948-north-dakota-fighting-sioux-to-lose-school-nickname
4. Lederman, D. (2005, August 24). *Flip-flop on Florida State.* Retrieved from http://www.insidehighered.com/news/2005/08/24/mascot
5. Foucault, M. (1980). *Power/knowledge: Selected interviews and other writings 1972–1977.* New York, NY: Pantheon Books, p. 131.
6. Baxter Magolda, M. B., & King, P. M. (2004). *Learning partnerships: Theory and models of practice to educate for self-authorship.* Sterling, VA: Stylus; Pascarella, E. T., &

Terenzini, P. T. (2005). *How college affects students: A third decade of research* (Vol. 2). San Francisco, CA: Jossey-Bass.

7. hooks, b. (2003). *Rock my soul: Black people and self-esteem.* New York, NY: Atria Books.

8. Matsuda, M. J., Lawrence III, C. R., Delgado, R., & Crenshaw, K. W. (1993). *Words that wound: Critical race theory, assaultive speech, and the first amendment.* Boulder, CO: Westview Press.

9. hooks, *Rock my soul*, p. 50.

10. Hill Collins, P. (1997). Defining Black feminist thought. In L. Nicholson (Ed.), *The second wave: A reader in feminist theory* (pp. 241–259). New York, NY: Routledge.

11. Foucault, *Power/knowledge*, p. 119.

12. Lorde, A. (1995). Age, race, class, and sex: Women redefining difference. In J. Arthur & A. Shapiro (Eds.), *Campus wars: Multiculturalism and the politics of difference.* Boulder, CO: Westview Press, p. 191.

13. Lorde, Age, race, class, and sex.

14. Ibid.

15. MacLeod, J. (1995). *Ain't no makin' it: Aspirations & attainment in a low-income neighborhood.* Boulder, CO: Westview Press.

16. Rhoads, R. A. (1995). *Coming out in college: The struggle for a queer identity.* Westport, CT: Bergin & Garvey.

17. Fairclough, *Language and power*, p. 68.

18. Kegan, R., & Lahey, L. L. (2001). *How the way we talk can change the way we work: Seven languages for transformation.* San Francisco, CA: Jossey-Bass, p. 67.

Words: The Windows to
Our Assumptions and Truths

Ebelia Hernandez, Rutgers University

"What's the difference between *dorm* and *residence hall?* You know what I mean!" Yes, we may know students are referring to their living space when they use either residence hall or dorm, yet words do more than communicate simple ideas. Stephen Quaye in his essay aptly stated that "the words we use are a big deal and implicitly convey our values, beliefs, and assumptions" (p. 289). Indeed, our words are powerful, as they are the windows for others to ascertain what we believe our truths to be, even those truths we unconsciously believe. To critically examine the words we use is to examine our own values, truths, and assumptions that color our worldviews. Challenging our students to think of the words they use can be an opportunity for them to discover their own truths and assumptions, which is a very different task from asking them to substitute one word for another in an effort to be more politically correct.

In this essay, I extend Quaye's discussion about the significance of language to apply the ideas that he presented to a personal investigation of the words we use to identify ourselves, identify others, and identify objects, items, or concepts.

Quaye effectively started the conversation by laying a foundation for this exercise that explored the significance and power of language. Yet we must continue thinking through what this means for us at the personal and professional levels. In writing this response essay, I more closely examined my own word use and that of my students, and colleagues, by asking questions about the words they use and listening to their conversations about this topic. I challenge you to also critically examine your own truths and assumptions by examining your own language use. Doing this personal work ourselves is necessary to be good company for our students when we challenge them to critically examine their own words.

Identifying Self: I Am _____.

Choosing how we identify ourselves is a very personal process. The words we choose to identify ourselves are ever changing as our sense of self, values, and beliefs continuously evolve. Life events, such as moving to a new town, starting a new job, or beginning graduate school, can all be prompts for us to reevaluate who we are and what our chosen labels mean to us. Our labels are generally those aspects of ourselves that are most salient, which is often influenced by our environment.[1] As I reflect on how I identify myself, which ethnic label best fits me—Hispanic, Latina, Mexican American, or Chicana? Each of these labels seems to generally mean the same thing, but I recognize that each one refers to particular perspectives about one's cultural background, historical legacies, and political ideologies.

To critically examine the words we use is to examine our own values, truths, and assumptions that color our worldviews.

A different sense of self emerges from each of these labels. Some feel oppressive, others empower me. Quaye pointed out in his references to Rhoads's work how claiming an identity can be empowering, especially in transforming labels that once were derogatory to ones that evoke pride.[2] He discussed how the word queer transformed from being an oppressive label to one that the lesbian, gay, bisexual, and transgender community took ownership of and redefined to identify sexual orientation and a political perspective. Similarly, the term *Chicano* had a negative connotation until the Chicano movement of the late 1960s through the early 1970s when Mexican American activists reclaimed it to identify their Mexican American background and a nationalistic ideology that advocated ethnic pride, recognition of indigenous roots, and a commitment to political action for the uplifting of their community.[3] Chicano and queer are often not labels that others give us—they are labels we can choose for ourselves because they identify more than characteristics; they declare a particular level of political consciousness and active resistance to the status quo.

The college experience is a time for discovery and examination of the words that can define one's own identities. The courses students enroll in, the campus environment, and the people they interact with all play a role in the student's developing sense of self. Students try on identities, trade one for another, and discard ones that no longer fit with their new perspectives. We can see this process play out in the words on clothes they wear: T-shirts with statements as bold as "This is what a feminist looks like," sweatshirts with Greek letters to signify membership in a particular organization, or clothes with their school name proudly front and center.

"I am _____" spoken out loud or displayed on what you are wearing can be a powerful statement that requires not only acknowledgment of owning a certain identity but living it and realizing the consequences of claiming that identity. Indeed, labels—such as gay, woman, leader, athlete, African American—are all words, but they all have their own power in what they convey about who we claim to be and how others will respond to us.

As you reflect on the words you use to identify yourself, you may understand the power of words by thinking about the labels you are proud to claim and the labels that make you uncomfortable. Quaye's conclusion about the power of being able to name ourselves is a double-sided coin—the words we use to identify ourselves can be empowering, but they can also create exclusivity and distance from our colleagues and students. How do you identify yourself? How has it changed over time? Who could you potentially attract and distance from the ways you choose to identify yourself? What consequences have you experienced from claiming these identities?

Identifying Others: You Are _____.

We also use words to identify others. Quaye stated that language conveys messages to people about their worth. What worth, privilege, assumptions about maturity, and ability do we convey when we use the following terms:

- for those we aim to educate—students, kids, or learners;
- for those who work in student affairs—professionals, educators, staff, or colleagues;
- for those in their first year of college—freshmen, first-years, or frosh?

How we identify others also reveals our evaluation of who they are in relation to ourselves. In other words, when you label someone, you reveal what you perceive to be his or her worth, status, and abilities in relation to yourself, and you also indicate your relationship to the other person in the label you choose to identify him or her. For example, it can be argued that if you choose to identify those we aim to educate as kids, you are perceiving this group as young, immature, and requiring an authority figure to take care of them, and you are also inferring yourself as older, more mature, and taking on a parental role in the way you choose to interact with them. How could your word choices to identify others set the stage for the type of relationship you expect to have and the role you will play?

Often, we do not realize we reveal these subtle messages. This can be a problem because the words we use to identify others can be empowering or oppressive. I challenge the notion of labels being neutral (hence the purpose of this chapter). Not examining the words we use means we may not realize how we may perpetuate stereotypes, assumptions, or other messages about someone's worth or abilities, or how we leave social norms unexamined and unchallenged. For example, take the word *freshman*. This word is generally perceived as harmless; most students would probably not object to being called one or recognize any negative associations with it. Yet, like any label, it carries assumptions, historical legacy, and values. A colleague posted on Facebook the issue he had with using the term *first-year* instead of freshman in a report. He struggled with others not recognizing how his choice of terms reflected his choice to use a nongendered identifier for a population of people who in fact are now the majority—women. His word choice could have been interpreted as being politically correct or even trendy without having the knowledge of the intent behind his decision. The significance of a gendered term may play out even more strongly for students who attend a women's college or in other educational spaces where women have felt exclusion, separation, or marginalization. Freshman indicates the historical roots of men having had exclusive access to higher education, and when women entered higher education, the gendered term persisted.

Here is where things can get tricky. As Quaye said, "Often those who insist on particular language choices do not know why they prefer these terms nor offer a clear and persuasive rationale for these word choices" (p. 283–284). My colleague believed that he was engaged in a conversation with someone who had not critically examined his or her preference for freshman over first-year. The question here is not which word is better. How do we engage in conversations with our colleagues, supervisors, and students about word choice that go beyond being politically correct to a more meaningful analysis of language, intent, and how your words convey your values and beliefs? How do you identify those you aim to educate? Those you work with? Do these word choices indicate the relationships you hope to cultivate with them and how you value these relationships?

Defining Things: This Is _____.

Consider these terms: *bonehead math, remedial math, developmental math*. They all refer to that class that some students may have to take as a prerequisite for college-level math. These different terms used to name the same thing powerfully illustrate how the words we use are charged with value. Each of the terms indicates an evaluation of this class's worth, the perceived ability of the students who take the course, and the role of the instructor. What type of student would you imagine taking bonehead math? What sense of academic ability can we determine when a student states he or she is enrolled in bonehead math? Could we come to some type of conclusion on the particular approach to teaching based on the term an instructor for such a class may use?

Words are like windows that let others see into our personal worldview, which reflects the assumptions and truths we hold.

Again, to think of word choice as a process of choosing the least offensive term does not provide the opportunity to reflect on how words can influence our sense of self. I can see how Quaye's discussion of how words can be internalized to become the truth of who you are plays out in this example.

Being aware of the power of language, monitoring our words, and occasionally changing the words whenever we deem it appropriate may start to change our thinking, because consciously thinking of our words leads to a critical examination of what these words mean to us. In other words, reevaluating the words we use and changing our vocabulary to more accurately reflect our values and perspectives extend beyond just being politically correct.

Continuing the Conversation About Words

What do your words say about you? What messages do you give to others about your values, your worth, and your place in this world? What are the consequences of using these words for you and for others? This response essay examined the power of words Quaye addressed by more closely examining who we are, how we identify others, and how we identify things.

Words are like windows that let others see into our personal worldview, which reflects the assumptions and truths we hold. Our words are the best tools we have to share with others who we are. They communicate so many things about us, particularly our perceived identities and our perception of others. Realizing this, it is worthwhile to take a closer look at the words we use so we can more fully recognize the messages we send others. How can we continue this reflection about the words we use? What questions should we ask ourselves to reveal our worldview that colors our language? I suggest that we begin by listening: Listen to the words you speak; consider the words you write in essays, notes, or e-mails. Even the words on the clothes you wear are all ways of communicating who you are. We can then accompany others to reflect on how their words communicate their perspectives by asking them the provocative questions we asked ourselves. Dorm or residence hall? Woman or girl? You make the choice, but understand that your words reveal more than a general meaning; they reveal who you are and your understanding of this world.

Notes

1. Jones, S. R., & McEwen, M. K. (2000). A conceptual model of multiple dimensions of identity. *Journal of College Student Development, 41*(4), 405–414.

2. Rhoades, R. A. (1995). *Coming out in college: The struggle for a queer identity.* Westport, CT: Bergin & Garvey.

3. Muñoz, C., (1989). *Youth, identity, power: The Chicano movement.* New York, NY: Verso.

Further Reading and Related Blog

Jeff Manning, Fordham University

Bohm, D. (1996). *On dialogue.* New York, NY: Routledge.

Bohm defines dialogue as finding meaning through words. This book describes dialogue and the intricacies of participating in this type of discussion. Dialogue examines and changes thought processes via understanding the various ways of constructing these complex thoughts and ideas. Bohm outlines the vision for dialogue and some of the necessary components to engaging in successful and meaningful dialogue with others.

Delgado, R., & Stefancic, J. (2004). *Understanding words that wound.* Boulder, CO: Westview Press.

This book describes the harm and hurt that words and hateful speech can cause. The authors examine the frequency and theories behind the use of these types of words. This type of language is present on college campuses across the nation and negatively affects the overall college climate—at times embodied in mascots and other prominent campus symbols.

Hyde, B., & Bineham, J. L. (2000). From debate to dialogue: Toward a pedagogy of nonpolarized discourse. *Southern Communication Journal,* 65, 208–223.

This article details one class's experience with a pedagogy involving dialogue as opposed to debate and the various ways to create the fundamental components necessary to participate in dialogue. Typically the pedagogy of debate yields polarization of opinions. The class used a different method involving dialogue to combat the polarization of opinion and thought while examining students' ability to engage in meaningful dialogue.

Blog URL: contestedissues.wordpress.com or
Corresponding Chapter Post: tinyurl.com/contestedissues15

16

What Are the Implications of Providing Special Considerations to Particular Students?

Special Considerations for a Universal Problem: Campus Accommodations

Deborah McCarthy, University of South Florida

I remember the first day of second grade—exciting and special—so special that I could choose what we would have for dinner. As I waited to go home, a classmate bounded down the stairs of our school and stopped to stare. She looked at the braces on my legs and said, "Those are ugly. You belong in special school." I remember thinking, "Schools can be special?" and "What's wrong with this school? I like it here." The reality of special schools, where those with disabilities were set apart from the other students, was not part of my young consciousness. I did not understand the idea that my braces made me special.

I recognized that I walked differently and that I did not like (nor could I play) the same physical games as my classmates, but I didn't feel special. I remember looking at the classmate and thinking, "Why don't you think I belong here?" Perhaps that is why, after living with cerebral palsy for many years, after K–12, college, and graduate school in mainstream education and a career dedicated to student affairs and disability work, the idea of special considerations makes me cringe.

My first reaction to the question, What are the implications of giving special considerations to some students? is a concern about language. The word *special* generates feelings of separateness and pity. In the context of disability, special students are a curiosity to be examined, admired or avoided. *Special considerations* is a phrase that connotes exception rather than inclusion; the term highlights limitations. The implication of special considerations is that there is some reason a student cannot meet regular requirements; the student is less than the norm.

Thinking that perhaps my reaction indicates oversensitivity to language based on my own experience, I asked several students who work in my disability services office what they thought of the phrase. Unanimously, these students reacted negatively to special considerations. They all said, "That doesn't seem very politically correct," and favored *accommodations* or *academic adjustments*. Wondering how a student who needed accommodations would react, I asked Justin, a student who uses a wheelchair, "What do you think about defining the tools you have received from disability services, as special considerations?" He groaned and said, "Accommodations is a better word because it's more PC, but it still sets students who use disability services apart from everyone else. Why do we always focus on what is different? It's 2010. Regardless of what we call it, real accommodations are about an attitude of equality."

If Justin is correct, as I believe he is, and the tools for success and the attitude of equality are paramount, then our use of language is important. Disability scholar Steven Brown says of the recent trend toward more politically sensitive language, "As far back as I can recall, I believe the language debate to be a vital one, not because of the words themselves, but instead because the words represent one's sense of personal, social and political identity."[1] As student affairs professionals, we routinely affirm the whole student. We base the validity of our profession on the notion of developing not just a student's academic experience but also his or her out-of-classroom experience. That out-of-classroom experience includes historical, personal, political, and social factors that define our assumptions about disability.

Are Special Considerations Fair?

Four models shape society's understanding of and response to disability: the moral lens, the medical/rehabilitation lens, the civil rights or legal lens, and the social lens.[2] Society's understanding of disability began with the moral lens and continues to evolve toward the social lens. To fully examine the implications of providing accommodations for students with disabilities, it is helpful to take a closer look at each lens. According to the moral view, disability is the result of personal or familial sin, and the individual with a disability either deserves his or her affliction or is a sinner deserving of pity or scorn. From this lens, disability is a wrong to be addressed by divine intervention or punishment. Certainly student affairs professionals do not perceive disability as punishment. We seek to provide appropriate tools for our students. Yet, a subtle examination of this historical lens reveals disturbing implications. The moral model challenges us to examine the concept of fairness. Is it fair to have special considerations for some students and not for others? Are students who need accommodations held to the same standard as their peers without disabilities? Do students who need accommodations deserve to be in higher education? Is it essential that we as educators treat students with fairness? These are only a few of the complicated questions that arise in the moral lens of disability.

Consider Michael. In 2004 he was a B plus student with aspirations to become president of his fraternity. At a party during his first year, Michael drank too much, fell down a flight of stairs, and landed unconscious. After many weeks in a coma, Michael emerged with neurological and physical limitations. Years of therapy allowed Michael the ability to speak, walk, and physically care for himself. Determined to finish his degree, Michael returned to the university. With an electric scooter to assist with mobility and a computer to assist with note taking, Michael reentered the classroom. As his disability services coordinator, I believed in Michael's ability to pursue his degree. I armed Michael with additional time on his exams, copies of notes from a classmate, and a reduced-distraction testing environment.

Yet neither Michael nor I was prepared for the reaction. At the beginning of every semester, one of Michael's faculty members would call me and awkwardly say, "I don't want to be unwelcoming or discriminatory, but I don't see how Michael can be in this class. It isn't fair to me or the other students." I would respond by asking the caller the question, "What seemed unfair?" Answers included grading issues, the amount of time needed to provide instructions to Michael, and the belief that other students would complain that Michael was being treated differently. Regularly I challenged the instructor to consider how much time he or she spent with a star student. Usually, at least one student in the class, because of an increased interest in the subject matter or an affiliation with the instructor, consumed more of the instructor's time. "How is spending time with Michael different from spending time with this star student?" There were no satisfactory answers to this question, but the most pervasive response was, "I'm afraid that someone [a student or a colleague] will accuse me of not being fair."

In the context of disability, special students are a curiosity to be examined, admired, or avoided. Special considerations *is a phrase that connotes exception rather than inclusion; the term highlights limitations.*

A double standard prevails in higher education. Accommodating a star student is often a worthwhile investment. Providing a tutor for a popular campus athlete too seems appropriate to many. Students, faculty, and student affairs professionals alike readily make exceptions for athletic talent. Accommodating students with disabilities, however, raises concerns about fairness. Some of Michael's faculty and peers do not perceive him as having a special talent that will benefit the university. "That wouldn't be fair" becomes a common excuse for not adapting our university environment, teaching styles, or program standards to students with disabilities. One of the primary implications of providing accommodations is that we as educators must begin to examine our assumptions about fairness. We must examine the relationship between difference and equality. What is fair is not what allows a student with a disability to be an equal peer. As disability studies historian Paul Longmore observes, "[In America], equality means identical arrangements and treatment. It is not possible in American society to be equal and different, to be equal and disabled."[3]

What happens, though, when adjusting our concept of fairness meets head-on with the common perception that students with disabilities work harder and longer and are thus more deserving of academic success because of having to overcome a disability? Are our students rewarded for effort or results? An instructor called me about Samantha, a graduate student with a processing disability. One of the essential components of her ethics course is the ability to debate issues verbally and in writing. Samantha must articulate her own original thoughts quickly and succinctly. The instructor said that Samantha is failing the course because she parrots the verbal responses of her peers and fixates on minor elements in her writing rather than discussing broader issues. It seemed that Samantha did not display the critical thinking skills necessary to be successful in the course. In speaking with her instructor, I asked, "What do your colleagues who previously instructed Samantha say about her work?" Samantha's instructor replied that previous colleagues responded with pity by awarding her higher grades than what Samantha earned.

What do we do when accommodations are insufficient? The moral lens encourages us to do whatever we can to ease the burden of a student with a disability. How do we as professionals balance what is fair and what is reasonable and appropriate? How do we gauge a student's academic ability? How do we avoid acting from pity?

Just Cure the Problem

In the medical model we avoid pity and appease our notions of fairness by eliminating the disability. If we fix the defect, then the individual will be normal and will fit into society. This argument is the centerpiece of the medical/rehabilitation lens. Those who have the medical knowledge to cure are the ones most likely to perpetuate this disability lens. Critics of the medical/rehabilitation lens assert that by focusing on a cure, society forces individuals with disabilities to conform to societal norms that do not include the imperfections of disability. By approaching disability solely as a medical problem, we imply that those with disabilities are inferior. In his book, *A Matter of Dignity: Changing the World of the Disabled*, Andrew Potok highlights advocate Rosemary Garland Thomas's quote, "Disability is a broad term which disadvantage(s) people by devaluing bodies that do not conform to cultural standards. Thus, disability functions to preserve designations such as beautiful, healthy, normal, fit, competent [and] intelligent."[4] The problem with these designations is their exclusivity. The same individual is not pretty and ugly, healthy and ill, disabled and normal. The person with a disability cannot be disabled and well or whole. It is a system of binaries. The medical professional has the cure and the individual with the disability is a passive patient.

Passive Education

A similar passivity permeates the United States educational system. The prominent philosophy of the K–12 system is that all students can be successful. Thus, students receive special considerations as a matter of course. Entire teams of teachers, parents, therapists, and specialists gather to develop an individualized education plan (IEP) for the student. These teams modify assignments; shorten exams; change curriculum; and, when necessary, provide one-on-one coaching, counseling, or therapy. Rarely if ever do these professionals involve students in this process. The IEP becomes a student's prescription for success. Just as a medical professional dispenses a prescription, so too does the K–12 educational system dispense plans for academic success.

A primary tenet of our student affairs profession is balancing challenge and support for our students. The medical lens of disability and the experience of most students in the K–12 system perpetuate the belief that the individual who requires accommodation is a passive recipient. Many day-to-day practices of a disability services office also perpetuate this passivity. We perform a cursory examination of a student's documentation, reach into our tool bag of accommodations, and create a treatment plan of standard accommodations. In higher education, we require that the student at least request assistance. But what happens when a student asks for special considerations and is approved for accommodations in higher education? How often do we invite students to reflect on whether accommodations are necessary? Do we revisit accommodations as our students grow and develop, or do students receive the same accommodations letter each semester regardless of personal growth? Do we view our students as equal partners in an educational process or as clients who receive a standard service?

Stewards of the Law

Providing services on demand is the basic tenet of the legal lens. Because the law requires accommodations, institutions must provide them. The Americans With Disabilities Act (ADA) is primarily responsible for the sense of entitlement that permeates conversations about accommodations.[5] Touted as one of the greatest pieces of civil rights legislation since *Brown v. the Board of Education*, the preamble of the ADA states that the original intent of the legislation is "To provide a clear and comprehensive national mandate for the elimination of discrimination against individuals with disabilities."[6] Accommodations for students with disabilities are now a legal mandate. How do we respond when a student we've coached to be an advocate says, "You have to allow me to the retake the exam; it's the law!"?

Frequently, we defer to the legal language of the ADA and explain that the law allows for reasonable accommodations; we emphasize it is the institution that dictates what is reasonable. We defer to the attorneys and legal counsel. None of these approaches truly addresses a fundamental reality of providing accommodations to students in 2010. The implications of the legal mandate range from issues of entitlement to academic freedom and fiscal responsibility. As the stewards of this mandate, disability services professionals are simultaneously enforcers and advocates.

Nearly every campus of higher education has an ADA coordinator, whose role is to protect individuals from discrimination and to enforce appropriate legal mandates. Any disability services provider will say that the enforcement of the ADA begins at a much lower level. Unreasonable requests and aggravated constituents are par for the course. Because the government mandates accommodations does not mean that a university has no standards. In fact, one implication of the legal mandate is that decisions become a complicated balancing act. University admissions processes are an example of the need for educators to balance special considerations for students, legal mandates, and the standards of an institution. Accommodations apply after a student is admitted. Students must be "otherwise qualified" to participate in higher education. It is appropriate for staff at an institution to say no to any student—even one with a disability. One of the more unfortunate implications of the legal lens is the assumption that saying no is an illegal and thus unacceptable answer. Even more frustrating is the perception that educators who work toward equal application of standards and equitable decisions are barriers to a student's academic success.

On the positive side, the presence of a legal mandate allows for services educators have previously not considered. Today captioning and sign language services are common at university events. Students with chronic medical conditions have the option to pursue medical withdrawals without financial penalty should their conditions flare midsemester. Blind or low-vision students have access to course materials via computer technology. Lab tables, classrooms, food counters, and residence hall rooms are more accessible to those who use wheelchairs. Individuals with psychological disabilities can request a reduced course load to accommodate medication schedules. Tools for educational success that were once too much trouble or too expensive are now standard practices.

At What Cost?

While it is a myth that all special considerations are financially expensive, there is no denying that services such as captioning and transcription are costly. One of the far-reaching implications of the legal lens is that universities must plan ahead. Knowing that the law requires higher education to provide access to classrooms, course materials, and events, educators must find ways to fund the accommodations process. Educators in general and student affairs professionals in particular have a responsibility to steward our finances and employ our fiscal creativity so that money is no longer the reason for failure to comply with the legal mandate to provide accommodations.

Beyond the Law: A Universal Approach

Many critics of the ADA contend the law does not go far enough. They say that attitudes are more important than legalities. Those who promote the social or cultural lens of disability believe that the challenge of accepting, accommodating, and welcoming those with disabilities as equal and valued community members belongs to the entire university community. As the author of the memoir *Awakening to Disability* observed, "Because disability is a universal experience, creating a barrier-free world eventually involves everyone."[7]

Advocates of the social model contend that disability is an element of diversity and that societal attitudes are the primary barrier. Deborah Kaplan quotes advocate and universal design expert David Pfeiffer:

> Paralyzed limbs may not particularly limit a person's mobility as much as attitudinal and physical barriers. . . . Most people will experience some form of disability, either permanent or temporary, over the course of their lives. Given this reality, if disability were more commonly recognized and expected in the way that we design our environments or our systems, it would not seem so abnormal.[8]

What happens then if society rejects pity, cures, and legal mandates in order to embrace disability as an element of diversity? How do our educational systems and practices change if instead of providing a special consideration because we have to, we allow accommodations because doing so welcomes our students? How do we encourage self-advocacy? These questions lie at the heart of the social model of disability. There are no definitive answers to these questions. There are, however, tools of success that student affairs educators might employ to further embrace the social model of disability.

One such tool is the concept of universal design: "The design of products and environments to be usable by all people, to the greatest extent possible, without the need for adaptation or specialized design."[9] We see some of the influences of universal design in building projects. Many architects include automatic doors, family restrooms, accessible landscaping, and, where appropriate, technological advances designed to enhance everyone's experience. These are visible and high-profile indicators that the social lens of disability is gaining ground. Disability is part of being human.

Allowing for disability as a human characteristic challenges us to do more than offer support. The social model of disability dictates that we have a responsibility to encourage advocacy and to promote education by engaging with our students. The social model calls educators and student affairs professionals to "be good company for our students with disabilities as they learn to speak about their needs and integrate 'the disability thing' into their views of self and the world around them."[10]

Engaging in Advocacy

How do we respond when, in an effort to promote this understanding, our students and colleagues choose methods that render more pity than awareness? How do we respond when well-intentioned members of our community want to spend a day in a wheelchair to know what it's like to have a disability? From the perspective of the social lens, simulations are a throwback to the moral and medical models. The majority of participants in simulations come away saying, "I had no idea life could be so hard," or "Gosh, people who use chairs are so brave." These assumptions belittle the real experience of a person with a disability. For individuals with disabilities, the simulation does not end. Simulations do not represent our real experience. Instead, these activities move understanding of disability culture backward, generate pity, and create misunderstanding.

We have the opportunity and the responsibility to engage in dialogue with our students, colleagues, and friends with disabilities so their experiences become part of the history of student affairs.

Dialogue is the key to advancing our understanding of disability and accommodations. Disability theologian Eiesland commented,

> The concept of minority group provides a theoretical lens of understanding how such factors as negative stereotype, prejudice, and discrimination affect the lives of persons with disabilities. Such understanding is the first step toward real communication and ultimately a change in the negative attitudes and [special] treatment of persons with disabilities."[11]

Disability deserves the respect and reflection student affairs professionals and educators at large offer to other marginalized groups.

The final implication of the social lens is one of responsibility. Through the social lens, the responsibility of engaging a student in the accommodations process does not belong to a specific instructor, office, or department. Instead, it is a universal responsibility. Each of us has an opportunity to ask questions, to share observations, and to value the experience of the individual with a disability in such a way that there is an exchange of ideas, frustrations, and possibilities. We have the opportunity to meet those who use accommodations in their real experience. We can acknowledge that the issue of special considerations for students in higher education has come a long way and that there is still work to be done.

The social lens is the preferred lens for disability work, but as this discussion demonstrates, it is not the only lens. We have the opportunity and the responsibility to engage in dialogue with our students, colleagues, and friends with disabilities so their experiences become part of the history of student affairs. By providing support with active dialogue rather than with pity, cures, or laws, we will be able to ask a far more powerful question, What are the implications of a universally accessible educational system?

Notes

1. Brown, S. E. (2003). *Movie stars and sensuous scars: Essays on the journey from disability shame to disability pride.* Lincoln, NE: iUniverse, p. 161.

2. Connections for community leadership. (2007). *Models of disability.* Retrieved from the Communities of Power: http://www.copower.org/leader/models.htm

3. Longmore, P. K. (2003). *Why I burned my book and other essays on disability.* Philadelphia, PA: Temple University Press.

4. Potok, A. (2002). *A matter of dignity.* New York, NY: Bantam Books, pp. 177–178.

5. Americans With Disabilities Act of 1990, 42 U.S.C. 12101§ 1201 (1990).

6. Ibid.

7. Stone, K. G. (1997). *Awakening to disability: Nothing about us without us.* Volcano, CA: Volcano Press.

8. Kaplan, D. (1999). *The definition of disability: Perspective of the disability community.* Retrieved from the People Who website: http://www.peoplewho.org/debate/kaplan.htm

9. Story, M. F., Mueller, J. L., & Mace, R. L. (1999). *The universal design file: Designing for people of all ages and abilities.* Raleigh, NC: Center for Universal Design, p. 2. Retrieved from http://www.ncsu.edu/www/ncsu/design/sod5/cud/pubs_p/docs/udffile/intro.pdf.

10. McCarthy, D. A. (2007). Teaching self-advocacy to students with disabilities. *About Campus: Enriching the Student Learning Experience, 12*(5), 10–16, p. 10.

11. Eiesland, N. L. (1994). *The disabled god: Toward a liberatory theology of disability.* Nashville, TN: Abingdon Press, p. 66.

Finding the Union of Success and Access
A Focus on Learning for Students With Disabilities

Peter J. Haverkos, Miami University Hamilton

Deborah McCarthy provides a foundational overview of disability theory and considerations for individuals working in the disability services field at higher education institutions. While this review is a starting point for graduate students and new professionals in student affairs, a deeper look reveals the profoundly intricate issues in disability services that are more complex in practice and specifically in the field of academic support. McCarthy's disparate view of the four lenses in the field of disability studies does not address the interconnectedness some of these lenses often have for students, faculty, parents, and others involved in promoting student success in higher education. While I agree with McCarthy's privileging and promotion of the social lens and her identification of the important question, What are the implications of a universally accessible educational system? her questions and ideas only touch the surface of the complicated nature of working for success and access related to learning for all students engaged in higher education. In this essay I contrast disability services at 2-year and open-access institutions with 4-year traditional universities and colleges. I also call for a focus on learning at all levels of an institution, which provides more equity and support for all students in general and students with disabilities in particular.

As an academic support professional in learning assistance at a 2-year regional campus, I often collaborate with students with disabilities, faculty, and staff where a multitude of factors and the lenses McCarthy described are at play. Students struggle to find the appropriate strategies that maximize their learning and balance their right to accommodations without eliciting pity from faculty and staff to be treated as special cases. Two-year institutions have a long history of serving groups who are often marginalized at traditional 4-year institutions, such as historically underrepresented students, English-language learners, adult learners, and students with disabilities.

Faculty at these 2-year institutions have wrestled with differences in learning, differences in students, and have had to reconsider or redefine their teaching and curriculum to be a more flexible enterprise, broadening definitions of success and learning. Faculty at 2-year institutions understand students' varied life experiences, which could include being a student parent with a disability, and the stress it entails or the time demands of a full-time working adult responsible for the household. As an academic support professional at an open-access institution I frequently meet with students, their faculty, and the disability services staff to resolve issues and concerns related to learning. It may not involve adjustments in assignments or testing but rather involves open communication and developing an understanding of a student's learning and life context including the student's individual strengths, weaknesses, and goals.

Students struggle to find the appropriate strategies that maximize their learning and balance their right to accommodations without eliciting pity from faculty and staff to be treated as special cases.

These faculty and staff members sometimes work in a more collaborative fashion with students and are more willing to work with accommodations for all students. This flexibility and openness can also be a problem in 2-year colleges; sometimes faculty and staff are too accommodating, not holding high expectations for student learning because they use McCarthy's moral or legal lens of disability and show pity for the student instead of setting a level of learning in their classroom that is applicable to all students.

Conversely, officials at 4-year traditional institutions, often because of their selective status and their reliance on standardized test scores for admittance, have only slowly had to consider how faculty and students need to teach and learn differently in courses. Most students at these residential institutions enter higher education directly after graduating from high school. In my work experience at a selective, traditional, residential university, faculty did not intend to create barriers or be discriminatory, but their construction of the way that college is supposed to be interferes with students who learn differently. Whether teaching is a traditional lecture format or a more collaborative style, when we use our own experience of education as a gauge and do not deeply consider individual learners we privilege and promote learning for the few—the good test takers and those who excel at this game called school. The past experiences of faculty as undergraduate and graduate students, coupled with their teaching experience as new faculty, create expectations of how college works, and unfortunately this framework does not serve all students, particularly students with disabilities. How can we all reimagine our understanding of college to simultaneously hold high expectations of learning and success while also being earnest in our attention to access?

A large gap exists between the K–12 system and postsecondary education. In primary and secondary school, personnel and parents advocate for the students, while in colleges and universities students must advocate for themselves. It is the student's responsibility in postsecondary education to self-identify and register with the appropriate disability office on campus. Although staff members in disability services and academic support offices aid students, the primary onus is on the student. McCarthy calls for dialogue as a first step, but how do institutions move beyond dialogue into the complexities of action? Individual students in conjunction with faculty and academic support personnel, including student affairs practitioners, must delve into what learning means, entails, and requires for each student.

Society has been advocating for all high school students to attend college. This aim is admirable and problematic. Higher education administrators must realize we are all responsible for student learning; this includes the student, faculty, staff, and institution. Personnel from traditional 4-year institutions could gain from open dialogue about the successes and challenges their 2-year colleagues experience. Open-access institutions, including community colleges, junior colleges, and regional campuses, are at the front lines of the complexity of access and success and the intersection of learning and disability. Students with significant disabilities, including psychological, cognitive, and developmental, are entering postsecondary education as the means to personal and economic transformation.[1] Faculty and staff at open-access institutions have developed ways to help these students make the transition to the institutional complexities of higher education.

With classrooms full of diverse learners (e.g., student parents, adult learners, first-generation students, minority students, and English language learners) faculty at 2-year institutions constantly reconsider and rework their teaching and the learning happening in the course. Students' lives outside the classroom have a profound impact on classroom performance and learning, and faculty at 2-year institutions strive to find the delicate balance of challenge and support while remaining flexible within the system of higher education. My experience as an academic support professional on a 2-year campus finds faculty willing to work in conjunction with students through the extenuating circumstances and barriers they encounter in higher education. Whether a student faces problems related to child care or employment or learning English or struggling through basic math, faculty examine their expectations and goals for learning via their courses, assignments, and tests. We often cannot see through our own systems and perspectives to imagine what higher education might be not only for students with disabilities but for all students. Drago-Severson said, "A self-transforming knower has the capacity to be less invested in identity, point of view, and standards and is more open to other's perspectives."[2] She wrote: "Self-transforming knowers have the capacity to examine issues from multiple points of view and, most important, to see the way seemingly opposing perspectives overlap."[3] A community of self-transforming knowers will be able to look at issues surrounding learning from multiple perspectives and address the needs of all the learners in that community. To meet the needs of all students, how might student affairs staff and faculty be more self-transforming knowers?

As McCarthy said, universal design is an excellent frame for faculty and institution officials to examine their syllabi, processes, and design. Universal design is a good first step, encouraging all faculty and students to consider who they are in the teaching and learning process as they begin to develop into self-transforming knowers. As Drago-Severson pointed out, "Challenging . . . knowers toward growth could take the form of encouraging them to be more flexible and to follow alternative pathways to a goal or problem."[4] Universal design and the flexibility associated with it make some students uneasy, but it also challenges them as knowers. They must consider who they are, where they are going, and what type of assignment might extend their learning. Some students struggle with connecting the course and learning to their goals. It is far easier to complete a specific assignment, get the grade, and obtain the degree without truly considering one's place in the whole system.

While universal design provides flexibility, it remains important to directly address the learning needs of students with disabilities. Disability services personnel typically meet with students individually and determine the accommodations the university is willing to provide. These accommodations are often globally applied to the student's education and are not designed to meet the needs of specific course and content material.[5]Accommodations may be providing a benefit to a student's learning in some circumstances, and in other cases, as with students with physical disabilities, accommodations can be paramount and the only vehicle that provides equity and access to education. Extended time, separate testing location, and note takers are common accommodations, but do these really address the specific needs of the individual?

When do disability services staff meet with the student *and* faculty to address how the course is structured and ways to effectively meet faculty and student goals? Senior disability services staff often obtain contextualized knowledge about courses and instructors through years of service, but time on the job cannot be the only key to student learning success. Systematic processes must be established that allow all the factors to be considered with the student. How can institutions move toward a more personalized academic plan for all students including those with disabilities? How can we bring advising structures, disability services, and faculty into an interconnected system at an institution? By creating a space to explore the unique learning strengths and challenges associated with each class and the student, higher education institutions can engage in the complex realities of learning. The student must be in the driver's seat; we must not provide education *to* students with disabilities. Rather, we must teach and learn in conjunction *with* each other.

When faculty and staff at an institution can focus on an individual student's learning in a course, and do so consistently, they are much better situated to engage in a larger discussion of learning. Mission statements that promote access and the transformative experiences that higher education can offer to individuals are more powerful when real learning values are enacted. Mezirow said, "Commitment to the common good is understood not as a final state but rather as a stance of openness to necessary and ongoing dialogue with those who differ or who may not yet be full participants on the commons."[6] Students with disabilities are advocating to be full participants on the commons, and while our learning environments still have barriers, we must commit to the commons, to the learning of all students, and to the self-reflective processes that allow us to all become self-transforming knowers.

Notes

1. Ankeny, E., & Lehmann, J. P. (2010). The transition lynchpin: The voices of individuals with disabilities who attended a community college transition program. *Community College Journal of Research and Practice, 34*(6), 477–496.

2. Drago-Severson, E. (2009). *Leading adult learning: Supporting adult development in our schools.* London, UK: Sage, p. 49.

3. Ibid., p. 50.

4. Ibid., p. 57.

5. Kurth, N., & Mellard, D. (2006). Student perceptions of the accommodation process in postsecondary education. *Journal of Postsecondary Education and Disability, 19*(1), 71–84.

6. Mezirow, J., & Associates. (2000). *Learning as transformation: Critical perspectives on a theory in progress.* San Francisco, CA: Jossey-Bass, p. 105.

Further Reading and Related Blog

Peter M. Magolda and Marcia B. Baxter Magolda,
Miami University

Davis, L. J. (2010). *The disability studies reader* (3rd ed.). New York, NY: Routledge.

This collection of essays offers a comprehensive look at essential topics in disability studies. Several essays explore disability in the United Kingdom, which provides U.S. readers with opportunities for meaningful comparisons. This text is an excellent resource for higher education professionals with minimal exposure to the field of disability studies.

McCarthy, D. (2007). Teaching self-advocacy to students with disabilities. *About Campus, 12*(5), 10–16.

This article combines personal narrative, personal experience, and real-life practice, and introduces the disability services provider to the necessity and value of self-advocacy. Educators have an opportunity to use the article as a catalyst for reflection and discussion on assumptions, appropriate questions, and how educators might promote self-advocacy skills in the teacher/student relationship.

Shapiro, J. P. (1994). *No pity: People with disabilities forging a new civil rights movement.* New York, NY: Times Books.

Shapiro provides a comprehensive review of the impact of the Americans With Disabilities Act on American culture. He discusses disability history, disability cultures, and the politics of the disability rights movement. Many of the struggles (e.g., inadequate support services, disability myths, victimization, patronization, segregation, prejudices) in 1994 persist in 2011. Individuals interested in a disability rights movement primer will find this text useful.

Blog URL: contestedissues.wordpress.com
Corresponding Chapter Post: tinyurl.com/contestedissues16

17

What Are the Responsibilities and Limits of Student Affairs Educators' Roles in Addressing Burgeoning Student Mental Health Issues?

Supporting Collegians' Mental Health: Collaboration and Role Differentiation

David B. Spano, University of North Carolina at Charlotte

S hortly after starting my first job as a counseling center director, I attended the 1996 annual conference of the Association of University and College Counseling Center Directors (AUCCCD) in Seattle. One of the prominent concerns discussed at the conference was a fear that because of budget entrenchments and a narrowing mission, student affairs and other university administrators were marginalizing counseling services and considering outsourcing these services to private entities. The rise of managed care in American medicine led some to believe that higher education would embrace a managed care model for campus counseling and health services. Some directors argued that to resist the push toward outsourcing we needed to match managed care in its cost-efficient delivery of services to clients. Several models of service delivery emerged with an eye on the bottom line that would demonstrate that counseling services could offer a cost per hour that would compete with the managed care model.

Some counseling center directors argued that the way to ensure the continued viability of campus counseling services was to reject the burgeoning medical model and instead return to our mission—roughly as it was defined at the beginning of the student personnel movement—and infuse the work we do more deeply into the academic and student development missions of our institutions. Managed care, after all, focuses primarily on treating individual clients with mental health concerns. These directors felt we should return to our roots, grounded in student development theory, focused on the whole person, attending to individual strengths and not just pathology, and serve as consultants and partners with administrators, faculty, and other staff members. This group felt that counseling centers were, at their essence, far more than isolated mental health clinics. Beside the remediation of mental health problems, these professionals envisioned counseling center activities to include workshops and outreach programming, social justice advocacy, training, research, and a close connection to institutional goals such as student learning and retention.

Specialization of Counseling Services

Counseling services and the field of counseling psychology have long been an integral component of the broader work of student affairs. As far back as 1937, *The Student Personnel Point of View* included the philosophical statement that one of the obligations of institutions of higher education was to "consider the student as a whole . . . [including] his [sic] emotional make up."[1] The statement also noted that "an effective educational program includes . . . determining the physical and mental health status of the student [and] providing appropriate remedial health measures."[2] The 1949 update of the monograph went further. Among the essential elements of a student personnel program, the authors included "service to the student of trained, sympathetic counselors to assist him [sic] in thinking through his [sic] educational, vocational, and personal adjustment problems" as well as "physical and mental health services whose orientation is not only the treatment of illness but also . . . an educational program of preventive medicine and personal hygiene counseling."[3]

Because of practical considerations, counseling services became more central to student personnel services on campuses following World War II after the passage of federal legislation, the GI Bill, which rewarded veterans for their service by providing financial support for them to attend college. Waves of veterans enrolled in universities without a clear sense of their academic or occupational goals, and universities provided vocational guidance to assist them. Concurrently, college counselors, often operating out of dean of students' offices or academic departments, began integrating social and personal counseling into the vocational services provided for these veterans.[4]

In the decades since, counseling has become a more specialized service, operating within but in some ways walled off from other student affairs departments and the rest of the university. This professionalization of counseling center personnel has paralleled the evolution of counseling psychology into a field that has moved closer to clinical psychology in its focus on the assessment, diagnosis, and treatment of psychological disorders and away from its roots in the vocational guidance movement, which focused on client strengths rather than pathologies. Despite the historical links between counseling services and other student affairs functions, the evolution of the profession has created cultural and practical boundaries that have resulted in sometimes contentious relationships between counseling center personnel and their colleagues in and outside the student affairs division.

Differences in Professional Preparation Programs

Differential graduate preparation training programs have helped create these boundaries. Over the past several decades, student affairs preparation programs have shifted from a somewhat reactive focus on student personnel services to a more proactive promotion of student learning with an emphasis on the study of student culture and student and organizational development. During the same period, counseling preparation programs—which in their vocational guidance origins focused primarily on individual strengths—have added an emphasis on the more clinical identification and treatment of mental health problems among students. While many student affairs preparation programs offer courses in basic counseling skills, these are often aimed to help practitioners relate to students in informal arenas, advise residence hall and other student staff, and enhance basic relationship-building skills to strengthen practitioners' interactions with collegians. Those entrusted with the actual counseling work in higher education obtain their professional training in counseling or, increasingly, in clinical psychology programs or schools of social work, which may but typically do not have formal affiliations with student affairs preparation programs, and where the identification and treatment of mental disorders is of paramount importance. As the mental health needs of students have become more complex, as demand for services has increased, and as administrators, faculty, parents, and others are calling for measures to help ensure individual and community safety, enhanced skills in assessment and treatment have become even more essential.

The intersection of the academic preparation of counseling center staff and other student affairs staff may consist of, at best, a few basic counseling courses and elementary research and statistics courses. It is now common practice for counseling center staff members to possess terminal degrees and licenses to practice psychology, counseling, or social work. With the exception of senior leadership and some department heads, it is uncommon for student affairs staff members to have terminal degrees, and very few outside counseling centers possess the credentials, to assess and treat mental health issues.

Policy development can bind or divide student affairs professionals and their counseling center colleagues.

Counseling center personnel are thus positioned as the only staff on campus who can credibly recognize, assess, and treat mental health concerns, and personnel outside counseling have been reluctant to involve themselves with students on mental health issues out of fear they will miss something, make an error, or be held liable for an unintended negative outcome. These attitudes, while understandable, have often led to tension between those in and outside our counseling centers. Some student affairs educators and faculty members do not perceive that their jobs include involvement with student mental health issues. Stress levels of counseling center staff have increased as concerns over campus safety and student mental health issues have become a more central institutional concern and as demand for services has grown. While many institutions have done an admirable job of allocating additional resources to counseling services, demand for services often outstrips the supply. Even centers that comply with staffing recommendations from the International Association of Counseling Services (IACS), a body that accredits over 170 university and college counseling centers, employ one counselor for every 1,000 to 1,500 students, and many IACS-accredited centers have ratios that fall short of these guidelines.[5]

Growing Mental Health Concerns

As specialization and separation of counseling services has progressed, and as debates about the role of counseling centers and their service delivery models have continued, events have occurred that have dramatically transformed the role of counseling centers on university campuses and changed the relationship between counseling services and other parts of the campus community. First, and perhaps most significantly, there has been a steady rise in the number of students who use counseling services, and those who use counseling present with increasingly complex concerns. These trends have been documented in surveys conducted by AUCCCD, the American College Health Association, the Center for the Study of Collegiate Mental Health, and Robert Gallagher from the University of Pittsburgh.[6]

A number of factors have converged to contribute to this increase in utilization and deepening complexity of student issues. Better treatments for conditions such as major depressive disorders and provisions of the Americans With Disabilities Act have allowed more students who have psychological concerns to attend college. Effective new medications and new evidence-based therapies have helped students improve functioning to the point where they can succeed in college. Concurrently, the federal government has been requiring universities to provide reasonable accommodations to students with diagnosed disabilities, including psychological disabilities. These students, not surprisingly, frequently need ongoing support from counseling staff to maintain a level of functioning needed to succeed in college.

The other events that have led to the increased prominence of counseling services on campus are well known to the general public: disturbing suicides and murders at elite universities; the impact of the events of

September 11, 2001; the resultant stress of wars and economic doldrums; and, of course, the mass murders at Virginia Tech and Northern Illinois University. Numerous state and local task forces have issued recommendations aimed squarely at providing more effective counseling services to our students and connecting students to support services through education, outreach, and referral. Universities have formed behavioral intervention and threat assessment teams and are doing case management—following up with students who are referred to psychological services to be sure they remain connected to those services and are making progress in their recovery—to ensure students remain safe from harm and function in a way that allows them to succeed as students. A growing number of students are taking advantage of counseling, and they seem to be less worried about the negative stigma attached to seeking help.

Thus, on today's campuses, we find ourselves examining more closely than ever the role counseling services play in our divisions of student affairs and our universities. The events of the past 15 years have required administrators of institutions to rethink the way they approach the identification, assessment, and remediation of student mental health issues. There is a clear directive from administrators, legislators, and others for counseling services and other campus departments to develop responsible and effective ways to share information and assume joint responsibility for addressing student mental health concerns. Increased attention to mental health concerns has offered campuses an opportunity to develop a more collaborative approach that can empower student affairs professionals (as well as other staff and faculty) to form partnerships with counseling professionals to help students overcome mental health concerns so they can optimize their academic, developmental, and interpersonal growth.

Collaboration on Student Mental Health Concerns

Counseling services personnel and student affairs staff must share responsibility for creating these collaborative relationships, and these responsibilities start in our preparation programs and continue into our continuing professional development activities and the development of best practices.

With demand exceeding resources and with concerns about mental health increasing, counseling center staff cannot be the sole possessors of the skills and expertise needed to identify and respond to students with psychological needs. Student affairs preparation programs must emphasize the development of communication skills to enhance the ability of professionals to engage with students and inquire about their mental health, their personal safety, and the safety of the community. Student affairs staff must be more comfortable with asking difficult questions (e.g., "Are you thinking of killing yourself?") and understanding when a consultation or referral is necessary.

These skills need to be honed and developed in student affairs professionals as their careers develop, and counseling center personnel must provide the types of training experiences staff need to enhance these skills. New models of so-called gatekeeper training have been developed, and many universities are using these trainings to improve campus safety and facilitate campuswide communication. Training in Question, Persuade, Refer (QPR), a suicide prevention protocol developed by the QPR Institute, has been available since the late 1990s.[7] More recently, specific gatekeeper training programs aimed at university faculty and staff are widely available. Campus Connect is a suicide prevention program developed at Syracuse University with the support of a grant from the Substance Abuse and Mental Health Services Administration of the U.S. Department of Health and Human Services.[8] Another example is an interactive web-based simulation called *At Risk*, developed and marketed by Kognito Interactive.[9] These two programs and others like them help to train non-counseling personnel in the skills needed to identify, approach, and refer students who may be at risk for mental health problems. These programs capitalize on the relationships that many student affairs staff, other staff, and faculty members have already developed with students before the emergence of concerns. These connections are invaluable in gaining the trust and cooperation of students as they address their issues.

There are training issues for counseling center staff as well. While young professionals receive excellent training in clinical assessment and treatment skills, training in consultation rarely gets adequate attention in graduate training programs. At the University of North Carolina at Charlotte Counseling Center, we have invested significant professional development time to consultation training so all staff members can understand our goals and roles as consultants to others on campus. Counseling personnel are taking increasingly active roles in the establishment and delivery of gatekeeper training programs on our campuses. It is the responsibility of counseling center staff to identify a gatekeeper training program that aligns with the campus's mission and culture, advocate for the budget allocations to bring these resources to campus, gain the expertise needed through train-the-trainer opportunities, and then facilitate the implementation of these programs.

Sharing Information While Maintaining Privacy

The successful implementation of consultation and gatekeeper programs on campus can enhance relationships between student affairs and counseling staff, but their success is dependent on building trust and clear communication on potentially contentious issues that can cause disconnections.

The maintenance of privacy and confidentiality is one such contentious issue. By law and according to ethical principles, counseling centers may not release information about who is seeking their services nor the content of those services without informed consent of the client (except in rare circumstances where imminent danger of harm is a concern). These confidentiality policies serve to create a safe environment for students to explore mental health concerns as well as a potential communication barrier between counseling services and other university offices.

From the perspective of student affairs educators—especially the chief student affairs officer who is concerned about the well-being of students and wants to be assured that professionals in the division are doing all they can—it can be understandably disconcerting to be barred from knowing whether students are getting the mental health services they need. While other departments in the division operate with relative transparency, counseling services can seem like a black hole when it comes to acquiring information.

Across this divide are counseling professionals who must abide by state privacy laws and professional ethics and who believe that confidentiality is a cornerstone of a successful mental health practice. To these professionals—who know that breaches of confidentiality not only have legal and ethical consequences but can create a chilling effect on a student's willingness to seek help—any effort on the part of another professional to request disclosure of confidential information can be seen as a sign of disrespect for the legal and ethical principles of the field and cause mistrust to develop.

So how do parties prevent conflicts in this area and resolve those that might occur? First, it is important that all sides understand the applicable laws and ethical guidelines. Counseling personnel can be explicit in sharing the provisions and rationale of their state laws with regard to confidentiality and its limits as well as the relevant ethical principles of their professional groups. Other student affairs professionals can then place their wish to receive information from counseling professionals in the context of these specific legal and ethical requirements.

Yet, counseling personnel need to consider reasonable requests from others for information. Privacy laws allow the release of information in specific instances (e.g., when there is imminent danger of harm to self or others) and when a student gives informed consent to release the information. When a residence hall staff member, a dean of students, or a chief student affairs officer reaches out to a student and gains the student's trust through the consultation and referral process, a counselor might do well to consider asking the student to grant permission to share some very basic information with that referring staff member, including simply whether the student followed through with the referral and if the student seems to be doing better as a result. The referring professional learns that the process is working, a student's circle of care is widened, and the relationship between the counselor and the other staff member improves. The vast majority of students are perfectly willing to consent to these limited disclosures. And even in the absence of informed consent, a counselor can share information about how similar issues are generally handled, which can be reassuring to all involved. It is rarely acceptable to respond to inquiries with a simple, "I'm sorry, but I cannot tell you anything."

Understanding the provisions of the Family Educational Rights and Privacy Act (FERPA) is also important.[10] FERPA allows information, classified as education records, to be shared across departments of an institution on a need-to-know basis, and student affairs professionals must evaluate their ethical obligation to share information when a student raises concerns. While FERPA exempts counseling records from these regulations, information that comes from other sources (e.g., the communication between a student and a residence hall staff member) is not confidential and should not be treated as such. Sharing information across departments can ensure that information silos do not exist on campus and that pieces of information about a student can be connected. Staff outside counseling centers should take responsibility for sharing important information with supervisors, deans of students, and counseling center staff.

Developing Trust in Community

Student affairs staff who are charged with building community, whether in residence halls, student group advisement, or other activities, are also advised to encourage students to look out for each other, as Kadison and DiGeronimo effectively argue in their book, *College of the Overwhelmed.*[11] Helping to create a culture of care, in which students discuss their concerns about other students with student affairs staff and others and take responsibility for their own mental health, is a relatively new twist on the ways student affairs staff can assist with the development of the students they work with.

Added to this mix is the growing diversity of our student bodies and the need to develop multicultural competencies in presenting and delivering mental health services. Responsible and effective counselors spend significant amounts of time in professional development not just honing their general clinical skills and keeping up with research but also in ensuring they are offering culturally sensitive and responsive services to all campus populations. Student affairs preparation programs often include training in multicultural issues as part of their core curriculum. And some student affairs professionals, specifically those who work in multicultural resource centers, are among the campus experts in multiculturalism. The development of a core set of competencies in multiculturalism across the division, including those in and outside counseling services, is another area that is ripe for deepening collaborative relationships.

Faculty, staff, and students should think of counselors as partners in the delivery of effective student development programs on campus.

Policy development can bind or divide student affairs professionals and their counseling center colleagues. Universities' campus behavior intervention teams are trying to understand appropriate responses to students who may pose a risk to themselves or others. It is sometimes a point of contention whether to remove from campus a student who exhibits mental health issues that may pose a risk. Operating under a shared understanding of threat-assessment principles can help us work together to the common end of enhancing campus safety, and many of us across student affairs divisions have been involved in a crash course in these principles. Gene Deisinger, deputy chief of police at Virginia Tech and a clinical psychologist and campus threat assessment expert, argues that our campuses have placed an overreliance on control-based strategies, and we should never equate separation with safety.[12] Deisinger argues that engagement, including intervention and monitoring, are management strategies that we sometimes abandon when we too hastily use suspension and expulsion for students who raise concerns. The best way to interact with a student who raises concern is through the collaborative approaches many campuses are developing in their intervention teams, which involves counseling center staff, other student affairs staff, and faculty and staff from across campus.

None of the collaborative efforts and skill-building training will be effective unless staff forge relationships where trust and open communication are the daily norm. Faculty, staff, and students should think of counselors as partners in the delivery of effective student development programs on campus. Counseling center staff members must be visible and accessible on campus, through outreach programs, committee memberships, and presence at important university functions. They must educate themselves about campus politics outside their counseling centers and understand the larger student affairs' mission, goals, and objectives.

Other student affairs staff can assist with building relationships by formalizing liaisons with counseling staff, including counselors on various divisional committees and task groups, and, most importantly, learning about counseling services, understanding privacy and confidentiality issues, and developing skills in identifying, responding to, and referring students of concern. Staff on both sides of the potential divide must openly communicate about the goals and processes they will consult on regarding student concerns and make their partnerships essential elements of the effective practice of their disciplines.

Notes

1. American Council on Education. (1937). *The student personnel point of view.* Washington, DC: Author, p. 39.

2. Ibid., pp. 40–41.

3. American Council on Education. (1949). *The student personnel point of view.* Washington, DC: Author, pp. 27–28.

4. Hodges, S. (2001). University counseling centers at the twenty-first century: Looking forward, looking back. *Journal of College Counseling, 4,* 161–173.

5. Boyd, V. S., Hattauer, E., Brandel, I., Buckles, N., Davidshofer, C., Deakin, S., et al. (2003). Accreditation standards for university and college counseling centers. *Journal of Counseling and Development, 81,* 168–177.

6. Barr, V., Rando, R., Krylowicz, B., & Winfield, E. (2010). *The Association for University and College Counseling Center Directors Annual Survey.* Retrieved from http://aucccd.org/img/pdfs/directors_survey_2009_nm.pdf; American College Health Association. (2010). *American College Health Association–National College Health Assessment II: Reference group data report fall 2009.* Baltimore, MD: Author; Center for the Study of Collegiate Mental Health (2009). *2009 pilot study executive summary.* State College: Pennsylvania State University; Gallagher, R. P. (2009). *National survey of counseling center directors: 2009* (Monograph Series No. 8R). Arlington, VA: International Association of Counseling Services.

7. For details, see the QPR Institute website at http://www.qprinstitute.com/

8. Syracuse University Counseling Center. (2010). *Campus Connect: A suicide prevention program for gatekeepers.* Retrieved from http://counselingcenter.syr.edu/index.php/campus-connect/

9. Kognito Interactive. (2010). *Online gatekeeper training simulations.* Retrieved from http://www.kognito.com/atrisk/

10. Family Educational Rights and Privacy Act §20 U.S.C. § 1232g; C.F.R. Part 99 (1974).

11. Kadison, R., & DiGeronimo, T. F. (2004). *College of the overwhelmed: The campus mental health crisis and what to do about it.* San Francisco, CA: Jossey-Bass.

12. Deisinger, G. (2010, April 9). *Threat assessment: Best practices for institutions of higher education.* Paper presented at the fourth annual meeting of the North Carolina Higher Education Safety Symposium, Greenville.

Moving Toward a Cross-Campus Wellness Model for Student Mental Health

Lori E. Varlotta, California State University, Sacramento, and Paul M. Oliaro, California State University, Fresno

As responding coauthors to David Spano's essay and as executives who lead comprehensive student affairs divisions, we concur with many of the issues he has raised and the dilemmas they pose for student affairs professionals. We use this essay to amplify Spano's call for "shared responsibility" by proposing that counseling center professionals, student affairs colleagues, and related staff across campus join forces to promote the mental wellness of students. To advance a wellness model for student mental health, various university staff must work together to offer proactive services that foster the types of healthy decisions that reduce the likelihood that problems emerge in the first place and reactive ones that address existing needs and issues. We explain how counseling centers and other campus entities can move beyond their traditional roles and responsibilities to support this model.

Role and Responsibilities of Counseling Center Staff

The key responsibility of today's counseling centers is tripartite: to meet the needs of students with serious psychological issues as well as those with milder concerns while offering outreach or educational services that promote overall mental wellness. In meeting this multifaceted responsibility, counseling staff must attend to

- ▶ risk management concerns stemming from high profile campus tragedies and the growing interest from the campus community to provide outreach, education, and training that helps counseling staff and others identify and address potential problems;
- ▶ increased emphasis on academic success and retention, which prompts staff at centers to see students with mild psychological issues who may achieve academic success if provided with assistance;

- ▶ the complexity of issues, including increased reliance on psychotropic prescriptions and the very serious problem of college suicide;
- ▶ economic conditions leading to campus and community budget reductions.

Faced with these challenges, many counseling center administrators find themselves at a crossroads. On the one hand, they react to issues that come their way and cannot be delegated to others, and on the other, they want to offer more proactive, educational services that reduce the chance that harm occurs. Often, the public, parents, and campus community pressure staff of contemporary centers to prioritize those issues most likely to result in crises (e.g., severe depression, acting-out behaviors, suicide ideation). In this mode, they embrace a model that centers on deficits, disorders, or pathology. This deficit model is in opposition to a wellness model, which focuses not only on existing problems but on prevention and education. It works to proactively address the less visible, seemingly less pressing mental health issues (e.g., personal development problems, adjustment/transition difficulties, relationship concerns) that can impede student retention and timely progress toward degree. To move toward a wellness model, counseling center staff must address concrete issues presented by students who seek their services while simultaneously promoting the safety and wellness of all students. Striking a balance that addresses these dual priorities can be very difficult.

This collaborative and proactive approach to student mental wellness creates tremendous opportunities for counseling centers, residential life, judicial affairs, university police, and other offices to make good use of limited resources.

On many campuses, striking a balance means that counseling centers become the primary focus of change. Accordingly, center personnel may attempt to address competing priorities by delivering more efficient and timely services; developing triage programs to identify students who are perceived as being unable to wait, and setting aside time daily to see students who are in crisis; identifying alternatives to the traditional 50-minute session; and focusing on evidence-based practice. While these four measures can enhance the efficacy of counseling centers, involving cross-campus partners can be even more effective—in cost and benefit—in promoting student wellness. Simply stated, counseling centers should certainly be a focal point in creating a wellness model, but no single entity should be charged with maintaining an approach that is as comprehensive and far-reaching as the one proposed here.

To address more broadly and proactively the emerging and less visible mental health concerns of students who are not being treated in the center, counseling professionals must work with university leaders to provide information and training to key staff from appropriate offices. After being trained, these "gatekeepers" can offer educational programs, help identify potential concerns, and make timely and appropriate referrals. In addition to working with other offices, counseling staff can help train the campus crisis response or behavioral intervention team that exists on most campuses today. Typically, this is a cross-divisional team of professionals who help identify problems and intercede when students are threatening harm or causing disruptive incidents in the classroom, at sporting events, during social activities, or in residence halls. By coordinating structured processes that allow various campus constituents to communicate with each other and initiate timely actions or interventions, low-risk and at-risk students might be identified before they become more vulnerable to serious health concerns or cause harm to others. This collaborative and proactive approach to student mental wellness creates tremendous opportunities for counseling centers, residential life, judicial affairs, university police, and other offices to make good use of limited resources.

Role and Responsibilities of Student Affairs and Related Staff

Counseling centers do a good job by and large of working with and reacting to students who walk in. However, many at-risk students and many suffering from lesser concerns never step foot in a counseling center. Therefore, counseling centers must rely heavily on student affairs colleagues and others to assist with mental health outreach and wellness programs that might reach this at-risk population. As a division leader, the vice president for student affairs (VPSA) frequently sets the tone and context for the development of such programs and services. Furthermore, the VPSA office is often the first point of contact for parents, faculty, and staff who express concern about students. Staff in many VPSA offices coordinate the cross-departmental crisis teams, and they can augment the reactionary roles these teams play with more proactive ones (e.g., providing positive feedback and reinforcement and train-the-trainer sessions). In addition, VPSAs design, coordinate, and formalize—through resource allocation and strategic planning—many of the partnerships that enhance mental wellness. Thus, the VPSA can play a key role in advancing a wellness model that prompts the campus population to see itself as a community of attentive individuals invested in the well-being of the whole. There are many ways to structure and formalize this community approach to wellness.

Many of the relationships between counseling centers and other campus entities are traditional and well known. One of the most prominent is the relationship between counseling centers and health centers. Sometimes these two centers share physical space, a common administrative director, and clientele. Additionally, health centers may provide via their primary care physicians a significant amount of mental health care and psychiatric medication evaluations and follow-ups. Beyond these traditional functions that still rely on students' seeking help of their own volition, health centers, perhaps more than other campus units, routinely provide proactive services that promote wellness.

Consider the health education and awareness programs on alcohol, tobacco, and other drugs that many health centers conduct during new student orientation. Frequently, health centers also provide resident assistant (RA) training so RAs can function as peer health educators, form partnerships with local law enforcement and community groups to sponsor harm reduction programs, and deliver information (via face-to-face workshops, web pages or podcasts, interactive webinars, or paper flyers, and brochures) about healthy diet, sleep, and exercise. Additionally, some health centers sponsor and house violence and sexual assault prevention services. These staff may also act in response mode to crisis situations on their campus. It is important that new student affairs professionals view counseling and health centers as not only partners in the day-to-day business of treating students but in promoting cross-campus wellness that de-escalates risk and reinforces healthy and responsible decision making.

Most counseling centers also interact with campus judicial affairs offices in a variety of ways. In a reactive mode, the judicial office staff may require students who violate campus policies to participate in mandated assessment or counseling, or they may be involved in removing (temporarily or permanently) disruptive, risk-posing students from campus. But judicial affairs officers can become partners with counseling centers to take a more proactive approach as well. The offices can join forces to offer workshops during new student and new faculty orientation about how students and faculty alike might identify behavior that should be reported to an appropriate campus official. New faculty in particular are usually very interested in understanding what is acceptable and unacceptable classroom behavior, whom to consult when things feel uncomfortable or get out of hand, and where to refer students in the case of disciplinary action. In summary, such training helps faculty create and maintain learning environments that foster healthy classroom discussions and interactions.

Beyond the classroom, housing and residential life staff play a crucial role in supporting student mental wellness. Mental health-related issues, many of which occur after business hours, can be particularly disruptive in the densely populated living environments that mark most campus housing facilities. Residential life staff have frequent and informal contact with students at all hours of the day and night, and in this sense they have their finger on the pulse of what is going on in the lives of the students with whom they live. Given the nature of their living and working environments, these staff are often the first ones who recognize potential issues; as such, they may have the opportunity to immediately address the issue and prompt changes in attitudes and behavior. To maximize this opportunity, most residential life staff could benefit from additional training from campus psychologists, from an increased presence of a counselor or psychiatrist who could serve as a liaison to the residence halls and assist them in dealing with the more serious behavior, and from after-hours and weekend support when necessary.

In addition to the somewhat reactive role of observing and responding to less than ideal behavior, RAs can reinforce healthy behavior and positively affect future behavior especially in the case of freshmen. RAs have the capacity to formally influence student behavior through policies, procedures, and if necessary, disciplinary measures. But as they get to know their residents, they can use informal, friendly check-ins and gentle inquiries to reinforce good choices and praise students who are making healthy decisions. In unstructured, casual ways and in more formal ways such as workshops, RAs can help students make the connections between physical and mental wellbeing and academic success.

In addition to collaborations between counseling centers and health centers, judicial affairs, and housing and residential life, other connections can be equally fruitful in promoting student wellness. One such partnership is between counseling centers and recreation sports. Many reliable health sources recommend regular exercise, adequate sleep, and a healthy diet as being as effective or more effective than prescription drugs in regulating mood, reducing mild symptoms of depression, and diminishing stress—all of which increase satisfaction and contentment. Counseling center staff can quickly and easily refer students to fun and healthy activities offered through recreation sports. Disability offices are another common collaborator with counseling centers, since campuses across the country are facing increased student requests for physical and psychological accommodations. Some disability offices employ psychological counselors to work with students seeking Americans With Disabilities Act services or accommodations. If disabled students obtain services early in the semester, they may be less likely to become frustrated or put themselves or others in vulnerable positions, and more likely to experience overall well-being.

In closing, we not only reiterate but underscore David Spano's point that campuses must encourage shared responsibility for identifying, confronting, and assisting students who manifest mental health problems. Moreover, we suggest that such collaboration be harnessed into a wellness model that is informed by current data and careful assessment of the scope and nature of emerging and existing problems. If education, outreach, training, and gatekeeper systems are to be on target, then they must be accurately focused on the real and substantiated needs of students.

Further Reading and Related Blog

Amanda Wilson, University of Iowa

Jablonski, M., McClellan, G., & Zdziarski, E. (Eds.) (2008). *In search of safer communities: Emerging practices for student affairs in addressing campus violence.* Washington, DC: National Association of Student Personnel Administrators.

This report is a comprehensive overview of best practices to ensure campus safety, with sections on the role of faculty and other student affairs administrators in campus safety prevention, mental health interventions, and response to campus tragedies.

Jed Foundation. (2008). *Student mental health and the law: A resource for institutions of higher education.* New York, NY: Author.

This document provides campus professionals with a summary of laws and professional guidelines and recommendations related to best practices in responding to student mental health concerns.

Kadison, R., & DiGeronimo, T. F. (2004). *College of the overwhelmed: The campus mental health crisis and what to do about it.* San Francisco, CA: Jossey-Bass.

This is a widely cited book whose authors argue that everyone associated with a university—faculty, staff, parents, even students themselves—is responsible for coping with the burgeoning mental health needs of students.

Blog URL: contestedissues.wordpress.com
Corresponding Chapter Post: tinyurl.com/contestedissues17

18

What Roles Should Student Affairs Educators Play in Attending to Students' Religious and Spiritual Needs?

Creating Space for Spirituality and Religion in Student Affairs Practice

Alyssa Bryant Rockenbach,
North Carolina State University

This past spring I ventured into new territory by teaching a course on spirituality and religion as an elective in my department's higher education administration graduate program. The name of the course, Qualitative Approaches to Studying Spirituality in Higher Education, reflected the dual purposes I was aiming (somewhat ambitiously) to accomplish: explore emerging issues surrounding religion and spirituality in higher education and conduct a collaborative narrative inquiry study designed to examine how people of diverse worldviews come together in spiritual exchanges across differences. The research component of the class involved pairing the graduate students in the course with undergraduates on campus who identified with different faiths and worldviews. The dyads engaged in three discussions over the semester about their different spiritualities, and our goal was to study the nature of their exchanges.

One of the challenges we encountered right from the start was making sense of the elusive terms *religion* and *spirituality*. Based on our reading and conversations in class, we agreed that religion takes shape in organized traditions of belief and practice. This is not to say that religion is inherently institutional. In fact, religious experiences can be intensely personal, but often they have at their foundation a doctrinal basis linked to particular scriptures, rituals, and deities. Spirituality may encompass religion—but not necessarily. Core dimensions of spirituality include meaning, purpose, wholeness, authenticity, transcendence, and connectedness.

The semester represented many firsts for me as a 4th-year assistant professor. Though I had been curious about spirituality in higher education for many years and committed most of my scholarship to probing these issues, I had never taught a class explicitly devoted to the subject. Neither had I integrated my research and teaching in a course format. Yet another first—one that became increasingly evident as the semester progressed—was the level of energy and authentic sharing the course demanded of my students and me. Though rewarding, our journey together was not an easy one. Our discussions challenged us academically as we sought to make sense of an area of scholarship that transcends disciplinary boundaries; our discussions challenged us personally as they revealed our deepest values, beliefs, biases, hurts, and hopes.

I share this experience to highlight what is possible when we provide space for spirituality in higher education. Although the topic of spirituality is considered by some in higher education to be beyond the bounds of appropriate discourse, conversations and educational settings that acknowledge and welcome all dimensions of the human experience take on a synergistic quality, sometimes to the surprise of those participating. In our case, the course's holistic inclusion of academic and personal objectives enriched our learning. The students became versed in emerging issues in our field, they assumed active roles as members of a research team, and (here is the synergistic part) they learned about themselves through telling and making sense of their spiritual stories—and through listening to the stories of others. As their teacher, my learning was similarly rich with an added element that surprised me: changes in the very nature of my teaching. During my first few years as a faculty member, I struggled to be myself in the classroom. Because I was close in age to my students and not far removed from the graduate school stage of life, I differentiated myself from them, perhaps unintentionally, with a measured degree of interpersonal distancing. To be the "expert" and to establish my legitimacy, I revealed little about who I was as their teacher, focusing instead on the facts of the course content and what the material meant for them (not me) as emerging higher education and student affairs professionals. But the spirituality class changed that for me. I had created the course with collaboration in mind. We were a team and I was part of the circle, not a distant facilitator. I asked students to write their spiritual narratives and discuss them openly. As a member of this learning community, I was unable to hide behind my neutral professorial facade. It only made sense for me to share my spiritual narrative in return and to be as vulnerable with them as they were with me. The distance that had characterized my former pedagogy fell by the wayside, and I gladly embraced a new way of teaching and being myself in the classroom.

In short, when asked what role educators should play in meeting students' religious and spiritual needs, my immediate response is, "a central one." But to me the larger question is *why*. My firsthand experience with teaching a class on spirituality and religion has convinced me that infusing these issues into our classroom discourse energizes and transforms those who partake in the conversation—the students and instructors. Beyond personal and professional transformation, there are other important reasons to address religion and spirituality in higher education and student affairs. In the next section I delineate a rationale and follow with reflection on the roles of student affairs professionals in meeting students' spiritual and religious needs, along with practical strategies for taking on those roles.

Why Are Spirituality and Religion Relevant to Student Affairs Work?

Even a cursory look at the history of U.S. higher education and student affairs reveals that spirituality and religion have been present in colleges and universities from their inception. The nine colonial colleges, early prototypes of what would later evolve into a diverse and intricate system of higher education, had Protestant Christian beliefs and values woven into their mission, purpose, and practice. Many students attending these first colleges received training for the ministry. Learning in the colonial colleges emphasized Christian moral philosophy, and administrators and faculty recognized the character development of their students as one of the core functions of higher education. Diminished emphasis on religious values occurred as colleges became universities in the late 19th and early 20th centuries. Values consistent with modern science (e.g., naturalism, positivism, and empiricism), and the German university model that scholars studying abroad brought back to the United States, broke the denominational hold on institutions aspiring to become universities.

While it may seem that higher education became effectively secularized during the rise of the American university, compelling evidence suggests otherwise. Surely, the nature of religious influence has changed substantially, but religion is still present in colleges and universities even if not in the form of official denominational affiliation. Cherry, DeBerg, and Porterfield describe a trend toward voluntary religion and pluralism on campus, with the "ethos of decentered, diverse, religiously tolerant institutions of higher education [serving as] a breeding ground for vital religious practice and teaching."[1] Likewise, as the student affairs profession emerged and took shape, it assumed a fundamental responsibility for the whole student. In step with the college-to-university transformation, faculty became increasingly professionalized and focused on disciplinary specialization and graduate student education. Thus, the personal development of students became the purview of the burgeoning student personnel profession. Codified in the 1937 and the revised 1949 *Student Personnel Point of View* (*SPPV*), religious values and spiritual development have long been one of the profession's concerns. As the authors of the 1949 *SPPV* state, "The student personnel point of view encompasses the student as a whole. The concept of education is broadened to include attention to the student's well-rounded development—physically, socially, emotionally, spiritually, as well as intellectually."[2] One of the fundamental reasons religion and spirituality are relevant to the work of student affairs educators is that both are components of the profession's historical legacy of valuing students as whole individuals.

Mentors and peers who make space for big questions and who are comfortable with the ambiguity that is integral to spiritual questing make ideal companions along the way.

In addition to what we can glean from the history of higher education, another rationale for addressing students' religious and spiritual needs in student affairs practice concerns the interests and expectations of present-day college students. The University of California, Los Angeles (UCLA) spirituality in higher education study has provided a national perspective on how students today approach the religious and spiritual dimensions of life. Initiated because of concerns that students' materialistic leanings had superseded their commitment to meaning and purpose, Alexander Astin, Helen Astin, and Jennifer Lindholm, the study's directors, sought to explore students' interior lives and learned that the instrumentality and materialism that students exhibit are not representative of the full picture.[3] Rather, as students enter college they report that spirituality is relevant to them: "Four in five indicate 'having an interest in spirituality' and 'believing in the sacredness of life,' and nearly two-thirds say, 'My spirituality is a source of joy.'"[4] Importantly, college students *expect* their institutions to be responsive to their needs with as many as two thirds claiming that it is "essential" or "very important" for their college to "enhance their self-understanding (69%), prepare them for responsible citizenship (67%), develop their personal values (67%), and provide for their emotional development (63%)."[5] Close to half underscore the importance of having their college encourage personal expression of spirituality.[6] In fact, attending to the spiritual climate on campus and responding to students' needs result in higher satisfaction levels among students. Specifically, ensuring that the institution is religiously diverse, open to spiritual expression, and free of interreligious divisiveness and conflict improves students' satisfaction with the campus climate.[7]

As educators, it is our hope that students leave college with inclinations toward health and well-being, engaged citizenship, compassion for others, and pluralism and inclusion. Several of these outcomes align with spiritual development, which the college experience has the potential to shape in myriad ways. According to the UCLA spirituality in higher education study, students become less religiously engaged during the first 3 years of college but exhibit growth along several dimensions characterized as spiritual, including quest (searching for meaning and purpose), equanimity (feeling peaceful and centered even during hardships), ethic of caring (relating compassionately to others), and ecumenical worldview (being open to others of different faiths/life philosophies).[8] The latter outcome—ecumenical worldview—involves having an interest in diverse worldviews, accepting others, and believing in human interconnectedness, and is particularly salient in light of ongoing discussions among student affairs practitioners about enhancing students' competencies in the area of global citizenship. Two studies found that peer undergraduate socialization processes that challenged rather than reinforced religious and spiritual perspectives, as well as challenging diversity experiences, encountering religion and spirituality in academic contexts, and experiencing religious/spiritual struggles, predicted students' development of an ecumenical worldview.[9] The numerous experiences that appear to shape students' ecumenicism are within the realm of student affairs practice. Thus, it makes sense for us as educators to understand the ways students' involvement shapes spiritual outcomes, especially those relating to global citizenship, and adjust our practices accordingly to maximize student potential in these key areas.

What Roles Should Student Affairs Professionals Assume in Meeting Students' Religious and Spiritual Needs?

I base my threefold justification for addressing religion and spirituality in student affairs practice on historical traditions in higher education and early student personnel work, current students' interests and expectations, and promising college outcomes that may be achieved in conjunction with spiritual development. With a rationale in place, I return to the central question at hand: What roles should student affairs educators play in meeting students' needs, and how might they take on these roles in their day-to-day practice? I propose five approaches for student affairs educators to consider as they seek to incorporate religion and spirituality in their work with students:

1. Modeling authenticity
2. Opening the door to religious and spiritual dialogue
3. Creating a mentoring environment
4. Providing and pointing the way to resources
5. Understanding nuanced institutional contexts and audiences

The five approaches are by no means exhaustive, and educators will surely tailor their roles in ways that are situation appropriate and congruent with their professional responsibilities. Nonetheless, I offer these recommendations as a starting point for those hoping to make the most of their interactions with students by enhancing spiritual development.

The first of the five approaches, modeling authenticity, begins with an inward reflection on the spiritual and religious dimensions of our own lives as educators. Too often the demands of our personal and professional lives encroach on time to contemplate who we are, where we have been spiritually and religiously, where we are going, and what we believe and value. It is incredibly difficult—if not impossible—to address students' needs if we cannot identify the cornerstones of our interior lives. Self-understanding, in other words, is a critical step toward supporting and guiding students along their religious and spiritual journeys. Writing a spiritual autobiography can be a particularly illuminating exercise to explore the dimensions of self that lie below the surface of daily routines and busy schedules. The spirituality course I described earlier began with an assignment in which each of us constructed a written narrative about the evolution of our personal worldviews. We came to discover that the facts and comprehensiveness of the stories we weave are not as important as the insight we glean about the significant experiences in our lives and the meaning we make of them. So much self-learning can take place simply by examining how we construct our stories and integrate the disparate pieces.

The internal work of exploring our religious and spiritual selves autobiographically becomes externally oriented once we begin to translate our self-understanding into self-disclosure. A critical component of modeling authenticity is openness with students about who we are and where we are in our spiritual journeys. Communicating to students that their inner lives are an important part of the college experience entails demonstrating that we too value our inner lives and strive for wholeness in the ways we live and express ourselves to others. Finding balance in authentic self-expression is surely challenging. As educators, we have a responsibility—ethically and legally—to remain ever mindful of the dangers of indoctrination whenever religion and spirituality are broached in contexts where power imbalances exist. Our expectations of students influence them, which is why we must continually remind them that the purpose of our sharing is to give credence to spiritual and religious experiences—theirs and ours—and that our sharing is not meant to elevate one particular faith, worldview, or spiritual path above any others. In short, we model authenticity so students understand they are free to do the same.

Modeling authenticity is arguably one way to initiate the second approach: opening the door to religious and spiritual dialogue. Beyond the honest relaying of our own journeys, there are abundant possibilities for opening (and holding open) the door to dialogue. The primary aim is to create space for meaningful conversation to occur. I facilitated a professional development seminar on spirituality among a group of student affairs professionals at a university near my home institution. During a particularly fruitful conversation about strategies to engage students spiritually, one participant reflected aloud about the value of safe space placards used on many campuses to signal offices and people who accept and welcome lesbian, gay, bisexual, and transgender (LGBT) people. She suggested we use a similar approach to identify safe spaces for spiritual and religious conversations. Educators who elect to place a spiritual space sticker or placard on their doors or in their offices would effectively be indicating receptivity to talking about matters of the inner life. Analogous to the intent of LGBT safe spaces, spiritual space stickers and placards should communicate commitment to religious/worldview pluralism in addition to general openness to spiritual conversations.

Numerous contexts in higher education represent ideal openings for dialogue. Community service activities, whether in conjunction with service-learning courses or cocurricular volunteer endeavors, challenge students to evaluate core dimensions of meaning, purpose, and values— often in relation to closely held religious and spiritual beliefs. Reflection, which is frequently recognized as the essential element of transformative community service involvement, goes hand in hand with spiritual development. Like service work, just about any encounter that incites reflection—for example, study abroad, formal or informal hot topic dialogues, or engagement with diverse peers—has the potential to initiate conversations that lead to the questions and concerns of the inner life.[10]

Understanding the student body of a given institution—and subcultures in the larger culture—is imperative to shaping meaningful opportunities to engage the inner life.

A third approach to addressing religion and spirituality in student affairs practice involves creating a mentoring environment. This approach stems from the writing of Sharon Parks who characterizes mentoring environments as hearthlike spaces that effectively reflect higher education's long-standing mantra to balance challenge and support in nurturing student development.[11] Mentoring communities, which "are particularly essential to the formation of an adult faith," have at their core a number of distinctive features that educators can seek to put into practice: a network of belonging, big-enough questions, encounters with otherness, important habits of mind (e.g., dialogue, critical and connective thought, contemplativeness), worthy dreams, and access to key images.[12] A mentoring environment is critical for students who happen upon unforeseen challenges to their faith and way of life. Typically in the first few weeks of college, students encounter people and experiences that call into question the foundations of their worldview or religious perspective. The surety of prior conviction is replaced with the disquieting unknown. Disequilibrium can be fertile ground for exploration and discovery among college students, but is best traversed in the company of others. Mentors and peers who make space for big questions and who are comfortable with the ambiguity that is integral to spiritual questing make ideal companions along the way. By providing a mentoring environment, student affairs educators foster students' searches for meaning and purpose at the same time they offer guidance and encouragement during the darker phases of struggle in students' spiritual journeys.

Student affairs educators assume a collaborative role as part of the fourth approach, providing and pointing the way to resources. More often than not, the resources students need to facilitate their spiritual growth are dispersed in compartmentalized spaces across campus rather than in a single one-stop-shop location. Educators can seek to establish a multifaceted support network for students by forming partnerships with faculty, counselors, campus or local clergy, and campus-based or community religious organizations. These partnerships can assume many forms. For example, an administrator seeking to help students negotiate religious and spiritual struggles, a common phenomenon among young adults, might convene a panel of campus ministers, counselors, and upper-division students willing to talk about their experiences.[13] The panel format would not only elevate awareness of an issue that many students navigate alone, it would also draw upon and integrate the expertise of people who have had firsthand experiences with spiritual struggles or who have supported and counseled struggling individuals.

It is also important to bear in mind that opportunities for religious and spiritual enrichment may exist in spaces not explicitly devoted to these purposes. For instance, although units, centers, and organizations focused on community service projects, study abroad, or student identities (e.g., gender, sexual orientation, race/ethnicity, and culture) may not consider spirituality and religion as central to their mission, students' inner development undoubtedly surfaces in these settings. Being cognizant of these spaces and connecting regularly with those who oversee them will enable student affairs educators to encourage students to draw upon the constellation of resources available.

The fifth and final approach I would like to put forth to student affairs educators committed to addressing students' religious and spiritual needs is that of understanding nuanced institutional contexts and audiences. The myriad possibilities educators may consider as they model authenticity, open the door to dialogue, create a mentoring environment, and provide and point the way to resources will vary considerably in their effectiveness (and suitability) from one campus to the next. The sheer diversity of institutions in the U.S. system of higher education ensures that successful initiatives will assume different forms depending on the institutional context.

Our first responsibility as educators is to consider the legal and ethical mandates in our particular context. For instance, what are the legal bounds of addressing religion and spirituality in public, private nonreligious, and private religious settings? Constitutional provisions and subsequent court decisions have tended toward a twofold message: Although the establishment clause of the First Amendment disallows public institutions' entanglement with religion and requires religious neutrality, the free speech and exercise clauses enable students to express themselves religiously and spiritually through noncoercive student-led campus activities.[14] Even so, the legal environment is continually in flux as new court rulings refine the rights of individuals and mandates governing institutions.

Our second responsibility is to understand the students we work with. What does spirituality mean to them and to what extent is it relevant? Some students gravitate toward conversations on faith and spirituality; others may feel that religion has played an oppressive role in society and view the *S* word with disdain. Understanding the student body of a given institution—and subcultures in the larger culture—is imperative to shaping meaningful opportunities to engage the inner life. Quantitative and qualitative assessments of students' needs may be useful to gauge their perspectives and expectations of student affairs.

In the end, my assertions that spirituality and religion have a place in student affairs practice extend from my own transformative experiences with creating spaces attuned to these dimensions, along with historical and empirical observations of the profession and student development. To ensure that needs are met as we engage students religiously and spiritually, we must practice authenticity, open doors to dialogue, create mentoring spaces, identify and integrate resources, and pay careful attention to context.

Notes

1. Cherry, C., DeBerg, B. A., & Porterfield, A. (2001). *Religion on campus.* Chapel Hill: University of North Carolina Press, p. 295.

2. American Council on Education. (1937). *The student personnel point of view.* Washington, DC: Author; American Council on Education. (1949). *The student personnel point of view.* Washington, DC: Author, p. 2.

3. Astin, A. W., Astin, H. S., & Lindholm, J. A. (2010). *Cultivating the spirit: How college can enhance students' inner lives.* San Francisco, CA: Jossey-Bass.

4. Astin, A. W., Astin, H. S., Lindholm, J. A., Bryant, A. N., Szelényi, K., & Calderone, S. (2005). *The spiritual life of college students: A national study of college students' search for meaning and purpose.* Los Angeles, CA: Higher Education Research Institute, p. 4.

5. Ibid., p. 6.

6. Ibid.

7. Bryant, A. N., & Mayhew, M. J. (2011). *The collegiate religious and spiritual climate: Predictors of satisfaction among students with diverse worldviews.* Unpublished manuscript.

8. Astin, A. W., Astin, H. S., & Lindholm, J. A. (2010). *Cultivating the spirit: How college can enhance students' inner lives.* San Francisco, CA: Jossey-Bass; Astin, Astin, & Lindholm, *Students experience spiritual growth during college;* Bryant, A. N., Choi, J. Y., & Yasuno, M. (2003). Understanding the religious and spiritual dimensions of students' lives in the first year of college. *Journal of College Student Development, 44,* 723–745.

9. Bryant, A. N. (2010). *The impact of campus context, college encounters, and religious/spiritual struggle on ecumenical worldview development.* Unpublished manuscript; Mayhew, M. J. (2010). *Spirituality as inclusive: A multi-level examination into the role colleges play in shaping the development of ecumenical worldviews.* Unpublished manuscript.

10. Nash, R. J., Bradley, D. L., & Chickering, A. W. (2008) *How to talk about hot topics on campus: From polarization to moral conversation.* San Francisco, CA: Jossey-Bass.

11. Parks, S. D. (2000). *Big questions, worthy dreams: Mentoring young adults in their search for meaning, purpose, and faith.* San Francisco, CA: Jossey-Bass; Sanford, N. (1966). *Self & society: Social change and individual development.* New York, NY: Atherton Press.

12. Parks, *Big questions, worthy dreams,* p. 135.

13. Bryant, A. N., & Astin, H. S. (2008). The correlates of spiritual struggle during the college years. *Journal of Higher Education, 79,* 1–27.

14. Kaplin, W. A., & Lee, B. A. (2009). *A legal guide for student affairs professionals* (2nd ed.). San Francisco, CA: Jossey-Bass.

The Student Affairs Educator as a Mentor for Religio-Spiritual Meaning

Michele C. Murray, Seattle University, and Robert J. Nash, University of Vermont

Do student affairs educators have a role to play in attending to students' religious and spiritual needs? Yes, unequivocally. As Bryant Rockenbach reminds us, religion and spirituality contribute to the whole person we are committed to educate, and so we agree with Bryant Rockenbach's assertion that the role of educators to engage students' religio-spiritual questions is a central one. For us, religion and spirituality are essential pathways for students (and educators) to make meaning of their experiences and search for answers to their deepest questions.[1]

Religion and spirituality, as Bryant Rockenbach points out on p. 341, are "the cornerstones of our interior lives," and sometimes they are the cause of, and key to, the darkest corners of our inner selves. If educators are to serve students as they develop habits of mind, body, spirit, and purpose, they need to be prepared to attend to their religio-spiritual needs.

Because the student affairs professional mandate is to educate the whole person, educators need to free themselves from the boundaries—whether perceived lack of expertise, need to protect and respect believers and nonbelievers of all types, fear of offending, or desire to avoid conflict between and among differing belief systems—that sometimes preclude them from engaging students' religious and spiritual questions, doubts, and discoveries. Bryant Rockenbach proposes five approaches for opening the door to the religious and spiritual dimensions of college students. We support her wise suggestions and have reflected on how we incorporate each of her approaches in our own work with students. In the sections that follow, we share our ideas with the hope of contributing to the conversation on how best to educate college students today.

Modeling Authenticity

Bryant Rockenbach advises that if educators are to teach about religion and spirituality, then they must begin with "an inward reflection on the spiritual and religious dimensions of our own lives as educators" (p. 341).

We could not agree more strongly, with the caveat that religio-spiritual reflection extends beyond the professional life to the personal as well. In our own work, we try to be crystal clear about what our (personal) beliefs and biases about this controversial subject matter might be. We are well aware of the dangers of becoming a nonbiased pretender, or worse, an agenda-driven religio-spiritual ideologue who consciously or unconsciously chooses sides. Our interior journeys have included much personal writing and consultation with trusted others who have helped us shed light on our own belief systems and how they influence our interactions with students. Collectively their advice was invaluable. In summary, it could be reduced to a few catchphrases: Be honest, be knowledgeable, listen in order to draw out students, make personal and practical connections whenever appropriate, and, as one religious studies scholar warned Robert: "Don't preach, leech, or screech. You'll just scare students away."

Beyond the inward journey, Bryant Rockenbach identifies self-disclosure as critical to modeling authenticity. Personal sharing with students, within prudent reason of course, demonstrates trust, communicates the value of religio-spiritual questions, and provides an example of how one person has approached a similar question or circumstance. We have found that sharing a bit of our own stories reminds students that we are whole people and gives them permission to be the same. However, modeling authenticity is not tied solely to self-disclosure. The journey toward self-understanding ultimately provides an opportunity for deepening personal integrity—that is, aligning foundational beliefs so they inform one's worldview and guide practice. Students are watching to see if their educators' actions match their words, and in this way they detect who is, and who is not, authentic. Aligning head, heart, and hand is as critical a component of modeling authenticity as is personal sharing—perhaps even more so.

Opening the Door to Religious and Spiritual Dialogue

Bryant Rockenbach states that the primary aim of this approach is to create space "for opening (and holding open) the door to dialogue" (p. 342). As with the lesbian, gay, bisexual, and transgender safe spaces Bryant Rockenbach mentions, we urge student affairs professionals to become more knowledgeable about a variety of religio-spiritual worldviews. Although Bryant Rockenbach did not emphasize this point, we believe that building a safe conversational space for students to talk about religious difference requires content-area competence in a number of religio-spiritual belief and nonbelief systems. In a post–September 11, 2001, world, we hold that a religiously literate educator is the sine qua non not just for helping students to create meaning but to become religious pluralists as well.[2]

As whole-person educators, student affairs professionals need a variety of tools—not rules—to meet students' religious and spiritual needs in whatever institutional context they find themselves.

Constructing safe spaces in this context entails creating vibrant and self-reflective conversational places where students can share their evolving religio-spiritual development without fear of ridicule, judgment, or criticism. To this end, we use a dialogue format Robert created called *moral conversation*. This method requires that educators and students respond to one another using only *conversation starters*, and *conversation sustainers*, not *conversation stoppers*.[3] Our conversation stopper rules include these proscriptions: no name-calling; no making others look bad so you, the speaker, can shine; and no positioning oneself on the highest moral ground.[4] The conversation starter and sustainer rules feature these prescriptions: explain, clarify, question, rephrase, respect, and affirm; be generous at all times without exception; attribute the best motive; and look for the truth in what you oppose and the error in what you espouse.[5] The rules, like open and honest dialogue, take time to master, and we learn alongside our students. When done well, learners and seekers can communicate across difference in a way that enriches, rather than encroaches upon, one another's perspectives and experiences.

Moral conversation creates an environment for multifaith, as well as absence-of-faith, expression to occur without fear of unwittingly trampling upon belief systems or enflaming religio-spiritual conflict. In the same way, moral conversation contributes to students' developing the ecumenical perspective Bryant Rockenbach supports without slipping into the territory of relativism where religio-spiritual beliefs amount to very little. As Bryant Rockenbach observes, opportunities for religio-spiritual moral conversations abound in higher education: Service-learning, education abroad, and a host of additional immersion experiences offer important entry points for making meaning, many of which have religious and spiritual dimensions.[6]

Creating a Mentoring Environment

Like Bryant Rockenbach, we value Sharon Daloz Parks's concept of mentoring and have honed our own thoughts on mentoring for meaning.[7] Defined less by expertise, meaning mentors are fellow spiritual seekers and questioners. We may be older and more knowledgeable about the content of the world's major and minor religions and spiritualities than our students, but we are not necessarily wiser or more practiced in these matters. After all, Robert is a secular humanist who himself has been engaged in a decades-long search for meaning, and Michele is a Roman Catholic who adheres to a particular worldview. We may have few answers for our students, but in our role as meaning mentors we are able to provide a comfortable refuge and an open-ended conversational space for questioners and seekers of all persuasions—whether agnostic, atheist, theist, or polytheist.

Mentoring for meaning does not clone the mentor's spiritual identity; rather, it is a way of accompanying students as they search the depths and heights of their own spiritual quests. The meaning mentor does not provide answers so much as hold the student's questions and provide a safe harbor for exploring, prodding, and sensitively turning the questions upside down and inside out. The meaning mentor follows a spirituality of teaching, which is driven by Alfred Lord Tennyson's conviction that a genuine faith must somehow find a way to wrestle with the demons of honest doubt.[8] The objective is not to overcome doubt, because this is neither possible nor desirable, but to fully incorporate it into any final declaration of belief and call to action. In this way, mentoring—and teaching—has a spirituality of its own. The spirituality of mentoring simply calls for the student and the mentor to undertake in trust an inward journey together whose ultimate purpose is to fashion a deeper, personal response to the mystery of existence.

Providing Resources

Bryant Rockenbach is quite helpful in her advice about connecting students with on- and off-campus resources that are competent and willing to give students the support they need to seek answers to the existential and metaphysical questions that emerge and reemerge throughout their lives. Indeed, partners in the meaning-making venture, whether faculty, campus ministers, or community religious leaders, are necessary for students' religio-spiritual growth. Support networks are everywhere, and students need to know how to take full advantage of them as they struggle with their deepest meaning questions. Furthermore, forming partnerships with local and campus resources helps dissipate the pressure to be experts in religious and spiritual matters. Having referral resources at the ready recognizes the personal limitations each educator has in the religio-spiritual realm. Rather than deflecting their questions, referring students gives them access to multiple perspectives and different areas of expertise.

A dynamic learning environment engages students at every turn—in coffeehouses, cafeterias, classrooms, residence halls, chapels, cultural centers, and service-learning sites. The same is true for creating an environment that asks, considers, and wrestles with religious and spiritual questions. Film discussions, speaker panels, guided reflection, and colloquia where students, faculty, and staff make presentations on meaningful topics connect students with one another and with religio-spiritual resources in nonthreatening circumstances where they can explore their deep questions at their own pace.

Understanding Nuanced Institutional Contexts and Audiences

Bryant Rockenbach understands well the nuanced (and nonnuanced) challenges of getting support for religio-spiritual meaning making from a variety of on- and off-campus groups. Legal constraints and institutional affiliation may shape the way educators respond to students' religious and spiritual needs, but they do not diminish the need to respond. Similarly, as Bryant Rockenbach points out, student cultures and subcultures range in their tolerance for explicitly, or even implicitly, religious or spiritual language. However, regardless of their contextual landscape, students cycle through deep metaphysical questions that raise doubt and cross the threshold to the transcendent. As whole-person educators, student affairs professionals need a variety of tools—not rules—to meet students' religious and spiritual needs in whatever institutional context they find themselves.

In our work on meaning-making, we outline several strategies educators can employ with students in one-on-one settings, in the classroom, and outside the classroom.[9] These tools, such as asking philosophical questions, telling stories, and creating purposeful silence, create the mental, psychological, spiritual, and sometimes physical space for deep-meaning learning to occur, and they have the capacity to adjust to any institutional environment and student population. We encourage all educators to use these tools and develop their own, so they might respond to the religious and spiritual needs of the students they serve while upholding their legal and ethical professional obligations.

In short, we support Bryant Rockenbach's position that student affairs educators play a central role in attending to students' religious and spiritual needs. Students' religio-spiritual development is inextricable from their development as whole people, an ideal the profession is committed to. It is not a matter of whether students have religio-spiritual questions. Instead, it is a matter of where, how, and with whom. The tools and approaches we discuss here address the questions of where and how, and it is the student affairs educator who has the ability to address the question of with whom.

Notes

1. Nash, R. J., & Murray, M. C. (2010). *How to help college students find purpose: The campus guide to meaning-making*. San Francisco, CA: Jossey-Bass.

2. Nash, R. J., & Bishop, P. A. (2010). *Teaching adolescents religious literacy in a post-9/11 world*. Charlotte, NC: Information Age.

3. Nash, R. J., Bradley, D. L., & Chickering, A. W. (2008). *How to talk about hot topics on campus: From polarization to moral conversation*. San Francisco, CA: Jossey-Bass.

4. Ibid.

5. Ibid.

6. Nash & Murray, *How to help college students find purpose*.

7. Parks, S. D. (2000). *Big questions, worthy dreams: Mentoring young adults in their search for meaning, purpose, and faith*. San Francisco, CA: Jossey-Bass.

8. Nash, R. J. (2001). Constructing a spirituality of teaching: A personal perspective. *Religion and Education, 28*, 1–20.

9. Nash & Murray, *How to help college students find purpose*.

Further Reading and Related Blog

Peter M. Magolda and Marcia B. Baxter Magolda,
Miami University

Astin, A. W., Astin, H. S., & Lindholm, J. A. (2010). *Cultivating the spirit: How college can enhance students' inner lives.* San Francisco, CA: Jossey-Bass.

This book summarizes a 5-year study of the spiritual growth of college students—in particular the role that college, as well as specific collegiate experiences, plays in the development of students' spiritual qualities. The authors carefully define dimensions of spirituality, illuminate the role spirituality plays in student learning and development, identify strategies for enhancing students' development, and encourage universities to explicitly address the spiritual needs of students.

Nash, R. J., & Murray, M. C. (2010). *Helping college students find purpose: The campus guide to meaning-making.* San Francisco, CA: Jossey-Bass.

This book pays tribute to the power of the college years to explore deep questions of meaning. Using real-life vignettes, the authors explore the role of faculty and administrators in mentoring students for meaning. They also outline theoretical approaches to meaning making as well as offer concrete tools for applying the theory and practice of meaning making to a variety of classroom and campus settings.

Parks, S. D. (2000). *Big questions, worthy dreams: Mentoring young adults in their search for meaning, purpose, and faith.* San Francisco: CA: Jossey-Bass.

Parks explores faith development in the era of young adulthood, highlighting the challenges young adults face in making meaning of their lives. She introduces the concept of faith as meaning making and discusses the role of higher education and mentoring to provide good company to young adults as they explore forms of knowing, dependence, and community.

Blog URL: contestedissues.wordpress.com
Corresponding Chapter Post: tinyurl.com/contestedissues18

19

How Do Campus Administrators Go Beyond the First Amendment in Achieving Balance Between Free Speech and Civil Discourse?

Putting the Hammer Down

Tobias W. Uecker, Kenyon College

In a frequently paraphrased line from *The Psychology of Science*, Abraham Maslow said, "I suppose it is tempting, if the only tool you have is a hammer, to treat everything as if it were a nail."[1] Indeed, given a single tool to solve all problems, it seems natural to find ways to make that tool apply in every case. Some might view the ability to adapt a single tool to many functions as an exemplar of the ingenuity that is crucial in an ever changing field like student affairs. However, I view Maslow's point as more of a caution than a suggestion. Everything is not a nail, so how effective is any approach that assumes universal nailness? Rather than treating everything as a nail, the person with only a hammer would be better served to seek out other tools or perhaps to begin honing the blunt instrument at hand into something more multifaceted.

The First Amendment to the U.S. Constitution serves as the hammer in resolving questions of free speech throughout society, including on college campuses. This first concept in the Bill of Rights is an effective blunt instrument; there is nothing inherently complex in its assertion, "Congress shall make no law . . . abridging the freedom of speech, or of the press; or of the people to peaceably assemble."[2] Court decisions over two centuries have created nuances in applying the First Amendment, but even these nuances fail to address every tension that might arise in the course of public discourse. Case law hones the First Amendment hammer a bit but still leaves day-to-day decision makers a relatively blunt instrument to hammer out challenging questions and answers.

Unfortunately, a blunt instrument in the hands of students, faculty, and administrators looking for easy answers and widely applicable truisms becomes a wildly swinging cudgel, as likely to smash the fragile balance of civil discourse as to pound in the nails that strengthen that balance. As we resolve the question of how student affairs educators protect freedom of speech while ensuring civil discourse, we must acknowledge the different contextual hardware we encounter and hone the blunt implements we may find in our problem-solving toolboxes into precision instruments we can draw upon at different times and in different situations to best serve our diverse student populations.

This essay examines two periods of campus controversy in the last half century. Responses to the 1960s' free speech movement and the implementation of speech codes in the late 1980s and early 1990s drive existing case law regarding free speech on campus and illustrate how the blunt application of First Amendment legal precedent inadequately addresses the tension between freedom of expression and civil discourse. I also explore two cases where different restrictive—rather than discursive—approaches to controversy allow opportunities for educational conversation to pass by in favor of blanket definitions of appropriate speech. Finally, I advance a framework that offers campus constituents access to an environment that is simultaneously open to controversial—even offensive—ideas and respectful of the need for civility in creating a welcoming and supportive campus environment.

The Campus Free Speech Movement: Forging First Amendment Protections

Richard C. Ratliff said, "A rash of free speech cases in the federal and state courts in the late 1960's [sic] underscored the fact that the 'speech' provision of the first amendment embraces more forms of expression than mere oral communication."[3] Thus, free speech protection or regulation on a college campus can apply to things ranging from words written on a residence hall whiteboard to the length of a student's hair to a symbol on an article of clothing. Because of the breadth of these situations, I choose to use the broader term *freedom of expression* in discussing the application of the First Amendment on campus.

The cases Ratliff referred to in describing how the concept of freedom of expression developed in a campus setting came largely as the result of what is called the free speech movement of the late 1960s. Students stretched into their newfound freedoms in the wake of the "legal death of the *in loco parentis* doctrine *vis-à-vis* college students."[4] Because the Supreme Court no longer legally defined administrators as having a parental authority, students could speak up and act out with less threat of punishment from campus authorities.

Writing a few years after the free speech movement case law came down from the nation's courts, Ratliff pointed out that the courts of the late 1960s were largely willing to defer to college and university educators. The case law acknowledges that as in the broader society, students on a college campus do not have unfettered free speech rights. However, the balance between free speech and the mission of a college or university mean that decisions about how to limit free speech need the nuanced eye of an administrator with contextual knowledge of each situation. In a sense, the free speech movement case law tells college officials that court rulings alone are too blunt to provide adequate answers in the case of free speech on the college campus.

If the reason we call on speech codes is that conflicting and intensely held opinions make discourse challenging, to expect an entire community to buy in to a single set of proscribed expressions defies logic.

Free speech movement case law also upheld long-standing legal precedents that placed public and private institutions in different constitutional contexts. William Kaplan cited an 1819 Supreme Court case overruling an intended state takeover of Dartmouth College that declared, "Private schools have been spared any governmental encroach-ment that impairs their charters of incorporation."[5] Still, many private institutions take pride in protecting free speech at the same level as their public counterparts.[6] Thus, Robert M. O'Neil said, "The guiding princi-ple for virtually all institutions of higher learning is that free speech must be protected, even when the speech for which the freedom is sought may be offensive or disruptive or at variance with the campus mission."[7]

Campus Speech Codes: Working Around the First Amendment

When free speech conflicts with creating a welcoming campus environ-ment—particularly for underrepresented populations—student affairs professionals face some of their toughest work in finding the appropriate educational tool. Ronald J. Rychlak estimated as many as 200 schools adopted speech codes in the 1980s and 1990s to directly address the ten-sion between free speech and the sort of insensitive expression that harms equality, diversity, and civility.[8] Donald Alexander Downs argued that such codes minimized free speech values, saying, "Free speech has lost status to the university's drive for diversity: when certain forms of dis-course are deemed harmful for equality and diversity, the institutional commitment to free speech falters."[9]

Speech codes explicitly state what forms of expression are and are not tolerable in the pursuit of civil discourse and holistic learning. Speech code advocates often justify their position by saying that the prohibited forms of speech are fighting words, which add nothing to the public discourse and are so threatening to public morality and social order that they warrant exclusion from conversation.[10] Many speech codes failed to pass constitutional muster in the 1990s, but those that managed to stay within constitutional limits on speech regulation represented what cam-pus officials felt were reasonable restrictions aimed at balancing free speech and civil discourse.

The limited success of some speech codes was insufficient to convince Evan G. S. Siegel of the codes' propriety:

> Enacting policies that punish the perpetrators of ugly verbal abuse may help improve matters if such codes meet constitutional scrutiny. A whole-sale, content-based prohibition of entire categories of speech and ideas,

however, will only gloss over existing problems and undoubtedly will create new ones.[11]

Siegel's assessment paints speech codes as another example of using too blunt a tool to address an issue of context and details.

With its effort to apply a single interpretation of what constitutes acceptable speech on campus, the speech code movement suffers from the same sweeping bluntness as a First Amendment–exclusive approach to upholding free speech with reasonable limitations. Both seek to address a big issue, but they do so in a way that can function too readily as a formula for addressing the distinctly nonformulaic nuances of human communication and its contexts. Robert C. Post warns us, "These formulas cast an illusion of stability and order over First Amendment jurisprudence, an illusion that can turn dangerous when it substitutes for serious engagement with the question of why we really care about protecting freedom of expression."[12]

Placing too much attention on formulas is especially frustrating because it is not in the finite variables of the specific words themselves that the chief challenge to civil discourse on campus exists. Rather, it is in the nuances of understanding and interaction that the offense and the damage occur. José Ortega y Gasset offers this artful explanation:

> The real meaning of a word appears when the word is uttered and functions in the human activity called speech. Hence we must know who says it to whom, when and where . . . what we call language forms only one, if a relatively stable, constituent which must be supplemented by the vital setting.[13]

Because this vital setting changes in infinite and unpredictable ways, no codified list of permissible and forbidden forms of speech can fully address the harmful effects of insensitive or hurtful campus expression. In addition to the illusion of order, the presence of a speech code sends a message of finality in the debate between free speech and civil discourse. Administrators can opt to hide behind a code and its process to escape harder conversations about why students choose to use certain words or why specific expressions cause such grief to members of the campus community.

E. David Hyland highlights the worthy goal at the heart of the speech code movement. He said, "What many speech code advocates are seeking is simple: a way of enlisting a whole community in creating an environment where people are not attacked and injured on the basis of their

---

Without addressing the complexity of those things we find most offensive on campus, we risk ending up as cudgel-wielding thought police rather than as skilled educational architects, able to call upon multiple tools in the process of interacting with students with challenging ideas and opinions.

---

identity."[14] However, this goal seems troubled from the start. If the reason we call on speech codes is that conflicting and intensely held opinions make discourse challenging, to expect an entire community to buy into a single set of proscribed expressions defies logic. A student's commentary from 1971 reminds us that "the era of consensus politics on campus is over. The university must determine how to handle adversary relationships without promoting violence or destroying itself."[15] This assessment may be a disappointment for those who prefer a more idealist view of our campus communities; unfortunately, it seems as accurate today as it was decades ago. Rather than seeking or creating false consensus about what is and is not permissible to say or do, we must satisfy ourselves with finding meaningful ways to bring disparate ideas into engagement with one another.

Shouting Down Discourse: The Irvine 11 Controversy

The difference between the sort of engagement at the heart of civil discourse and the sort of engagement that entrenches disparate viewpoints is evident in cases involving controversial campus lecturers. At the University of California, Irvine (UCI), students who disapproved of Israeli Ambassador Michael Oren's university-sponsored speech on campus disrupted the event by shouting their views during his presentation. Eventually, officials arrested the 11 students who stood up to shout Oren down. Further controversy followed, as supporters of the Muslim Student Union protesters argued that administrators had violated the students' free speech rights, while the students' detractors called on UCI to expel the students for their disrespectful actions.[16]

Erwin Chemerinsky, dean of the UCI School of Law, noted shortly after the incident that a blunt application of the First Amendment offers clear support for disciplinary action against the student protesters.[17] Their speech would have restricted the ambassador's own right to free speech if the students had been allowed to proceed: "The government, including public universities, always can impose time, place and manner restrictions on speech. . . . Freedom of speech, on campuses and elsewhere, is rendered meaningless if speakers can be shouted down by those who disagree."[18]

The week after the controversial speech at Irvine, students at Kenyon College sent dozens of outraged comments to an all-campus e-mail distribution list criticizing the planned appearance of British National Party Chair Nick Griffin, whose connection to White supremacist groups, dismissal of the Holocaust, and condemnation of Islam, students argued, were incompatible with the school's espoused values.[19] These critics prompted the members of the Robert A. Taft Society who had invited Griffin to campus to cancel the speech, citing safety concerns. While Kenyon president S. Georgia Nugent told the *Kenyon Collegian*, "In general, I do not believe that heckling and shouting down is a good use of free speech," the student uproar in some ways shouted Griffin down without his even setting foot on campus.[20] In the days following the cancellation, Taft Society president Taylor Somers captured the challenge many administrators face in dealing with issues of free speech and civility, saying, "It's hard to draw a line arbitrarily of what is an acceptable level of controversy."[21]

Conversation: The Multifaceted Tool for Student Affairs Educators

The acceptable level of controversy on any campus depends in large part on how well educators have prepared campus community members for conversing with each other. Administrators of colleges and universities must recognize that acting as free speech regulators or civil discourse referees relinquishes the educating power of conversation. While lessons exist in barring a certain word or shutting down a student protest, it is our shared responsibility to foster learning experiences rather than considering our duty done once we have made a specific decision or taken a specific action. Robert M. O'Neil put it this way: "Above all, universities should approach racism, homophobia, sexism, and anti-Semitism [ideologies that form the basis for many free speech controversies] through what they do best—education. Special programs and even courses may be developed with an eye to increasing intergroup understanding across campuses."[22] An emphasis on civil discourse should be at the heart of that educational mission and those special programs.

Jonathan Zimmerman conceptualized civil discourse as a set of shared ground rules for interaction, "and when we forsake these ground rules, we lose our ability to communicate—literally, to 'make common'—with each other."[23]Additionally, Zizi Papacharissi described civil discourse as imperfect.[24] Exploring civility in online communications, Papacharissi said, "Sanitized and controlled conversation does not fully capture the conditioned illogic of human thought. Civility standards should promote respect for the other, enhance democracy, but also allow human uniqueness and unpredictability."[25]

A framework that meets Zimmerman's and Papacharissi's standards for civil discourse is the concept of moral conversation that Robert J. Nash, DeMethra LaSha Bradley, and Arthur W. Chickering used in *How to Talk About Hot Topics on Campus*.[26] Moral conversation moves participants away from the sort of formulaic approaches that ask students to assess words and consequences rather than meanings and intentions.

Moral conversation is about students sharing the stories that inform who they are and how they make meaning of the world around them. Nash, Bradley, and Chickering describe moral conversation this way:

> A moral conversation is literally a manner of living whereby people keep company with each other and talk together in good faith, in order to exchange sometimes agreeable, sometimes opposing, ideas. Above all, however, moral conversation is a mutual sharing of all those wonderful stories that give meaning to people's lives.[27]

Certainly, moral conversation will not be effective if applied solely in the face of existing controversy. To come into a simmering debate about offensive language and ask everyone involved to "[begin] with an assumption that there is nothing inherently erroneous or immoral about any initial presumption of a particular truth,"[28] would do little to resolve the situation. However, a campus that foundationally emphasizes moral conversation prepares its students to engage in controversial issues with a level of civility that can feel more like the norm than like a special approach to crisis. For this approach to be effective at keeping student affairs educators from living the reactionary life of First Amendment interpreters, moral conversation must be a part of everyday civil discourse. As Susan Herbst stated,

> the fundamental problem of incivility is not about one-time behaviors and events, but about norms and culture. . . . Teaching civility, so that you don't have to worry so hard on fitful campus events, will minimize the trauma that comes with mean speech. And in doing so, all this will help to produce the citizens we say we make at a university.[29]

Moral conversation's chief virtue is the way it digs beneath the surface level of words—where speech codes and First Amendment case law would have us operate—and grapples with the deeper meanings and contexts Ortega y Gasset describes.[30] First Amendment advocate Nat Hentoff said, "An essential part of . . . education is to learn to demystify language, to strip it of its ability to demonize and stigmatize. . . . The way to deal with bigoted language is to answer it with more and better language of your own."[31] Enlisting moral conversations in place of simple speech codes or court rulings enables us to rise to Hentoff's educational expectations.

Conclusion

Carolyn J. Palmer, Sophie W. Penney, Donald D. Gehring, and Jan A. Neiger stated that we as student affairs educators must look beyond the legal lens as we address free speech questions on campus.[32] Though they apply their concluding analysis to upper-level colleagues, their words apply to all who engage with college students around controversial issues:

> [Senior student affairs officers] would be wise to approach the issues of hate speech and hate crimes by using a balanced approach that takes into account all legal requirements and carefully considers the ethical, moral, and educational implications of all programs, policies, and procedures designed to address these important issues.[33]

The important realization for campus partners involved in creating a balance between free speech and civil discourse is that looking purely to constitutional protections is insufficient. Certain words or forms of expression may fall under the protection of the First Amendment, but that does not mean all protected forms of speech and expression inherently contribute to the meaningful exchange of ideas. Alternatively, administrators might reasonably limit some words or forms of expression, based on sound constitutional interpretations. However, simply limiting forms of expression fails to address the ideas and meanings that lie beneath controversy. Without addressing the complexity of those things we find most offensive on campus, we risk ending up as cudgel-wielding thought police rather than as skilled educational architects, able to call upon multiple tools in the process of interacting with challenging ideas and opinions.

Notes

1. Maslow, A. H. (1966). *The psychology of science*. New York, NY: Harper & Row, p. 15.

2. U.S. Const. amend. I.

3. Ratliff, R. C. (1972). *Constitutional rights of college students*. Metuchen, NJ: Scarecrow Press, p. 172.

4. Ibid., p. 162.

5. Kaplan, W. A. (1978). *The law of higher education*. San Francisco, CA: Jossey-Bass, p. 20.

6. O'Neil, R. M. (1997). *Free speech in the college community*. Bloomington: Indiana University Press.

7. Ibid., p. 15.

8. Rychlak, R. J. (1992). Civil rights, Confederate flags, and political correctness: Free speech and race relations on campus. *Tulane Law Review, 66*, 1411–1434.

9. Downs, D. A. (2005). *Restoring free speech and liberty on campus*. Cambridge, UK: Cambridge University Press, p. 114.

10. O'Neil, *Free speech in the college community*.

11. Siegel, E. G. S. (1990). Closing the campus gates to free expression: The regulation of offensive speech at colleges and universities. *Emory Law Journal, 39*, 1351–1400, p. 1399.

12. Post, R. C. (1991). Free speech and religious, racial, and sexual harassment: Racist speech, democracy, and the First Amendment. *William & Mary Law Review, 32*, 267–327, p. 278.

13. Ortega y Gasset, J. (1946). *Concord and liberty*. New York, NY: Norton, p. 12.

14. O'Neil, *Free speech in the college community*, p. 7.

15. Kessler, D. (1971). The students. In G. W. Holmes (Ed.), *Law and discipline on campus* (pp. 27–31). Ann Arbor, MI: Institute of Continuing Legal Education, p. 31.

16. Twair, P. & Twair, S. (2010). Irvine 11 face unprecedented penalties for "dissing" Israeli ambassador. *Washington Report on Middle East Affairs, 29*(4), 36–37.

17. Chemerinsky, E. (2010, February 18). Free speech and the "Irvine 11." *Los Angeles Times,* p. A17.

18. Ibid., p. A17.

19. Steigmeyer, A. (2010, February 18). Nick Griffin visit canceled: Heated debate over politician's controversial views raised safety concerns. *Kenyon Collegian,* p. 1. Retrieved from http://www.kenyoncollegian.com/news/nick-griffin-visit-canceled-1.1925647

20. Ibid., p. 1.

21. Ibid.

22. O'Neil, *Free speech in the college community,* p. 25.

23. Zimmerman, J. (2010, February 28). You don't say: To teach students the value of free speech, sometimes we must restrict it. *Newsday,* p. A34.

24. Papacharissi, Z. (2004). Democracy online: Civility, politeness, and the democratic potential of online political discussion groups. *New Media & Society, 6*(2), 259–283.

25. Ibid., p. 265.

26. Nash, R. J., Bradley, D. L., & Chickering, A. W. (2008). *How to talk about hot topics on campus: From polarization to moral conversation.* San Francisco, CA: Jossey-Bass.

27. Ibid., p. 8.

28. Ibid.

29. Herbst, S. (2010, August 15). Rude democracy. *Inside Higher Ed.* Retrieved from http://www.insidehighered.com/views/2010/08/05/herbst

30. Ortega y Gasset, *Concord and liberty.*

31. Hentoff, N. (1991). "Speech codes" on the campus and problems of free speech. *Dissent, 38*(3), 546–549, p. 548.

32. Palmer, C. J., Penney, S. W., Gehring, D. D., & Neiger, J. A. (1997). Hate speech and hate crimes: Campus conduct codes and Supreme Court rulings. *NASPA Journal, 34*(2), 112–122.

33. Ibid., p. 121.

Drafting a Community-Wide Blueprint for Civil Discourse

Katie Sardelli, Winthrop University

In today's society of lawsuits and controversy, many believe that ensuring First Amendment freedom of speech while also ensuring constructive conversations on a college campus are incompatible. University administrators often fall into the trap of guaranteeing the rights provided by the First Amendment at the cost of facilitating conversations where productive dialogue seldom occurs, or restricting free speech and creating a sanitized, limiting, and less than constructive conversation involving collegiate communities. However, if one purpose of a liberal education is to encourage students to explore ideas from multiple perspectives, we must model such behavior in the way we initiate and guide civil discourse.

Approaching campus conversations in terms of absolutes limits speech or allows for it to proceed unchecked—two approaches that seldom result in constructive conversation. While Tobias Uecker suggests administrators need to find tools beyond the hammer, we must first decide why and for what we are using our tools and draft a blueprint for productive conversation on campus. Many administrators possess or can access the precision instruments Uecker suggests we hone, yet run into roadblocks by not considering what we are building and the potential complications of using these tools.

Before we can design a blueprint for our campuses, we must recognize our goals. Many envision liberal education as a marketplace of ideas where individuals can evaluate multiple perspectives to develop their own stance. However, we must consider Barbara Applebaum's argument that "the liberal belief in freedom of expression and a market-place of ideas is compelling only if all viewpoints have an equal opportunity to have their voices matter."[1] Thus, if a university is this marketplace, its officials must find a way to ensure equal opportunity for as many perspectives as possible to be heard and evaluated.

The First Amendment outlines the rights of the individual regarding expression—individuals have the opportunity to speak their mind, as long as the speech does not include fighting or hate words. Yet if we were to simply allow our community to speak with minimal parameters, conversation would stall as the individual with the biggest hammer dominates discussion, and attempts to facilitate dialogue disintegrate into power plays aimed at advancing one's own agenda. If the purpose of a student's education is to engage in the marketplace of ideas, we must assist our students in understanding that blindly following this freedom does not necessarily further their agenda. Students and administrators must learn that, although they can, it is rarely beneficial to cling to the protection provided by the First Amendment if they truly wish to engage in meaningful dialogue.

Henry Louis Gates Jr. suggested that the "First Amendment absolutism has never entailed absolute devotion to free expression; the question has always been where to draw the line."[2] Administrators have sought to draw this line distinctly to counteract the breakdown of conversation that can occur when dialogue is left with minimal guidelines. Administrators picked up the hammer and brought down the speech codes of the 1980s and 1990s or chose to restrict speakers or art exhibitions from campus to lessen controversy. Such tactics prove to be counterintuitive and counterproductive to the free exchange of ideas.

Many administrators have encountered situations where students challenge administration-imposed expectations. In residence halls, it typically proves more challenging to enforce a departmentally imposed quiet-hour policy than one self-determined by residents. During student organization meetings, many advisers encounter resistance from students when trying to impose regulations set by the administration because the students do not understand the purpose of the restrictions. Similarly, students will view any attempt to draw a line for acceptable speech as an administratively enforced rule, thus reducing the likelihood for students' buying in to any regulations. In many cases students will challenge any attempts by administrators to define acceptable speech and will act out in manners that will be more detrimental to the community.

By restricting speech, we negate any opportunities for students to learn how to engage in dialogue by simply addressing the specific words used rather than tone and implication. For example, if an administrator approached a student about using an offensive phrase without clarifying why that phrase is destructive, the student only learns not to say the phrase around that administrator. By restricting certain words or imposing a set of parameters for expression on campus (without a clearly stated rationale), we eliminate any teachable moments.

Attempts to define acceptable expression, even though established with an overarching goal to allow all voices to be heard, will in fact sometimes

Students and administrators must learn that, although they can, it is rarely beneficial to cling to the protection provided by the First Amendment if they truly wish to engage in meaningful dialogue.

silence some. While such parameters aim to guide those outspoken students toward productive dialogue, they also restrain more hesitant students. Limiting expression on campus in absolute terms sends a clear message that there are certain topics, issues, or words that are off limits. Those students who are already hesitant to engage in difficult dialogue out of fear of using inappropriate terminology or becoming involved in potential conflict will only have those feelings reinforced by the message that there are wrong words or topics too provocative to discuss.

Administrators' addressing student speech in absolute terms accounts only for student interaction at a macro level. Student conversations are not limited to classrooms or official university events that administrators can supervise to ensure all their expectations are met. Rather, they occur at all hours of the day—at lunch in the cafeteria or 2:00 a.m. in a residence hall room.

The desire for administrators to have a clearly defined approach to expression on campus is appealing at face value. However, allowing unchecked free speech or restricting speech are methods riddled with potential missteps that can create unintended consequences. We must set aside taking a restrictive or reactionary approach to speech and expression on campus in favor of a proactive community-based approach to an educational exchange of ideas. In a similar vein, Uecker argues for the educating power of conversation and fostering learning experiences rather than simply enforcing a set of standards.

Robert Corrigan argued, "Free expression is a matter of balancing rights with responsibilities."[3] Achieving this balance of rights and responsibilities begins by creating a campuswide understanding of what civil discourse truly means. Civil discourse must be understood as a respectful exchange of views, with active listening, no interruptions, no inflammatory language, and no ad hominem attacks.[4] Civil discourse is not a sanitized, noncontroversial interaction. In fact, Manuel N. Gomez suggested we do not want our campus to shy away from controversy, as tension instructively highlights the personal investment students have in their beliefs and ideas.[5] Universities must educate faculty, staff, and students on the true nature of civil discourse.

A community commitment to civil discourse, and an understanding of how it advances liberal arts education, is a necessary yet complicated task. Administrators cannot simply expect students to automatically invest themselves or understand the role civil discourse plays in a campus community when they enter college. Many students, according to Marcia Baxter Magolda, enter college with an absolute view on the world and only over time do they learn to recognize the validity of new perspectives.[6] It is our responsibility as educators to assist our students in opening themselves to new perspectives. However, we must also have a safety net in place, since as Gomez stated, "If students believe they are being harassed or feel unsafe it is an administrative responsibility to ensure that there are mechanisms in place to investigate any claims quickly and carefully. Administrators also must make the campus community aware of these mechanisms."[7]

J. Herman Blake argued, "One of the best preventative approaches is a sense of community. In a community you don't wait for the offended person to intervene; the potentially offended person needs to know that many voices will be raised on his or her behalf."[8] Such a community cannot be formed by administrative edicts for the same reasons that speech codes fail—students are not invested. We must step away from regulation and move toward creating a community norm of free exchange of ideas, constructive dialogue, and as Uecker suggests, interacting civilly over controversial issues.

How do we create such a norm of positive dialogue among our students to assist them in developing their opinions and to engage in civil discourse so all perspectives are heard and respected? One suggestion offered by Lawrence White is, "The university should encourage constant open discussion of its commitment to diversity."[9] We must find mechanisms to allow students to express their opinions without fear of recourse. Taking it one step further, Gomez said, "Certainly students need a safe place in which to learn. . . . But a community is not safe when speech is chilled and certain ideas are not free to be heard, examined or evaluated."[10]

If campus administrators truly value civil discourse, they must extend this commitment to the entire campus community—they must draft the blueprint that encourages students to engage in constructive conversations. Jodi Fisler and John Foubert said, "If a college aims to instill certain values in students, those values should be made clear to prospective students as well as those already on campus."[11]

Administrators can create a sense of investment in their students by creating universal classroom, residence hall, and organization norms that value constructive dialogue; holding campuswide conversations on hot topics; and addressing violations of campus expectations as a community. They can also adopt a values code, similar to an honor code, advocating commitment to dialogue and constructive expression, which all students must agree to honor upon entering the university.

Students must also ask themselves, according to David M. Estlund, "What kind of restraint ought I to exercise in my political expression, and under what conditions might the appropriate standards be more or less permissive?"[12] Essentially, we must encourage students to consider the following question: When engaging in discussion, what type of expectations must I adopt for myself to be part of this community—not because I am told to, but because I am committed to the values espoused by the institution and I have committed to growing as an educated member of the university?

Until true civil discourse becomes a community-wide priority, tension involving free speech and civil discourse will always exist. Because of their developmental stage, students entering college cannot be left without guidance on how to hold constructive conversations. Conversely, administrators cannot take it upon themselves to prescribe or dictate the interactions that can occur between students. Rather, a community-wide commitment is necessary to create a positive learning environment, in which all parties buy in to the concept that all members are entitled to their opinion, the only way to strengthen one's own opinion is to interact with those who hold different beliefs, and that everyone values hearing everyone's voices. We must ask ourselves, what does our blueprint look like, and how do we educate our community members on how we can continually draft it together?

Notes

1. Applebaum, B. (2003). Social justice, democratic education and the silencing of words that wound. *Journal of Moral Education*, *32*(2), 151–162, p. 159.

2. Gates, H. L., Jr. (1994, January–February). Truth or consequences: Putting limits on limits. *Academe*, *80*(1),14–17, p. 14.

3. Corrigan, R. (2006, spring). At the heart of the academy lies balance. *The Presidency*, *9*(2), 28.

4. Bornstein, R. (2010, winter). Promoting civil discourse on campus. *The Presidency*, *3*(1), 27–30, p. 30.

5. Gomez, M. N. (2008, March–April). Imagining the future: Cultivating civility in a field of discontent. *Change*, *40*(2), 11–17.

6. Baxter Magolda, M. B. (1992). *Knowing and reasoning in college: Gender-related patterns in students' intellectual development.* San Francisco CA: Jossey-Bass.

7. Gomez, Imagining the future, p. 15.

8. Hentoff, N., Gubar, S., White, L., & Blake, J. H. (1994, January–February). Forum: Discouraging hate speech without codes. *Academe*, *80*(1), 18–19, p. 19.

9. Ibid.

10. Gomez, Imagining the future, p. 17.

11. Fisler, J., & Foubert, J. D. (2006, November–December). Teach me, but don't disagree with me. *About Campus*, *11*(5), 2–8, p. 7.

12. Estlund, D. M. (2001). Deliberation down and dirty: Must political expression be civil? In T. R. Henseley (Ed.), *Boundaries of democracy: Freedom of expression and order in America* (pp. 49–67). Kent, OH: Kent State University Press, p. 52.

Further Reading and Related Blog

Craig Berger, Miami University

Downs, D. A. (2005). *Restoring free speech and liberty on campus*. New York, NY: Cambridge University Press.

Downs provides a history of free speech on college campuses and argues that higher education administrators have unfairly prioritized certain groups in the university community by creating speech codes. Downs uses four case studies to frame and illuminate his argument, indicating that speech codes do more harm than good.

Gomez, M. N. (2008, March–April). Imagining the future: Cultivating civility in a field of discontent. *Change, 40*(2), 10–17.

Gomez, vice-chancellor of student affairs at the University of California, Irvine, offers a practical exploration of how to balance freedom of speech in the university setting with the need to educate students on engaging in civil discourse. Gomez draws on his experiences working at a campus that has had its share of politically charged incidents; he describes the positive impact of dialogue on a college community.

Nash, R. J., Bradley, D. L., & Chickering, A. W. (2008). *How to talk about hot topics on campus: From polarization to moral conversation*. San Francisco, CA: Jossey-Bass.

The editors provide readers—presumably faculty, staff, and students—with a framework for facilitating conversations on controversial issues. This work emphasizes the need for a campuswide culture of conversation that welcomes varying perspectives and values. The editors stress that the moral conversation outlined in their work does not emphasize persuasion but instead encourages participants to listen and engage in open and civil dialogue.

Blog URL: contestedissues.wordpress.com
Corresponding Chapter Post: tinyurl.com/contestedissues19

PART FOUR

Organizing Student Affairs Practice for Learning and Social Justice

20

Why Is the Gap So Wide Between Espousing a Social Justice Agenda to Promote Learning and Enacting It?

What Could Student Affairs Educators Do to Genuinely Enact a Social Justice Ideology? Moving Beyond Good Intentions

Joel D. Zylstra, Center for Transforming Mission

My intent in this essay is to extend an invitation to a conversation about what it means for you, your office, your institution, and the larger student affairs profession to interpret and address issues of social justice in higher education, not to offer a blueprint for how to address this popular yet elusive term. We can all think of specific issues, causes, and commitments that are important to us. Race, gender, sexuality, social class, and ability often dominate the discussion about issues of social justice in the field, but I wonder what it would be like to step back, to conceptualize the commonalities among them, and to consider ourselves in a broader pursuit of a just world.

I joined students, staff, and faculty at a town hall meeting to discuss an insensitive off-campus theme party. The party, commonly referred to as Ghetto Fest, celebrates the end of the spring semester through the depiction of what students refer to as "urban culture," using music, dance, alcohol, and attire to represent life in the ghetto. While I have numerous concerns about such an event, one of the strongest opponents of Ghetto Fest left me with a lasting impression. Prompted by an invitation to direct questions to a panel of students, faculty, and administrators, a student stood up and reamed party organizers for their lack of concern for students whose identities were being undermined through this gathering. I do not recall much of what she said, as I fixated on the message printed on the front of her shirt. "Redskins Forever" it read, a counterstatement to the university's decision to change the mascot from Redskins to Redhawks 10 years ago. I do not claim to know what motivated this student's choice of apparel that day, nor her rationale for challenging Ghetto Fest organizers, but the contradiction between her spoken words and the message symbolically conveyed through her clothing flooded my mind with questions about what it means to espouse and enact one's social justice values.

I imagine that while you and I can conceal biases a bit better, we are not that different from this student. We live in a world plagued with issues of inequity and injustice, and continually address certain issues while neglecting others. While this student privileged issues of injustice inherent in a themed party over the historical and social implications in mascot representation, educators often do the same by diminishing some issues to lift up others. My impetus for acknowledging this is not to divert readers' attention and contributions away from the issues that are most important to them, but to acknowledge that despite our good intent, we are all guilty of ignorance in various arenas of social justice. What are the issues of justice you are committed to in and outside student affairs? Equally as important, what issues of justice are you ignorant about, lazy toward, or perhaps silent about because of its benefit to you? As we learn to acknowledge our own shortcomings, we can begin to create a space where social justice is more than a buzzword, more than a rant against theme parties, and more than what Ivan Illich described in an address to a group of Peace Corps volunteers as ignorance disguised by good intentions.[1]

Past and Present Panoramic Views of Social Justice

The concept of social justice has been around a long time. Ranging from Catholic teachings about caring for the poor to political and economic theories about the distribution of wealth and power, the breadth of usage of this term has fostered great debate.[2] Despite disagreement over the scope of its reach, this term historically has been used to address issues of human rights, equity, and access to resources and power. Most people position their own ideas about justice on a continuum seeking a proper balance between public equality and personal freedom. For some, this affirms stances on public health care, same-sex marriage, and affirmative action, while others lean toward a meritocracy that encourages individuals to fend for themselves. It would be disingenuous to think we know the true origins of this concept, as Winston Churchill reminded us that "history is written by victors," recognizing that it is possible and likely the voices of the real pioneers of social justice were silenced. Instead, we are left with the remnants of those who have written about it out of their own conviction as opposed to those who advocated for justice out of necessity.

Social justice entered the American public education system during the formation of the common schools in the 1800s. Educators originally designed American schools to create a common experience where all students could have access to education and opportunities to succeed equally, regardless of their geographic location and social class. Despite well-meaning education pioneers, these schools failed to address equity and access as they neglected youth that extended beyond the White Protestant European, male mold. From this vantage point, we quickly realize that the foundations of America's public schools were not so common after all and contributed to the process of producing victors to write the future.

Enacting a social justice pedagogy requires us not only to speak out against injustices but also to situate ourselves as benefactors of inequality.

Social justice in education was never confined to what we now refer to as the K–12 arena; it seeped into higher education from its conception. Joseph Soares highlighted the distorted illusion that higher education provides access to all who are interested through his historical analysis of unjust enrollment procedures in Ivy League schools.[3] Like other institutions, higher education falls prey to reinforcing society's current structure rather than allowing students to reconstruct our world. In other words, higher education often replicates familial circumstances from one generation to the next rather than permitting students from different backgrounds to have equal opportunities to participate and succeed in a system open to everyone. Perhaps this is why student affairs educators continue to emphasize the importance of supporting first-generation students, as we recognize that higher education is not designed in an equitable way for all students to succeed.

Higher education plays a unique role in society. It is often referred to as the academy, an impenetrable entity that exists in isolation from the rest of the world. In this vein, addressing issues of social justice in higher education (and student affairs) becomes multifaceted, looking inward at the institution and outward at the institution's relationship with the rest of society. Internally, issues of justice permeate the university, representing inequitable situations for students, staff, departments, and divisions. Most student affairs educators tend to focus on these issues, situating themselves as an oppressed entity in the university structure, underrespected by faculty, underresourced in comparison with other offices, and underappreciated by the broader campus community. Outsiders seldom recognize these power differentials in university structures and instead focus on the academy's privileged place in society because of the acquired power it maintains through education, wealth, and societal respect. Many people wonder why officials of universities spend millions of dollars on brick buildings to maintain their image, question the ability of scholars to solve real problems, and question why politicians, funders, and innovators seek counsel from the academy before approaching the general public. While those inside the system recognize power differentials among student groups, staff and faculty, and different departments, those on the outside categorize the university as elite, out of touch, and liberal.

From this vantage point, student affairs educators must hold in tension the areas of justice we represent. Advocating for underrepresented students to initiate some type of equity on campus is vitally important from an institutional perspective. Conversely, we often forget to consider our commitment to human rights outside the university, since according to the U.S. Census Bureau, only 27% of Americans over the age of 25 have a bachelor's degree, and 10% have an advanced (masters, professional, or doctoral) degree.[4] Given these numbers, student affairs educators can no longer afford to simply consider the role of social justice in institutions but must also consider what it means to educate for equity, opportunity, and justice beyond the confines of the academy.

Perhaps the lesson in all of this is that we are all in the midst of multiple political struggles, which inherently reveal issues of injustice. While we might be marginalized in one category (i.e., politics in the university), we are seen as powerful in other categories (i.e., educational capital in the broader society). Portraying ourselves as vulnerable in all circumstances diminishes our ability to seek social justice among the students we serve, the structures we work among, and the systems we maintain. An honest reflection likely yields the realization that we have become educators because we have somehow found a way to avoid being pushed aside in the schooling process and have found ways to succeed through favor, power, and resources through teachers, curriculum, and educational systems. Enacting a social justice pedagogy requires us not only to speak out against injustices but also to situate ourselves as benefactors of inequality. I would imagine that student affairs educators like myself who have graduated from master's programs have somehow inherited an undeserved advantage that is not available to everyone. When we begin to see ourselves in this light, we begin to recognize power as something that cannot be altogether given away but ultimately a gift that requires thoughtful and intentional stewardship.

Glenn Beck, a conservative TV pundit, brought the term *social justice* into the national spotlight because he deemed it to be code language for "Communism, Marxism, and Nazism."[5] If the debate on social justice is indeed about the level of public equality versus personal freedom as suggested by educators in the early 19th century, I find it ironic that his statement merges two fundamentally oppositional extremes. Not only does his statement raise questions about the actual meaning and scope of the term, but it also captures a societal push toward demoralizing issues of justice, pushing them out of the mainstream and into radicalism. Beck's comments infuriated enough religious, political, and educational leaders to warrant several responses giving different perspectives on social justice.

Carl Grant and Christine Sleeter's *Turning on Learning* offers a continuum on multicultural education that runs parallel to how many educators might conceptualize the issue of social justice.[6] They highlight four narratives on multiculturalism, ranging from an assimilation approach where equality is built around uniformity to a critical multiculturalism that addresses sources and conflicts of power within relationships. They suggest that many educators employ a human relations outlook built around tolerance, acceptance, collaboration, and learning to become comfortable with one's self and diverse others. Others conceptualize multiculturalism from a single-groups studies perspective (i.e., Black studies, women's studies, queer studies), which seeks to advocate for marginalized groups from their own perspective, equalizing inequities through the voices that have historically been silenced. Multicultural education advocates a sense of pluralism that integrates individuals with groups outside their own and helps them to understand the social, political, and historical influences that have shaped their identity. Finally, Grant and Sleeter suggest that multicultural social justice education seeks to address inequities by promoting critical questioning, democracy, the analysis of systems of oppression, and engagement in social action.[7] Most of us can think of situations in which at least one of these approaches has been employed.

The latter of these perspectives has gained traction over the past 40 years following the libratory work of Paulo Freire through teaching Brazilian peasants to read and exposing the oppressive structures that continually marginalize them.[8] Later scholars like bell hooks, Ira Shor, and Henry Giroux have expanded on his work under the name of *critical pedagogy*, problem-based learning that seeks to liberate the learner from the oppressive societal structures that impede learning.[9] While they center their work on K–12 education, Robert Rhoads, Kathleen Manning, and Dan Butin have explored these perspectives in higher education, specifically considering the realm of student affairs.[10] While several scholars have applied critical pedagogy to the service-learning realm, few have expanded on what it means to apply critical theory in the broader student affairs arena.

An Invitation to Risky Business

I hope some of this context offers a landscape for us to consider practical solutions to bridging the gap between the ability of student affairs educators to espouse and enact social justice in the world and through our work with students. The following section highlights some of the ways I have come to think about social justice. They are not the right way, nor are they the only way, but they are a way for each us to take seriously our roles as educators, reformers, and advocates of justice.

An Ethic of Imperfection

Like the student who spoke out during the town hall meeting, I too am guilty of completely missing the boat in numerous areas of justice. Like

---

Student affairs educators must begin to see their work in terms of advocacy rather than awareness.

---

many of you, I do not know enough about the companies I support through my purchases, the food I eat, the health care I receive, the politicians I elect, and so on. Despite my attempts to be socially just, I have a damaging footprint on the rights of human beings in my own community and afar. In recognizing this, we move away from the divisive dualisms that suggest that educators are either socially just or not and into an arena that acknowledges we are all imperfect, which creates space to learn more and to address issues in meaningful ways. I am continually reminded of this when I attend conferences. Those interested in environmental justice might be appalled by some of the unsustainable practices of those attending a conference centered on race or gender equality. Similarly, those advocating for economic justice might cringe at something said at a conference about sustainable living. Let us first acknowledge that we cannot be expert proponents of justice for all causes.

Far too often student affairs educators create dualisms regarding values, pitting one agenda against others by saying things like: "Other offices on campus are failing to address issues of race and gender equality," "The athletic department discriminates against nonheterosexual students" or "We are trying to change the culture of this campus, but they just aren't buying it." While these statements might be true, they also suggest we have all the answers, that we are doing everything we possibly can to make sure we address these issues, and that these areas of social justice trump all the other institutional and societal issues. This is not to suggest that some individuals do not have a stronger conscience on issues of justice than others but rather to help us recognize that we too are on a spectrum, perhaps sensitive to some issues while remaining ignorant on others. We often see this among individuals and groups as we pit our marginalized camp against others, eventually straining both groups. Who is more marginalized on this campus? Nonheterosexuals? First-generation students? Students of color? Women? International students? The very nature of these questions reinforces the dominant culture's superiority and diminishes our collective ability to work toward equity.

Awareness Has Limitations

To begin to shift toward enacting means of social justice, student affairs educators must begin to see their work in terms of advocacy rather than awareness. The current boom in social networking and accessible information has helped to connect higher education with issues of justice in and outside the university structure. What do we do with this information and ability to communicate now that we have it? Access to information does not translate to enacting values of social justice but rather to a sense of awareness about the issues.

Advocacy requires sacrifice. I cannot be a true advocate for something unless I am willing to give up something in order to advance a cause. Advocates for social justice are willing to offer time, energy, money, respect, or power on behalf of something. In this vein, student affairs educators must consider their work with students as a means of advocacy rather than simply building awareness about issues. It requires educators and students alike to recognize their own power and realize we have the potential to steward this power in ways that are advantageous to ourselves or others.

Perhaps an example might help. Julie Neururer and Robert Rhoads challenge the role of service-learning in local communities.[11] In many cases, higher education educators present service-learning in the name of social justice even though it is usually designed to promote development and learning among the students who participate. Studies show most service-learning yields minimal transformation for communities yet has a profound impact on the lives of students. The reality of most service-learning experiences is that most students are not addressing issues of justice, but rather they are developing an awareness for their surroundings that may allow them to be advocates for something in the future. This is not to suggest that we should not develop learning opportunities that invite students to build awareness, but rather that these types of experiences are insufficient to advance issues of social justice.

WHY IS THE GAP SO WIDE?

Programs Are Not the Solution

Student affairs educators are rarely assessed on their ability to foster communities where students build relationships in ways that address issues of justice. Most assessments of social justice initiatives privilege the types and number of programs, the number of participants, ability of the organizers to collaborate with other offices on campus, and a rationale for how the program fits the division or institutional mission. Sound familiar? Rarely do evaluators ask student affairs educators to provide insight on the role they are playing in making a more just, healthy, and intercultural community.

Think reflectively about your own experience. How did you develop a commitment to issues of justice? Was it through a class? A program? A relationship? A combination? Two experiences stand out for me as I consider the origins of my justice orientation. First, while taking a year off after high school before going to college, I lived with a gay Mexican American who was shunned by others in our apartment complex. The second was a series of bus rides through my hometown where I found myself sitting next to the same person on a weekly basis, learning about the city from her perspective. In both cases, the relationships shaped my perspective. It was not the apartment nor the bus ride but the relationships themselves that offered meaning and perspective about the experiences of those who do not reflect my own.

According to research, student retention has a direct correlation with students' "sense of belonging" in a school.[12] Students rarely feel a sense of belonging as a result of programming but rather through the relationships they develop among peers, staff, and faculty. We sustain a commitment to justice during and after college through the relationships we develop with those who represent different sociocultural and historical experiences. These relationships serve as a bridge linking one's decisions to the effects they will have on others.

Think Systemic

The field of cultural studies invites student affairs educators to recognize a connection between everyday interactions and the systems that frame the underside of the university. Educators maintain and disrupt the status quo through these daily occurrences. As educators, we focus on the triumphs and feats that occur, even though the underlying structure of the university remains quite static most of the time. One student's epiphany and advancing of justice does not shift the entire structure of the university. However, if this happens repeatedly, or many students respond in the same way, we might begin to see a shift in how the institution operates as a whole. When we consider this, student affairs educators' work is no longer limited to enhancing an individual's student learning but also about leveraging our work to develop university systems that promote and demand human equality.

My analysis of the town hall meeting tells us a great deal, not only about the student who spoke out against the theme party but also about the institution as a whole and how it systemically confronts issues of justice. The theme of the party might suggest a disconnect between students who are familiar with life in the ghetto and those who are not. We might wonder why more African American students showed up at this meeting than any other gathering hosted by the administration during the school year. From this vantage point, student affairs educators are not only interested in addressing concerns about the annual celebration, but we position ourselves as an intermediary to confront institutional realities that hinder human equality. Paulo Freire's *Pedagogy of the Oppressed* highlights the role of libratory educators in helping students develop the "awakening of critical awareness" not only by addressing their individual learning but also by exposing the oppressive systems, structures, and interests that prohibit students from being free.[13]

Freedom From Isolation

Higher education is no different from any other profession in that there is a tendency to zoom in on our field and ignore what is happening elsewhere. Student affairs educators are notorious for not creating personal and professional boundaries for themselves and are often fixated on work-related issues. This becomes dangerous when considering social justice since many issues of justice are outside the academy. If our commitment to human equality remains confined to the workplace, how does this promote justice elsewhere? Furthermore, we can learn and develop as advocates through our relationships and work with those outside higher education. If our commitment to justice stops when we leave work, we fail to make important connections across different sectors of society.

Additionally, it is important that university educators seek connections with the broader K–12 education system, the foundation for students to enter college. A failure to acknowledge what is happening in these schools is a failure to recognize the social, cultural, historical, and political realities of these students.

Are there ramifications for enacting social justice? Well, yes. In fact, that is the point. Justice requires us to leverage, steward, and take chances with the power we have to honor human equality. Perhaps this is where we as student affairs educators get hung up. We are aware of the issues, we help students become aware of the issues, and we try hard not to damage human equality through the lives we lead, but we stop there.

Conclusion

Enacting values of social justice requires something else. To begin, it requires us to be vulnerable enough to recognize that we too are perpetuators of injustice. Even though I take a stand against sexual assault and work tirelessly on issues of higher education access, I fall short in other areas and maybe even promote inequality for others. It also requires us to sacrifice our human capital to honor others. The stakes are high. We run the risk of losing some of our accumulated power and damaging important relationships around us. My supervisor might not trust me to coordinate student leadership training because she is worried my justice agenda might eclipse her agenda, or students might avoid approaching me about a program or event because they know I will challenge them to think about how nondominate groups on campus will interpret its purpose.

These are the risks we take when we enact social justice. It is not safe work, and it requires us to extend beyond inclusive words to bold actions that reveal our willingness to take risks on behalf of our commitments. What are those commitments for you? What are those commitments for your office? What are you willing to risk on behalf of those commitments?

Notes

1. Illich, I. (1968). *To hell with good intentions.* Retrieved from http://www.swaraj.org/illich_hell.htm

2. Curran, C. (2002). *Catholic social teaching 1891–present: A historical, theological and ethical analysis.* Washington, DC: Georgetown University Press.

3. Soares, J. A. (2007). *The power of privilege: Yale and America's elite colleges*. Stanford, CA: Stanford University Press.

4. Crissey, S. R. (2009). *Educational attainment in the United States: 2007*. Washington, DC: U.S. Census Bureau. Retrieved from http://www.census.gov/prod/2009pubs/p20–560.pdf

5. Beck, G. (March 23, 2010). *What is 'social justice?'* Retrieved from http://www.foxnews.com/story/0,2933,589832,00.html

6. Grant, C., & Sleeter, C. (2007). *Turning on learning: Five approaches for multicultural teaching plans for race, class, gender, and disability* (4th ed.). Hoboken, NJ: Wiley.

7. Ibid.

8. Freire, P. (1970). *Pedagogy of the oppressed*. New York, NY: Continuum.

9. hooks, b. (1994). *Teaching to transgress: Education as a practice of freedom*. London, UK: Routledge; Shor, I. (1992). *Empowering education: Critical teaching for social change*. Chicago, IL: University of Chicago Press; Giroux, H. (1997). *Pedagogy and the politics of hope: Theory, culture, and schooling, a critical reader*. Boulder, CO: Westview Press.

10. Rhoads, R. (1997). *Community service and higher learning: Explorations of the caring self*. New York, NY: SUNY Press; Manning, K. (1994). Liberation theology and student affairs. *Journal of College Student Development, 35*(2), 94–97; Butin, D. W. (2008). *Service-learning and social justice education*. New York, NY: Routledge.

11. Neururer, J., & Rhoads, R. A. (1998). Community service: Panacea, paradox, or potentiation. *Journal of College Student Development, 39*(4), 321–330.

12. Hausmann, L., Ye, F., Schofield, J., & Woods, R. (2009). Sense of belonging and persistence in White and African American first-year students. *Research in Higher Education, 50*(7), 649–669.

13. Freire, *Pedagogy of the oppressed*, p. 15.

Beyond Awareness

Student Affairs Educators as Social Justice Advocates

Nana Osei-Kofi, Iowa State University

In Joel Zylstra's essay on social justice work in student affairs, he expresses concern over what he describes as a gap between declaring a social justice agenda among student affairs educators and the actualization of such an agenda. To address this fissure, Zylstra emphasizes the need for student affairs educators to recognize commonalities among different forms of social injustice, to adopt a more global understanding of social issues, and to move from simply creating awareness of social injustice to actively working for social justice.

Overall, I deem Zylstra's observations of the state of social justice work in student affairs to be timely and accurate. Many of the issues he identifies are critical to student affairs educators' becoming social change agents. Concurrently, it is necessary to expand upon as well as trouble some of the ideas Zylstra presents, if student affairs educators are to play a significant role in advancing social justice in institutions of higher education and beyond. Hence, to begin to complicate further what it means for student affairs educators to work for social justice through what might be viewed as a difficult dialogue, I focus on three critical issues that surfaced in my reading of Zylstra's essay, namely, the relationship of awareness to understanding, the role of self-reflexivity, and the relevance of structural thinking in social justice work.

In offering these comments, my perspectives are informed by my experiences as a woman of color and by my view of "social justice as a process and an objective of ending oppression and domination at the individual, institutional, and systemic levels."[1] For me, to work for social justice means adopting a praxis that advances equitable policies and practices that challenge and transform the multiple ways oppression and domination manifest socially, politically, culturally, and economically.

Awareness and Understanding

Zylstra argues that through social networking and other means, student affairs educators today have significant access to information on social justice issues and do well creating awareness of these issues among students. However, he maintains that this emphasis on awareness is void of mechanisms that translate into advocacy on the part of student affairs educators and the students with whom they work. Subsequently, he believes that student affairs educators need to center their work on advocacy rather than building awareness.

Inspired by Paulo Freire's contention that "liberating education consists of acts of cognition, not transferrals of information," I believe it necessary to more closely scrutinize the relationship of information and awareness to advocacy in the promotion of action for social justice.[2] It is imperative to recognize that the availability of information does not necessarily create awareness, and awareness does not by definition equate to understanding, which is imperative for meaningful action or what Zylstra describes as advocacy. For example, just because I have awareness of the existence of racism, this does not mean that I am *knowledgeable* about the consequences of racism, and even though I may be knowledgeable about the ramifications of racism, this does not in itself mean I *understand* racism. To understand racism, to the extent possible if this is something I have not experienced myself, means that I understand the multiple ways racism manifests itself and shapes our society. It also means that I recognize how I am situated in relation to racism. Through a continuous process of moving toward critical consciousness, I am able to see larger social patterns and their applicability to different contexts and situations beyond the specific. Hence, to agitate for social change, a focus on cultivating deep levels of understanding is pivotal.

Self-Reflexivity

A deep level of understanding of how we are located within our social structure, and how this informs not only why we do social justice work but also the types of social justice work we do, is critical to advancing social change. In our 24/7 society it is important to guard against leaping from concern for social justice to action without forethought. Developing our own critical consciousness and self-reflexivity must precede seeking to develop the same in students. Do we understand the issues we are seeking to address? What worldview informs our perspectives? How may we be implicated in the conditions we seek to change? What fears do we have about doing social justice work? Have we done our own work of internal healing in relation to the social justice issues we seek to address? To become effective agents of social change, we must begin with ourselves.

Having said this, I view it necessary to problematize self-reflexivity in Zylstra's essay. Overall, I did not find that self-reflexivity received the attention I believe is necessary to approach social justice work with the utmost consciousness and diligence. Without doing our own intellectual, emotional, and spiritual work, despite good intentions, we can easily cause more harm than good. Zylstra touches only briefly on his own social location, suggesting that student affairs educators "like him" as holders of advanced degrees are beneficiaries of unearned privilege and must engage with this recognition in their work. Beyond this it is unclear what it means to be like him and what unearned privileges this might entail.

To work for social justice means adopting a praxis that advances equitable policies and practices that challenge and transform the multiple ways oppression and domination manifest themselves socially, politically, culturally, and economically.

In this same vein, I find it unsettling that all the examples Zylstra uses to illustrate what sparked his commitment to social justice are based on external experiences made possible through contact with the "Other." What makes me apprehensive about these types of examples is that when we see our own commitment to social justice work as the result of coming to know the Other without implicating ourselves in what we come to know, we position the Other as what is to be known in the service of our transformation while erasing any acknowledgment of the social conditions that structure relationships between dominant and oppressed groups.[3]

Building from this construction of the Other, Zylstra's overall discussion is framed as one in which student affairs educators, positioned as the collective "we," should engage in social change work on behalf of the Other, consider the impact of their actions on the Other, and extend their attention to the Other, beyond their immediate professional responsibilities. As a woman of color, I am particularly struck by this framing of social justice advocacy. For me, there is little separation between my social justice work in higher education and my everyday life experiences. My social location limits my possibility of viewing myself as working on behalf of the Other, and it is also a position I reject in light of the ways I believe we are all implicated, albeit differently, in our current social realities.

Inherent in the idea of working on behalf of the Other is the danger of what Sherene Razack describes as stealing the pain of others. To steal the pain of others is to view oneself as understanding the pain of others by being a compassionate witness, in no way implicated in the situation. In so doing, speaking on behalf of others brings with it a sense of moral authority as a result of deeply feeling the other's pain. It is a situation in which we view our vulnerability to these conditions as what marks us as social justice advocates. We become the subjects of the issue, while those we supposedly advocate for are simply objects that facilitate the story we tell about ourselves.[4] For all these reasons, self-reflexivity is critical to working for social transformation and must go beyond what is discussed in Zylstra's essay so that we fully come to understand our own motivations in doing social justice work.

Structural Views

Throughout Zylstra's essay, one of the issues he brings forth that I want to expand upon is what I have come to think of as *manufactured fragmentation*. In the place of scrutinizing issues of social injustice structurally, Zylstra makes salient what I would describe as the ways "political, social, and economic concerns are seen as distinct and unrelated issues shaped by inevitable, individually defined and often abstract forces," the consequences of which are a great hindrance to social transformation.[5] For instance, in lieu of recognizing how structural arrangements shape the marginalization of different groups of students, fragmented approaches to identifying and seeking to address socially unjust practices often result in different groups being pitted against one another. Instead of fighting in collectivity for the resources needed to shift oppressive structural conditions while embracing a politics of difference, individual groups fight one another for already insufficient resources. The outcome of this type of horizontal hostility is what Audre Lorde would describe as "endless kitchen wars" that ultimately benefit the status quo.[6] Similarly, college and university administrations often address injustices that result from oppressive structural arrangements on campuses as interpersonal issues resulting from differences among individuals.[7] Hence, approaches that focus on changing individual behaviors are centered as preferred practices for combating injustice rather than addressing structural arrangements that produce and perpetuate oppression. To shift these realities, it is crucial that student affairs educators adopt a structural analytic approach to social justice work that takes into full account the ways "human behavior is shaped by the collective forces of history and the social/political/economic structures that make up . . . society."[8] For example, instead of viewing bullying gay students simply as resulting from individuals' hatred of homosexuals, a structural analytic perspective would suggest that these acts are not solely about hatred expressed by individuals; instead they are about the enforcement of larger societal gender norms, thus reflecting the hegemonic expectation of heteronormativity. That is to say, bullying gay students represents learned forms of social control of deviance that function to reinforce a hierarchical gender structure. Hence, while education and conflict resolution focused on individuals may be a part of addressing the bullying of gay students, a structural analytic approach requires that the ways institutions produce and reproduce gender hierarchies and heteronormativity be engaged in order to begin to address the root causes of these expressions of violence.

Social institutions such as government, religion, and education function to maintain and reproduce our existing (unequal) social structure. Therefore, to approach an understanding of social injustice structurally necessitates becoming keenly aware of the history and culture of the institutions we function in. It also means becoming conscious of the systemic mechanisms, such as norms and values, that uphold everyday institutional practices which, while oppressive, are largely taken for granted. The consequences of failing to adopt such an approach, failing to understand oppression as structural, results in complicity with modes of power that perpetuate oppression and domination, even when we might believe we are contesting these powers.

Conclusion

Doing social justice work, whether in student affairs or any other setting, is a continuous process of reflection, understanding, listening, questioning, challenging, strategizing, analyzing, organizing, acting, learning, and growing as an advocate for social transformation. Doing social justice work calls for a critical understanding of issues of injustice relationally, historically, and contextually. Doing social justice work is about clarity of vision, knowing what it is we mean by social justice and why we choose to do the work. Doing social justice work is to be able to think beyond the moment, to imagine a different future, to use knowledge for social transformation, and to collectively intervene to make institutions, society, and the world a better place for all inhabitants.[9]

Notes

1. Osei-Kofi, N., Shahjahan, R., & Patton, L. (2010). Centering social justice in the study of higher education: The challenges and possibilities for institutional change. *Equity & Excellence in Education, 43*(3), 326–340, p. 329.

2. Freire, P. (2000). *Pedagogy of the oppressed.* New York, NY: Continuum, p. 79. (Original work published 1970).

3. Ahmed, S. (2000). *Strange encounters: Embodied others in post-coloniality.* New York, NY: Routledge.

4. Razack, S. (2007). Stealing the pain of others: Reflections on Canadian humanitarian responses. *Review of Education, Pedagogy, and Cultural Studies, 29*(4), 375–394.

5. Osei-Kofi, N. (2003). *In the image of capital: The making of the corporate university* (Unpublished doctoral dissertation). Claremont, CA: Claremont Graduate University.

6. Lorde, A. (1984). *Sister outsider.* Freedom, CA: Crossing Press, p. 48.

7. Mohanty, C. (1994). On race and voice: Challenges for liberal education in the '90s. In H. Giroux & P. McLaren (Eds.), *Between borders: Pedagogy and the politics of cultural studies* (pp. 145–166). New York, NY: Routledge.

8. Bishop, A. (2005). *Beyond token change: Breaking the cycle of oppression in institutions.* Halifax, Nova Scotia, Canada: Fernwood Publishing.

9. Davis, A. (2006, October). *How does social change happen?* Speech presented at the University of California, Davis, CA.

Further Reading and Related Blog

Sue Ann Huang, University of Washington

Giroux, H. A., & Giroux, S. S. (2004). *Taking back higher education: Race, youth, and the crisis of democracy in the post–civil rights era*. New York, NY: Palgrace MacMillan.

The Giroux's book strives to combat several attitudes facing society today: apathy and cynicism toward national politics, and skepticism toward education. The authors view these two issues as interrelated and suggest that politics and education cannot be separated nor can pedagogy, power, and culture. They present a call to action for educators and society to reclaim higher education as a space for critical engagement.

Johnson, A. G. (2005). *Power, privilege, and difference*. Mountain View, CA: McGraw-Hill.

Johnson's book provides an introduction to concepts of power, privilege, oppression, and difference. He provides a way to think about these institutional systems of privilege and oppression and proactive ways to work to change the system. He encourages everyone to take responsibility for changing the system and provides an accessible way to think about these difficult concepts and how to start the change.

Rhoads, R. A., & Black, M. A. (1995). Student affairs practitioners as transformative educators: Advancing a critical cultural perspective. *Journal of College Student Development, 36*(5), 413–421.

Rhoads and Black present a critical cultural perspective as a way to practice student affairs. The authors provide a history of various ideologies that forms a framework for their perspective, tracing various critical perspectives. They describe the benefits of their perspective and transformative education, and they present their perspective as a way to change institutional culture.

Blog URL: contestedissues.wordpress.com
Corresponding Chapter Post: tinyurl.com/contestedissues20

21

What Would Student Affairs Organizational Structures Look Like If They Supported Inclusive, Learning-Centered Practices?

Advancing Inclusive and Learning-Centered Practice: Redesigning Student Affairs Work

John P. Dugan, Loyola University Chicago

In my current faculty appointment I have the great blessing to teach courses on social justice. Each year the thoughtful self-exploration of students and their consideration of how issues of privilege and oppression manifest themselves in the higher education context impresses me. However, in the final weeks of the semester a critical question regularly emerges: How do we move education grounded in social justice from an idealistic concept to a practical reality? After a semester of deep personal reflection and increasing experiences in the field via internships and assistantships, this question haunts students. In all fairness, it haunts me as well. Alumni return to campus and regularly express frustration with organizational systems that purport the centrality of learning and justice but at the same time constrain substantive progress in these areas.

Certainly higher education in general and student affairs in particular have made important gains in response to issues of inclusivity and learning centeredness in recent years. Increasing diversity of staff, enhanced accountability by documenting learning, policies requiring equity in hiring and compensation, and organizational structures with dedicated services for traditionally underrepresented student populations all are evidence of a growing investment and attention to inclusivity and learning. However, these important changes can at times feel like cosmetic fixes masking more fundamental problems, which may be where frustrations begin to take root. As one student so eloquently stated, "How can we expect other contexts to embrace and support the values of social justice when we can't even model it in our design and delivery of student affairs practice?" Why is it so difficult to enact the organizational changes necessary to reshape our work?

What would student affairs organizational structures look like if they supported learning-centered, inclusive principles? This essay reflects an assumption that inclusivity is insufficient on its own and best serves educational practice when grounded in the broader concept of social justice, which Joseph Zajda, Suzanne Majhanovich, and Val Rust situate as inherently concerned with how individuals can contribute to "a more equitable, respectful, and just society for everyone."[1] Specifically, I provide an abbreviated history outlining the organizational design of student affairs work, barriers impinging on the effective infusion of inclusivity and learning-centered approaches, and recommendations for enhancing learning-centered and inclusive practice.

Evolving Conceptualizations of Student Affairs Organizations

Student affairs educators have a long tradition of aligning organizational structures with the core values informing their work, and numerous scholars situate a focus on learning and inclusivity as central tenets. A wide array of factors, including historical considerations regarding the role of student services, organizational theory, and empirical research, inform the choice of how to structure student affairs practice to achieve this aim. Historically, the organization of student affairs work largely reflected its perceived function and value within the larger institutional context. Arthur Sandeen and Margaret Barr offered a thoughtful overview of how these perceptions changed over the years based on societal influences and institutional goals along with the resultant shifts in organizational structures.[2] They identified two primary considerations administrators of institutions debate in the struggle to enhance effectiveness. These considerations included whether to centralize or decentralize the delivery of services and whether student affairs should report directly to the president or through the provost. A danger exists in these dichotomizations, however, as effectiveness can easily be interpreted as retaining the maximum institutional influence or greatest resource acquisition rather than how each model contributes to the educational gains of students.

---

*How do we move education grounded in social justice
from an idealistic concept to a practical reality?*

Of particular importance to student affairs practice should be an understanding of how different organizational structures contribute positively to student learning. Organizational theory provides a lens for understanding how people in complex systems identify and work toward goals, engage in decision making, respond to internal and external stakeholders, and navigate change—issues that are at the center of historical concerns about how to structure student affairs practice. Numerous scholars have explored organizational theory as well as its application to higher education and student affairs.[3]

Most scholars agree that organizational theories typically fall within two distinct paradigms, the conventional and the postconventional. George Kuh suggested that conventional organizational theories are characterized by hierarchical structures, predictable interactions, and clearly delineated expertise and authority while postconventional theories reflected heterarchical structures, dynamic and unpredictable interactions, and interdependence within and between systems.[4] The two paradigms are not mutually exclusive, though, and elements of each can be seen simultaneously in a single organization. This is an observation often left unstated that perpetuates an oversimplification of organizational dynamics.

To their benefit, postconventional theories do typically direct significantly more attention to understanding cultural dimensions of organizations (e.g., artifacts, values, assumptions) as opposed to emphasizing structural components (e.g., policies, reporting lines, standard operating procedures). William Tierney suggested that higher education would be better served by focusing greater attention on cultural properties of organizations consistent with postconventional theories, and less on the simple structural considerations that much of the historical literature addressed.[5] This is an astute observation as it enhances the role that individuals play in the cultural formation of organizational life. However, overzealous educators should be cautioned that Tierney is not likely suggesting the use of one theoretical frame over the other but emphasizes using both frames.

The inability of either historically evolving student affairs structures or organizational theory to provide clear evidence of how best to structure student affairs practice for student learning contributed to empirical research on the subject. Arthur Sandeen found little consistency in the organizational structures of student affairs divisions at institutions where he identified the chief student affairs officer as highly successful. The organizational design and delivery varied significantly based on an institution's specific context.[6] Although the results of this study support nonprescriptive approaches to organizing student affairs work, I struggle with the design itself, which seems leader centric and overly fixated on structural dimensions. Could it be that while organizational structures varied significantly at institutions, the behaviors of individual actors within those structures were consistent?

The Documenting Effective Educational Practices research project offered perhaps the most comprehensive analysis of student affairs organizational models with a specific emphasis on student affairs practice at educationally engaging institutions. Kathleen Manning, Jillian Kinzie, and John Schuh identified 11 unique approaches to organizing student affairs work.[7] The models map nicely onto organizational theory paradigms and reflect evolving perceptions of the role and value of student affairs. Six of the models are unsurprising and emerged from the existing literature reflecting more traditional organizational structures. Five distinctive models also emerged reflecting innovative approaches to the design and delivery of student affairs work. These models stress human interactions and the philosophical approach to organizational work as much as, if not more than, structural considerations. Most important, though, was the finding that no one model fit all institutional contexts. In both of the previously mentioned studies, scholars advocated for institutions to create organizational structures that aligned with the institutional mission, supported collaborative practices, and advanced a learning-centered approach. They did not, however, suggest there was a singular structure that best achieved this.

Neglected Influences in Student Affairs Organizational Designs

If one size does not fit all in the organization of student affairs work, it seems to beg the question of whether this is truly a contested issue. There certainly appears to be agreement that variation in organizational delivery is appropriate. However, most educators would probably also agree that we are hardly there yet in terms of supporting the foundational principles of learning centeredness and inclusivity.

Perhaps then the issue lies less in organizational structures and more with the individual actors who bring to life organizational behaviors. I concede that my scholarly interests and inherent biases favor the arena of social psychology and understanding how individuals in systems work interdependently toward goals that advance social change. In this case, however, my bias may offer a window into understanding how structural considerations in organizing student affairs work may lead to enhanced effectiveness across principles that are broadly identified as acceptable. Student affairs practice that is learning centered and inclusive likely falls in a gray area, though. The values may be perceived as socially desirable but can also be experienced as individually threatening. Dealing with issues of power, privilege, oppression, and one's own perceived competence as a knower inherently involves the ego. These are principles that are easy to accept in the abstract but require vulnerability and accountability to integrate into practice. At the core of this is a process of reevaluating and restructuring the self-concept, a process that often triggers avoidance. Thus, individual educators may engage in behaviors that externally project a shared valuing of learning centeredness and inclusivity but also consciously or subconsciously undermine work to achieve them.

As a means to explore the central question of this essay, it seems appropriate to first take a step back and consider barriers related to individuals within systems that complicate the pursuit of learning-centered and inclusive practice. Four considerations seem to emerge: overemphasis on organizational structures, lack of acknowledgment of political dimensions, ownership of social justice, and collusion of graduate preparation programs.

Over-Emphasis on Organizational Structures

Drawing on the work of organizational theorists, George Kuh deftly points out the important differences between organizational structures and organizational behaviors, with the latter reflecting how individual actors in organizations actually bring to life the culture, values, and shared identity.[8] The emphasis in practice, however, often falls on the former with the use of policy and structural designs as catalysts for change and advancing critical goals. William Tierney pointed out that "structure follows vision, it cannot precede it."[9] Vision, in turn, is enacted at an individual level. Thus, an organization can provide structural evidence that it values learning-centered and inclusive practices, but individual actors must also embrace these practices for them to manifest in meaningful ways. Until organizations begin uniquely targeting both structures and behaviors, it will be difficult to fully integrate learning-centered and inclusive practices.

An example of the overemphasis on organizational structures lies in the espoused versus actualized values associated with hiring practices. Search committees are routinely charged with seeking out diverse candidate pools, provided training on how to do this, and supported by policies. These structural supports are often insufficient, though, as conscious and subconscious behaviors on the part of individual actors can diminish their effect. I recall sitting on multiple search committees as a student affairs professional in which the final candidate pool lacked nearly any racial or gender diversity and individuals habitually offered "perfectly logical answers" to explain this away, often placing the blame on marginalized communities in the process. In these cases the structural interventions could not overcome the power of individual and group behaviors.

Lack of Acknowledgment of Politics

In addition to confounding organizational structures and behaviors, the lack of acknowledgment of the deeply political nature of learning-centered and inclusive practice makes structuring organizational life difficult. As

Adrianna Kezar noted, addressing and advancing complex issues related to diversity requires an acknowledgment of and ability to navigate political considerations.[10] This includes understanding how to anticipate and address a variety of ways resistance can arise from within and outside the organization. Failure to consider how political dynamics may influence learning-centered and inclusive practices at the individual and organizational levels significantly limits the likelihood of deep or meaningful change. This may contribute to the creation of structures that are largely symbolic and lack any tangible effect on the organization, which can do more harm than good in shaping organizational culture.

Ownership of Social Justice

Creating an organizational structure characterized by learning-centered and inclusive practice necessitates an examination of how normative assumptions in student affairs may constrain effectiveness. Student affairs educators have long advocated on behalf of marginalized voices and ideas in the larger higher education context. This includes the importance of learning beyond traditional classroom boundaries and advancing diversity and multicultural competence. Student affairs educators often serve as the arbiters of these issues on campus. There is a danger in this role, however, as it infers expertise in a topical area predicated on lifelong learning and the need for continuous, critical self-reflection. Does perceived expertise effectively let student affairs professionals off the hook for their own learning? Similarly, the role of arbiter of social justice can also insinuate that others fail to understand and must be educated.

I once observed the staff of a multicultural student affairs unit address issues of cultural competence with a group of faculty. The student affairs staff members' assumptions prior to the meeting were clearly that faculty were lacking in this domain. The reality, however, was that this particular group of faculty was actively engaged in research on social justice topics and specifically interested in advancing classroom pedagogical approaches using critical theory. The faculty certainly had more to learn but did have a solid foundation and were interested in learning with their student affairs colleagues. The staff's presumption of a lack of competence, condescending approach, and inability to validate the faculty as knowers in their own right was immediately distancing and diminished the two groups' desire to work together in the future.

Ownership of knowledge related to social justice and the tendency to classify others based on whether they are perceived to get it is dangerously

---

Strategies for comprehensive and transformational change need to target individual behaviors and organizational structures simultaneously.

---

counterproductive. Jason Laker and Tracy Davis problemize the issue further by noting the ease with which those advancing multicultural campus communities can fall into self-congratulatory behaviors.[11] These behaviors contribute to an oversimplification of issues, us-versus-them mindsets, and patriarchal ways of interacting that erode opportunities for shared learning and meaningful dialogue. Why is it so difficult to extend the same developmental ethics of care and patience to our fellow colleagues we so readily offer to students?

Collusion of Graduate Preparation Programs

The role of student affairs educators as inherent arbiters of social justice represents a false self-concept that is internalized at some point in the professional socialization process. Graduate preparation programs play a significant role in shaping professional identity and potentially collude in this. Most preparation program curricula offer course work in student development and multiculturalism that targets the facilitation of student learning. To what degree, though, do programs train new professionals to engage in and with this work personally? Furthermore, to what extent do these curricula emphasize knowledge acquisition over knowledge integration? It is easy to assume the role of expert and arbiter if one intellectualizes issues of learning centeredness and inclusivity, as intellectualization can provide a sense of false certitude as well as distance from the issues. Paulo Freire stresses the essential role identity plays in learning and the need for educational approaches that stress cognition and critical self-reflection over the simple transfer of information.[12] The extent to which we practice this not only shapes the socialization process of student affairs educators but also has a direct effect on their abilities to engage in the organizational behaviors necessary to support structures characterized by learning-centered and inclusive practices.

These four issues represent potential barriers that impinge on the ability of student affairs organizations to fully support learning-centered and inclusive practices. They also suggest the need to broaden the view of organizational development beyond simple structural considerations. Individual behaviors within systems and the socialization processes that inform those behaviors must also be addressed for comprehensive change to occur.

Envisioning a Different Future

So how can student affairs organizations be structured to better support learning-centered and inclusive practices given what we know from the prior literature and the barriers identified here? A starting point is to avoid the either/or approaches to organizational development that typically overemphasize structural considerations. Strategies for comprehensive and transformational change need to target individual behaviors and organizational structures simultaneously.

Without a doubt, organizational structures must be used as a vehicle for advancing the principles of learning centeredness and inclusivity. This includes the application of postconventional organizational theories that support the further reduction of functional silos and disrupt traditional structural features that reinforce unequal power dynamics. Kathleen Allen and Cynthia Cherrey advocate an approach that reconceives traditional ways of being within organizational systems.[13] They assert that human relationships provide the connective tissue in organizations and create an interconnected web informing how work is accomplished. This is not to say that traditional hierarchies are ineffective or should be flattened, but that how individuals interact in hierarchies can largely shape the effectiveness of an organization. This perspective contributes greatly to advancing learning-centered and inclusive practice by providing an opportunity to disrupt conventional assumptions regarding organizational life. The following are just a few of the ways increased interaction across levels may have an impact on the organization:

> ► It increases the likelihood that core values are more accurately transmitted, contributing to more effective socialization into the organizational culture.

> ► It disrupts traditional models of authority that constrain dialogue and processes by stipulating who is privileged to know.
> ► It enhances perceptions of shared responsibility for organizational goals as opposed to carving them into discrete duties of specific units.

These are just some of the benefits associated with aligning organizational structures more closely with postconventional organizational theory. Advancing learning-centered and inclusive practices will also require policies, evaluative processes, and reward systems that continue to support individual behaviors within the organization. Too often policies and structures are symbolic in nature with no established mechanisms for measuring their effectiveness. The creation of these policies and structures needs to be accompanied by concrete evaluative measures, accountability plans, and implications for success or failure.

A need persists to better attend to organizational behaviors if administrators and staff of student affairs units wish to enhance learning-centered and inclusive practices. At the core of this is training actors within systems to understand and to have agency concerning these critical issues. Maurianne Adams, Lee Anne Bell, and Pat Griffin suggest the goal of social justice education is

> to enable people to develop the critical analytical tools necessary to understand oppression and their own socialization within oppressive systems, and to develop a sense of agency and capacity to interrupt and change oppressive patterns and behaviors in themselves and in the institutions and communities of which they are a part.[14]

This goal necessitates a learning-centered approach and is routinely directed at students. How often, though, is it turned inward and applied to the educators themselves? Actors within systems do not automatically have agency related to social justice simply because the system suggests it is important and adopts policies and structures to promote it. The concept of agency reflects an individual's internal belief system and must be intentionally cultivated.

Moving individuals within systems from actors to agents regarding the issues of learning centeredness and inclusivity is a complex process that begins by addressing the problem at its root. This involves rethinking the process and delivery of graduate preparation program curriculum. At the core of this is reconsidering the extent to which programs prepare students to engage in lifelong learning and critical self-reflection. It also requires a curriculum that teaches not only multicultural competence but also the tenets of social justice, which provide the framework for understanding why multicultural competence is important, one's positioning within broader systems, and how to develop agency. This represents a significant pedagogical shift and requires the support of not just graduate preparation faculty, but professional staff and national associations as well.

Individual organizations must also model a learning-centered approach and provide substantive opportunities for continuing education. It merits restatement that organizations cannot assume that individuals have agency or even functional knowledge about how to engage in learning-centered and inclusive practice. Student affairs professionals represent a variety of disciplinary backgrounds and may or may not have been prepared to engage in this work. If an organization's leaders suggest learning-centeredness and inclusivity are important, then what are they functionally doing to prepare educators to engage in it? Student affairs organizations need to provide platforms for educators to participate in personal and values-based conversations about these topics if they wish to reduce perceptions of threat, and advance authentic dialogues and a professional practice characterized by lived principles. Professional development cannot be the domain of graduate preparation programs or national associations alone. Student affairs units have a responsibility to create opportunities for exploration of these topics as well.

I have been proud to be part of an organizational culture at Loyola University Chicago that increasingly attempts to address organizational structures and behaviors as it advances learning-centered and inclusive practice. This occurs in my academic unit as well as at the institutional level and in the student affairs division. As a mission-based institution that holds social justice at its core, the educational context espouses the values of inclusivity and learning centeredness. Recently, however, the university placed these values at the forefront via a renewed emphasis on transformational education. Institutional conversations established a clear definition of the concept that could be adopted and endorsed university-wide. Clear objectives were established for making transformational learning an institutional reality, and structural changes (e.g., new policies, identification of responsible parties, and mechanisms for evaluating progress) were implemented to support this. Simultaneously, individual units engaged in extensive discussions about how this intersected with their personal values as well as with the specific functions of their units. This provided an opportunity to address individual and collective organizational behaviors and explicitly examine how they might influence various objectives associated with advancing a transformational educational approach.

Meaningful progress in organizing student affairs practice around learning-centeredness and inclusivity requires a fundamental shift from the end goal to process orientation. The climate itself must change so that learning and inclusivity are in the foreground of how people interact with one another. This personalizes the issues, elevates their importance beyond times of convenience, and acknowledges individual and organizational responsibility.

Conclusion

The quest continues for the student affairs organizational model that best contributes to effectiveness and educational gains. Part of this undoubtedly reflects our need for parsimonious and neat solutions to complex problems that do not have concrete answers. My own yearning and that of my students for greater congruence between espoused values and practical realities reflect this need. It also reflects our shared desire to serve our students and one another well. Certainly progress has been made in the organizational design and delivery of student affairs practice to better reflect the values of learning centeredness and inclusivity. However, if we intend to live the espoused values of our field, we need to begin coupling interventions that address organizational structures and organizational behaviors. This increases the likelihood that systems will adopt the values and enact the intended processes necessary to advance learning-centered and inclusive practice.

Notes

1. Zajda, J., Majhanovich, S., & Rust, V. (2006). Introduction: Education and social justice. *Review of Education, 52*, 9–22, p. 13.

2. Sandeen, A., & Barr, M. J. (2006). *Critical issues for student affairs: Challenges and opportunities*. San Francisco, CA: Jossey-Bass.

3. Birnbaum, R. (1988). *How colleges work: The cybernetics of academic organization and leadership*. San Francisco, CA: Jossey-Bass; Bolman, L. G., & Deal, T. E. (2003).

Reframing organizations: Artistry, choice, and leadership (3rd ed.). San Francisco, CA: Jossey-Bass; Morgan, G. (2006). *Images of organizations.* Thousand Oaks, CA: Sage; Schein, E. H. (2004). *Organizational culture and leadership* (3rd ed.). San Francisco, CA: Jossey-Bass.

4. Kuh, G. D. (2003). Organizational theory. In S. R. Komives & D. B. Woodard Jr. (Eds.), *Student services: A handbook for the profession* (4th ed., pp. 269–296). San Francisco, CA: Jossey-Bass.

5. Tierney, W. G. (1999). *Building the responsive campus: Creating high performance colleges and universities.* Thousand Oaks, CA: Sage.

6. Sandeen, A. (2001). Organizing student affairs divisions. In R. B. Winston Jr., D. G. Creamer, & T. K. Miller (Eds.), *The professional student affairs administrator: Educator, leader, and manager* (pp. 181–209). New York, NY: Brunner-Routledge.

7. Manning, K., Kinzie, J., & Schuh, J. (2006). *One size does not fit all: Traditional and innovative models for student affairs practice.* New York, NY: Routledge.

8. Kuh, Organizational theory.

9. Tierney, *Building the responsive campus,* p. 23.

10. Kezar, A. (2008). Understanding leadership strategies for addressing the politics of diversity. *Journal of Higher Education, 79,* 406–441.

11. Laker, J. A., & Davis, T. L. (2009). Continuing the journey towards multicultural campus communities. In G. S. McClellan & J. Stringer (Eds.), *The handbook of student affairs administration* (3rd ed., pp. 242–264). San Francisco, CA: Jossey Bass.

12. Freire, P. (2003). *Pedagogy of the oppressed.* New York, NY: Continuum. (Original work published 1970)

13. Allen, K. E., & Cherrey, C. (2000). *Systemic leadership.* Lanham, MD: University Press of America.

14. Adams, M. J., Bell, L. A., & Griffin, P. (2007). *Teaching for diversity and social justice* (2nd ed.). New York, NY: Routledge, p. 2.

Changing Student Affairs Through Organizational Sense Making

Tatiana Suspitsyna, The Ohio State University

Reconceptualizing organizational structures to support inclusive learning-centered practices is an ambiguous task when one is uncertain about the building materials. Are they structural or are they cultural? Do structures shape the cultural norms expressed in practices? Or is it culture that creates supportive organizational structures? With such an array of building blocks, the question about student affairs structures that support inclusive learning-centered practices is somewhat of a chicken or the egg problem. By strengthening the inclusive and learning-centered culture, practitioners can transform the structure of student affairs; by changing organizational structures, they can foster the culture of inclusiveness and learning centeredness. The solution of this dilemma and what John Dugan deplores as practitioners' overemphasis on structure at the expense of individual behaviors may be found in a social constructivist position that recognizes the mutually constitutive and enacted nature of organizational structure and culture. It is from that theoretical perspective that I respond to Dugan's essay and propose a vision of inclusive and learning-centered student affairs. I will begin by outlining my conceptual framework and then discuss the constraints and possibilities of constructing learning-centered and inclusive structures and cultures.

Student Affairs as Cultures

With organizational structures understood broadly as divisions, departments, and jobs, Gareth Morgan's metaphor of organizations as cultures is central to my approach. In his influential *Images of Organizations*, Morgan views culture as a process of reality construction and an interpretative paradigm individuals use to make sense of new situations and their own behavior.[1] Linda Smircich, who concluded that culture is not what an organization has but is what an organization is, also noted this property of culture to govern organizational reasoning and behavior.[2] In other words, as culture, an organization is a collective accomplishment of its members who through their social interaction continuously reconstruct and enact rules, regulations, norms, beliefs, patterns of practices, and structures—everything that makes up the organization.

To reflect the continuous and ongoing nature of that construction and enactment, Karl Weick abandoned the term *organization* altogether in favor of its verbal form *organizing*.[3] Echoing Morgan, Weick viewed organizing in cognitive terms of sense making, a social, ongoing, and retrospective process grounded in individual identities that involves noticing and selecting cues in the environment for interpretation and results in enactment of that interpretation in practice. Sense making activates organizational members' interpretative schemas, their mental models of the world. The schemas help individuals understand new information and diagnose a new problem, and at the same time constrain their interpretation and action to the boundaries of what is already known, tried, and tested. Translated into the context of higher education, Weick's perspective on organizing through sense making draws attention to the root of colleges' and universities' impermeability to rapid transformation: the tenacity of old interpretative schemas and the meanings, norms, and practices these schemas generate and maintain.

Weick's sense making provides a useful framework for understanding the relationship among student affairs structure, culture, and practices by linking individual and organizational dynamics through the production of meaning and action. Unlike other perspectives reviewed in Dugan's essay, sense making does not pit organizations against individuals, nor does it assume the preeminence of structure over cultural and behavioral norms in organizational analysis and planning. Rather, it focuses on the process of organizing, that is, constructing, sustaining, and enacting organizations on a daily basis. If student affairs is a culture in Smircich's sense, then the central question of this essay can be rephrased: How can student affairs be enacted in an inclusive and learning-centered way? Next, I outline key processes of that enactment.

Organizing Student Affairs for Inclusiveness and Learning Centeredness

The process of making sense of something and enacting inclusiveness and learning centeredness has individual and organizational dimensions. At the individual level, the sense making opens up individual interpretative schemas for revision and modification. Student affairs practitioners have to learn to recognize and make diversity, social justice, and student centeredness relevant to their identities, activities, and pedagogies. Repeated and accepted as appropriate interpretations, these changes in individual cognition and action lead to institutionalization of the new meanings and practices and produce new routines—stable patterns of decision making and courses of action—which are infused with values of social justice and learning. Magnified to the organizational level, the performance and maintenance of the new routines require adjustments and innovations in hiring practices, job descriptions, division of responsibilities, communication channels, and so on. In other words, the culture and structure of student affairs change as members adopt and act upon new knowledge and values and then retain those practices in the organizational memory as standard operating procedures and appropriate behaviors.

For example, according to the Transgender Law & Policy Institute, in the past 5 years, the number of colleges and universities that added gender identity/expression to their nondiscrimination policies grew from 55 to over 300.[4] The increasing recognition of the needs of transgender populations on campus has marked a cultural shift and resulted in structural changes that affect a wide range of operations from registrar to health care to housing and recreation. Gender-neutral bathrooms, housing options and locker rooms, counseling and hormone replacement therapy for transitioning students, and procedures for changing gender designation in campus records are some of the services colleges and universities now provide. These practices and procedures in turn reinforce the culture of diversity and increase the visibility of transgender issues in higher education.

Enacting student affairs in a learning-centered and inclusive way requires more than a strategy. It calls for an overhaul of old interpretative schemas and the accepted norms and standards of organizational decision making and action.

This view of mutually constitutive cultural and structural change has some discomforting implications for student affairs practitioners and administrators. First, it means there is no quick fix, no easy strategy for transforming student affairs structures. Organizational scholar Barbara Czarniawska reminds us that contrary to the penchant of managers for quick impact, research suggests that all profound and lasting organizational change is slow and piecemeal.[5] Second, and I strongly agree with Dugan here, change has to target the individual, leaders as well as rank-and-file employees, who recreates the field and service of student affairs in his or her daily work. Although sense making is an organizational process, the individual does the interpreting, acting, and remembering; organizations act and remember only metaphorically. Finally, no single student affairs structure or individual behavior can best serve the cause of inclusiveness and learning centeredness. This last point is worth elaborating on, as it departs in spirit from Dugan's quest for best practices.

The tacit knowledge of what student affairs is and how it runs as a unit inside a larger college or university organization is the basis of the everyday operation of student affairs offices. Part of that knowledge comes from graduate programs in counseling, student affairs, and higher education, which, as studies suggest, shape practitioners' understanding of the field and mold their expectations of newcomers.[6] Central to forming a professional identity and workable interpretative schemas of student affairs, the socialization pressures exerted by graduate preparation programs may nevertheless produce negative effects. As Dugan astutely observes, inculcation of norms and values may foreclose opportunities for self-exploration and questioning, particularly with regard to diversity and multiculturalism.

Another part of the tacit knowledge is specific to individual organizations. There is ample evidence that institutional size, mission, and structure affect the ethos and job responsibilities of student affairs professionals. Employers at different types of institutions are known to look for different skill sets in their applicants for entry-level student affairs positions.[7] Student affairs professionals make different sense of their jobs and environments depending on the school's culture and institutional type. As Joan Hirt demonstrates in her illuminating exploration of the field, from standard bearers at liberal arts colleges to guardians at historically Black colleges and universities to specialists at research universities, student affairs administrators conceive of and perform their roles in congruence with their employers' culture, legacies, and goals.[8] For that reason, the wide range of effective organizational forms and structures found by Arthur Sandeen among successful student affairs offices is not surprising; with their diverse cultures and missions, campuses resist cookie-cutter prescriptions.[9] For that reason also, the answer to Dugan's question of whether individual behaviors are consistent across diverse structures is yes and no—the behaviors converge on the norms learned during graduate studies but acquire institution-specific characteristics during socialization into the culture of the employer.

So far I have sketched out the complexities and difficulties of enacting student affairs. I discuss three of them here. First, transformation of old mental models requires a concerted effort at delegitimizing practices that lead to exclusion and inhibit learning. Student affairs practitioners cannot accomplish this task alone without help from the faculty, guardians of the curriculum and pedagogy, and students. Expansive and purposeful liaisons with faculty across academic disciplines, policy making based on institutional and student assessment research and data, continuous and consistent involvement of student organizations in intercultural conversations, and above all, creation of a vibrant public sphere for contestation and discussion of ideas are among the measures that can collectively devalue and terminate harmful practices.

The work of the Bias Assessment and Response Team (BART) at the Ohio State University (OSU) is an example of intentional sense making in the service of diversity. A joint venture of the Office of Student Life and the Office of Diversity and Inclusion, BART serves as a watchdog of existing policies and practices and provides a timely and qualified response to incidents of harassment, prejudice, and hate crime on campus. The BART core team of top student affairs administrators, intercultural specialists, and student staff works with faculty members, professionals, students, and student organizations across campus, drawing on their expertise and their interpretative schemas to diagnose and eliminate prejudice on a case-by-case basis.

Second, student affairs administrators need to facilitate the culture of shared experience to build a common stock, the cultural glue that bonds members and ensures continuity and coherence in decision making and action. The glue does not come from shared meanings but from working side by side, collaborating, forming partnerships, and doing things together. After all, the meanings that individuals make of the world are specific to them, and imposing a uniform interpretation can lead to homogeneity and more exclusion. Shared experiences also allow a safe space for verbalizing one's reasoning and behavior, or as Weick would put it, for "talking the walk," and uncovering one's biases, assumptions, and expectations to keep them in check.[10] National Coalition Building Institute (NCBI) training, staff retreats, and communal events and celebrations are some activities conducive to reducing prejudice and building shared experience in organizational units on campus.

Third, as a medium of sense making, language frames issues, names problems, and directs the focus of attention. Developing and advancing organizational vocabulary and imagery of successful learning-centered and inclusive environment and action, student affairs practitioners create a unifying vision of change that is sensible and meaningful across multiple interpretative schemas. Endorsed and employed by top college and university leadership, this vocabulary and imagery guide sense making in student affairs and beyond, and move administrators, staff, faculty, and students to recognize, adopt, and enact inclusiveness and learning centeredness.

For example, OSU promotes a vision of diversity as a source of excellence.[11] The idea that diversity and institutional excellence are mutually constitutive has underpinned a series of high-profile programs that aim to enhance OSU's competitiveness in science, technology, engineering, and mathematics (STEM), and to increase the numbers of underrepresented populations in these areas. In the past 5 years, OSU cofounded an experimental high school to build a diverse STEM-oriented pipeline, formed a partnership to establish the Battelle Center for Science Education and Mathematics Policy, launched Project ASPIRE to enhance the quality of science education in central Ohio, cofounded Ohio's STEM Ability Alliance to recruit students with disabilities, and opened the Todd Anthony Bell National Resource Center on the African American Male to cultivate and retain its own talent. As noted in the OSU Diversity Action Plan 2007–2012, however, for this vision to continue as a unifying framework for future initiatives it has to be repeatedly articulated, explained, and popularized by the university leaders.[12]

Conclusion

Enacting student affairs in a learning-centered and inclusive way requires more than a strategy. It calls for an overhaul of old interpretative schemas and the accepted norms and standards of organizational decision making and action. David Siegel captured this problem well in his book on universities' social partnerships:

> The way we organize our solutions to society's most intractable problems has a lot to do with how we are *already* organized and institutionalized, which is to say that we tend to solve problems—to identify them, frame them, weigh alternatives for addressing them, and finally select what we deem to be appropriate solutions—based on how we define our organizations or sectors.[13]

Thus, the task of creating structures to support inclusive and learning-centered practices is the problem of disrupting and delegitimizing old meanings, definitions, and practices, and institutionalizing new ones in their place. In the process of making sense of, enacting, and institutionalizing inclusiveness and learning centeredness, individuals undergo changes in their own identities and mental models. Student affairs practitioners are therefore creators of change, and they are the change themselves. Student affairs as an organization and culture is a living laboratory for advancing the causes of student development and social transformation in higher education.

Notes

1. Morgan, G. (2006). *Images of organizations*. Thousand Oaks, CA: Sage, p. 134.

2. Smircich, L. (1983). Concepts of culture in organizational analysis. *Administrative Science Quarterly, 28*(3), 339–358.

3. Weick, K. (1995). *Sensemaking in organizations*. Thousand Oaks, CA: Sage.

4. Transgender Law & Policy Institute. (2010). *Colleges/universities*. Retrieved from http://www.transgenderlaw.org/college/index.htm#policies

5. Czarniawska, B. (2003). Forbidden knowledge: Organizational theory in times of transition. *Management Learning, 34*(3), 353–365.

6. Herdlein, R. J., III. (2004). Survey of chief student affairs officers regarding relevance of graduate preparation of new professionals. *NASPA Journal, 42*(1), 52–71.

7. Kretovics, M. (2002). Entry-level competencies: What student affairs administrators consider when screening candidates. *Journal of College Student Development, 43*(6), 913–920.

8. Hirt, J. B. (2006). *Where you work matters: Student affairs administration at different types of institutions*. Lanham, MD: University Press of America.

9. Sandeen, A. (2001). Organizing student affairs divisions. In R. B. Winston Jr., D. G. Creamer, & T. K. Miller (Eds.), *The professional student affairs administrator: Educator, leader, and manager* (pp. 181–209). New York, NY: Brunner-Routledge.

10. Weick, *Sensemaking in organizations*, p. 82.

11. *The Ohio State University key initiatives*. (n.d.). Retrieved from http://www.osu.edu/initiatives/

12. Ohio State University. (n.d.). *Diversity action plan. Renewing the covenant: Diversity objectives and strategies for 2007 to 2012.* Retrieved from http://www.osu.edu/diversityplan/index.php

13. Siegel, D. (2010). *Organizing for social partnership: Higher education in cross-sector collaboration.* New York, NY: Routledge, p. 5.

Further Reading and Related Blog

Ashya Majied, Miami University

Adams, M. J., Bell L. A., & Griffin P. (2007). *Teaching for diversity and social justice* (2nd ed.). New York, NY: Routledge.

This book uses a hands-on approach in tackling issues centering on social justice teaching in America. Adams, Bell and Griffin also offer a pedagogically sound and theoretically sophisticated framework.

Kuh, G. D., Kinzie, J., Schuh, J., & Whitt, E. (2005). *Student success in college: Creating conditions that matter.* San Francisco, CA: Jossey-Bass.

Based on the Documenting Effective Educational Practice project, this book offers six features common to 20 institutions that enhance student achievement and success. These features form the foundation for policy and practice to promote student learning and engagement.

Schein, E. H. (2004). *Organizational culture and leadership* (3rd ed.). San Francisco, CA: Jossey-Bass.

Schein defines culture and how it changes. He also emphasizes how understanding culture can lead to changing it.

Tierney, W. G. (1999). *Building the responsive campus: Creating high-performance colleges and universities.* Thousand Oaks, CA: Sage.

This work critiques the state of academia in the 1990s while offering an innovative framework for how to improve the quality of higher education. The author also outlines important and effective insights to achieving an educational community.

Blog URL: contestedissues.wordpress.com
Corresponding Chapter Post: tinyurl.com/contestedissues21

22

What Forms Would Supervision Take to Model Inclusive, Learning-Oriented Practice?

The Case for Developmental Supervision

Michael G. Ignelzi, Slippery Rock University

vividly remember a conversation I had with a potential employer a few years ago, who was conducting a reference check on one of my graduating master's students. He wanted me to assure him that this individual would not need any supervision because he was too busy with his own work to devote time to supervising staff. He needed staff that could hit the ground running and work independently with minimal support. Unfortunately for him, I informed him that I could not provide such an assurance for this student or any of the other talented graduates that have completed our graduate preparation program in my 17 years of teaching because such individuals do not exist. Embedded in this professional's request is the assumption that supervision is not as critical as other student affairs work tasks. While his view is extreme, it has been my experience that many in the higher education community, especially within student affairs, narrowly define work as a product (e.g., a program or service). Regularly meeting with staff to reflect on their work, understandings, challenges, and professional or personal goals is considered to be a less important use of a supervisor's time, particularly when compared with other tasks demanding attention. Too often my graduate student interns, who are clearly invested in learning, report that internship site supervisors cancel supervisory meetings and typically do not reschedule them.

Published research centering on the frequency of supervision provided to student affairs professionals supports my anecdotal experience. An extensive survey of student affairs supervisors from almost 500 higher education institutions found that the frequency of supervisory sessions conducted by supervisors for their professional student affairs staff was quite varied. Sixty-four percent of supervisors reported monthly or more frequent sessions with their supervisees; however, 14% reported 4 to 6 supervisory sessions a year, 12% reported 1 to 2 sessions per year, and 11% conducted no supervisory sessions with their staff members.[1] A later, similar survey found that only 49% of student affairs staff reported having supervisory sessions with their supervisor monthly or more frequently. Four percent reported supervisory sessions 6 to 11 times a year, 16% reported 3 to 5 times per year, 24% reported sessions 1 to 2 times per year, and 7% reported having no supervisory sessions in the last year.[2]

In my first staff meeting as a young student affairs professional, my new supervisor announced to me and the other new resident directors that we were no longer learners but now student affairs professionals and educators. While I understood her intent—to have us focus on delivering services and programs to students—her statement seemed extreme to me. Doesn't our learning continue after we become a professional? Can't I be a professional and a learner, and, in fact, won't some focus on my ongoing learning make me a more competent professional? Doesn't the degree to which I see myself as a learner connect me and make me sensitive to the corollary learning process of students? If I aspire to be an effective role model to students in their learning, don't I need to demonstrate my ongoing learning orientation? My answer to these questions is a resounding yes.

Unfortunately, the research data on using supervision as an opportunity for learning are discouraging. Surveys from the two studies—one from supervisors' viewpoints and one from supervisees—indicate that current and near term work assignments or tasks and information sharing dominate discussion during supervisory sessions. Survey respondents reported that other topics related to the enhancement of professional and personal development were discussed infrequently or not at all. "Supervision seems to be perceived simply as an instrument to get the job done, not as an important way to foster the betterment of staff."[3]

A troubling assumption among many student affairs supervisors on when learning ends for supervisees seems to be that learning ends with graduation from a student affairs preparation program, as shown by their supervisory views and behavior toward professionals they supervise. There also appears to be a widespread assumption that supervision, when it occurs, should be almost exclusively aimed at the particulars of getting current work tasks successfully accomplished. These assumptions run counter to the holistic and developmental view of learning that serves as the philosophical and operative basis of our profession.

A Learning View of Supervision

The developmental theories and models that so heavily influence our understanding of and work with students collectively espouse and document a lifespan view of development. We never stop learning and developing throughout our lives; the process is continuous, only the developmental tasks and our understandings of them change. We are all works in progress. Student affairs professionals should embrace this role as they have in their work with students. Student affairs professionals are intentional in their efforts to enhance student learning and development. Likewise, supervisors of student affairs professionals should be intentional in attempting to enhance the continuing learning and development of their supervisees.

In *Improving Staffing Practices in Student Affairs*, Roger Winston and Don Creamer define supervision as "a management function intended to promote the achievement of institutional goals and to enhance the personal and professional capabilities of staff."[4] This definition acknowledges that staff learning is a central goal of student affairs. Implicit in this definition is the assumption that enhancing the capabilities of staff assists in the achievement of institutional goals. I concur with this view because in the student affairs profession the quality of programs and services delivered to students depends on the personal and professional capabilities of the staff that designs and provides those programs and services.

Winston and Creamer's synergistic supervision model includes a "dual focus on accomplishment of the organization's goals and support of staff in accomplishment of their personal and professional development goals."[5] The synergistic supervision model has a clear focus on learning, both professional and personal. This approach to supervision advocates having a growth orientation toward supervisees in which their enhanced development is one of the important goals of supervision. According to the model, to promote effective job performance of student affairs staff, quality supervision that supports the developmental needs and goals of supervisees is required and possible.

We never stop learning and developing throughout our lives; the process is continuous, only the developmental tasks and our understandings of them change. We are all works in progress.

Developmental Supervision

Following Winston and Creamer's lead, I advocate for reframing our view of supervision in student affairs to one that is developmental and focused primarily on learning. I call this *developmental supervision* to emphasize its focus and underlying philosophy. In developmental supervision, relevant developmental theory and assumptions are at the heart of how student affairs educators conceptualize and deliver supervision.

A key developmental assumption is that the learning needs of individuals vary based upon how they understand or make meaning of their experience. This includes how they make meaning of themselves, others, and the world around them. These understandings evolve over time and from experience, and directly influence a person's personal and work-related capacities and capabilities. Developmental supervision requires some assessment of an individual's current method of making meaning so that appropriate learning and supervision needs can be determined.

Developmental theory and assumptions influence my own research on student affairs professional development and supervision.[6] I devised a model of student affairs professional development based on extensive interviews of 30 research participants. This model reveals how these individuals understand and make meaning of their work with students, the supervision they receive, and their use of theory in practice. The model has three developmental levels or perspectives that align closely with the developmental orders proposed by Robert Kegan in his theory of meaning making.[7] The model describes how development is manifested in the supervisory context and provides guidance on how a supervisor might better understand and support her or his student affairs supervisees consistent with their developmental level.

An Illustration

To illustrate developmental supervision, I present interview excerpts from two student affairs professionals who discussed how they evaluate their work performance. Stephanie talked about the criteria she used:

> Well, if there's an outcome, how was that outcome? Like if it's a personal counseling situation I'm doing with a student and we're talking about things and she's . . . I've asked her or we've worked on her going to her, or approaching her roommate to talk to her about a situation or going to a counselor, did she follow through with that outcome? . . . Interactions with that student beyond that, I mean, when I meet them in the hall or talk with them in a different situation, how is that interaction? And does she seem to want to talk to me again? I mean, is she cold? Is she open to talking with me further? I don't think I have any direct ways that I measure it. Just a feeling I have and how I interact with that student again. If she's in favor of continuing contact with me or not. Just basic vibes I get.
>
> Interviewer: And you feel like you're usually pretty right about those vibes given that . . .
>
> I think, I'm okay about it. I'm sure at times I tend to err on, I think she doesn't like me more than she does like me. I don't think I err on the side that she likes me more. I think that it might be that maybe I had an interaction with a student where I had to tell her something that she didn't want to hear. And I thought, oh, she hates me. But I'm probably, it's probably not the case.
>
> Interviewer: Um hum. So those are the main ways that you feel like you evaluate?
>
> Yes.[8]

Another professional, Sarah, spoke about using other criteria to evaluate her work performance:

What I know, I guess about myself, my own performance, using like the year before as a benchmark, as far as what is it that I then want to achieve in addition to that or areas that I want to improve on for my own frame of mind. I guess that's one thing—my own experience. Another is feedback that I get from the student and the student staff and the advisors. Also, feedback that I get from my supervisor and also, I would say, just my own—not only my own experience but my own observations about myself, about my work style, about my strengths and weaknesses.

Interviewer: Okay. How do the evaluations from students and your supervisor then play into that? You have your own evaluation about how you're doing with those goals, and then you have these other external evaluations coming from these other sources. I'm wondering how those get put together for you.

I think part of that is also me seeking that out. And I do this pretty consistently with the advisors and with my supervisor, of finding out, you know, here's my perception of how I'm doing. What feedback, what ideas do you have at this point? I feel like here are the areas that I'm doing well in; here are the areas that I continue to work on. What's your perception of that? And so part of that, I think, is me, like taking the initiative to do that. But then, like at evaluation time, with the formal evaluation process, really then taking into, I guess, consideration: What do I think, and how does that fit or not fit with my supervisor, the student staff, the advisory staff? And what do I do with that information, just as far as like Do I feel that's an accurate perception? Is that something that can change? Is that something inherent in my style? What is that?[9]

Stephanie and Sarah evaluate their work performance very differently. Stephanie evaluates her work with students using two main criteria— whether students follow through with what she has worked on with them and whether she feels that students like her following their interaction(s) with her. Her evaluation of her work seems totally derived from her perceptions of student actions or attitudes toward her; she reports no personal standards or views that assist her in interpreting the feedback she observes. Stephanie uncritically accepts student actions and reactions she believes are related to her. Alternatively, Sarah evaluates her work by first setting her own performance goals, and then she compares feedback from students with other sources of feedback as well as her own observations in determining its consistency and accuracy. She ultimately decides the value of such feedback in evaluating her performance as well as how it gets integrated into her view. Sarah is no less interested in student feedback than Stephanie (in fact, she actively solicits it); however, she brings her own views to bear in interpreting and using it.

Sarah is at a more advanced developmental level than Stephanie on the issue of evaluating work performance and many other professional issues (e.g., view of professional role, meeting student' expectations, supervisor structure required, dealing with disagreements and conflicts, reflection on use of theory) as assessed using my model of student affairs professional development. Sarah's professional development is reflective of Perspective 3 in my model while Stephanie's corresponds with Perspective 1. Interestingly, Sarah and Stephanie are similar in age and both have between 3 to 5 years of full-time professional student affairs experience. It is also of note that both are alumnae of respected student affairs graduate preparation programs. My research suggests that simply age or number of years of experience does not determine a supervisee's current developmental level and supervision needs.[10] How an individual constructs her or his understandings determines that individual's developmental level, which can vary among those within the same experience or age group. Therefore, a supervisor needs to carefully listen to a particular supervisee to determine her or his level of professional development and the form of supervision she or he needs to feel supported and appropriately challenged to achieve more complex understandings.

What forms of developmental supervision do Stephanie and Sarah need regarding the issue of work performance evaluation? In other words, what form of developmental support and challenge do each need? I list support before challenge because individuals must first feel accepted and supported in their current ways of understanding before they will be open to considering alternatives. In *The Evolving Self* Robert Kegan contends that to be of effective help to another, we need to be able to communicate that we understand how situations are experienced by that person.[11] This ability, is one of the most powerful ways to connect with and provide meaningful support to a supervisee. Developmental challenge involves providing learning experiences for the supervisee that exposes her or him to alternative ways of understanding consistent with a slightly more advanced level of development.

To support Stephanie in her current way of understanding, her supervisor needs to acknowledge the value of her focus on student feedback in her work with them. Having concern for how students respond to our work with them is important because it keeps us aware of and sensitive to their experience and needs and is one measure of our success. When an uncritical focus on student reactions is the only measure, however, it can create problems. Often, student affairs professionals need to take positions and actions with students in the interest of their learning or safety that students will disapprove of. One can imagine these situations are difficult for Stephanie and may be costly to her sense of accomplishment and competence because she currently has no other means beyond her perceptions of student reactions to evaluate her work. A supervisor could discuss with Stephanie how she experiences such situations and explore her interest in working toward a change. Working collaboratively with Stephanie, her supervisor could help her identify and set performance goals based on more extensive and varied criteria than she currently uses. This would be the first step in developmentally challenging her to begin creating and considering her own performance standards. Her supervisor would also need to regularly meet with Stephanie to engage her in informal evaluation on her performance goals and model a process of how she might use multiple criteria and take increased responsibility for evaluating herself.

A supervisor needs to carefully listen to a particular supervisee to determine her or his level of professional development and the form of supervision she or he needs to feel supported and appropriately challenged to achieve more complex understandings.

Stephanie's method of evaluating her performance may take considerable time to evolve to the more internalized and complex method Sarah employed. Stephanie's supervisor, however, can assist her in taking critical steps in that evolution and in the meantime provide her with another source of valuable feedback to help her gauge her work performance. This is not only important for Stephanie's development but is critical to ensuring the quality of her work. Perspective 1 supervisees want supervisors who take personal interest in them and their learning. For such supervisees, a supervisor's influence is directly proportional to the quality of the relationship developed. This requires an authentic investment of time and energy by the supervisor and supervisee.

It may appear from Sarah's interview excerpt that she does not need any supervision related to evaluating her work performance. She demonstrates an ability to set performance goals, solicit relevant feedback from multiple sources, and interpret that feedback in relation to her own internal views. Sarah has her own self-generated theory about what constitutes successful work performance. Even so, Sarah can still benefit from supervision in her continuing development, though that supervision needs to have a very different form from Stephanie's. Perspective 3 supervisees want broad autonomy in defining and carrying out their job responsibilities; however, they still value their supervisor as a resource and consultant. To be developmentally supportive of Sarah, her supervisor needs to respect her theory and related views and provide feedback as requested by Sarah on her progress toward achieving her performance goals. Perspective 3 supervisees can become too entrenched in their own theory about what constitutes important work goals and successful work performance and behave as though no other equally valuable theories exist. To developmentally challenge Sarah, her supervisor could invite her to take part in ongoing discussions aimed at reflecting upon not only her interpretation of the feedback she receives in relation to her theory of work performance but on the theory itself.

Relevant Research and Implications

One study concluded that absent a theory-based approach to supervision, supervisors tailored their supervision to their own preferences and needs, which were different from the needs of their less experienced supervisees.[12] A developmental approach to supervision, like the one illustrated previously, assists supervisors in getting beyond their own personal constructions to more clearly see a supervisee's understandings and needs from the supervisee's perspective. There is some limited research evidence that supervision activities consistent with a developmental learning approach have a positive effect on supervisee perceptions of the supervision they receive and on the job satisfaction and retention of new student affairs professionals.[13]

So how can developmental supervision and regularized supervision in general become more widely practiced in student affairs? First, it requires that student affairs professionals acknowledge that they are learners and their continuing development improves their professional practice. Related to this, the importance of supervision as a learning context worthy of our time and energy needs to be legitimized. It is shortsighted and impractical to poorly supervise staff when supporting supervisees' developing capabilities through quality supervision can contribute to increasing their competence and ability to effectively accomplish their work. Reflecting on my experience as a practitioner and supervisor, providing quality supervision to my staff members actually saved work time because of their increased abilities to competently handle issues without my direct involvement.

Second, administrators of student affairs preparation programs and professional associations need to provide increased education and training on supervision. In one survey of student affairs supervisors, only half reported receiving formal training in supervision, and of this half only 55% reported receiving that training in their graduate preparation programs.[14] We should either teach existing supervision models or translate and apply the developmental and leadership learning theories already taught in graduate programs to the supervisory context.

Last, supervisors should model the same learning orientation toward supervision that they want their supervisees to model in their work with students. This learning orientation should be sensitive to and inclusive of developmental differences as well as other demographic and cultural differences. Developmental supervision that provides different forms of support and challenges appropriate to a supervisee's learning needs mirrors and reinforces our profession's best practices and central mission.

Notes

1. Winston, R. B., & Creamer, D. G. (1997). *Improving staffing practices in student affairs*. San Francisco, CA: Jossey-Bass, p. 109.

2. Saunders, S. A., Cooper, D. L., Winston, R. B., & Chernow, E. (2000). Supervising staff in student affairs: Exploration of the synergistic approach. *Journal of College Student Development, 41*(2), 181–192, p. 186.

3. Ibid., p. 188.

4. Winston & Creamer, *Improving staffing practices in student affairs*, p. 186.

5. Ibid., p. 196.

6. Ignelzi, M. G. (1994). *A description of student affairs professional development in the supervisory context and an analysis of its relation to constructive development.* (Unpublished doctoral dissertation). Harvard University, Cambridge, MA.

7. Kegan, R. (1994). *In over our heads: The mental demands of modern life.* Cambridge, MA: Harvard University Press.

8. Ignelzi, *Description of student affairs professional development*, pp. 110–111.

9. Ibid., pp. 200–201.

10. Ignelzi, M. G., & Whitely, P. A. (2004). Supportive supervision for new professionals. In P. M. Magolda & J. E. Carnaghi (Eds.), *Job one: Experiences of new professionals in student affairs* (pp. 115–135). Lanham, MD: University Press of America.

11. Kegan, R. (1982). *The evolving self: Problem and process in human development.* Cambridge, MA: Harvard University Press.

12. Barham, J. D., & Winston, R. B., Jr. (2006). Supervision of new professionals in student affairs: Assessing and addressing needs. *The College Student Affairs Journal, 26*(1), 64–89.

13. Saunders et al., Supervising staff in student affairs; Tull, A. (2006). Synergistic supervision, job satisfaction, and intention to turnover of new professionals in student affairs. *Journal of College Student Development, 47*(4), 465–480.

14. Winston & Creamer, *Improving staffing practices in student affairs*, p. 111.

Scholar Practitioners Model Inclusive, Learning-Oriented Supervision

Patricia A. Perillo, Davidson College

I support Michael Ignelzi's assertion that a greater emphasis on providing regularized, quality supervision for all professionals is needed. I base this appraisal on my 25 years of supervisory experience in student affairs. Almost 40 years ago, Stamatakos and Oliaro reported that research supporting the value of professional development in student affairs was scarce.[1] In 1990 Komives and Woodard reported that "workers of the future, particularly those in human development fields, will have high expectations for a caring, nurturing supervisor."[2] Ten years ago Saunders, Cooper, Winston, and Chernow said that research on professional development, particularly when linked to supervision, was still limited.[3] And in 2004 Ignelzi and Whitely stated that "within the student affairs supervision literature, there is a paucity of published work on the topic of supervision."[4] In this book Ignelzi argued that supervision has received insufficient attention in student affairs practice. Little has changed over the past 40 years. If our profession values supervision, why is the research on supervision in student affairs so scarce? Even worse, as Ignelzi noted, why is supervision such a low priority?

When I asked my staff why quality supervision was the exception rather than the rule as Ignelzi reported, they replied that supervisors don't have the time or don't know how to do it. My supervisory experience supports their assertions. And perhaps it is related to why Dalton states that "supervision is one of the most difficult tasks of student affairs leadership."[5]

Let's examine the argument of not having time to supervise. It is well known in the human resource management scholarly arena that staff members who increase their knowledge and grow professionally are more likely to be effective in their work and relationships. High energy and enthusiasm can be maintained when staff members have opportunities for personal renewal and development.[6] Ultimately, the more one supervises the less one supervises; this has proven to be true for me as a supervisor. My weekly investment of time with each staff member individually and collectively matters. Compared to colleagues who do not supervise actively, I have spent less time managing others' mistakes, doing another's work, or managing staff turnover. Staff members who have clarity of purpose and feel supported generally do great work and commit to organizations. Investing time in and with staff ultimately saves time.

Next, let's address the assertion that people don't know how to supervise well. Ignelzi's model for a developmental approach to supervision is a rare and good one. However, I remain unconvinced that our colleagues know how to translate these ideas into practice. As we know from *Powerful Partnerships*, "Learning is a social activity, and modeling is one of the most powerful learning tools."[7] Supervisors attain positions without necessarily having had good supervision modeled. And because of this, they often do not know how to serve as an effective supervisor or create learning-oriented environments.

Ignelzi asserts that "student affairs professionals are intentional in their efforts to enhance student learning and development. Likewise, supervisors of student affairs professionals should be intentional in attempting to enhance the continuing learning and development of their supervisees" (p. 418). While I agree that supervisors should apply learning in the supervisory context, I am reluctant to assume that professionals are intentional about fostering student learning. While serving as the American College Personnel Association (ACPA) president and preparing for our annual convention, I invited two senior colleagues—Elizabeth Whitt and Terry Piper—to develop a student learning primer for senior student affairs officers (SSAOs). Knowing that many SSAOs either graduated decades ago or lack formal student affairs training, Elizabeth, Terry, and I thought SSAOs would embrace this idea. After surveying many of them, we discovered that enriched understanding of student learning was not a primary focus or priority. If SSAOs are not facilitating student learning-centered divisions, is it safe to assume they are not promoting staff learning-centered environments? Does the next level of staff supervise without the context of divisional priorities steeped in our profession's mission and simply supervise to achieve the current goals of the current SSAO?

When SSAOs promote learning environments, the experience is transformative for institutions of higher learning. While Terry Piper served as an SSAO, he placed the division's mission and priorities on students and student learning; he aligned divisional work with students' work in the classroom. He recognized that meaningful learning occurs outside the classroom and developed a learning outcome model that measured these experiences.[8] His work provides evidence that inclusive, learning-oriented environments transform the college environment; my own work, as a senior-level administrator at public and private institutions has revealed the same. So let's call the question: What forms would supervision take to model inclusive, learning-oriented practice? Using the scholarship of our profession, let us consider and agree upon the following forms.

Supervisors must commit to their own and others' learning, be culturally competent, hold themselves and others accountable, and establish mutual partnerships with staff members so that supervision is learning oriented and inclusive.

Supervisors must commit to their own learning. Effective supervision begins with oneself; we cannot take people further developmentally than we have taken ourselves. If you are unfamiliar with the scholarship of supervision, learn it. Given the scarcity of literature about supervision in higher education, I recommend studying supervision scholarship in other academic disciplines. If you have not had good supervision modeled for you, locate mentors who exemplify it and learn from them.

Supervisors must meet with staff members regularly. An important precursor to achieving any endeavor is simply showing up. Providing effective supervision, at a minimum, requires that supervisors meet with supervisees. Professional and personal goals should take center stage. Winston and Creamer emphasize that supervisory sessions should focus on the twin areas of advancement of the institutional mission and goals, and the personal and professional advancement of the individual.[9] Supervisors are responsible for the performance and growth of their staff, and subsequently students, and achieving a balance of support and challenge is a key component to employee development.

Coconstructing expectations of the supervisory relationship is imperative. Supervision is mutual and requires explicit understanding of each other's styles, preferences, and goals. This is often difficult for hierarchically centered supervisors who are uncomfortable yielding power; establishing a mutual relationship with shared responsibility can be scary at times. Coconstructing expectations acknowledges both people as learners and explicitly affirms that the supervisor is not the expert.

Developmental supervision is essential. As Ignelzi says, it is important to assess a supervisee's current way of making meaning so that appropriate learning needs can be determined. Student affairs professionals apply constructive developmental theories "to better understand how students make sense of their experience and themselves, as well as what that understanding suggests for creating environments supportive of students' learning and development."[10] Scholar practitioners use developmental theory when interacting with students and staff. Constructive developmental theory supports Winston and Creamer's focus on personal and professional development, as they are both influenced by the same underlying meaning-making structure.[11]

Supervision requires holding each other accountable. How do we learn best if we don't acknowledge mistakes or areas of growth? Perhaps this is why Dalton stated that supervision is the most difficult task of leadership. Too many supervisors avoid conflict. Consequently, we have senior-level leaders in our profession who weren't held accountable and do not know how to hold others accountable. Several years ago, after working at a university for a few years, I accepted a request to supervise a colleague who had been there for over 25 years. Many people did not speak well of her performance, yet prior supervisors never had performance conversations with her. As we worked together, we discussed her passions, strengths, and goals. I invested in her, and we discovered how her capacities were not aligned with her work. She told me I was the first supervisor to care enough to talk with her and help her understand that the position she was in did not acknowledge her strengths. Subsequently she left the college, sought work in the private sector and was happier than she had been in years. Holding each other accountable is an act of care that provides inordinate learning for those involved.

Supervisors must focus primarily on learning, and clearly one way to do that is to apply Ignelzi's developmental approach to supervision. Another way is to discover avenues to translate theory into practice with staff. For example, when writing this essay, I invited staff to read several articles on supervision, and we conferred during our meetings and discussed their supervisory experiences; situating the scholarship in their own experience enhanced our learning. Including theories more directly in campus discussions encourages staff to think more critically.

Inclusive practice involves multicultural competence. Increasing human diversity requires supervisors to be culturally competent. Colorblind supervision minimizes human experience and can easily make staff members feel invisible. For example, when we discussed supervision as a staff in preparation for this essay response, I was keenly aware that my diverse staff members have experienced supervision in different ways, partly because of the social identities most salient for them. Understanding and managing diversity is essential to the successful attainment of organizational goals and thus should be of significant concern to supervisors.[12]

Supervision should be more regularized and developmental. I also underscore that supervisors must commit to their own and others' learning, be culturally competent, hold themselves and others accountable, and establish mutual partnerships with staff members so that supervision is learning oriented and inclusive. Given our current state of affairs, we are not making good on our promise to help students develop and learn; we cannot deliver on this promise until we commit to the staff we supervise, who are undoubtedly our greatest organizational resource.

Notes

1. Stamatakos, L. C., & Oliaro, P. M. (1972). In-service development: A function of student personnel. *NASPA Journal, 9*, 269–273.

2. Woodard, D. B., Jr., & Komives, S. R. (1990). Ensuring staff competence. In M. J. Barr & M. L. Upcraft (Eds.), *New futures for student affairs* (pp. 217–238). San Francisco, CA: Jossey-Bass.

3. Saunders, S. A., Cooper, D. L., Winston, R. B., & Chernow, E. (2000). Supervising staff in student affairs: Exploration of the synergistic approach. *Journal of College Student Development, 41*(2), 181–192.

4. Ignelzi, M. G., & Whitely, P. A. (2004). Supportive supervision for new professionals. In P. M., Magolda & J. E. Carnaghi (Eds.), *Job one: Experiences of new professionals in student affairs* (pp. 115–135). Lanham, MD: University Press of America.

5. Dalton, J. C. (2003). Managing human resources. In S. R. Komives & D. B. Woodard (Eds.), *Student services: A handbook for the profession* (pp. 397–419). San Francisco, CA: Jossey-Bass.

6. Ibid., pp. 399–400.

7. American Association for Higher Education, American College Personnel Association, & National Association of Student Personnel Administrators. (1998). *Powerful partnerships: A shared responsibility for learning.* Washington, DC: Author.

8. For details see Koester, J., Hellenbrand, H., & Piper, T. D. (2005). Exploring the actions behind the words "learning-centered institution." *About Campus: Enriching the Student Learning Experience, 10*(4), 10–16; Koester, J., Hellenbrand, H., & Piper, T. D. (2008). The challenge of collaboration: Organizational structure and professional identity. *About Campus: Enriching the Student Learning Experience, 13*(5), 12–19.

9. Winston, R. B., Jr., & Creamer, D. G. (1997). *Improving staffing practices in student affairs*. San Francisco, CA: Jossey-Bass.

10. Ignelzi & Whitely, Supportive supervision for new professionals.

11. Winston and Creamer, *Improving staffing practices in student affairs*, p. 133.

12. Pope, R. L., Reynolds, A. L., & Mueller, J. A. (2004). *Multicultural competence in student affairs*. San Francisco, CA: Jossey-Bass.

Further Reading and Related Blog

Sarah Meagher, Miami University

Allen, K. E., & Cherrey, C. (2000). *Systemic leadership: Enriching the meaning of our work.* Lanham, MD: University Press of America.

Allen and Cherrey skillfully apply complexity, chaos, and systems theories to help readers understand how technology has ushered in new ways to consider relationships in an organization and how to best get things done. They emphasize that problems need to be solved holistically because we live and lead in a networked, knowledge-based, and connected world where communication and information are ever changing.

Ignelzi, M. G., & Whitely, P. A. (2004). Supportive supervision for new professionals. In P. Magolda & J. Carnaghi (Eds.), *Job one: Experiences of new professionals in student affairs* (pp. 115–135). Lanham, MD: University Press of America.

Ignelzi and Whitely synthesize the importance of supporting graduates professionally and personally as they transition into their roles as student affairs practitioners. They use three case studies to exemplify how supervisors can support these professionals; each young professional requires supervisors who get to know them personally and understand them developmentally to foster their roles as student affairs practitioners.

Winston, R. B., Jr., & Creamer, D. G. (1997). Supervising and managing staff. In R. B. Winston & D. G. Creamer, *Improving staffing practices in student affairs* (pp. 180–218). San Francisco, CA: Jossey-Bass.

Winston and Creamer suggest moving away from the negative perception that supervision serves as a tool for preventing inevitable failure by a supervisee and toward a positive relationship for supporting and challenging the supervisee. Winston and Creamer introduce *synergetic supervision* as a possible approach; this framework guides supervisors to tailor their supervision to the needs of each supervisee and continue to amend this supervisory relationship as appropriate for motivating the supervisee to achieve and develop professionally.

Blog URL: contestedissues.wordpress.com
Corresponding Chapter Post: tinyurl.com/contestedissues22

23

Why Do Student Affairs Educators Struggle to Set Professional Boundaries?

Establishing and Maintaining Healthy Professional and Personal Boundaries

Kate Linder, Indiana University of Pennsylvania

lthough it was nearly 25 years ago, I vividly recall the desperation and exhaustion I felt as I finished my second year as a residence hall director at a large midwestern public institution. For two years I had devoted myself passionately to the cause of students, working long hours to provide guidance, support, and an appropriate level of challenge to promote the personal growth of the collegians I interacted with. I developed and implemented meaningful programs and provided thoughtful group advisement as a way to foster the development of as many of my 1,000 residential students as possible. I was readily available to them and to office workers, resident assistants, graduate assistants, and administrators. If I was not in the building, I responded to needs, questions, and concerns by phone. With my supervisor's urging, I devoted time to stay current in my knowledge and understanding of higher education issues, embraced learning about diverse student populations, and worked to integrate theory with practice.

At the end of my first year as a residence director, my accomplishments and experiences pleased me. Receiving the Outstanding Residence Hall Director of the Year award made me proud. My supervisors formally and publically acknowledged my competence, leaving me honored and gratified. These accolades motivated me to strive even harder to improve the quantity and quality of my work with residents. I developed additional goals and objectives, volunteered for more committees, and spent my limited social time in the company of other residence directors, debriefing our work adventures. I adopted a Western approach to work that equates time spent working with dedication and success and immersed myself in residence life and student affairs professionally, personally, and socially. One year after completing my graduate studies, being a residence hall director was no longer a job or a career path, it was the primary way I defined myself.

Midway through my second year, residents failed to embrace my carefully crafted judicial interventions, attendance at building programs declined, and I struggled to keep pace with the demands of my position. My professional dedication was not furthering the achievement of my ambitious goals and objectives. In addition, my supervisor encouraged me to assume more responsibilities in the student affairs division, and I felt tremendous pressure to continue to maintain my outstanding residence hall director status. My stress level heightened. I spent my limited leisure time with residence life peers enumerating the problems with students, the administration, and the student affairs field. I began to question myself—why had I chosen a career characterized by ceaseless demands from residents, paraprofessionals, faculty, and staff colleagues, supervisors, and upper-level administrators? How could I successfully perform infinite job responsibilities to my satisfaction and consequently demonstrate my unfailing competence and professionalism to others? When would I enjoy a weekend without the on-call phone endlessly ringing, requiring me to pause in my meager personal pursuits to address an unpredictable potpourri of problems and crises?

Convinced that I needed to change my circumstances to avoid an emotional breakdown, I updated my résumé and pursued a new job elsewhere. I expected that in a midlevel position at a smaller institution the demands would ease and a balanced, happy life would naturally follow. Within 3 months, I succeeded in securing a residence life coordinator position at a midsize public institution and soon realized that my vision of making the transition to a naturally balanced existence was sheer fantasy. My career in student affairs was under way, as was my struggle to set professional boundaries.

Understanding the Roots of My Struggle

As defined by mental health counselor Anne Katherine, a boundary is a limit that protects "the integrity of your day, your energy and spirit, the health of your relationships, the pursuits of your heart. . . . Boundaries provide a clear moral compass. They keep us on track. They protect the important, tender parts of ourselves."[1] In retrospect, I understand that multiple internal and external factors inhibited my ability to establish and adhere to healthy boundaries as I began my professional career in student affairs. As a helping profession, the field of student affairs is inherently demanding of those individuals who embrace it fully and strive to effect a positive difference in the personal growth and development of college students. Residence life as a core student affairs function requires staff to work long hours during paraprofessional training and opening and closing weekends and to complete break inspections, provide coverage during special campus events, support evening and weekend programs, and generally meet the needs of residents as they arise, often during late-night and weekend hours. Senior staff members expect new student affairs professionals to fulfill weekend and evening commitments, to live on campus, and to function in unstructured work schedules that make the pursuit of outside interests and relationships challenging.[2] Acceptance of a residence life position implies agreement to and understanding of the adoption of a work life characterized by an unpredictable schedule and inevitable peak work periods. Thus residence life staff cannot choose peak periods to set a boundary without significant negative political and social ramifications (except for a family emergency). For example, Ben, a residence director colleague, took an extended break from campus during a fall opening weekend to visit with friends. He left his paraprofessional staff with minimal directions to handle the onslaught of families during the move-in period. Consequently, they relied on intermittent assistance from other busy building directors. Problems abounded, and Ben returned to a frustrated staff, dissatisfied families, exasperated colleagues, and an angry supervisor. His neglect of basic job responsibilities earned him a job warning and cost him the respect of colleagues.

Understanding and accommodating the fundamental demands of student affairs core functions, whether in residence life, campus events,

---

Setting boundaries effectively is an internal process, but as humans we are vulnerable to the influence of compelling external factors.

---

admissions, or any other area, is an important aspect of developing professional boundaries. Professional staff cannot chose to fulfill only select, desired aspects of job descriptions but must accommodate position responsibilities and institutional needs while striving to create balanced lives. Working out an alternate weekend with his supervisor would have been a better way for Ben to accommodate his personal needs.

Like many new professionals, I eagerly demonstrated competence, dedication, and success. I invested in meeting the needs of my residents, prioritizing their needs above my own. Rather than establish a healthy boundary that provided time for me to refresh and renew myself after working through a peak period, I continued logging equally long hours, convincing myself that I should capitalize on my high level of motivation. Despite fatigue, I continued to work, not recognizing that exhaustion compromised my efficiency—longer hours did not necessarily translate into greater productivity or quality results.

My second year as a residence director produced positive outcomes, and I continued to be rewarded for overextending myself and failing to set appropriate boundaries. My supervisor disseminated initiatives I developed as examples for my peers, and various administrators sought my feedback regarding ideas for improving practices. The attention and respect I enjoyed from seasoned student affairs practitioners energized and motivated me—in the short term. I do not recall anyone discussing the notion of setting healthy boundaries with me during this time period. When I scanned the workplace, I witnessed clear rewards being bestowed upon staff who devoted the most time and energy to work by sacrificing significant time with family and friends and foregoing personal pursuits. I also noticed subtle disapproval of staff who chose to leave work promptly to cultivate personal relationships and activities. Key university administrators interpreted the nurturance of non-work-related pursuits as lacking passion and commitment for workplace achievement.

By the time I left my first professional student affairs position, I had learned destructive lessons that discouraged the establishment of healthy boundaries. I had developed work habits based on external factors in an environment that rewarded the unbalanced commitment to my job I expressed through working an average of 80 hours weekly. No union existed to advocate for professional and personal balance. I was not sufficiently self-aware or assertive to raise the issue with my supervisor, nor was I prepared to assume the risks associated with setting boundaries. For me, balance was not yet worth risking loss of recognition for excellence at work. I lacked the courage to establish healthy boundaries in defiance of my institution's culture. Often when I was not on the job, I was sleeping in an effort to regain stamina so that I could work longer and harder the next day. I had failed to develop an internal capacity to understand how to accomplish my professional goals while also achieving personal goals. Fortunately, my experience as a midlevel residence life manager in a supportive work environment surrounded by positive role models, caused me to alter these destructive habits.

Lessons of a Supportive Work Environment

In my new position as a residential life quad coordinator, I continued to form my primary social relationships with professional colleagues and was fortunate to develop a close friendship with Linda, a more experienced colleague who often used humor to make a point. Shortly after I arrived at my new institution, I was at my desk working diligently around 9:00 p.m., having begun the day at 8:00 a.m. and taken only a brief break for lunch. My phone rang, startling me. When I answered, Linda's voice playfully chastised me, "Hey, what are you still doing in the office?! You're making the rest of us look bad—go home!" After a good laugh, I heeded her advice and walked across the hallway to my apartment to recuperate.

Linda became a mentor and ally in helping me realize that setting boundaries was not simply important—it was essential to long-term survival. Unlike many of my colleagues before and after her, Linda effortlessly socialized with student affairs professionals without centering the interactions around aspects of work. We became good friends, discussing relationships, family, hobbies, dreams, and other personal topics. We occasionally digressed into conversations about work-related matters but were cognizant of keeping them brief. Linda enjoyed students and committed herself to work but concurrently valued her mental and physical health, the development of her relationship with her partner, and the cultivation of many varied friendships and personal interests.

Regardless of context, Linda infused a sense of fun and lightheartedness into situations. She was a talented and respected student affairs professional who, through role modeling balanced priorities, promoted the growth and development of students and staff. Linda served as my personal role model as I began to consciously develop priorities for my own life. I now realized that I had some ability to influence my work environment, but more importantly, I controlled my reaction to all facets of life. I had the capacity to establish healthy personal and professional boundaries and needed to develop them by shifting my focus from external factors to internal growth, a process that would be easier to conceptualize than to implement.

Fortunately, as I began to intentionally develop an awareness of my values, priorities, and needs, the institutional culture of my workplace promoted the development of healthy boundaries between professional and personal time and relationships. My supervisor incorporated discussions about balance, stress and time management, and general wellness into our individual meetings. Professional development training sessions regularly included these topics, and if residence life staff appeared to be violating these norms, a colleague or supervisor challenged them to reassess their choices. Departmentally and divisionally the demands of work were rigorous and often complex, but the culture established by upper-level administration gave student affairs professionals significant control over how they fulfilled responsibilities, embraced creativity, rewarded achievement, and promoted the attitude that mistakes were an inevitable, invaluable tool to promote continuous learning and improvement.

Typically, student affairs professionals increased their own workload as a result of implementing inspired initiatives, but when new tasks needed to be assigned, supervisors at this institution delegated equitably and fairly based on an awareness of staff skill levels and the capacity for staff to reasonably absorb and sustain the work. Supervisors held employees to a high standard of accountability. Finally, the administration promoted the ongoing development of community in student affairs by structuring opportunities to collaborate on projects and committees, promoting attendance at divisional professional development sessions, and collectively celebrating achievements by gathering to socialize at each semester's end. The institutional culture promoted positivity and productivity and minimized the potential for burnout that results from a lack of boundaries.[3]

These optimal external circumstances supported my ability to establish priorities reflective of my values and beliefs while honoring my personal and professional needs and fulfilling my job responsibilities. As an experiment, I explored ways to work fewer hours by eliminating administrative and organizational tasks I perceived as important but were not valued in the department or division. I endeavored to work in a more directed, efficient manner. To my surprise, I spent less time working, felt refreshed, produced positive outcomes, and maintained the respect of colleagues and administrators. I continued to be rewarded formally and informally for my achievements and delighted in positively affecting students' lives.

Rediscovering Life Outside Student Affairs

Within 3 years of assuming the quad coordinator position, two significant personal events accelerated my commitment to establishing and implementing healthy personal and professional boundaries. First, I met my partner, Carolyn, and embarked upon a rewarding, loving relationship. Carolyn, 10 years my senior and a seasoned faculty member, was highly skilled at rendering decisions that reflected her values and beliefs and respected the constraints imposed on her by multiple health concerns. Through action and comment, she challenged me to seize control over my decisions. Carolyn encouraged me to define my priorities and intentionally shape the landscape of my life through thoughtful choice and mindful adoption of attitudes. If I complained about an aspect of my professional life, Carolyn challenged me to act to change my circumstances. If change was not a realistic option, she suggested I empower myself to respond to my circumstances in a way that honored my knowledge, values, and beliefs.

Although my blossoming partnership with Carolyn was an external factor that facilitated the establishment of improved professional and personal boundaries, the first time professional commitments vanished from my consciousness was when my mother died unexpectedly. As I prepared to oversee the implementation of a weekend-long resident assistant selection process, I received the news of her death. Under any other circumstance, my fulfillment of these core job responsibilities would have been crucial. Without hesitation, colleagues immediately arranged to cover my work and I departed campus with no concern about my professional

In the absence of strategic planning, higher education institutions assume a pattern of doing more with less and create a climate in which setting well-defined personal and professional boundaries is extremely challenging and politically risky.

responsibilities—it no longer mattered to me when, how, or if the department implemented the selection process. My roles as daughter and sibling to my grieving father, brother, and sisters—and my own overwhelming grief—eclipsed my identity as a student affairs professional. Reflecting later on this crisis, I realized that I valued my identity as a student affairs professional less than my identities as a partner, daughter, sister, and friend. When my life ended, I wanted to be remembered first as a loving, caring woman as reflected in the quality of my relationships and second as a competent student affairs professional. That realization established a firm foundation for the choices I have made when setting personal and professional boundaries for the past 20 years.

Setting Boundaries Is a Continual Process

The epiphany I experienced from beginning my partnership with Carolyn and saying good-bye to my mother further encouraged me to look inward in the process of establishing personal and professional boundaries. As Marcia Baxter Magolda writes in *Authoring Your Life*, "These challenges require figuring out what you believe and value, how to define yourself, and how you relate to others."[4] I had begun the process of authoring my own life by using my internal voice to guide my decision making around boundaries. While it would be comforting to relay that as a result I established a clear set of effective, healthy boundaries and maintained them through the present day, the truth is more complicated. Setting boundaries effectively is an internal process, but as humans we are vulnerable to the influence of compelling external factors. The changes that occur around us influence the ease or struggle with which we establish and maintain healthy boundaries. Personally, love relationships begin and end; we become parents, guardians, and grandparents of children and pets; our parents age and require our care; family members and friends die leaving us to grieve and navigate the aftermath; friendships change; our values and beliefs shift; our knowledge expands; and our intellectual, emotional, spiritual, and physical needs change. Professionally, we change jobs; we are willingly or unwillingly promoted, downsized, reorganized, and reclassified; we seek advanced academic degrees, certification, and training; we serve an increasingly diverse population; the expectations of students, their parents, and colleagues change; the conditions of our workplace are fluid; institutional leadership, priorities, challenges, and resources change; technology expands; the need for adaptability increases; and the world evolves culturally, financially, politically, and socially.

As my career has progressed, my work environment has changed, and I have grown older and regularly readjusted my personal and professional boundaries in response to the many changing circumstances that make up my life.

Challenges to Setting Boundaries in the 21st Century

Each generation of student affairs professionals has faced challenges, but none seem more daunting than issues that have arisen or intensified since the start of this millennium. The devastating terrorist attacks on the World Trade Center complex and the Pentagon on September 11, 2001 engendered an increased sense of vulnerability and insecurity nationwide and catalyzed outrage and fear on university campuses. Multiple campus shootings at Virginia Tech in 2007 and Northern Illinois University less than a year later cemented the need for campus safety and security protocols, student behavioral intervention teams, and the development of a constant state of readiness to respond to crises at a macro level. Parents and guardians accompanied their students to campus, often intervening on their behalf, expecting to receive the immediate attention of student affairs professionals in resolving their students' issues and believing that they would automatically obtain a more effective response.[5] Millennial students, more diverse in personal characteristics than previous generations, arrived with their own high expectations, including quick customer service, full integration and access to the newest technology, and the ability to have instant, ongoing access to staff via e-mail, instant messaging, and other cyber communication as a supplement to or replacement for face-to-face meetings.[6]

Add to these issues the precarious state of financial affairs in higher education resulting in job losses, reorganization of work responsibilities, downsizing, and declining economic and human resources; the high level of accountability demanded by state and federal governments; increased expectations by the public; media scrutiny; and the litigiousness of American society, and the current challenges for student affairs professionals can easily seem insurmountable.[7] Levels of expectation and accountability from multiple constituents have increased, while shrinking resources have forced service delivery to be significantly altered or eliminated. Student affairs professionals are compelled to justify their mission and values, cost-effectiveness, and their impact on student learning—in short, to defend their relevance in higher education.

In the absence of strategic planning, higher education institutions assume a pattern of doing more with less and create a climate in which setting well-defined personal and professional boundaries is extremely challenging and politically risky. If remaining employed or advancing professionally is a primary goal, saying no is not always a viable option for student affairs practitioners in times of scarcity. However, student affairs professionals who passively allow the mindless erosion of personal and professional boundaries can experience exhaustion, cynicism, depression, anger, anxiety, hopelessness, and physical illness.[8] For the sake of students, self, and the profession, student affairs practitioners must prioritize establishing and living within healthy boundaries.

Strategies for Establishing Healthy Boundaries

Each student affairs professional's circumstances are unique and serve as the genesis for establishing healthy personal and professional boundaries. Personal characteristics (e.g., gender, race, ethnicity, religion, sexual orientation, age, ability), personality traits (e.g., extroversion, introversion, temperament), self-awareness, motivation, and physical and mental health in combination with external factors such as institutional culture, core job functions, family considerations, and economic and political realities determine the extent to which setting boundaries is a struggle.

Student affairs professionals must take charge of navigating their professional and personal responsibilities. I offer select strategies to facilitate the effective, continuous establishment, implementation, and revision of healthy personal and professional boundaries. On the surface these may appear mundane, but look closer. They require authentic personal assessment, dealing with ambiguity, tough choices, and action to manage one's commitments. These strategies are not easy, but they are crucial for professional and personal effectiveness.

1. *Engage in regular and authentic self-assessment and reflection.* Devoting time to reflection is critical, exploring questions such as, What do I value? Do my daily choices reflect my priorities? Am I content with the quality of my work life? How do I feel about my personal life? What changes do I need to make to increase my overall satisfaction? If I became critically ill tomorrow, what aspects of my life would I change?

2. *Assess the potential to affect external factors at work and at home.* If core job responsibilities are not regularly compatible with personal needs, pursue a change in position or career. If personal relationships falter, develop a specific plan for investing time and energy toward healing, or decide to alter or end relationships.

3. *Identify gaps between priorities and behavior and make changes to align them.* If more quality time is needed to spend on personal issues or relationships, identify work responsibilities to alter or eliminate them without disregarding core job functions. Assess the consequences of postponing or eliminating select tasks, considering whether real or imagined ramifications exist. Gauge the inevitable risks and potential impacts of implementing change. If work requires more quality attention, evaluate family roles and responsibilities. Is missing a child's dance recital or baseball game worth generating greater likelihood of a promotion at work? Would a promotion enable funding of a family vacation that provides optimal time together? Or would missing a child's activity be an irreplaceable loss?

4. *Prioritize quality over quantity of time spent in various situations.* Eliminate activities that lack value. Thoughtfully plan the creation of meaningful personal and professional experiences and outcomes. Be selective in assuming new responsibilities.

5. *Let go of the desire to satisfy everyone else's needs and expectations.* Pressures at home and at work are inevitable. Replace an external

focus on automatically fulfilling the needs and expectations of others with an internal focus on assessing the appropriateness and legitimacy of others' needs, then respond (or choose not to) accordingly. Cultivate this internal voice and trust it to guide decision making.[9] Through practice, develop comfort in the absence of external forms of affirmation. Learn to carefully listen and follow your heart and mind.

6. *Recognize that personal and professional circumstances change and establishing boundaries is a continual process.* Life is fluid. The process of setting boundaries is dynamic and requires periodic reflection and adjustment.

With commitment, practice, and trust in their internal voice, student affairs professionals can manage the struggles associated with establishing and honoring appropriate personal and professional boundaries, enhance the quality of home and work experiences, and role model healthy behaviors.

Notes

1. Katherine, A. (2000). *Where to draw the line: How to set healthy boundaries every day.* New York, NY: Simon & Schuster, p. 14.

2. Nobbe, J., & Manning, S. (1997). Issues for women in student affairs with children. *NASPA Journal, 34*(2), 101–111.

3. Maslach, C., & Leiter, M. (1997). *The truth about burnout: How organizations cause personal stress and what to do about it.* San Francisco, CA: Jossey-Bass.

4. Baxter Magolda, M. B. (2009). *Authoring your life: Developing an internal voice to navigate life's challenges.* Sterling, VA: Stylus, p. 41.

5. Kennedy, K. (2009). The politics and policies of parental involvement. *About Campus: Enriching the Student Learning Experience, 14*(4), 16–25.

6. Oblinger, D. (2003). Boomers, gen-xers, & millennials: Understanding the new students. *EDUCAUSE Review, 38*(4), 37–47.

7. Altbach, P. G., Berdahl, R. O., & Gumport, P. J. (Eds.). (2005). *American higher education in the twenty-first century: Social, political, and economic challenges.* Baltimore, MD: John Hopkins University Press.

8. Maslach & Leiter, *The truth about burnout.*

9. Baxter Magolda, *Authoring your life.*

Establishing Boundaries Beyond Time Management

Kristina Mickel Clement, Georgia State University

In Kate Linder's essay, she discusses the struggles many student affairs educators experience in setting appropriate boundaries to establish work-life balance. She attributes some of the time management struggles to the Western approach to work, which "equates time spent working with dedication and success" (p. 435). Linder received recognition for her outstanding time and dedication to her residence hall during her first year as a residence hall director. As a result, she dedicated even more time and energy to her work in the following year. When I began my first graduate assistantship, much like Kate I believed success would be a result of long hours of work and selfless dedication to my students.

The beliefs that Linder and I held regarding work and success are not unique to the field of student affairs. Gayle Porter reports that Westerners—especially Americans—work more than individuals in any other culture.[1] Porter asserts that many people blame global competition for the increase in hours, but she argues that individuals too are responsible for this trend. According to Porter, "Work has become such an integral part of personal identity that some people invest their entire sense of well being in work-related activity."[2] Linder provides evidence of this philosophy in her essay when she states that "being a residence hall director was no longer a job or a career path, it was the primary way I defined myself" (p. 435). Given the tendency to define ourselves by our work, it is not surprising that establishing professional boundaries is so difficult for student affairs educators.

Linder offers advice to help student affairs educators who are struggling to establish professional boundaries and tells her story as an example of the importance of setting boundaries and continually evaluating those boundaries. I agree with the advice she offers, especially regarding the need to engage in regular reflection to determine your personal values and priorities. In a field focused on the holistic development of students, it is important for professionals to regularly assess themselves, so they recognize how their beliefs and values influence their work with students. Regular reflection also helps to deal with another set of boundaries I find particularly challenging as a professional—those involving relationships with students.

When Friendships Cloud Professional Judgment

During my first year as a graduate assistant in residence life, I developed close relationships with the 10 women I supervised. We scheduled regular individual meetings, shared meals, and conversed each and every day. These resident assistants encountered many situations I also experienced as an undergraduate paraprofessional. While we regularly talked about residents, the women also confided in me about their romantic relationships, struggles with family, and personal financial problems. In some ways, I began to feel like an older sister to these women. At the time, I did not see this as a problem, but in retrospect I concluded these relationships clouded my judgments and professional decisions.

At the end of my first semester, the Office of Residence Life notified me that a woman on my staff did not meet the minimum grade point average (GPA) requirement to continue in her role as a resident assistant. The news upset me because I had to terminate her position based on her poor academic performance. She had done an amazing job building community on her floor, and I also knew she struggled financially and needed this job to offset collegiate expenses. I had developed a particularly strong relationship with this student; I feared I could not follow through with the termination. I spoke with my supervisor and asked that the woman remain on staff for the spring semester. I agreed to follow up with her regularly to monitor her academic progress to ensure she met the minimum GPA requirement at the end of the spring semester. As a result of my plea, the director allowed the student to remain on staff.

Reflecting on this experience, I based my decision more on my personal feelings and relationship with the staff member—not what was in the best interest of the staff member, her residents, and the department. Many times in the years that followed, I terminated students based on their failure to meet minimum grade requirements. I came to understand the necessity for minimum standards and the importance of being fair and consistent to all students. I concluded it was easier to uphold termination decisions when I separated my personal feelings about the students from their academic performance. Decisions such as these are difficult, but focusing on my professional responsibilities instead of my personal feelings ensures the decisions I make are in the best interest of the student and the department I represent.

The Need for Boundaries

In the age of in loco parentis, the role of the student affairs educator was much clearer. As David A. Hoekema wrote in *Campus Rules and Moral Community*, the role of the administrator was like a parent, "flexible yet firm, benevolent but not indulgent."[3] Staff at colleges and universities determined the standards they expected their students to follow in everything from dress to residence hall visitation hours. A clearer sense of the role of staff as authority—not friend—prevailed. As colleges and universities abandoned in loco parentis, student affairs educators began to focus less on establishing rules to control student behavior and more on creating opportunities for student learning and success.

Early in my graduate studies, I learned the role of a student affairs educator was to be involved in the holistic development of college students.[4] I focused on their personal, social, mental, and intellectual lives. My studies of student development theory taught me to understand students on their developmental journeys and offer appropriate levels of challenge and support.[5] What was not so apparent in textbooks was a clear answer to the question of where to draw the line in relationships with students.

Given the tendency to define ourselves by our work, it is not surprising that establishing professional boundaries is so difficult for student affairs educators.

In this social networking age of Facebook and Twitter, when everyone wants to be your friend, it is even more challenging to navigate personal and professional boundaries with students. In a profession that concerns itself with student success, developing positive relationships is crucial to the overall success of the profession. In times like these, it is more important than ever to establish boundaries so we can effectively build relationships with students while upholding professional obligations and trust. In the following section, I offer advice on establishing boundaries with students as well as suggestions for administrators of graduate preparation programs to address this issue with emerging professionals.

Building Professional Relationships

As Linder notes in her essay, "The field of student affairs is inherently demanding of those individuals who embrace it fully and strive to effect a positive difference in the personal growth and development of college students" (p. 436). In such a demanding field, it is helpful to set boundaries early in your career so you can best serve the students you interact with. While I offer the following advice, I recognize some colleagues may disagree with me based on varying degrees of comfort in developing relationships with students. You will have to decide for yourself how far you will go in relationships with students.

1. *Regularly evaluate your relationships with students.* In much the same way that Linder suggests engaging in regular self-assessment and reflection, I recommend professionals set aside time on a regular basis to reflect on their relationships with students. The following questions might be considered in your evaluation. What kinds of relationships have you developed with students? Are you closer to some students than other students? Are you treating all students fairly in regard to the decisions you make? Are you putting your personal relationships with students ahead of your role as a campus administrator? If you have concerns about a developing relationship and whether it is headed in an unprofessional or uncomfortable direction, ask others for their opinion. Outsiders can help you see if you have crossed the line from professional to personal.

2. *Communicate your personal boundaries to students as you begin to develop relationships.* In my own experience, I have witnessed varying degrees of comfort regarding the boundaries professionals set in relationships with students. It is important to consider your comfort level so you can specify your boundaries with students and they can understand the kind of relationship they might have with you. Let students know where you draw the line, and they will be less willing to challenge your personal boundaries. The following questions represent common situations you might find yourself in as a

professional, and it would be helpful to know in advance where you stand. Will you socialize with students outside of the university environment? Will you allow students access to your personal phone numbers so they can reach you at any time? Would you be willing to consume alcohol with students who are legally allowed to consume alcohol?

3. *Consider how you will use emerging technologies to interact with students.* As Linder mentions in her essay, those of the Millennial generation have embraced emerging technologies and often use e-mail and other online tools to communicate with student affairs educators. Students are more connected than ever through smart phones, social networking sites, and online class websites. All of this connectivity has resulted in the expectation that student affairs educators are accessible at all hours. In my experience, students today are more likely to send you a message on Facebook than call you on the telephone.

   As many student affairs divisions and departments have embraced social networking sites as a means to connect with students, students have begun to extend friend requests to student affairs educators with accounts on Facebook, asked them to connect on LinkedIn, or started to follow staff members' posts on Twitter. For some student affairs educators, this increased connection with students is advantageous, but others are not as comfortable with it. As a professional you must consider if you are open to interacting with students through social networking outlets. If so, do you prefer to connect on social media through a personal or professional account? Be consistent so you do not send conflicting messages to students.

4. *Graduate preparation programs should include discussions on personal and professional boundaries in their curriculum.* As emerging professionals are establishing their professional philosophies, it would be helpful to encourage them to consider the types of boundaries they might set in relationships with students. In my graduate experience, we spent a great deal of time talking about the importance of mentoring students and encouraging them along in their developmental journeys. It would have been helpful to discuss gray areas that might arise in developing relationships with students. One suggestion would be for program staff to review the ethical standards of the

profession and discuss with students how they might handle situations that fall on the border of ethical and unethical. Discussions such as these would challenge students to consider where they would stand on issues faced as student affairs educators. Establishing their professional boundaries early would benefit students as they advance in their career.

I intend for these suggestions to help student affairs educators establish meaningful and rewarding relationships with students. They serve also as a warning to always be conscious of your primary role as a student affairs educator. It is our role to safeguard and further the development of students, which should always be the primary focus of our relationships. Setting professional boundaries will ensure that we uphold our duty and responsibility to students and our profession.

Notes

1. Porter, G. (2010). Work ethic and ethical work: Distortions in the American dream. *Journal of Business Ethics, 96*(4), 535–550.

2. Ibid., p. 538.

3. Hoekema, D. A. (1994). *Campus rules and moral community: In place of in loco parentis.* Lanham, MD: Rowman & Littlefield, p. 13.

4. Nuss, E. (1996). The development of student affairs. In S. R. Komives, D. B. Woodard Jr., & Associates (Eds.), *Student services: A handbook for the profession* (pp. 22–42). San Francisco, CA: Jossey-Bass.

5. Evans, N. J., Forney, D., & Guido-DiBrito, F. (1998). *Student development in college.* San Francisco, CA: Jossey-Bass.

Further Reading and Related Blog

Jeff Manning, Fordham University

Baxter Magolda, M. B. (2009). *Authoring your life: Developing an internal voice to navigate life's challenges.* Sterling, VA: Stylus.

Based on a 24-year longitudinal study, this book illustrates the process of developing an internal voice to navigate life's challenges. Participants' narratives reveal life experiences that prompted them to take responsibility for coordinating external influences with their own internal belief systems and values. This internal voice is critical for effectively establishing and maintaining appropriate and healthy personal and professional boundaries.

Katherine, A. (2000). *Where to draw the line: How to set healthy boundaries every day.* New York, NY: Simon & Schuster.

Boundaries differ depending on the environment and relationships involved. This book defines boundaries and addresses over 20 different situations in which establishing boundaries can be important and difficult. When boundaries are created, they can be crossed out of error or purpose. This book addresses these boundary lines to help individuals navigate daily life—no matter what the situation.

Porter, G. (2010). Work ethic and ethical work: Distortions in the American dream. *Journal of Business Ethics, 96*(4), 535–550.

This article describes the uniqueness of the American combination of democracy and capitalism and the effect it has on work ethic and balance. Most Americans have subscribed to the assumption that hard work pays off in the end, leading to the American dream. However, this dream has been met with contradiction and questionable ethics. A shift to work smarter not harder has caused many individuals to attempt to beat the system or find alternative means to achievement, sometimes at the expense of others.

Blog URL: contestedissues.wordpress.com

Corresponding Chapter Post: tinyurl.com/contestedissues23

24

How Do Professionals Navigate Situations When Their Professional Beliefs Clash With Their Supervisors' or Organizations' Beliefs?

Engaging in Dialogues About Difference in the Workplace

Peter M. Magolda and Marcia B. Baxter Magolda,
Miami University

E very January, graduate students aspiring to complete their student affairs in higher education degree in May begin their quest to secure a job in higher education. Over the years we have listened to students discuss their employment search strategies. Comments such as "I want to secure an entry-level student activities position that pays at least $38,000 a year at a public institution in Chicago" are commonplace and reveal personal and professional values that guide new professionals' decisions. Most individuals have identified the functional area they want to work in (e.g., student activities). They are also keenly aware of the kinds of jobs (e.g., entry-level position) they are qualified for, their geographic and institutional preferences, and minimum salary requirements.

As these new professionals complete their first semester of work in student affairs, we hear many "if I knew then what I know now" stories as they retrospectively make sense of their job search and early days in the field. While most individuals appear highly satisfied with their employment search strategies and current work environments, they often confess they neither gained a complex understanding of the institution's ethos nor fully comprehended the wide-ranging influence of their supervisor until work began. One former student's e-mail message pointedly captures this pervasive sentiment:

> I am enjoying my job; however, I feel like I am living for my job. I also have been evaluating Creed University [pseudonym] and how it does and does not match up with my values. One major concept I learned in grad school was how to embrace difference and how a diversified group of people can make a stronger bond than people who are all the same. Creed is ethnically diverse, but in other areas of diversity they are very homogeneous.
>
> Christianity is a HUGE thing in people's lives here. Of course there is no room for anyone that is gay on this campus. I find myself being very careful here because people are so strong in their faith that it leaves little room for discussion on certain topics. For example, the only CDs I have at work are instrumental because I do not know if it would offend some people if I listen to secular music. Also, movies . . . I can't really talk with my co-workers about an "R" rated movie that I enjoyed. In some ways I should have known this coming into this job; I guess I was so excited that I did not think deeply enough about the negatives.
>
> I am not writing this to portray that I am unhappy. I am actually very happy. I just find it interesting that I am working for a school that I would not want my own kids to attend because people are too much the same. This is my first challenge with my job.—Ned

Ned's message mirrors the realization of many new and veteran professionals—uneasy feelings based on value differences are inevitable in work contexts. Ned, a Christian, aspired to work at a religiously affiliated college; we suspect this passion contributed to the realization of his dream as an admissions counselor at Creed University. Yet initially Ned did not recognize the wide variance of institutional types in the Christian college sector of higher education. He also elicited positive vibes from his eventual supervisor during the interview process, but as they forged a supervisor-supervisee relationship, he better comprehended her far-reaching influence on individual staff members and the office culture. Joseph Boehman defines *organizational commitment* as a person's capacity to internalize and work toward the attainment of the goals of the organization, as well as remain with the organization.[1] Ned's reluctance to commit to the values of Creed University is a primary source of his angst.

Moral, Ideological, and Political Tensions

Ned's confession raises an important question that almost everyone who works in higher education asks at some point in their career: How do professionals navigate situations in which their professional beliefs are inconsistent with their supervisors' or organizations' beliefs? There are three obvious glib responses to this question: (a) berate oneself for not recognizing the value gap sooner rather than later; (b) suck it up, repress your concerns, and do the job you agreed to do; or (c) leave. In the remainder of this essay we evaluate these three responses, then offer a fourth option that begins with a decision-making framework and concludes with a discussion about differences aimed at mutual understanding and coconstructed ethical resolutions.

An obvious (and not so helpful) hindsight reaction to this question is for new professionals to chastise themselves for not anticipating the tension. In Ned's case, there is some merit in self-criticism (e.g., asking insufficient questions about Creed's conceptualization of Christianity) and examining the past and learning from it. But ultimately, tensions persist if the sole intervention is self-analysis.

At the root of Ned's uneasiness are subculture differences. Ned's Christian subculture differs greatly from Creed's Christian subculture. Assessing organizational subcultures/cultures is easier said than done. Job seekers, like Ned, review institutional websites and download organizational charts, cost of living data, staff salaries, and real estate/rental information. Even with seemingly infinite amounts of information available on the Internet, extended on-campus interviews, testimonials from trusted colleagues, and keen participant observation skills, conducting what Elizabeth Whitt refers to as *cultural audits* (i.e., the systematic discovery of organizational values and assumptions) is complicated, confusing, and imperfect.[2] No doubt it is easier for an outsider to gain insights about the espoused goals of a culture than its enacted goals. The inevitable gap between espoused and enacted goals becomes clearer from within the organization once the individual begins work, which for some seems too late.

So then, how does one assess enacted values during a cultural audit? Whitt argued that auditors need to have a capacity to understand their own values before embarking on a quest to understand the values of others (an issue we discuss in-depth later in this essay). In Ned's instance, he had an intuitive sense of his values, which he incorrectly surmised aligned with Creed University's espoused values. It was not until he began work that the value gap between Creed University and Ned, as well as the gap between Creed's espoused and enacted goals, became apparent—contributing to Ned's ethical dilemma. Had Ned more carefully reflected on the details of his Christian values, he might have been more effective in conducting his cultural audit and unearthed some elements of the gap with enacted goals. Pursuing these values in more depth with his prospective supervisor might have revealed her influence on the office.

Being honest, making differences public, and ultimately negotiating those differences are bedrock foundations of our profession that can strengthen interpersonal relationships, improve communication, make competing values and differing interests clear, and illuminate individual and institutional priorities.

Should I stay or should I go? The second and third dismissive responses—suck it up or leave—reflect simple, dichotomous, and extreme solutions to resolve complex problems. Given two differing perceptions that appear to be mutually exclusive, professionals sometimes feel compelled to embrace one or the other. Selecting exclusively between binaries (e.g., suck it up or leave) severely limits one's capacity for high-quality ethical decision making. In Ned's situation, leaving seems like a draconian measure that would have serious implications for Creed University as well as for Ned's family; inevitably, value differences and subsequent tensions would follow Ned to his next work context. An equally unappealing alternative is for Ned to repress his concerns, since existing tensions will likely persist and manifest themselves in different Creed contexts. Complex problems warrant complex analyses and multilayered interventions.

While most of the responsibility for honing one's capacities for conducting proficient cultural/subcultural analyses, self-reflection, and deconstructing culture/subculture clashes rests with student affairs educators, student affairs preparation programs bear some responsibility for inadequately preparing graduate students for the challenges that await them in academia.

Ned's graduate faculty and practicum supervisors provided him with high-quality technical job search advice (e.g., feedback about his résumé, cover letter, interview, and networking). Ned's on-the-job uneasiness, rooted in a subculture clash of values, reveals a shortcoming of graduate preparation programs—faculty and students' supervisors are more proficient at coaching students about the technical aspects of a job search and adjusting to work responsibilities than they are with the moral, political, and ideological dimensions of work contexts.

Ned's e-mail began with the statement he is "living for his job." Deciding how much one devotes to work versus other life dimensions is a moral matter and not merely pragmatic or technical. Ned acknowledged a gap between Creed University's and his conceptualization of diversity. From Ned's perspective, Creed's ethnic diversity is an asset, but its homogeneity as it relates to social issues (e.g., condemning gays, eschewing secular music and R-rated films), troubled him. This value gap based on differing ideologies had political implications. Ned's decision whether to play secular music while at work or discuss R-rated movies with colleagues has political consequences. Assessing the potential political fallout from interjecting a competing ideology into a seemingly homogeneous work context often paralyzes new professionals. Marilyn Amey and Lori Ressor in *Beginning Your Journey: A Guide for New Professionals in Student Affairs* identified three overriding themes of paramount importance to new professionals: relationships, fit, and competence.[3] New professionals like Ned fear that calling attention to ideological differences—especially with a more powerful supervisor whose values appear to differ from his— could jeopardize relationships with colleagues and the supervisor, call into question one's fit with the office or institution, and raise competency doubts. Yet, as A.H. Hawley stated, "every social act is an exercise of power, every social relationship is a power equation, and every social group or system is an organization of power."[4] Hoping to avoid power imbalances in one's world of work is impossible; learning to negotiate power differences and ultimately make ethical decisions, although challenging, is necessary.

Ned's final statement—"I just find it interesting that I am working for a school that I would not want my own kids to attend because people are too much the same"—illustrates the nexus of moral, ideological, and political issues that are inevitable on the job. Graduate student affairs preparation program faculty must bolster efforts to address topics such as ethics, ideology, and politics and how to discuss them with a supervisor.

Before introducing a fourth, and more viable solution—acknowledging, understanding, discussing, and negotiating moral, ideological, and political differences leading to ethical decision making—it is essential we make clear that the dynamics showcased in Ned's e-mail are not unique to new professionals. Seasoned professionals also regularly experience value clashes that lead to turmoil. For example, the arrival of a new supervisor who reorganizes the office and institutes new policies incites some experienced professionals to romanticize about the past, lament about the present, repress uncomfortable feelings, and in extreme cases disassociate from the organization.

So why do new and seasoned student affairs professionals struggle to navigate situations in which their professional and personal beliefs clash with their supervisors' or organizations' beliefs? What's so frightening about conflict? A subtle and implicit implication persists that acknowledging or initiating conflict will damage morale, jeopardize organizational efficiency, and destabilize solidarity. We disagree; cultural/subculture conflicts are natural and normal. Being honest, making differences public, and ultimately negotiating those differences are bedrock foundations of our profession that can strengthen interpersonal relationships, improve communication, make competing values and differing interests clear, and illuminate individual and institutional priorities. These outcomes benefit all stakeholders, especially students. Mediating conflict is a risk worth taking, while acknowledging that such an action will not guarantee an amicable resolution. Still, repressing conflict has far more dire consequences than attempting to resolve it, even unysuccessfully.

A Decision-Making Framework to Address Workplace Tensions

Acknowledging and mediating subculture differences are purposeful acts that require sustained reflection. We propose beginning with keen self-awareness—an internal and reflective audit of sorts—aimed at achieving greater clarity of one's values and priorities and others' critiques of these self-held beliefs. In 1977 Robert Nash introduced an applied problem-solving method to enhance his student affairs graduate students' ethical literacy.[5] At first glance, the application of Nash's framework to explore the question of how professionals navigate situations in which their professional beliefs are inconsistent with their supervisors' or organizations' beliefs seems contrived. Yet carefully studying this question reveals the numerous ethical dilemmas at the root of this question, and understanding these ethical tensions are essential as one navigates differences with the other.

Ten questions are the centerpiece of Nash's framework aimed at systematically recognizing and analyzing ethical dilemmas, competing ideologies, and political quagmires in a specific case. The scope of this essay neither permits us to substantively summarize the model nor address each question. Instead, our abridged summary and analysis (using Ned as a case study and frame of reference) models ways for student affairs educators to better understand their own core values and beliefs and what they deem to be good.

Nash's opening question—What are the moral themes in the case?—is a purposefully broad question aimed at bringing order to the chaos associated with the myriad of ideas embedded in moral dilemmas. Examples of implicit moral themes in Ned's e-mail message include professional responsibility, institutional allegiance, and personal integrity. Having accepted Creed University's job offer, Ned has a professional and moral duty to fulfill his job responsibilities as an admission recruiter. In this capacity he must convey a genuine allegiance to Creed and its mission, for if he does not believe in Creed, how can he expect prospective students to believe in Creed? Unfortunately his uneasiness with some of Creed's values (e.g., intolerant views regarding gay students) created an internal conflict, which begins to answer Nash's second question: What are the conflicts in the case that make it an ethical dilemma? Ned's dilemma centers on lessening the gap between being loyal to Creed's beliefs and loyal to his own. Creed's mission statement asserts its members "will display the highest level of integrity. We will develop bonds based on trust and endeavor to maintain that trust with faculty, staff, students and others who interact with us." If Ned represses his feelings, he runs the risk of peers' and prospective students' perceiving him as disingenuous and lacking integrity. If he openly expresses his beliefs, he runs the risk of appearing to be an unfaithful rebel.

The framework's third question—Who are the major stakeholders?—reminds one of the far-reaching influences the resolution of a single ethical dilemma has on multiple stakeholders. In Ned's context, he is a primary stakeholder, as are his supervisor and colleagues. Yet, so too are Ned's family, the Creed community, and prospective students. Ned's resolution has consequences for these stakeholders, which is the essence of Nash's fourth question—What are some foreseeable consequences of the possible choices in the case?

Without intending to appear melodramatic, if Ned opts to quit his job, the decision would affect multiple stakeholders. Future employers could perceive Ned as a quitter. Being unemployed, even temporarily, would burden Ned and his family. Creed administrators might not have the capacity to quickly rehire a replacement, which would jeopardize their new-student recruitment initiatives. If Ned stays the course and remains silent, his muted passion and apprehensions about Creed could undermine his recruitment efforts. If Ned made his concerns public and tensions arose, it could fracture the camaraderie of the admission office and marginalize him. If his supervisor responded positively to Ned's concerns and remedied them, an outcome might be a less repressive and more inclusive office ethos. The previous discussion centering on options such as berating oneself, sucking it up, leaving, or mediating the conflict reveals answers to the framework's fifth question, What are some viable alternatives to the possible courses of action in the case?

Nash's sixth question, What are some important background beliefs you ought to consider in the case? is at the heart of how professionals navigate situations in which their professional beliefs are inconsistent with their supervisors' or organizations' beliefs. Our lives include our life story, family upbringing, religious or secular training, and educational experiences; these are but a few influences on our worldviews, which continually calibrate our moral compass (i.e., internal mechanisms that guide one's views of right and wrong). These worldviews and life experiences influenced Ned's decisions to pursue a career in student affairs and work at a Christian university. Nash advocates a multiple and integrative approach to ethical analysis, one that "features consideration of consequences, principles, background beliefs, acting in character, and a professional code of ethics."[6] In Ned's context, religion and honesty are two competing values that are of crucial importance. Ned's job musings in his e-mail message make implicit reference to his principles, consequences, beliefs, and personal code of ethics. This amalgamated (although stream of consciousness) analysis illustrates Nash's vision of an integrative analysis.

Nash embeds sage advice in questions seven and eight—What are some of your initial intuitions and feelings regarding the case? and What choices would you make if you were to act in character in the case? He urges individuals to trust their instincts, intuitions, and feelings because they provide invaluable cues related to possible pursuits to resolve the dilemma. These two questions also remind individuals they belong to multiple moral communities that influence the direction they pursue. An examination of the choices one makes *in character* in a specific context reveals espoused, enacted, and aspirational conceptualizations of self.

The ninth question, What does the profession's code of ethics say regarding key moral principles? augments one's own moral compass by exploring the written ideals of the profession. As Nash said, "A good code of ethics, therefore, captures exactly what it is the profession thinks its practitioners ought to profess in morally anomalous situations."[7] For example, the American College Personnel Association's *Statement of Ethical Principles and Standards* states that student affairs professionals should

> contribute to their institution by supporting its mission, goals, policies, and abiding by its procedures. Seek resolution when they and their institution encounter substantial disagreements concerning professional or personal values. Resolution may require sustained efforts to modify institutional policies and practices or result in voluntary termination of employment. Recognize that conflicts among students, colleagues, or the institution should be resolved without diminishing respect for or appropriate obligations to any party involved.[8]

This document also states that student affairs professionals will "not discriminate on the basis of age, culture, ethnicity, gender, disabling condition, race, religion, or sexual/affectional orientation. They will work to modify discriminatory practices."[9] Not only does Ned find himself in conflict with his work colleagues; his professional association's code of ethics simultaneously suggests supporting Creed's mission while embracing multiple social identities.

The final question—What is your decision?—not so subtly conveys the urgency to act. If professionals carefully contemplated the nine questions preceding this final one, they would be more likely to be able to make an ethically grounded decision.

Our purpose in introducing this model is that we believe it is essential for new professionals to carefully explore their own values and the foundations of these values before initiating action. The tenets of the model remind us that decision making is not simply a pragmatic or technical task, but a moral, ideological, and political act. As Nash proposes, by examining ethical themes, identifying points of conflict and ethical dilemmas, recognizing stakeholders, anticipating consequences, generating viable alternatives, carefully examining core/background beliefs, valuing one's intuitions and feelings, exploring possible choices, and juxtaposing one's personal ethical principles and standards with the codes of professional organizations, the likelihood increases exponentially that sound decisions will result and a clearer sense of what is good will prevail.

The Role of Personal Authority in Decision Making

Self-reflection is a necessary but insufficient skill for navigating complex dilemmas that involve potential conflict. Navigating these dilemmas requires self-authorship—using one's internal voice and core personal values to guide one's life.[10] Nash's framework clearly demands careful analysis of one's beliefs and values, as well as those of others. Sorting out moral themes and issues requires acknowledging that multiple perspectives and outcomes are possible. Exploring background beliefs, feelings, and intuition suggests looking inward to clarify values. Balancing competing stakeholders' (including the self's) needs implies the capacity to function interdependently with others. These requirements reflect complex cognitive, intrapersonal, and interpersonal developmental capacities.

Our lives include our life story, family upbringing, religious or secular training, and educational experiences; these are but a few influences on our worldviews, which continually calibrate our moral compass.

Thus our fourth solution requires moving beyond relying on external authorities for what to believe and how to act. What we suggest here

means professionals have to listen to and cultivate their personal authority, a task easier said than done. Many participants in Baxter Magolda's
longitudinal study reported they spent most of their 20s learning to cultivate and trust their internal voices; this occurred in work settings where
supervisors asked them to function autonomously, using their own judgment in meeting the needs of their organizations.[11] Some experienced
conflicts similar to Ned's, and resolving them required bringing their
personal authority into conversation with external authorities (often their
supervisors). Those who encountered supervisors and colleagues who
respected their thoughts and collaborated with them to solve problems
found it easier to cultivate their internal voices. These partnerships resonate with Sharon Daloz Parks's depiction of a mentoring environment.
Among what she calls *gifts of a mentoring environment* are "creating
norms of discourse and inclusion that invite genuine dialogue, strengthen
critical thought, encourage connective-holistic awareness, and develop
the contemplative mind."[12] Mentoring environments are essential in
helping student affairs professionals develop self-authorship.

As Baxter Magolda's participants refined their beliefs, priorities, and
identities, they worked to rely less on uncritical acceptance of external
formulas and more on using their personal authority to coordinate external influences. Trusting their internal voices emerged when they realized
that while reality was beyond their control, how they reacted to reality
could be shaped by their internal voice. Trusting the internal voice, which
is the initial element of self-authorship, is key to the capacity to shift
cultural frames and engage in meaningful, interdependent relationships
with diverse others.[13] Ned's reluctance to express his authentic voice in
his new work setting implies that he may not yet fully trust his internal
voice. However, the fact that he is not completely miserable (e.g., "I am
actually very happy") also suggests that he may simply be unsure when
and how to express himself. Ned's e-mail makes no mention of a mentoring environment that would welcome his thoughts and encourage him to
express himself authentically. If he felt more comfortable with his supervisor, he might find her to be a resource in exploring the tensions he is
experiencing.

Self-authorship does not emerge full blown on a moment's notice.
Trusting one's internal voice enables one to begin to make commitments
that form a philosophy to guide one's life. Building this philosophy sometimes requires refining the internal voice. Baxter Magolda's participants
often noted they were able to conceptualize these philosophies before

they actually lived them naturally in everyday life—a process that continued well into their 30s and 40s.[14] This suggests that veteran student affairs professionals may still be working on the kind of self-authorship required for navigating conflicts of beliefs with their work settings. Thus it behooves not only staff and faculty of graduate preparation programs to intentionally provide mentoring environments for the growth of self-authorship, leaders of professional associations and student affairs divisions should also construct mentoring environments to support the personal growth that undergirds professional effectiveness.

Being self-authored also does not mean that the frequency of conflicts will decrease. It simply means that self-authored professionals are more likely to regard conflicting perspectives as natural, understand their internal perspectives more deeply, and be sufficiently secure in their own identities to authentically participate in mutual dialogues with others whose perspectives differ, including more powerful supervisors. These dialogues, and the opportunity to be welcomed into conversation regardless of one's perspective, are essential ways for professionals to work out their perspectives and participate effectively in communities of difference. The ability to do so enables professionals to model and engage undergraduates in these dialogues for the same purpose.

Navigating conflicting beliefs in work settings, or any setting for that matter, requires crossing boundaries. In *Teaching to Transgress*, bell hooks said, "To engage in dialogue is one of the simplest ways we can begin as teachers, scholars, and critical thinkers to cross boundaries."[15] hooks advocates the creation of communities or subcultures that struggle to understand the effects of power, the social construction of knowledge and identity, the meaning of education, and the need for social and cultural change. Nash's moral analysis framework and mentoring to enable self-authorship support creating these communities that would enable professionals to navigate conflicts among their and their supervisors' or organizations' beliefs, as well as model the communities we strive to create in student affairs contexts. What we propose leads to discomfort, yet in that uneasiness lies the comfort of knowing that learning is taking place, and that is what we are all about.

Notes

1. Boehman, J. (2007). Affective commitment among student affairs professionals. *NASPA Journal, 44*(2), 307–326.

2. Whitt, E. J. (1993). Making the familiar strange: Discovering culture. In G. D. Kuh (Ed.), *Cultural perspectives in student affairs work* (pp. 81–94). Lanham, MD: University Press of America.

3. Amey, M. J., & Reesor, L. M. (2002). *Beginning your journey: A guide for new professionals in student affairs.* Washington, DC: National Association of Student Personnel Administrators.

4. Hawley, A. H. (1963). Community power and urban renewal success. *American Journal of Sociology, 68,* 422–431, p. 422.

5. Nash, R. J. (1997). Teaching ethics in the student affairs classroom. *NASPA Journal, 35*(1), 3–19.

6. Ibid., p. 6.

7. Ibid., p. 8.

8. American College Personnel Association. (2006). *Statement of ethical principles and standards.* Retrieved from http://www2.myacpa.org/ethics/statement.php, p. 4.

9. Ibid., p. 5.

10. Baxter Magolda, M. B. (2009). *Authoring your life: Developing an internal voice to navigate life's challenges.* Sterling, VA: Stylus.

11. Ibid.

12. Daloz Parks, S. (2000). *Big questions, worthy dreams. Mentoring young adults in their search for meaning, purpose, and faith.* San Francisco, CA: Jossey-Bass, p. 141.

13. King, P. M., & Baxter Magolda, M. B. (2005). A developmental model of intercultural maturity. *Journal of College Student Development, 46*(6), 571–592.

14. Baxter Magolda, *Authoring your life.*

15. hooks, b. (1994). *Teaching to transgress: Education as the practice of freedom.* New York, NY: Routledge, p. 135.

Tempered Radicals

Managing Risks in Negotiating Differences

Rozana Carducci, University of Missouri

Peter Magolda and Marcia Baxter Magolda present a compelling response to the perennial question of how to navigate ideological and cultural conflicts in the workplace. Drawing upon the theories and practices of self-authorship, cultural audits, and Nash's ethical decision-making framework, the authors map out a process of self-reflection designed to help student affairs professionals first recognize their internal beliefs and values and then initiate productive dialogues about differences with supervisors and colleagues.[1] Magolda and Baxter Magolda acknowledge the significant power dynamics embedded in workplace conflicts, which pleases me, but their multilayered dialogue about differences framework does not adequately address the professional or personal risks assumed by individuals who decide to publicize tensions between personal beliefs and organizational norms, particularly if these conflicts are rooted in issues of identity (e.g., race and ethnicity, gender, religion, social class, sexual orientation).

As Magolda and Baxter Magolda note, professionals confronted with workplace conflict are often paralyzed by fear of the political fallout that may accompany voicing their concerns and opinions. Although cultivating one's internal voice via the self-reflective processes described in their essay may reaffirm the need for individuals to initiate dialogues about differences, these frameworks offer little insight into how to go about starting these conversations in ways that will preserve organizational relationships as well as minimize personal risk and negative political consequences. To address this important dimension of negotiating differences in the workplace, I introduce Debra Meyerson's framework of tempered radicals, a model of grassroots leadership that outlines specific strategies for successfully negotiating conflict, particularly identity-based tensions, from within organizations and without the benefit of formal authority or positional power.[2]

Tempered Radicals

In *Rocking the Boat: How to Effect Change Without Making Trouble*, Meyerson explores the following questions, How do individuals effect meaningful change from within organizations? and How do organizational members express identities and values that are different from the majority culture while fitting into that culture?[3] The correspondence between Meyerson's guiding questions and the focus of this student affairs contested issue dialogue is striking. Also similar are the response options Meyerson maps out for individuals who recognize incongruencies between personal beliefs and organizational practices: conformity and compromise (i.e., what Magolda and Baxter Magolda describe as the suck it up response); exiting the organization; flaming out or aggressively asserting beliefs and values without regard for existing organizational practices (a strategy likely to result in further organizational alienation or exit), and engaging in tempered radicalism or "small acts of self-expression" that raise organizational awareness of alternative beliefs and norms.[4] Although Meyerson does not explicitly use the language of self-authorship or ethical decision making to describe the work of fostering change from within organizations, student affairs professionals seeking to initiate the productive dialogues about differences, imagined by Magolda and Baxter Magolda, will likely find the spectrum of tempered radical strategies to be a meaningful framework of action.

Tempered radicals are everyday leaders who seek congruence between their personal beliefs and identities and their organizational environments.[5] What is distinctive about the actions of tempered radicals is their intentional pursuit of slow and steady incremental organizational change (hence the description of their efforts as tempered). Rather than seeking dramatic change overnight through the public pronouncement of organizational injustice, an act likely to further alienate the individual and raise the ire of supervisors, tempered radicals call attention to value differences and seek congruence via small-scale efforts of self-expression and negotiation. Meyerson identified and described a spectrum of tempered radical strategies that include resisting quietly and staying true to one's self, turning personal threats into opportunities, broadening the impact through negotiation, leveraging small wins, and organizing collective action.[6] It is this spectrum of possible actions that I find most useful with respect to extending and enacting the dialogue about differences framework proposed by Magolda and Baxter Magolda. More specifically, adopting the tempered radicals framework as a starting point for reflection on Nash's fifth ethical decision-making question (What are the viable alternatives to the possible course of action in this case?) presents the student affairs professional with numerous tangible options for translating self-awareness into meaningful action while simultaneously minimizing personal risk and political fallout.

Although the space limitations of this essay prevent a thorough review of all five tempered radical strategies, I illustrate the value of the framework as a tool in the negotiation of workplace ideological differences by applying three of the strategies to Ned's case story. As you recall, Ned is a student affairs professional experiencing conflict between his personal values and the homogeneous Christian culture of his employer, Creed University. Although cognizant of this tension, Ned noted he is actually very happy at work and espouses a desire to remain at the institution. What options does Ned have for productively navigating this conflict from within the organization?

Selecting from among the five possible strategies of tempered radicals leadership necessitates that Ned reflect on the desired scope (for example, influencing the behaviors and beliefs of a few coworkers or fostering a more sweeping organization-wide transformation) and the intention of his actions (ranging from preservation of self-identity to initiating broader organizational change in the name of social justice).[7] If Ned determines he is primarily interested in preserving his sense of self-identity and influencing the attitudes and beliefs of his immediate coworkers, he might opt to engage in a set of behaviors Meyerson describes as "resisting quietly and staying true to one's self."[8] For example, Ned might choose to enact his authentic identity at work by playing secular music in his office, displaying a quote on his door that celebrates different spiritual traditions, or openly sharing his perspective when office conversations turn to matters of faith. Meyerson recounts the stories of tempered radicals who quietly resisted organizational norms via their choice of clothing, office decor, and language. Additionally, Ned might choose to engage in psychological resistance, for example actively maintaining a positive self-identity by intentionally cultivating relationships with individuals (inside or outside Creed) who celebrate his unique spiritual perspective. Although narrow in scope and intention, Ned's efforts to resist quietly will serve to subtly disrupt organizational norms regarding individual expressions of faith and allow Ned to remain true to himself and a Creed employee.

If Ned's supervisor confronts him about the inappropriateness of playing secular music at work, Ned might engage in the tempered radical strategy of turning threats into opportunities and use this interaction as a time to raise the supervisor's awareness of potentially problematic organizational assumptions. More specifically, Ned might explicitly but tactfully name the issue and converse with the supervisor about Creed's

What is distinctive about the actions of tempered radicals is their intentional pursuit of slow and steady incremental organizational change.

Christian mission and the possibility of university employees' fulfilling that mission while expressing their unique identities.[9] Additional strategies for turning threats into opportunities include using humor as a means of calling attention to differences of opinion in a nonthreatening manner, interrupting the momentum of conversations that marginalize those with different perspectives, and correcting false assumptions as they surface in conversation, policy, and practice.[10] For example, if a lunchtime conversation turns to popular culture, and one of Ned's colleagues expresses the opinion that secular music is a root cause of immoral student behavior, Ned might interrupt the conversation by interjecting a humorous comment to respectfully highlight their difference of opinion or by asking the colleague to elaborate on the logic behind his or her statement. Once Ned has successfully interrupted the momentum of the conversation, he can maximize the learning potential of this interaction by sharing his own perspective on the relationship (or lack thereof) between popular culture preferences and expressions of faith. When deciding if and how to turn a threat into an opportunity for organizational learning, Meyerson reminds would-be tempered radicals to acknowledge they have a choice with respect to their actions. They may opt to interrupt the momentum of the conversation as it unfolds or wait for a more appropriate time and place to raise the issue.[11]

For those student affairs professionals who feel that resolving tension between their personal values and organizational beliefs necessitates actions of wider scope and intention, they may choose to adopt the tempered radical strategy of leveraging small wins. This strategy entails engaging in a "limited, doable project that results in something concrete and visible."[12] Ned might seek to leverage small wins by initiating a staff brown bag series on spiritual diversity or soliciting support from his supervisor to establish a Living Mission Award to honor department staff members who enact the Creed university mission in their daily practices. Both programs would provide Ned with a nonthreatening forum to initiate dialogues about different interpretations of faith within the campus community. Small wins not only foster hope, increase efficacy, and boost the self-confidence of tempered radicals, they pave the way for broader organizational change, as the cumulative effect of small wins add up over time and gradually shift organizational culture.

Cultivating Student Affairs Tempered Radicals

Having illustrated the relevance of the tempered radicals framework for navigating ideological tensions in the student affairs workplace, we now address the question of how student affairs preparation programs, professional associations, and staff development committees may facilitate the cultivation of tempered radicals. I concur with Magolda and Baxter Magolda that "self-reflection is a necessary but insufficient skill" (p. 462) for navigating ideological conflict. Although establishing the mentoring environments called for in the previous chapter will no doubt enhance participant self-authorship, fostering the courage and skills associated with the leadership of tempered radicals will likely require more than connecting student affairs professionals with mentors. What is needed is a comprehensive leadership development program that fosters the particular skills and strategies of tempered radicalism (e.g., assertive communication, negotiation, framing, public relations, networking, mobilizing, fund-raising).[13] The leadership curriculum must include not only opportunities to study and discuss the tempered radicals model, it should also facilitate the application and practice of these newfound skills via case studies, simulations, and role-playing activities.

Finally, although the aim of adopting a tempered, incremental approach to self-expression and organizational change is to minimize personal risk and political fallout, choosing to vocalize differences of opinion with institutional leaders is an inherently risky endeavor. Indeed, Meyerson dedicates a chapter of her book to the challenges that tempered radicals must overcome, including burnout, loneliness, anxiety, and accusations of hypocrisy.[14] Thus, in addition to helping student affairs professionals translate self-awareness into action, graduate preparation faculty and leadership mentors must also help individuals cultivate the skills, strategies, and resources of resilience and renewal in difficult times. These leadership lessons might include developing support networks within and beyond the organization, seeking out opportunities for rejuvenation (e.g., meditation, exercise, a hobby), and cultivating habits that will help the individual overcome the inevitable barriers of frustration and self-doubt (for example, patience, flexibility, and perseverance).[15]

As Magolda and Baxter Magolda wisely note, "Complex problems warrant complex analyses and multilayered interventions" (p. 456). Integrating the tempered radicals framework with the reflective processes of cultural audits and ethical decision making will help student affairs professionals recognize the multiple ways they can engage in self-authorship at work. Additionally, introducing student affairs professionals to a model of incremental tempered conflict resolution and organizational change will likely minimize the fear and risk associated with speaking up, and removing, or at least lowering, two significant barriers to initiating meaningful dialogues about differences.

Notes

1. Baxter Magolda, M. B. (2009). *Authoring your life: Developing an internal voice to navigate life's challenges.* Sterling, VA: Stylus; Whitt, E. J. (1993). Making the familiar strange: Discovering culture. In G. D. Kuh (Ed.), *Cultural perspectives in student affairs work* (pp. 81–94). Lanham, MD: University Press of America; Nash, R. J. (1997). Teaching ethics in the student affairs classroom. *NASPA Journal, 35*(1), 3–19.

2. Meyerson, D. E. (2008). *Rocking the boat: How to effect change without making trouble.* Boston, MA: Harvard Business Press.

3. Ibid., p. xi.

4. Ibid., p. xi.

5. Ibid.

6. Ibid., p. 8.

7. Ibid.

8. Ibid., p. 37.

9. Ibid., p. 61.

10. Ibid., p. 63.

11. Ibid., pp. 61–62.

12. Ibid., p. 102.

13. Kezar, A., & Carducci, R. (2009). Revolutionizing leadership development. In A. Kezar (Ed.), *Rethinking leadership in a complex, multicultural, and global environment: New concepts and models for higher education* (pp. 1–38). Sterling, VA: Stylus.

14. Meyerson, *Rocking the boat*, p. 141.

15. Ibid., p. 171.

Further Reading and Related Blog

Sarah Meagher, Miami University

Kegan, R., & Lahey, L. L. (2000). *How the way we talk can change the way we work: Seven languages for transformation.* San Francisco, CA: Jossey-Bass.

This book examines how our assumptions about ourselves and others keep us from accomplishing our goals. The step-by-step process introduced in the first four chapters guides readers in assessing their own immunity to change. The remainder of the book offers social languages that promote learning on the personal and organization levels. These languages offer a framework for understanding and addressing differences among people in the workplace.

King, P. M., & Baxter Magolda, M. B. (2005). A developmental model of intercultural maturity. *Journal of College Student Development, 46*(6), 571–592.

This article examines students' ability to work with and understand a diverse array of cultures and perspectives based on their intrapersonal, interpersonal, and cognitive development. Integrating theoretical perspectives from each of these three developmental dimensions, the authors describe a trajectory of initial, intermediate, and advanced intercultural maturity that can guide practice to help collegians acquire intercultural maturity.

Meyerson, D. E. (2008). *Rocking the boat: How to effect change without making trouble.* Boston, MA: Harvard Business Press.

The author offers five strategies for addressing differences in the workplace that range from quiet resistance to organizing collective action. Using the concept of tempered radicals, she suggests that moderating one's approach to work in a particular context leads to more effective negotiation and increases the likelihood of reducing inequality in the workplace.

Blog URL: contestedissues.wordpress.com
Corresponding Chapter Post: tinyurl.com/contestedissues24

CONTRIBUTORS

Ana M. Martínez Alemán is an associate professor of education and chair of the Department of Educational Leadership and Higher Education at Boston College. She is coauthor of "Online Social Networking on Campus: Understanding What Matters in Student Culture."

Victor J. Arcelus is an assistant dean of college life and the director of residence life at Gettysburg College. Victor earned his bachelor's degree and master's degree in counseling from Bucknell University and his PhD in higher education from The Pennsylvania State University. Victor's research focuses on how faculty and student affairs staff perceive their own and each other's roles as educators and how these perceptions influence the potential for developing a learning-centered campus.

James P. Barber is an assistant professor of education at the College of William and Mary. Prior to his faculty appointment he worked in student affairs administration, particularly with fraternity and sorority affairs, residence life, and student activities. His research interests include investigating integration of learning—how students make connections between ideas, skills, and knowledge across contexts.

Marcia B. Baxter Magolda is distinguished professor of Educational Leadership at Miami University. She received her master's degree and PhD in higher education from The Ohio State University. Her scholarship addresses the evolution of learning and development in college and young adult life, the role of gender in development, and pedagogy to promote self-authorship.

Mimi Benjamin is associate director in residential programs at Cornell University. She earned her PhD from Iowa State University where she was an adjunct faculty member in the higher education program. Mimi also served as coordinator of residence life, interim dean of students, and assistant to the vice president for student affairs. Her research interests include professional socialization, student-faculty interactions, and learning communities.

Gregory S. Blimling is vice president for student affairs at Rutgers University. He served as editor of the *Journal of College Student Development* and as president of the American College Personnel Association. He received his master's degree in student affairs from Indiana University and his PhD in higher education from The Ohio State University.

Lisa Boes is Allston Burr Resident Dean of Pforzheimer House at Harvard College and a lecturer in social studies. Living in residence with 400 undergraduates, she supports students' academic progress and their personal well-being. She also works closely with students dealing with academic difficulties or challenging personal matters. Lisa received her master's degree from Miami University and her EdD in learning and teaching from Harvard Graduate School of Education.

Victor John Boschini Jr. is Texas Christian University's 10th chancellor. Boschini served as president of Illinois State University from 1999 to 2003. From 1997 to 1999, he served as Illinois State's vice president for student affairs. Boschini received his bachelor's degree from Mount Union College, master's degree from Bowling Green State University, and PhD from Indiana University in higher education administration.

Ellen M. Broido is an associate professor of higher education and student affairs at Bowling Green State University. Her research focuses on the development and effects of undergraduate students' social identities on their collegiate experiences, the effects of the environment on students from targeted social groups, and on social justice issues on college campuses.

Rozana Carducci is an assistant professor of educational leadership and policy analysis at the University of Missouri. Her research and teaching interests include higher education leadership, academic capitalism, student affairs administration, and critical qualitative inquiry. Rozana's previous higher education administrative experience includes serving as the coordinator of Leadership Development at the University of Missouri–Columbia and as a research analyst in the University of California, Los Angeles Student Affairs Information and Research Office.

Jill Ellen Carnaghi is associate vice-chancellor for students and the dean of campus life at Washington University in St. Louis. She has worked at Washington University since 1997. Jill has also worked in residence life at the University of Vermont and the University of California Davis, as well as in the dean's office in the School of Education at Indiana University. She has held various leadership positions in ACPA including president in 2001, senior scholar (2009–2014), and cochair of the 1997 and 2007 ACPA/NASPA joint meetings. Jill's PhD is in higher education administration from Indiana University, MA in college student personnel administration from Michigan State Unviersity, and BA in human development and recreation from Purdue University.

Kristina Mickel Clement is assistant director for leadership development at Georgia State University. She received her bachelor's degree from Winthrop University and master's degree in college student personnel from Miami University. Kristina recently accepted an appointment in student activities after spending 9 years in residence life.

Mark R. Connolly is an assistant scientist with the Wisconsin Center for Education Research at the University of Wisconsin–Madison. Mark studies college teaching, postsecondary faculty, academic careers, and student learning at both the undergraduate and graduate levels. He is currently leading a 5-year longitudinal study of the effects of future faculty professional development programs on doctoral students in science, engineering, and mathematics.

Tracy Davis is a professor in the Department of Educational and Interdisciplinary Studies at Western Illinois University where he also coordinates the College Student Personnel Program. He also serves as director of the Center for the Study of Masculinities and Men's Development and received a PhD in student development in postsecondary education from the University of Iowa. His scholarship focuses on identity intersections, men's development, and social justice.

J. Michael Denton has been a student affairs practitioner at universities in Georgia, Florida, and North Carolina for the past 15 years. He earned his master's at Mississippi State University and is currently pursuing a PhD in student affairs in higher education at Miami University.

John P. Dugan is an assistant professor in the higher education program at Loyola University Chicago where he teaches graduate courses in leadership theory, student development theory, and social justice. He received his master's degree and PhD from the University of Maryland. John is the principal investigator for an international research program examining the influences of higher education on the development of students' capacities for socially responsible leadership.

Kelsey Ebben Gross is the coordinator for the Office of Limited Entry Programs at Central New Mexico Community College. She has held advising positions at the University of Michigan and Albion College. She coauthored *It's All About Jesus: Faith as an Oppositional Collegiate Subculture* with Peter Magolda in 2009. Kelsey received her bachelor's degree from St. Norbert College and her master's degree in college student personnel from Miami University.

Florence A. Hamrick is a professor and program director of the College Student Affairs Program at Rutgers University and was previously a faculty member at Iowa State University. Her research centers on higher education equity, access, and success for members of nondominant and traditionally underrepresented groups. She is a past editor of the *Journal of College Student Development*.

Peter J. Haverkos is the director of learning assistance at Miami University Hamilton, an open-access regional campus of Miami University. His office provides academic support to high-risk students, including adult learners, first-generation students, nonnative speakers of English, and students with disabilities. He received his master's degree and is currently pursuing a PhD in student affairs in higher education at Miami University.

Ebelia Hernandez is an assistant professor in the Department of Educational Psychology at Rutgers University. Her research centers on the Latina college student experience, particularly the interconnections between engagement and students' holistic development.

Michael G. Ignelzi is an associate professor and program coordinator of the Student Affairs in Higher Education Program at Slippery Rock University. He worked as a student affairs practitioner for 10 years while earning his EdD in human development and psychology at Harvard University. His research interests center on professional development and supervision of student affairs staff, professional ethics, and moral reasoning and education.

Laura Blake Jones is associate vice president for student affairs and dean of students at the University of Michigan. She previously held positions at the University of Oregon; the University of California, Berkeley; and the University of California, Davis. She earned her bachelor's degree at Miami University, her master's degree from the University of Vermont, and her PhD from the University of Oregon.

Patricia M. King is a professor in the Center for the Study of Higher and Postsecondary Education at the University of Michigan. Her teaching and research focus on college students' learning and development, with a special interest in the intersections among intellectual, identity, and moral development, and on the relationship between learning and development.

Jillian Kinzie is associate director in the Center for Postsecondary Research and the National Survey of Student Engagement Institute for Effective Educational Practice at Indiana University. She earned her PhD in higher education at Indiana University. Jillian coordinates research and project activities to facilitate the use of student engagement data to promote educational effectiveness and institutional improvement.

Jaime Lester is an assistant professor of higher education at George Mason University. Jaime earned her master's degree and PhD in higher education at the University of Southern California. Jaime's research agenda examines gender equity in higher education, with a specific interest in community colleges, the socialization of women and minority faculty, and work-life balance.

Heidi Levine is dean of students at Cornell College and president of the American College Personnel Association. Heidi has worked extensively in college and university counseling and health services. She earned her PhD in counseling psychology from Temple University.

Kate Linder is associate dean of students for student life and community engagement at Indiana University of Pennsylvania. She earned her bachelor's degree and master's degree from Miami University. Her student affairs background is in residence life, judicial affairs, and student life.

John Wesley Lowery is an associate professor in the Student Affairs in Higher Education department at Indiana University of Pennsylvania. John earned his PhD at Bowling Green State University. He previously served on the faculty at Oklahoma State University and the University of South Carolina. He was also the director of residence life at Adrian College and university judicial administrator at Washington University in St. Louis.

Peter M. Magolda is a professor in Miami University's Student Affairs in Higher Education Program. He received his bachelor's degree from LaSalle College, his master's degree from The Ohio State University, and his PhD in higher education administration from Indiana University. Peter's scholarship focuses on ethnographic studies of college students and critical issues in qualitative research.

Deborah McCarthy is director of students with disabilities services at the University of South Florida. She earned her master's degree in college student personnel from Miami University. She has a wide range of experience in student affairs, including work in residence life, conferencing and marketing, admissions, academic advising, and disability services.

Karen L. Miller is a doctoral candidate at the Institute of Higher Education at the University of Georgia. She received her bachelor's degree from Emory University and a juris doctorate from Harvard University. She has served in many senior administrative positions, including academic dean at John Marshall Law School in Atlanta and as senior vice president of administration at Morehouse College. Her primary research interest is in capacity building in higher education.

Chris Mundell is assistant dean of students for support services at the Columbus College of Art & Design. He oversees learning support services, disability services, and student conduct. Chris has also worked in academic advising, multicultural affairs, and learning assistance. He currently serves as president-elect of the Ohio College Personnel Association.

Michele C. Murray is associate vice president for student development at Seattle University. She provides leadership for engaging students in an educational environment that integrates their intellectual, spiritual, and emotional development. Michele earned her bachelor's degree from the University of Virginia, her master's degree from the University of Vermont, and her PhD from the University of Maryland.

Robert J. Nash is the Official University Scholar in social sciences and humanities. He is also a professor in the Higher Education and Student Affairs Administration Program at the University of Vermont.

Paul M. Oliaro is vice president for student affairs at California State University Fresno; previously he served as vice president for student affairs at West Chester University in Pennsylvania. He is a past president of the American College Personnel Association. He earned his master's degree and PhD in higher education administration from Michigan State University.

Nana Osei-Kofi is an assistant professor of social justice studies and a women's studies affiliate faculty member at Iowa State University. She earned her MA in applied women's studies and PhD in education at Claremont Graduate University. Her scholarship focuses on critical education, transnational feminist thought, cultural studies in education, and arts-based inquiry.

Julie J. Park is an assistant professor in the School of Education at the University of Maryland, College Park. She completed her PhD at the University of California, Los Angeles in education with a concentration in Asian American studies. Her research examines how race, religion, and social class affect the campus climate for diversity.

Lori D. Patton is an associate professor in the Higher Education Program at the University of Denver. She earned her PhD in higher education at Indiana University. Her research agenda focuses on the experiences of racially minoritized populations in higher education, issues of campus climate and culture, and college student development.

Patricia A. Perillo is the associate dean of students at Davidson College. A former president of the American College Personnel Association, she earned her bachelor's and master's degrees from the University of Delaware and her PhD from the University of Maryland. She has worked at the University of Maryland (College Park and Baltimore County), the University of Delaware, and the State University of New York (Plattsburgh and Albany).

Jonathan Poullard is the assistant vice-chancellor for student affairs and the dean of students at the University of California, Berkeley. As a senior administrator in the Division of Student Affairs he is instrumental in guiding collaborative efforts to support a diverse student body, promote academic and personal development, and provide direction for enriching the quality of student life.

Stephen John Quaye is an assistant professor in the College Student Personnel Program at the University of Maryland, College Park. His research concentrates on the influence of race relations on college and university campuses, specifically the gains and outcomes associated with inclusive racial climates, cross-racial interactions, and racially conscious pedagogical approaches.

Kristen A. Renn is an associate professor of Higher, Adult, and Lifelong Education at Michigan State University. She has also served as a dean in the Office of Student Life at Brown University. Her research and teaching interests include college student development, particularly in the areas of racial, gender, and sexual orientation identities.

Alyssa Bryant Rockenbach is an assistant professor of higher education at North Carolina State University. She earned her master's degree and PhD in higher education from the University of California, Los Angeles. Her research involves exploring issues of development, identity, and well-being in relation to the spiritual and religious dimensions of college students' lives.

Katie Sardelli works at Winthrop University in South Carolina as a residential learning coordinator and academic associate. She earned her bachelor's degree from the College of William and Mary and her master's degree in college student personnel from Miami University. She has worked in residence life as a resident director at Emerson College.

David B. Spano is the associate vice-chancellor for health programs and services and director of the Counseling Center at the University of North Carolina–Charlotte. He earned his master's degree from The Ohio State University and his PhD from the University of North Carolina at Chapel Hill. A licensed psychologist, David has also worked at counseling centers at the University of Texas at Austin, St. Edward's University, and Ithaca College.

Tatiana Suspitsyna is an assistant professor in the School of Educational Policy and Leadership at The Ohio State University. She earned her PhD from the University of Michigan. Her research interests include feminist poststructural perspectives, international students, accountability in education as rhetoric and a technology of governmentality, and economic advancement and engaged citizenship.

Kari B. Taylor is an associate director for student development in the University Honors Program at Miami University. In this role she has helped create and implement a learning outcomes–based, developmentally sequenced curriculum. Her key responsibilities involve helping students map out intentional steps to take toward their personal and professional goals.

J. Douglas Toma, professor of higher education at the Institute of Higher Education at the University of Georgia, is interested in issues of strategy and management in higher education, with special foci on legal issues, organization development, and athletics. He holds a PhD in higher education, an MA in history, and a JD from the University of Michigan.

Tobias W. Uecker is an assistant director of housing and residential life at Kenyon College. He has focused on First Amendment issues through study in journalism and political science and through work as managing editor for *The Collegian* while earning his bachelor's degree from South Dakota State University. Toby earned his master's degree in student affairs in higher education at Miami University.

Lori E. Varlotta leads a Division of Student Affairs in managing the university's enrollment and student life functions at California State University, Sacramento. Lori actively contributes to the state and national conversations on higher education assessment and accountability and university planning and budgeting. She has also participated in the design and implementation of the country's first voluntary system of higher education accountability, a project called the College Portrait.

Andrew F. Wall is an assistant professor of educational leadership at the University of Rochester. He teaches classes in evaluation and higher education policy and leadership, and is part of an interdisciplinary team in health profession education. Andrew focuses his research in the areas of college student health and learning, assessment and evaluation, and higher education policy and finance.

Michele M. Welkener is an assistant professor in the Higher Education and College Student Personnel Programs and is coordinator of the PhD program at the University of Dayton. She has served as an administrator of nationally recognized living-learning community, faculty development, and academic programs. Her major research interests include teaching and learning in higher education, faculty development, student development, and creativity.

Joel D. Zylstra continues to reconcile the connections between higher education and national and international social issues rooted in poverty and violence. Joel's ongoing work with training grassroots leaders in Kenya, Latin America, and several U.S. cities offers insight on how to bridge community development and student learning.

INDEX

483

Also available from Stylus

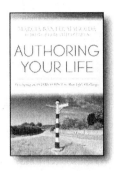

Authoring Your Life
Developing an Internal Voice to Navigate Life's Challenges
Marcia B. Baxter Magolda
Illustrated by Matthew Henry Hall
Foreword by Sharon Daloz Parks

"This book should be considered an essential addition to the library for the young professional just entering a career in academic advising. The emphasis placed on developing the skills to become a more independent thinker is essential to understanding the needs of college and university students who are in the early stages of understanding the complexities of becoming successful contributors to society as a whole."—*NACADA Journal* *(National Academic Advising Association)*

"No one has carried the concept of 'self-authorship' forward more richly, or with greater use for the reader, than Marcia Baxter Magolda. Anyone interested in supporting their own, or others', adult development will benefit enormously from this book."—*Robert Kegan, Meehan Professor of Adult Learning, Harvard University, and co-author of* Immunity to Change

Positioning Student Affairs for Sustainable Change
Achieving Organizational Effectiveness Through Multiple Perspectives
Linda Kuk , James H. Banning and Marilyn J. Amey

At a time of increasing student diversity, concern about security, demand for greater accountability, and of economic difficulty, what does the future hold for higher education, and how can student affairs organizations adapt to the increasing and changing demands? How can university leaders position existing resources to effectively address these and other emerging challenges with a sense of opportunity rather than dread? How can organizations be redesigned to sustain change while achieving excellence?

Intended for practitioners, graduate students, interns and student affairs leaders, this book presents the key ideas and concepts from business-oriented organizational behavior and change theories, and demonstrates how they can be useful in, and be applied to, student affairs practice—and, in particular, how readers can use these theories to sustain change and enhance their organization's ability to adapt to complex emerging challenges. At the same time it holds to values and perspectives that support the human dimension of organizational life.

Each chapter opens with a case study, and closes with a set of reflective questions.

22883 Quicksilver Drive
Sterling, VA 20166-2102

Subscribe to our e-mail alerts: www.Styluspub.com